Spiritual Solutions

to

America's Problems

Spiritualizing the World, vol 7

Spiritual Solutions to America's Problems

KIM MICHAELS

Copyright © 2019 Kim Michaels. All rights reserved. No part of this book may be used, reproduced, translated, electronically stored or transmitted by any means except by written permission from the publisher. A reviewer may quote brief passages in a review.

MORE TO LIFE PUBLISHING

www.morepublish.com

For foreign and translation rights,

contact info@ morepublish.com

ISBN: 978-87-93297-59-3

The information and insights in this book should not be considered as a form of therapy, advice, direction, diagnosis, and/or treatment of any kind. This information is not a substitute for medical, psychological, or other professional advice, counseling and care. All matters pertaining to your individual health should be supervised by a physician or appropriate health-care practitioner. No guarantee is made by the author or the publisher that the practices described in this book will yield successful results for anyone at any time. They are presented for informational purposes only, as the practice and proof rests with the individual.

For more information: *www.ascendedmasterlight.com* and *www.transcendencetoolbox.com*

CONTENTS

Introduction 9

Part 1 Aligning America with the mind of Saint Germain 13

1 | America is a cosmic experiment 15

2 | Invoking social awareness in America 33

3 | Taking America from human judgment to the discernment of Christ 65

4 | Invoking an exposure of the false leaders of Christianity 87

5 | Invoking a shift from judgment to discernment 111

6 | From the United States of America to the United Peoples of America 133

7 | Invoking the Unification of the People of America 151

8 | Invoking the transcendence of polarization 171

9 | What does it mean to be an American? 191

10 | Invoking an awareness of our basic humanity 209

11 | Invoking the New American Creed 229

12 | Winning the political game in the Golden Age 255

13 | Invoking an end to the obsession with winning 273

14 | Invoking the political changes of the Golden Age 297

15 | Total transparency in government 317

16 | Invoking transparency in government 329

17 | Freeing America from the slavery of capitalism 349

18 | Invoking freedom from the slavery of capitalism 367

19 | Invoking a post-capitalist economy 387

20 | Why Americans do not demand better leadership 407

21 | Invoking better leadership in America 421
22 | The power elite and American foreign policy 449
23 | Invoking the exposure of American foreign policy 461
24 | Americans have a right to demand better leaders 489
25 | Invoking non-dualistic leadership in America 501
Part 2 Freeing America from black-and-white thinking 519
26 | A higher form of democracy in America 521
27 | Invoking a more direct democracy in America 533
28 | The judgment of Christ upon the false Jesus 561
29 | Invoking the judgment of Christ upon
the false Jesus 575
30 | Is America a Christian or a Buddhist nation? 603
31 | Invoking freedom from judgment 617
32 | Consuming the records of war in America 637
33 | Freeing America from intolerance 655
34 | Freeing America from black-and-white thinking 675
35 | Freeing America from elitism 693

INTRODUCTION

This book belongs to the series *Spiritualizing the World*. The books in this series are given by the ascended masters as workbooks that provide the knowledge and practical tools we need in order to make a contribution to solving concrete world problems. This book contains the knowledge and the tools we need in order to solve many of the problems facing the United States today. These books do not contain foundational knowledge about ascended masters and their teachings. In order to make the most efficient use of this book, you need to have a general knowledge of the following topics:

- You need to know who the ascended masters are, how they give their teachings and how you can make the best use of them on a personal and planetary level. You can find extensive teachings on this in the books: *How You Can Help Change the World* and *The Power of Self*.

- You need to know how the earth functions as a cosmic schoolroom. You need to know your own role and the authority you have as a spiritual being in embodiment. You need to know the role of the ascended masters and how only we who are in embodiment can give them the authority to use their unlimited power to affect change on earth. You can find more on these topics in the first book in this series: *How You Can Help Change the World*.

- You need to know how to use the practical tools given by the ascended masters. You can find more on this topic in: *How You Can Help Change the World* and on the website: *www.transcendencetoolbox.com*.

- You need to know about the existence and methods of the dark forces who are ultimately responsible for creating problems on earth. You can find foundational teachings on this in: *Cosmology of Evil*.

How to use this book

There is no one way of using the teachings and tools in this book. However, if you want to make a significant contribution to solving America's problems, it is suggested that you start by following this program:

- You read one of the chapters in the book completely in order to increase your understanding of the topic.

Introduction 11

- You give the invocation associated with that chapter once a day for nine days while studying the same chapter again.

The reasoning behind this program is that the chapters in the book form a progression. As you give an invocation for one chapter, you are also clearing your own consciousness from certain energies and illusions. This makes it easier for you to absorb and apply the teachings from the next chapter.

You can, of course, also read the book all the way through and then select one or more invocation(s) that you give several times. It is always more powerful to give an invocation once a day for nine or 33 days.

PART 1 ALIGNING AMERICA WITH THE MIND OF SAINT GERMAIN

The dictations in Part 1 were given at a conference in Albuquerque, New Mexico in September 2018. The invocations were made based on the dictations. The theme for the conference was how to align America with the mind of Saint Germain.

1 | AMERICA IS A COSMIC EXPERIMENT

I AM the ascended master that you know as Mother Mary, and it is my great joy and my great privilege to open this conference. Of course, when I say "open," you have already opened the conference by opening up your hearts to share with each other. Some of you, my beloved, have the question in your mind: "But we haven't given an invocation yet so how can we be ready for a dictation?" What is the purpose of giving an invocation? Is it not to release light? And have you not released light when you shared so freely of your sorrows, your trials, your joys, your experiences?

My beloved, we have given teachings now for a very long time, at least if you measure with just one lifetime, since we started this dispensation of progressive revelation, of messengers who could speak the Word. You can look at these teachings, as some of you have done. You can study them. You can seek to understand them, as many students have done—and many students have grown in understanding. Yet my beloved, what is it we truly want to give to you? Is it understanding? Well, we do want to give you understanding but we realize very well that understanding will only get you so far on the path. It is, as has been said so many times: You cannot solve a problem with the state of consciousness that created the problem, you cannot get out of the dualistic state of mind through the reasoning, analytical faculties of the mind.

When students first find the teachings of the ascended masters, they often do so because they have questions that were never answered by the previous religions or teachings they had been exposed to. They want to understand, they want to have that intellectual understanding of some aspect of life. There is nothing wrong with this, but this will only get you to a certain point.

You see this in the story of Jesus' life where he encountered the scribes and the Pharisees who were so advanced in their intellectual understanding that they could not recognize the Living Christ when he stood before them. In fact, their sophisticated, intellectual, analytical reasoning blocked them from actually having the *experience* that was the highest potential of encountering the Living Christ. Namely, that they had an inner experience that there was something higher than their present level of consciousness.

How to tell other people about the path

What do we of the ascended masters really want to give to you? We want to give you that experience. Surely, many of you have had that experience while listening to a dictation or even reading it because you tuned in to our Beings, to our Presences. Do you not realize, my beloved, that when you talk about, as some of you did, reaching out to other people, telling other people about your path, you sometimes have a tendency to think that you need to give them understanding that they can grasp intellectually? But what is it you first of all need to give them? You need to give them an experience of your being, of your presence, of what you have internalized on the path, which means that you are at a higher level on the path than they are at. You are at a higher state of consciousness than they are at and if you can share that with them, then they will get something from you that they could never get if you tried to only give them the intellectual teaching.

Do you not realize that the session you had earlier, where you were so willing to share from the heart, this is the most powerful way to approach other people? To be willing to be open, to be willing to even be vulnerable, to be very honest and very direct about your own path: What you have learned, what you have experienced, what you have internalized. When they sense that you are genuine, many will be moved that would not be moved by the intellectual teaching. My beloved, some may still give you a negative reaction. This is where you have come to a point now on the path – and I include all of you who are here and all who have studied these teachings and been willing to open yourself to them – where you are ready to step up and say: "I'm not going to let those who are negative cause me to close myself off. I'm going to focus on those who are positive, who are open. I'm going to focus on those people that I can reach, those people I can help. I'm not going to be concerned about those I cannot help, I'm not going to even react to them."

If you find that you do react to them, then you follow what the messenger explained. He looked in himself: "Why am I reacting to these negative people? What is it in me?" If you can come to the point of resolving that, you will feel that now you are free to be who you are, to share who you are. This will transform people more than anything else.

Being an open door for the masters

What is it we have trained the messenger to do? We say he is an open door and, yes, he is an open door for many teachings that you can grasp with the intellect, but he is also an open door that allows us to shine some measure of our Beings, our light, through him so that you can experience it. But how many people can this messenger meet in the rest of his lifetime? Certainly, not as many people as all of you can meet. How are we going to reach many people on earth if there is only one person who can be an open door for us sharing our Presences through them? Therefore, we are not looking for all of you to do specifically what the messenger does and take dictations and bring forth teachings. We are looking – certainly – for all of you to be able to share you own presence, and in sharing your own presence also allowing us to shine through you. You all have the capacity to be the open door in that way.

Some of you may do other things as well, I am not putting a limitation on it that this is the only thing you can do. This is certainly something you can strive to do and that most of you are much closer to doing than you might think. As you can see, you could stand up and share. If you do it more times, if you work on your own reaction to doing it or having done it, you can get to this point of being an open door. It is not a matter of always (although you may do it sometimes) standing in front of a group of people. It is also one-on-one or with a few friends where you can share something from your heart that is beyond mere intellectual understanding.

How can you do this? You can do it by, as the messenger explained, working on this sense of ownership, the image of yourself. You can do it when you are setting other people free because you have set yourself free. You are setting them free to react any way they want because you have already set yourself free. However they react, you are not going to have a negative reaction to it. You do not own them, they do not own you but you are sharing.

What it truly means to give

You see my beloved, there is a very important concept to ponder because most people on earth have a distorted view of what it means to give. They think that if you give something to somebody, they either own the thing you are giving them or they own you because you are obligated to give them something else tomorrow. When you come to the point where you have set yourself free from the need to own other people, and you have accepted that nobody else can own you, then you can freely give. That is the real meaning behind Jesus' statement: "Freely ye have received, freely give."

How have you freely received? Because Jesus was free when he gave to his disciples. He did not have the sense that: "They are *my* disciples, I own them." He freely gave without any strings attached, without any expectations, any demands, any sense of ownership. What he wanted his disciples to do was to then give that gift to others in the same freedom, freedom from ownership.

"The prince of this world cometh and has nothing in me." How can you achieve that state of freedom? Well, you cannot let the prince of this world own you. How can you come to a point where the prince of this world has nothing in you whereby he can own you? You can come to that point only when you have given up the desire to own anything on earth. As long as there is something on earth that you want to own, then the prince of this world has something in you—and he will use it to exercise ownership over you.

The experiment of America

What does this have to do with the topic of this conference: "Aligning America with the Mind of Saint Germain?" Well, from a certain standpoint: *nothing,* from another viewpoint: *everything.* Is not America meant to be the land of the free? How can you be free if you want to own something on earth? How can America be free if it has such a strong desire to own something that it has to build a wall to protect it? Or that it has to erect other barriers and stop interacting with the world, trading freely, exchanging this or that freely? When you start closing yourself off, it is because you think you own something and you have to protect it. When you start building an army that can project force anywhere on the planet, it is almost as if you think that you not only own America, you own the world.

Who owns America, who can claim ownership of America? *What* is America? Is it a country? Is it a certain area on earth that you can draw a line around and say: "Inside of this is America, outside is not America?" Nay, America is an *idea.* Can you own an idea?

Who owns gravity? My beloved, America is not only an idea because even ideas have been misconstrued by people to be something final. You can see, for example, how the Catholic church will claim that its doctrines represent something final, something absolute, something that could never be improved upon because it is the highest truth or the only truth. You all know this is not the case. Then, look at America. Is the idea of America something absolute, something unchangeable, something that could never be improved upon? Nay my beloved, America is a *process,* it is not clearly defined. Not even Saint Germain has clearly defined America. He realizes that the destiny of America, the unfoldment of America, the evolution of America depends on the free-will choices of not only the people who live within its borders but many other people who are tied to it in various ways. America is an *experiment*.

The sponsorship of Saint Germain

Many of you have heard from previous ascended master teachings that Saint Germain is the primary ascended master who sponsored America. His sponsorship is not something absolute, not something final, not something that can be taken for granted. Saint Germain has not given a blank check to America and said: "Use it however you want and I will pay the karmic price for it." That is not what sponsorship means.

Why do you think that Jesus gave his parable about the three servants who were given different talents and two of them multiplied the talents and one did not? America has been given a sponsorship by Saint Germain. What he gave, and what he was allowed to give, was a certain portion of energy.

Now, you can see how that certain portion has driven a tremendous growth in America, but it is not something that will last forever or can be taken for granted. Whether or not more will be given (or how much more will be given) depends on whether Americans multiply what they were given in the first place. What Jesus gave 2,000 years ago was an absolute law. If you do not multiply the talents you have been given, what you have shall be taken away from you. One of the absolutely most tragic things that can happen on earth is that when a nation or a group of people have been sponsored by an ascended master, they start taking it for granted and they think they do not have to multiply the talents given.

Do you seriously believe that because Saint Germain has sponsored America once, he will continue to do this forever—regardless of how the people and the leaders use the gifts?

Indeed, there can come a point where everything that was given to America will be taken away because Saint Germain will not be able to renew his sponsorship of America. Now, I am not trying to create some scare scenario here. I am not trying to say that this is in the risk of happening tomorrow. I am trying to give the sense of realism that one of the main things that prevents America from being aligned with the mind of Saint Germain is that too many people in America take for granted what they have. They do not realize that the reason America has gained the position it has in the world (the riches, the development that it has) is primarily because of Saint Germain's sponsorship.

Why America must serve others

They think it is their own rugged individualism that has built this country, but it is not individualism as such that has built this country. Certainly, it is not *rugged* individualism that says: "I only care about myself and I don't care whatsoever about other people." What does it mean to multiply the talents? Well, what did Jesus say: "Do unto others, as you want them to do unto you." More than that, he also (between the lines) told (his disciples at least) to multiply what he had given them and then use it to do something for others.

My beloved, you could (even though it would be an artificial concept) look at America and you could sum up how much wealth is owned by people in America. Then, you could start looking at how America spends that wealth and you could say: "Is that wealth being used to do something for people? Is it being used to do something for the American people? Is it being used to do something for people outside America?" I know you could point to certain things here and there, and

America is doing this and America is doing that. I do not want to detract from what is being done.

What I am pointing out here is that if you looked honestly at the amount of wealth that is in this country and how it is being spent, you would see that over the last several decades the tendency is very clear. The wealth is being concentrated in the hands of fewer and fewer people and they are not using it to help others. They are just using it to build more wealth even though they already have more than they could possibly need for the rest of their lifetimes.

One or two people turning to philanthropy and giving away billions of dollars does not change this picture sufficiently. Again, not detracting from what they are doing, obviously it is better to turn to philanthropy than to keep accumulating wealth. Nevertheless, my point is that right now there is a small elite of Americans who think they have a right to own the wealth produced by this nation, to concentrate it in their own hands and to put it under their control, to decide essentially that they will take this wealth out of circulation.

The downward trend of money

What is the purpose of money? It is to circulate and to do something for others because that is how the talents are being multiplied so that the wealth of a nation can truly grow. What is happening right now in America is a downward trend where the wealth that is existing is not being used, it is not being multiplied to do something for others. Therefore, there can only come a point where the system crashes, as you saw it do in 2008. This is the only way right now that the wealth is going to be taken away from the elite. Unfortunately, this also has ramifications for the people because they are also affected by this but that is, again, because the people are allowing the elite to steal the wealth.

The wealth is primarily, again, an effect of Saint Germain's sponsorship but it is also an effect of the people's labor. Those who perform the labor should have a right to control how the money, or at least the majority of it, is spent. In this so-called capitalist system, this free enterprise economy that you think you have (wish it were free but it is not) there is no room for that. There is no room for sharing the wealth among all the people who help create it. Well, then, my beloved, how can the talents be multiplied? They cannot, and if they are not multiplied, how can the wealth keep growing?

If you were to look at this, you would be able to say that America has far greater wealth than it had twenty, thirty years ago. I would say: "Is that really so?" Because what is the wealth you have today that you did not have 30 years ago? It is the so-called value of stocks, bonds and other financial instruments. Where is that money, my beloved? It exists only as numbers on a computer screen, as zeros and ones on a server's hard drive, nothing else.

Egotism rules America

Is that wealth? Nay, it is simply numbers that serve to gratify the egos of those who have taken the so-called rugged individualism to its ultimate perversion of caring only about themselves and not about others. Egotism rules America and that is not what Saint Germain meant when he gave his sponsorship of this nation. It has nothing whatsoever to do with his vision for this nation. He did not mean to raise up a nation of spoiled brats who care only about themselves and who take for granted that they have a right to have what they have and do whatever they want with it, without any sense of responsibility for sharing with others.

How do you multiply the talents? Well, my beloved, when it comes to money, certainly you need to take care of yourself and your family. You need to have a place to live, you need to have a car to drive—if you live in America, the land of cars. Nevertheless, there comes a point where you have taken care of those needs—and it can be individual. I am not saying we are setting up a standard for how much money every family should have. We allow some individualism here but there comes a point where you have enough to take care of yourself and your family. From that point on, multiplying the talents means doing something to help other people. Of course, when you are spending money, you are also helping other people because you are keeping the economy growing.

What is it that the analysts on television always say when there is an economic downturn in America? Why is the economy not growing? Because there is not enough consumer spending, they say. Because consumer spending is two-thirds or more of the economy.

Well, why is there not consumer spending? Because the consumers are not the ones who have the money. It is concentrated in the hands of the elite who do not know how to spend the money because they have already bought all the mansions and all the yachts and all the Rolls Royces and all the Jaguars and all the Maseratis that anybody could possibly have—or the private jets or the this or the that.

There comes a point where you cannot spend more money on yourself. But if you have this obsessive-compulsive need to own the money, then you go into this mode of just accumulating more and more because what if you lost it? When do you ever feel secure? You *never* feel secure when you are in this state of mind.

A country not dominated by an elite

What needs to happen in America, in order to align it with the mind of Saint Germain, is that there has to be a sharing of the wealth. Now, this can be done in various ways. It does not have to be done only the way it has been done in Europe where you have the very high taxes that are being distributed by the government. That is not the only way that it can be done but it is certainly one way that has worked for many European countries to the point where they have secured a lower degree of poverty than what you see in America.

America is an idea, America is a dream. What was the idea that Saint Germain had in mind when he sponsored America? What was it that the Founding Fathers and many of those who gave their lives to create this country had in their minds? Well, it was to create a society that was distinctly different from the kind of societies you had in Europe at the time. You had the feudal societies with a very small power elite who had control of the majority of the wealth, meaning the land. You had the king who had absolute power to do anything. In other words, you had a completely elitist system.

The vision of Saint Germain and the Founding Fathers was to create a country that was not controlled by an elite but where all of the people had an opportunity to multiply their individual talents and be rewarded according to their willingness to make an effort. What has happened since then is that the power elite has, in various ways, eroded that freedom and they have taken the fruits of the people's labor to a very large degree. It now goes to corporations that are not owned by a single person or even to companies that may be owned by a single person. In any event, it concentrates the wealth in the hands of a small elite. That is not the kind of free, egalitarian, non-elitist society that Saint Germain sponsored.

Americans growing a conscience

What is it going to take to truly begin to move beyond this? Well, it is simply going to take that America and Americans need to develop a conscience, a social awareness. You will say: "Well, don't we have that already?" I would say: "Look around you." Look at some of the other countries where they have said: "We will not allow there to be people who are poor, who are starving to death, who are malnourished, who cannot afford to go to the doctor but must wait until they have a life-threatening illness to go to the emergency room. We do not want to have a society where we are only taking care of ourselves and not taking care of each other. We do not want to have a country that consists of 400 million individuals. We want a country that consists of people who realize we are in the same boat and we will all do better if we take care of each other."

You may say: "Are there not people who have this awareness in America?" Of course there are, but we have not yet reached a critical mass in America and how can you tell? Well, there is not healthcare available for all people, is there? There is not a social safety net for those who lose their jobs because some corporations care more about profit for the elite than salaries for the people. Unless we come over this critical mass of people who not only develop the social awareness but begin speaking out, then America cannot go beyond its present level.

If it cannot go beyond its present level, my beloved, it must decline because the talents are not being multiplied. If there is not a willingness to reform the system, then the system must be allowed to collapse. This entire colossus, that the power elite has built in this country, must be allowed to fail.

The government and the media, both of which are essentially owned by the elite, may think that the apparatus is too big to fail, but Saint Germain does not think it is too big to fail. If that is the only way to move America forward, then he will withhold or withdraw his sponsorship and let it all collapse in upon itself. The people will be free from the tyranny of the financial elite, which is essentially the same lifestreams that were embodied in medieval Europe as the feudal lords and the kings—the *mad* kings in many cases. One way or the other, the people will be free from this elite. Will it be the easy way or will it be the hard way? *That* is a question that Saint Germain cannot decide because it is up to the free will of the people.

Raising America beyond rugged individualism

Certainly, I am not trying to say here that there is a huge gap between where America is now and where it should be. There is, in fact, not such a large gap before that social awareness, that sense of togetherness, can begin to really dominate the American way of thinking. But we are not there yet. There needs to be someone who will go to the forefront, who will make the calls, as we always tell you to do.

You also need to look at yourselves, those of you who have grown up in America. See how you might have been, from an early age, indoctrinated with this sense of the American individualism and really start to look at this in yourselves and resolve it, as many of you have already started to do. Some of you have already completed this and started feeling this compassion for other people. Many of you, of course, are on this planet because you have compassion for the people. Some of you have still been affected by this American way of thinking where you still have not freed yourself from it. What I am saying is that you actually came into embodiment partly to take on this American way of thinking and help resolve it in the collective so that you can help raise the collective to the next level up.

America is not the most sophisticated democracy

My beloved, I know very well that there are many, many Americans who will vehemently reject what I will say here. It is a grand illusion of the ages when so many Americans think that America is the most sophisticated of the evolved countries, the evolved democracies. A realistic assessment will show that when it comes to developing a true functioning democracy, Canada and many of the nations in Europe have reached a higher level of maturity—in part, in *great* part, because there is that social awareness.

What is the meaning of a democracy, my beloved? I know some will say that America is not a *democracy,* it is a *republic,* but, nevertheless, you are voting for representatives, are you not? And that is one of the keystones of a democracy. So the essence of the current American model is that there is a small elite who manipulates the people into voting for either this party or that party, but both parties are owned and controlled by the elite. Therefore, they cannot enact a policy that overthrows the dominance of the elite. Is that a democracy? No. It is just a camouflaged dictatorial system that is ruled by a small elite.

How do you have a true democracy? Only when you develop a social awareness where the people realize: "We are in this together, and we function better when we all help each other, when we don't allow a small elite to manipulate us because we don't allow them to get away with setting themselves up as an elite." As I said, who created the idea of the rugged American individualism and the "America first" and the "America is the greatest nation in the world?" Well, the elite have because they are the ones who want to be completely egotistical, only think about themselves, not care about the consequences for anybody else and accumulate, accumulate, accumulate. They think they can own something on earth, but that is not individualism.

I am not talking about having a country where you give up being individuals and you blend into the mass consciousness and you all become automatons. That is not what social awareness is about. Social awareness is that you realize that you are an individual but you are not living in a bubble. You are living in a nation with millions of other people and you are your brother's keeper. Let those who are in the Cain consciousness stay in that consciousness but do not let them run your nation! You are all your brother's and sister's keepers because that is the only way that a free democratic, non-elitist society can be built.

My beloved, with this I have opened this conference, perhaps set a certain tone. Perhaps, Saint Germain will build on that tone, perhaps he will have his own. Nevertheless, I am grateful for the opportunity to have delivered this address, to be able to speak it into the collective consciousness and to use all of your chakras as loudspeakers to give it greater momentum, greater impact. In fact, it has reached to the far corners of the nation and it has had the impact that I desired it to have for now, based on the very complex equation we apply when we give a dictation—which is something I do not want to discourse on because it is too complicated for words.

I want you to know that we see a certain matrix for the potential for delivering a dictation. Part of that equation is how many people are at the conference but also how open are you, what is your level of consciousness. I can assure you, my beloved, that your willingness to be so open and share previously today has actually multiplied, with a not inconsiderable factor, what I was able to release through this dictation.

For this, you have my gratitude, you have my joy of being with you. I hope that if I have not given you an experience of my Presence during this release, you might tune in to me before you go to sleep and ask me to take you to the retreat Then, I hope that you will at some point have that experience of touching my Presence, of feeling that my Presence has touched you. With this, my beloved, go in peace. You have my total, unconditional acceptance of who you are right now.

2 | INVOKING SOCIAL AWARENESS IN AMERICA

In the name of the I AM THAT I AM, Jesus Christ, I use the authority that I have as a being in embodiment on earth to call upon Mother Mary to reinforce my calls and use my chakras to project the statements in this invocation into the collective consciousness and awaken Americans to the need to develop a stronger social awareness. Awaken Americans to the reality that we are spiritual beings and that we can co-create a new future by working with the ascended masters. I especially call for …

[Make your own calls here.]

Part 1

1. We cannot solve a problem with the state of consciousness that created the problem, we cannot get out

of the dualistic state of mind through the reasoning and analytical faculties of the mind.

> O blessed Mary, Mother mine,
> there is no greater love than thine,
> as we are one in heart and mind,
> my place in hierarchy I find.
>
> **O Mother Mary, generate,**
> **the song that does accelerate,**
> **the earth into a higher state,**
> **all matter does now scintillate.**

2. The scribes and the Pharisees were so advanced in their intellectual understanding that they could not recognize the Living Christ when he stood before them.

> I came to earth from heaven sent,
> as I am in embodiment,
> I use Divine authority,
> commanding you to set earth free.
>
> **O Mother Mary, generate,**
> **the song that does accelerate,**
> **the earth into a higher state,**
> **all matter does now scintillate.**

3. Their sophisticated, intellectual, analytical reasoning blocked them from having the inner experience that there was something higher than their present level of consciousness.

> I call now in God's sacred name,
> for you to use your Mother Flame,

to burn all fear-based energy,
restoring sacred harmony.

**O Mother Mary, generate,
the song that does accelerate,
the earth into a higher state,
all matter does now scintillate.**

4. Most people have a distorted view of what it means to give. They think that if we give something to somebody, they either own the thing we are giving them or they own us because we are obligated to give them something else tomorrow.

Your sacred name I hereby praise,
collective consciousness you raise,
no more of fear and doubt and shame,
consume it with your Mother Flame.

**O Mother Mary, generate,
the song that does accelerate,
the earth into a higher state,
all matter does now scintillate.**

5. When we set ourselves free from the need to own other people, and accept that nobody else can own us, then we can freely give. That is the real meaning behind Jesus' statement: "Freely ye have received, freely give."

All darkness from the earth you purge,
your light moves as a mighty surge,
no force of darkness can now stop,
the spiral that goes only up.

**O Mother Mary, generate,
the song that does accelerate,
the earth into a higher state,
all matter does now scintillate.**

6. Jesus was free when he gave to his disciples. He freely gave without any strings attached, without any expectations, any demands, any sense of ownership. What he wanted his disciples to do was to then give that gift to others in the same freedom from ownership.

All elemental life you bless,
removing from them man-made stress,
the nature spirits are now free,
outpicturing Divine decree.

**O Mother Mary, generate,
the song that does accelerate,
the earth into a higher state,
all matter does now scintillate.**

7. "The prince of this world cometh and has nothing in me." We cannot achieve that state of freedom if we let the prince of this world own us.

I raise my voice and take my stand,
a stop to war I do command,
no more shall warring scar the earth,
a golden age is given birth.

**O Mother Mary, generate,
the song that does accelerate,**

> the earth into a higher state,
> all matter does now scintillate.

8. The prince of this world has nothing in us whereby he can own us only when we have given up the desire to own anything on earth. As long as there is something on earth that we want to own, then the prince of this world has something in us—and he will use it to exercise ownership over us.

> As Mother Earth is free at last,
> disasters belong to the past,
> your Mother Light is so intense,
> that matter is now far less dense.
>
> **O Mother Mary, generate,
> the song that does accelerate,
> the earth into a higher state,
> all matter does now scintillate.**

9. America is meant to be the land of the free. How can we be free if we want to own something on earth? How can America be free if it has such a strong desire to own something that it has to build a wall to protect it? Or that it has to erect other barriers and stop interacting with the world, trading freely, exchanging this or that freely.

> In Mother Light the earth is pure,
> the upward spiral will endure,
> prosperity is now the norm,
> God's vision manifest as form.
>
> **O Mother Mary, generate,
> the song that does accelerate,**

**the earth into a higher state,
all matter does now scintillate.**

Part 2

1. When we start closing ourselves off, it is because we think we own something and we have to protect it. When we start building an army that can project force anywhere on the planet, it is because we think that we not only own America, we own the world.

> O blessed Mary, Mother mine,
> there is no greater love than thine,
> as we are one in heart and mind,
> my place in hierarchy I find.

> **O Mother Mary, generate,
> the song that does accelerate,
> the earth into a higher state,
> all matter does now scintillate.**

2. Who owns America, who can claim ownership of America? What is America? Is it a country? Is it a certain area on earth that we can draw a line around and say: "Inside of this is America, outside is not America?" Nay, America is an *idea*. Can we own an idea?

> I came to earth from heaven sent,
> as I am in embodiment,
> I use Divine authority,
> commanding you to set earth free.

2 | Invoking social awareness in America

**O Mother Mary, generate,
the song that does accelerate,
the earth into a higher state,
all matter does now scintillate.**

3. America is not only an idea because even ideas have been misconstrued by people to be something final. The idea of America is not something absolute, something unchangeable, something that could never be improved upon.

I call now in God's sacred name,
for you to use your Mother Flame,
to burn all fear-based energy,
restoring sacred harmony.

**O Mother Mary, generate,
the song that does accelerate,
the earth into a higher state,
all matter does now scintillate.**

4. America is a *process*, it is not clearly defined. Not even Saint Germain has clearly defined America. The destiny of America, the unfoldment of America, the evolution of America depends on the free-will choices of not only the people who live within its borders but many other people who are tied to it in various ways. America is an *experiment*.

Your sacred name I hereby praise,
collective consciousness you raise,
no more of fear and doubt and shame,
consume it with your Mother Flame.

> **O Mother Mary, generate,**
> **the song that does accelerate,**
> **the earth into a higher state,**
> **all matter does now scintillate.**

5. Saint Germain's sponsorship is not something absolute, not something final, not something that can be taken for granted. Saint Germain has not given a blank check to America and said: "Use it however you want and I will pay the karmic price for it." That is not what sponsorship means.

> All darkness from the earth you purge,
> your light moves as a mighty surge,
> no force of darkness can now stop,
> the spiral that goes only up.

> **O Mother Mary, generate,**
> **the song that does accelerate,**
> **the earth into a higher state,**
> **all matter does now scintillate.**

6. Jesus gave his parable about the three servants who were given talents and two of them multiplied the talents and one did not. America has been given a sponsorship by Saint Germain. What he gave was a certain portion of energy.

> All elemental life you bless,
> removing from them man-made stress,
> the nature spirits are now free,
> outpicturing Divine decree.

> **O Mother Mary, generate,**
> **the song that does accelerate,**

> the earth into a higher state,
> all matter does now scintillate.

7. That portion has driven a tremendous growth in America, but it is not something that will last forever or can be taken for granted. Whether or not more will be given depends on whether Americans multiply what they were given in the first place.

> I raise my voice and take my stand,
> a stop to war I do command,
> no more shall warring scar the earth,
> a golden age is given birth.
>
> **O Mother Mary, generate,**
> **the song that does accelerate,**
> **the earth into a higher state,**
> **all matter does now scintillate.**

8. What Jesus gave 2,000 years ago was an absolute law. If we do not multiply the talents we have been given, what we have shall be taken away from us. One of the most tragic things that can happen on earth is that a nation has been sponsored by an ascended master but people think they do not have to multiply the talents given.

> As Mother Earth is free at last,
> disasters belong to the past,
> your Mother Light is so intense,
> that matter is now far less dense.
>
> **O Mother Mary, generate,**
> **the song that does accelerate,**

> the earth into a higher state,
> all matter does now scintillate.

9. The fact that Saint Germain has sponsored America once, does not mean he will continue to do this forever—regardless of how the people and the leaders use the gifts. There can come a point where everything that was given to America will be taken away because Saint Germain will not be able to renew his sponsorship of America.

> In Mother Light the earth is pure,
> the upward spiral will endure,
> prosperity is now the norm,
> God's vision manifest as form.
>
> **O Mother Mary, generate,
> the song that does accelerate,
> the earth into a higher state,
> all matter does now scintillate.**

Part 3

1. One of the main things that prevents America from being aligned with the mind of Saint Germain is that too many people in America take for granted what they have. They do not realize that the reason America has gained the position it has in the world is primarily because of Saint Germain's sponsorship.

> O blessed Mary, Mother mine,
> there is no greater love than thine,

as we are one in heart and mind,
my place in hierarchy I find.

O Mother Mary, generate,
the song that does accelerate,
the earth into a higher state,
all matter does now scintillate.

2. Many Americans think it is their own rugged individualism that has built this country, but it is not individualism as such that has built this country. Certainly, it is not rugged individualism that says: "I only care about myself and I don't care whatsoever about other people."

I came to earth from heaven sent,
as I am in embodiment,
I use Divine authority,
commanding you to set earth free.

O Mother Mary, generate,
the song that does accelerate,
the earth into a higher state,
all matter does now scintillate.

3. Multiplying the talents means that we do unto others as we want them to do unto us. We multiply what we have been given and then use it to do something for others.

I call now in God's sacred name,
for you to use your Mother Flame,
to burn all fear-based energy,
restoring sacred harmony.

> O Mother Mary, generate,
> the song that does accelerate,
> the earth into a higher state,
> all matter does now scintillate.

4. The wealth owned by people in America is not being used to do something for the American people. It is not being used to do something for people outside America.

> Your sacred name I hereby praise,
> collective consciousness you raise,
> no more of fear and doubt and shame,
> consume it with your Mother Flame.

> O Mother Mary, generate,
> the song that does accelerate,
> the earth into a higher state,
> all matter does now scintillate.

5. Over the last several decades the wealth is being concentrated in the hands of fewer and fewer people and they are not using it to help others. They are just using it to build more wealth, even though they already have more than they could possibly need for the rest of their lifetimes.

> All darkness from the earth you purge,
> your light moves as a mighty surge,
> no force of darkness can now stop,
> the spiral that goes only up.

> O Mother Mary, generate,
> the song that does accelerate,

> the earth into a higher state,
> all matter does now scintillate.

6. I call forth the judgment of Christ upon the small elite of Americans who think they have a right to own the wealth produced by this nation, to concentrate it in their own hands, to put it under their control and decide that they will take it out of circulation.

> All elemental life you bless,
> removing from them man-made stress,
> the nature spirits are now free,
> outpicturing Divine decree.
>
> **O Mother Mary, generate,**
> **the song that does accelerate,**
> **the earth into a higher state,**
> **all matter does now scintillate.**

7. The purpose of money is to circulate and to do something for others because that is how the talents are being multiplied so that the wealth of a nation can truly grow.

> I raise my voice and take my stand,
> a stop to war I do command,
> no more shall warring scar the earth,
> a golden age is given birth.
>
> **O Mother Mary, generate,**
> **the song that does accelerate,**
> **the earth into a higher state,**
> **all matter does now scintillate.**

8. What is happening right now in America is a downward trend where the wealth that is existing is not being used, it is not being multiplied to do something for others. There must come a point where the system crashes, as we saw in 2008.

> As Mother Earth is free at last,
> disasters belong to the past,
> your Mother Light is so intense,
> that matter is now far less dense.
>
> **O Mother Mary, generate,**
> **the song that does accelerate,**
> **the earth into a higher state,**
> **all matter does now scintillate.**

9. This is the only way that the wealth is going to be taken away from the elite. This has ramifications for the people because they are also affected by this, but that is because the people are allowing the elite to steal the wealth.

> In Mother Light the earth is pure,
> the upward spiral will endure,
> prosperity is now the norm,
> God's vision manifest as form.
>
> **O Mother Mary, generate,**
> **the song that does accelerate,**
> **the earth into a higher state,**
> **all matter does now scintillate.**

Part 4

1. The wealth is primarily an effect of Saint Germain's sponsorship but it is also an effect of the people's labor. Those who perform the labor should have a right to control how the majority of the money is spent.

> O blessed Mary, Mother mine,
> there is no greater love than thine,
> as we are one in heart and mind,
> my place in hierarchy I find.
>
> **O Mother Mary, generate,**
> **the song that does accelerate,**
> **the earth into a higher state,**
> **all matter does now scintillate.**

2. In this so-called capitalist system, there is no room for sharing the wealth among all the people who help create it. The talents are not being multiplied, and if they are not multiplied, how can the wealth keep growing?

> I came to earth from heaven sent,
> as I am in embodiment,
> I use Divine authority,
> commanding you to set earth free.
>
> **O Mother Mary, generate,**
> **the song that does accelerate,**
> **the earth into a higher state,**
> **all matter does now scintillate.**

3. The wealth we have today that we did not have 30 years ago is the so-called value of stocks, bonds and other financial instruments. That money exists only as numbers on a computer, as zeros and ones on a server's hard drive, nothing else.

> I call now in God's sacred name,
> for you to use your Mother Flame,
> to burn all fear-based energy,
> restoring sacred harmony.

> **O Mother Mary, generate,**
> **the song that does accelerate,**
> **the earth into a higher state,**
> **all matter does now scintillate.**

4. This is not wealth. It is simply numbers that serve to gratify the egos of those who have taken the so-called rugged individualism to its ultimate perversion of caring only about themselves and not about others.

> Your sacred name I hereby praise,
> collective consciousness you raise,
> no more of fear and doubt and shame,
> consume it with your Mother Flame.

> **O Mother Mary, generate,**
> **the song that does accelerate,**
> **the earth into a higher state,**
> **all matter does now scintillate.**

5. Egotism rules America and that is not what Saint Germain meant when he gave his sponsorship of this nation. It has nothing whatsoever to do with his vision for this nation.

All darkness from the earth you purge,
your light moves as a mighty surge,
no force of darkness can now stop,
the spiral that goes only up.

**O Mother Mary, generate,
the song that does accelerate,
the earth into a higher state,
all matter does now scintillate.**

6. Saint Germain did not mean to raise up a nation of spoiled brats who care only about themselves and who take for granted that they have a right to have what they have and do whatever they want with it, without any sense of responsibility for sharing with others.

All elemental life you bless,
removing from them man-made stress,
the nature spirits are now free,
outpicturing Divine decree.

**O Mother Mary, generate,
the song that does accelerate,
the earth into a higher state,
all matter does now scintillate.**

7. Naturally, people have a right to take care of the needs of their families. There comes a point where we have taken care of those needs, and then multiplying the talents means doing something to help other people.

I raise my voice and take my stand,
a stop to war I do command,

no more shall warring scar the earth,
a golden age is given birth.

O Mother Mary, generate,
the song that does accelerate,
the earth into a higher state,
all matter does now scintillate.

8. When we are spending money, we are also helping other people because we are keeping the economy growing. Consumer spending is two-thirds of the economy, but the consumers are not the ones who have the money. It is concentrated in the hands of the elite who do not know how to spend the money because they have already bought all they need.

As Mother Earth is free at last,
disasters belong to the past,
your Mother Light is so intense,
that matter is now far less dense.

O Mother Mary, generate,
the song that does accelerate,
the earth into a higher state,
all matter does now scintillate.

9. There comes a point where people cannot spend more money on themselves. If they have an obsessive-compulsive need to own the money, then they just accumulate more and more because what if they lost it? People never feel secure when they are in this state of mind.

In Mother Light the earth is pure,
the upward spiral will endure,

prosperity is now the norm,
God's vision manifest as form.

**O Mother Mary, generate,
the song that does accelerate,
the earth into a higher state,
all matter does now scintillate.**

Part 5

1. In order to align America with the mind of Saint Germain, there has to be a sharing of the wealth. This can be done in various ways, not necessarily through high taxes.

O blessed Mary, Mother mine,
there is no greater love than thine,
as we are one in heart and mind,
my place in hierarchy I find.

**O Mother Mary, generate,
the song that does accelerate,
the earth into a higher state,
all matter does now scintillate.**

2. America is an idea, America is a dream. The idea that Saint Germain had in mind when he sponsored America was to create a society that was distinctly different from the feudal societies in Europe.

I came to earth from heaven sent,
as I am in embodiment,

I use Divine authority,
commanding you to set earth free.

**O Mother Mary, generate,
the song that does accelerate,
the earth into a higher state,
all matter does now scintillate.**

3. The vision of Saint Germain and the Founding Fathers was to create a country that was not controlled by an elite but where all of the people had an opportunity to multiply their individual talents and be rewarded according to their willingness to make an effort.

I call now in God's sacred name,
for you to use your Mother Flame,
to burn all fear-based energy,
restoring sacred harmony.

**O Mother Mary, generate,
the song that does accelerate,
the earth into a higher state,
all matter does now scintillate.**

4. Since then, the power elite has eroded that freedom and they have taken the fruits of the people's labor. It now goes to corporations that are not owned by a single person or even to companies that may be owned by a single person.

Your sacred name I hereby praise,
collective consciousness you raise,
no more of fear and doubt and shame,
consume it with your Mother Flame.

**O Mother Mary, generate,
the song that does accelerate,
the earth into a higher state,
all matter does now scintillate.**

5. The American system concentrates the wealth in the hands of a small elite. That is not the kind of free, egalitarian, non-elitist society that Saint Germain sponsored.

All darkness from the earth you purge,
your light moves as a mighty surge,
no force of darkness can now stop,
the spiral that goes only up.

**O Mother Mary, generate,
the song that does accelerate,
the earth into a higher state,
all matter does now scintillate.**

6. In order to move beyond this, America and Americans need to develop a conscience, a social awareness.

All elemental life you bless,
removing from them man-made stress,
the nature spirits are now free,
outpicturing Divine decree.

**O Mother Mary, generate,
the song that does accelerate,
the earth into a higher state,
all matter does now scintillate.**

7. Americans need to look at some of the other countries where they have said: "We will not allow there to be people who are poor, who are starving to death, who are malnourished, who cannot afford to go to the doctor but must wait until they have a life-threatening illness to go to the emergency room."

> I raise my voice and take my stand,
> a stop to war I do command,
> no more shall warring scar the earth,
> a golden age is given birth.
>
> **O Mother Mary, generate,**
> **the song that does accelerate,**
> **the earth into a higher state,**
> **all matter does now scintillate.**

8. Americans need to say: "We do not want to have a society where we are only taking care of ourselves and not taking care of each other. We do not want to have a country that consists of 400 million individuals. We want a country that consists of people who realize we are in the same boat and we will all do better if we take care of each other."

> As Mother Earth is free at last,
> disasters belong to the past,
> your Mother Light is so intense,
> that matter is now far less dense.
>
> **O Mother Mary, generate,**
> **the song that does accelerate,**
> **the earth into a higher state,**
> **all matter does now scintillate.**

9. America needs to have healthcare available for all people and a social safety net for those who lose their jobs because some corporations care more about profit for the elite than salaries for the people.

> In Mother Light the earth is pure,
> the upward spiral will endure,
> prosperity is now the norm,
> God's vision manifest as form.

> **O Mother Mary, generate,**
> **the song that does accelerate,**
> **the earth into a higher state,**
> **all matter does now scintillate.**

Part 6

1. Unless we have this critical mass of people who not only develop the social awareness but begin speaking out, then America cannot go beyond its present level.

> O blessed Mary, Mother mine,
> there is no greater love than thine,
> as we are one in heart and mind,
> my place in hierarchy I find.

> **O Mother Mary, generate,**
> **the song that does accelerate,**
> **the earth into a higher state,**
> **all matter does now scintillate.**

2. If America cannot go beyond its present level, it must decline because the talents are not being multiplied. If there is no willingness to reform the system, then the system must be allowed to collapse. This entire colossus, that the power elite has built in this country, must be allowed to fail.

> I came to earth from heaven sent,
> as I am in embodiment,
> I use Divine authority,
> commanding you to set earth free.
>
> **O Mother Mary, generate,**
> **the song that does accelerate,**
> **the earth into a higher state,**
> **all matter does now scintillate.**

3. The government and the media, both of which are essentially owned by the elite, may think that the apparatus is too big to fail, but Saint Germain does not think it is too big to fail. If that is the only way to move America forward, then he will withhold or withdraw his sponsorship and let it all collapse in upon itself.

> I call now in God's sacred name,
> for you to use your Mother Flame,
> to burn all fear-based energy,
> restoring sacred harmony.
>
> **O Mother Mary, generate,**
> **the song that does accelerate,**
> **the earth into a higher state,**
> **all matter does now scintillate.**

4. The people will be free from the tyranny of the financial elite, which is essentially the same lifestreams that were embodied in medieval Europe as the feudal lords and the kings.

> Your sacred name I hereby praise,
> collective consciousness you raise,
> no more of fear and doubt and shame,
> consume it with your Mother Flame.
>
> **O Mother Mary, generate,**
> **the song that does accelerate,**
> **the earth into a higher state,**
> **all matter does now scintillate.**

5. One way or the other, the people will be free from this elite. Will it be the easy way or will it be the hard way? That is a question that Saint Germain cannot decide because it is up to the free will of the people.

> All darkness from the earth you purge,
> your light moves as a mighty surge,
> no force of darkness can now stop,
> the spiral that goes only up.
>
> **O Mother Mary, generate,**
> **the song that does accelerate,**
> **the earth into a higher state,**
> **all matter does now scintillate.**

6. There is not a large gap before that social awareness, that sense of togetherness, can begin to dominate the American way of thinking. But we are not there yet.

> All elemental life you bless,
> removing from them man-made stress,
> the nature spirits are now free,
> outpicturing Divine decree.
>
> **O Mother Mary, generate,**
> **the song that does accelerate,**
> **the earth into a higher state,**
> **all matter does now scintillate.**

7. Many Americans have been indoctrinated with this sense of the American individualism. We need to resolve it and start feeling compassion for other people.

> I raise my voice and take my stand,
> a stop to war I do command,
> no more shall warring scar the earth,
> a golden age is given birth.
>
> **O Mother Mary, generate,**
> **the song that does accelerate,**
> **the earth into a higher state,**
> **all matter does now scintillate.**

8. Many spiritual people came into embodiment partly to take on this American way of thinking and help resolve it in the collective, so that we can help raise the collective to the next level up.

> As Mother Earth is free at last,
> disasters belong to the past,
> your Mother Light is so intense,
> that matter is now far less dense.

> O Mother Mary, generate,
> the song that does accelerate,
> the earth into a higher state,
> all matter does now scintillate.

9. It is a grand illusion of the ages when so many Americans think that America is the most sophisticated of the evolved countries, the evolved democracies.

> In Mother Light the earth is pure,
> the upward spiral will endure,
> prosperity is now the norm,
> God's vision manifest as form.

> O Mother Mary, generate,
> the song that does accelerate,
> the earth into a higher state,
> all matter does now scintillate.

Part 7

1. A realistic assessment will show that when it comes to developing a true functioning democracy, Canada and many of the nations in Europe have reached a higher level of maturity because there is that social awareness.

> O blessed Mary, Mother mine,
> there is no greater love than thine,
> as we are one in heart and mind,
> my place in hierarchy I find.

**O Mother Mary, generate,
the song that does accelerate,
the earth into a higher state,
all matter does now scintillate.**

2. The essence of the current American model is that there is a small elite who manipulates the people into voting for either this party or that party, but both parties are owned and controlled by the elite.

I came to earth from heaven sent,
as I am in embodiment,
I use Divine authority,
commanding you to set earth free.

**O Mother Mary, generate,
the song that does accelerate,
the earth into a higher state,
all matter does now scintillate.**

3. The two parties cannot enact a policy that overthrows the dominance of the elite. That is not a democracy; it is a camouflaged dictatorial system that is ruled by a small elite.

I call now in God's sacred name,
for you to use your Mother Flame,
to burn all fear-based energy,
restoring sacred harmony.

**O Mother Mary, generate,
the song that does accelerate,
the earth into a higher state,
all matter does now scintillate.**

4. We can have a true democracy only when we develop a social awareness where we realize: "We are in this together, and we function better when we all help each other, when we don't allow a small elite to manipulate us because we don't allow them to get away with setting themselves up as an elite."

> Your sacred name I hereby praise,
> collective consciousness you raise,
> no more of fear and doubt and shame,
> consume it with your Mother Flame.
>
> **O Mother Mary, generate,**
> **the song that does accelerate,**
> **the earth into a higher state,**
> **all matter does now scintillate.**

5. The idea of the rugged American individualism and the "America first" and the "America is the greatest nation in the world" was created by the elite because they are the ones who want to be completely egotistical, only think about themselves, not care about the consequences for anybody else and accumulate, accumulate, accumulate.

> All darkness from the earth you purge,
> your light moves as a mighty surge,
> no force of darkness can now stop,
> the spiral that goes only up.
>
> **O Mother Mary, generate,**
> **the song that does accelerate,**
> **the earth into a higher state,**
> **all matter does now scintillate.**

6. Social awareness is that we realize that we are individuals but we are not living in a bubble. We are living in a nation with millions of other people and we are our brother's keeper.

> All elemental life you bless,
> removing from them man-made stress,
> the nature spirits are now free,
> outpicturing Divine decree.
>
> **O Mother Mary, generate,**
> **the song that does accelerate,**
> **the earth into a higher state,**
> **all matter does now scintillate.**

7. We will not let those who are in the Cain consciousness run our nation! We are all our brother's and sister's keepers because that is the only way that a free democratic, non-elitist society can be built.

> I raise my voice and take my stand,
> a stop to war I do command,
> no more shall warring scar the earth,
> a golden age is given birth.
>
> **O Mother Mary, generate,**
> **the song that does accelerate,**
> **the earth into a higher state,**
> **all matter does now scintillate.**

8. Mother Mary, help more Americans tune in to your heart and experience how you love all people with a love that is truly unconditional.

> As Mother Earth is free at last,
> disasters belong to the past,
> your Mother Light is so intense,
> that matter is now far less dense.

> **O Mother Mary, generate,**
> **the song that does accelerate,**
> **the earth into a higher state,**
> **all matter does now scintillate.**

9. Mother Mary, help more Americans experience your Presence and experience the oneness of all life that is the strongest foundation for a social awareness.

> In Mother Light the earth is pure,
> the upward spiral will endure,
> prosperity is now the norm,
> God's vision manifest as form.

> **O Mother Mary, generate,**
> **the song that does accelerate,**
> **the earth into a higher state,**
> **all matter does now scintillate.**

Sealing

In the name of the I AM THAT I AM, I accept that Archangel Michael, Astrea and Shiva form an impenetrable shield around myself and all constructive people in America, sealing us from all fear-based energies in all four octaves. I accept that the Light of God is consuming and transforming all fear-based energies that make up the dark forces working against America!

3 | TAKING AMERICA FROM HUMAN JUDGMENT TO THE DISCERNMENT OF CHRIST

I AM the Ascended Master Jesus Christ, speaking through a human messenger. Now, imagine that this messenger was standing in front of a crowd made up of the leaders of the Christian churches in America. What would be their reaction to this opening line? They would be in instant denial. They would come up with a million excuses of why this could not be the real Jesus Christ. It has to be a false Christ, an impostor. It has to be the works of the devil and all of these other standard accusations that they come up with time and time again.

Can these people not look back at the stories of my life, described in the scriptures that they revere as the Word of God, can they not look at my life and see that what they are doing today is exactly what the leaders of the Jewish religion did to me when I did appear in the flesh and did not have to speak through a human messenger? Can they really not see this? They *cannot* or they *will not,* as the Scribes and the Pharisees and the leaders of the church back then *could not* and *would not.* Some *cannot,* I grant that, but too many *will not* and that I can do nothing about other than leave them behind. For how can I work with those who reject me when I respect free will? That is what I did to the leaders of the Jewish religion back then, and I went even further back then and allowed them to crucify me so that they would get the judgment of Christ.

Of course, I have on previous conferences pronounced the judgment of Christ upon the false leaders of Christianity [See Part 2]. I trust that those of you who know, respect and recognize who I am will make the calls for these invocations to reinforce that judgment of Christ. It is not my purpose here to bring any kind of judgment upon the false leaders of Christianity because I am not really so concerned about the false leaders. I am more concerned about their blind followers because I desire them to see the reality of who I am, and who I was and what *is* and *was* my true message.

Why America is not a Christian nation

Why am I speaking at this early stage of this conference where the topic is aligning America with the mind of Saint Germain? Well, it is because one of the major blocks to aligning America with the mind of Saint Germain is precisely Christianity in America. Why is it a greater block in America than in many (for example) European nations or in Canada?

Well, it is because there are so many people in America, and certainly the Christian leaders among them, who say that America is a Christian nation. Well my beloved, have they not bothered to read their own constitution? Does not the constitution make it very clear that America is *not* a Christian nation?

It is a *secular* nation because it is based on the separation of church and state. Do they not see that the Founding Fathers of America were very well aware of how things were and had been in Europe? For over a thousand years the Catholic church had a stranglehold on the nations of Europe and in many ways prevented their growth, and certainly was instrumental in preventing the freedom of the people. The Founding Fathers did not want to create a nation that could be dominated by one religion, like they had seen in Europe, and the Middle East with Islam. They wanted to create a nation where there was freedom *of* religion and freedom *from* religion if that was what people chose.

Certainly, they wanted a nation where the government had freedom from religion and was free to enact laws that were based on the desires and the will of the people and not what some religious authority imposed upon them—as had been done by the Popes throughout the Middle Ages. They saw the limitations of the system, they were very well aware of the need to separate church and state and this is the kind of country you are living in. Therefore, America, if it is true to its own constitution, can never be a Christian nation.

Would I or Saint Germain or any ascended master want America to be a Christian nation or be dominated by any other religion? Nay, we would not. What would be the reaction of the Christian leaders? "But didn't Jesus tell us 2,000 years ago to go out into all the world and preach the gospel and turn all people into his disciples?" Ah, yes I did, but did I say to go out into all the world and make all people members of a Christian religion? I think not, at least that is not how I read the scriptures.

Why do you read them differently? Ah, *there* is something that they will not ponder, those who claim to be representatives of Jesus Christ in America today. Are they willing to ponder whether there is a difference between the way *they* see Christ and the way *I* am? Are they willing to look at the most crucial place in the scriptures where I said to Peter: "Get thee behind me Satan?" Are they willing to consider why I did this? Are they willing to recognize that Peter was superimposing a man-made image upon the Living Christ and I refused to conform to it? Are they willing to see that they are doing the exact same thing today, superimposing a man-made image upon the Living Christ and I still refuse to conform? That is why I am speaking through a human messenger who is willing to not put an image upon me but let me be who I am.

Do Christian leaders know the real Jesus?

There are, of course, many of these leaders of the Christian churches who will say: "No, we have contact with Jesus, we have Jesus speaking through us or speaking to us, so we know the real Jesus." But do they? Are they willing to consider whether they know the real Jesus?

If they are, they need to look at the history of their own religion. They need to be willing to trace their roots back. Whether they are Christians or Anglicans or Calvinists or Lutherans or this or that, if you look at the history of the Christian religion, you cannot deny that all modern Christian churches are based on the foundation set by the Catholic church in the year 381. If you are, then, willing to look beyond that and go back to what I actually said, what I actually did, anyone who is willing to apply normal common sense, normal human intelligence, can see that there is a vast gap between what I preached, how I acted, and the image of me created by the Catholic church from the very beginning. I never claimed to be the *only* son of God. I did not deny that I am a son of God but you are all sons and daughters of God. I never set myself apart in a fundamental way and why is this? Because the essence of my message back then and now is that there is a path of initiation, a gradual path of initiation, that can lead any human being from the level of consciousness they are at right now, towards succeedingly higher stages of consciousness until they reach the state of consciousness that I demonstrated.

That is why I said: "Those who believe on me, (meaning truly those who are willing to internalize my teaching and apply it to themselves) ye can do the works that I did and even greater works." You can do greater works because I started a trend of raising the consciousness. As the collective consciousness is raised, it becomes easier and easier for people to reach higher levels of consciousness, which is why it is, despite the efforts of all the false preachers and all the dark forces, easier to manifest Christhood today than it was 2,000 years ago. That is why many more people have the potential to manifest it and express it.

How the gradual path of initiation was obliterated

Now, what has this got to do with America? Well, if you look at the historical facts, you will see that a considerable number among the Founding Fathers of this nation were Freemasons. This does not mean that Saint Germain wants all people in America to become Freemasons. The fact of the matter is that this is something that these Christian leaders do not want to look at because they, of course, consider Freemasonry a false religion. What is the essence of Freemasonry?

It is a gradual path of initiation that leads to higher levels. Now, the specifics of how the Masons do this are not particularly high and not particularly relevant in this age. They were what could be given at a time when the Catholic church aggressively and violently suppressed all other forms of religion. The Freemasons started as a secret society because that was all that could be created at the time, and the real purpose was to present people with a gradual path of initiation.

The very historical fact, which is undeniable for anybody who is willing to look at it, is that the Catholic church suppressed any form of religion that diverged from itself. Then, go back and look at the formation of the Catholic church and look at what actually happened in that process. What happened was that the entire idea of a gradual path to higher levels of consciousness, leading to a state of Christ Consciousness, was completely and absolutely obliterated from the Catholic church.

This was done by elevating me to being so above other human beings that they could not follow my footsteps because I was the *exception* not the *example*. This is something that the Christian leaders and their followers are not willing to look at, but it is not difficult to see this if you stop denying historical facts. The Catholic church completely obliterated the path of initiation, a path of initiation that had existed for thousands of years before my appearance in the flesh, and that existed in many other movements at the time throughout the Middle East. With the formation of the Catholic church this path was suppressed violently throughout the regions where the Catholic church had influence and it was that way for almost a thousand years.

For that matter it is still that way in the mainstream, but as you see in America, more and more people are rejecting that form of religion, which says you need an outside authority in the form of a church and its priesthood here on earth. It also says you need an external Saviour in the form of this "Jesus graven image" they have created, who comes and saves you.

Or you need the blood of Jesus to wash you clean from your sins. It is a total denial of the fact that your sin is a result of you making choices with your free will, and a total denial of the fact that no matter what choices you have ever made with your free will, you can come to make more aware choices and thereby free yourself from the consequences or the sin (or the karma or whatever you want to call it) of your previous choices. You can never make a choice from which you cannot free yourself by making a more aware choice.

Fallen beings in the churches of America

This is the very essence of free will, and it is exactly what the fallen beings and the dark forces have been attempting to deny and obliterate since they came to this planet. If you could see what I see from the ascended state, you would see that all of the major churches in America, and many of the smaller churches in America, are led by people who are either fallen beings in embodiment or who are well-meaning people whose minds have been completely taken over by demons in the emotional realm or by fallen beings in the mental or identity realm. If people could see this, if Christians in their churches could see what kind of leaders they have and what kind of non-material forces are behind those leaders, they would be shocked to the core of their beings and they would walk out of their churches, most of them instantly.

Why do you think that when I encountered the Scribes and Pharisees I called them "sons of the devil" and said that they would do the lusts of their father? Because they also were either fallen beings in embodiment or had their minds taken over by fallen beings in (or out of) embodiment. This, of course, is not something that I expect most Christians to accept but nevertheless, we intend for the dictations at this conference to be turned into a book and invocations to be made so that you can reinforce this and direct it into the collective consciousness. This can help those who are hypnotized by these false preachers to suddenly have a shift that makes them see what they cannot see now. You are your brother's keepers in the sense that you have seen the limitations and the fallacy of mainstream Christianity. It is only natural that you, then, use that to at least make the calls for your brothers and sisters to be free, as you have become free. This is not meaning that you are in any way forcing them to accept what you see but you are giving them the choice, then allowing *them* to have the choice.

Speaking to people about a higher teaching

That also relates very much to how I desire you to, so to speak tell, other people about what you know. Again, free will is free will—you do not want to force others. I do not want you to take the teachings I have given through this messenger and go into a fanatical state of mind, like you see with so many Christian preachers or even Christians who have been awakened and suddenly now think they have to go out and preach to everybody. I do not desire to see any of you go into this state of mind. I do not desire for you to feel *compelled* to tell other people. As Mother Mary said yesterday, when you freely share without having any intention of how other people should accept or not accept what you are saying, you have a much better opportunity to reach their hearts.

What is going to make a difference is reaching people's hearts, not speaking to their minds—or speaking to their fears as many of the leaders of the Christian churches in America are actually doing. It is valuable for you to share your own process of how you came to the realizations you have come to, but not with the purpose of converting others to a particular religion. We have purposefully not created an organization, not created a teaching that is clearly identified because what is there to convert people into here? There is no membership, right?

What does it mean to make people my disciples? It means that they understand the path of initiation, which can lead you to the Christ consciousness—or whatever you want to call it so that people can lock in to it. Many will (because of the false Christianity and its aggressiveness) reject the word "Christ." Well, then call it something else that they can accept. The words are not as important as conveying the central message that each human being has an opportunity to raise their awareness, and that by raising your awareness every aspect of your life will improve. As you will have experienced, many of you, that your lives have improved tremendously after you found the teachings and started applying them. You can, in fact, look back and see that you have actually been reborn spiritually, psychologically reborn and you have become what Paul called "a new being in Christ," whether it is in Christ or in the Universal consciousness. Christ was meant to be a universal word, it has become a sectarian word, but whatever word you use, you have become a new being. You are not the person you were before you found these teachings. That is what you can convey because that is what people are hungry for. They want to know that there is a way out of their troubles.

The increasing frustration of Americans

Look at America. More and more people are becoming dissatisfied with the state of government. More and more people are becoming dissatisfied with their daily lives. More and more people are feeling a pressure, they do not know what it is but they feel stressed. They feel pressure, they feel they cannot stand it—something must change. My beloved, all of this would have been unnecessary if Christianity had not been put on a false track by the fallen beings. If there had been a path of initiation, Americans would have been aware that this nation is the land of opportunity, meaning really the opportunity to raise your consciousness.

Back when America was founded, naturally the people of Europe had been suppressed by the feudal system, by them having no opportunity to improve their lives materially. What they saw as the land of opportunity was that they could come here and they would be given a piece of land on which they could grow their own food and live independently of any landlord who would come and take the fruits of their labor. It was a major revelation for them, a major opportunity and naturally they were focused on this.

Naturally, for the first several centuries of America's history people have been focused on improving the material way of life. Perfectly natural for a new nation, especially given the state of poverty that most people were in. If there had been just *some* understanding of a path of initiation, then Americans would have known the purpose for accumulating material wealth. A material high standard of living is not a goal, it is not an end in itself. The purpose is to give you free time so you can now focus on following that path of initiation and raising your awareness.

Of course, since the 1960's many people in the so-called New Age movements have found such a path. Ironically, in the "Christian nation" of America many have found it through eastern teachings because they still have some element of this path. Others have found it in other ways, including ascended master teachings. Many, many people have already discovered this path but many, many more are longing for it, are ready to discover it. If they could make that switch (which again you can make the calls for), then there could be a tremendous shift. So many of the problems you see in America could be changed very quickly. When people have a goal for their lives (they know where they are going and they know how to move towards that goal in a logical systematic step-by-step fashion), then their entire attitude to life changes, as many of you described yesterday. You had started out at a certain state of being depressed, being agnostic, being stressed out and then, when you discovered that there is a path, everything switched for you. This is what you can describe to other people, as I talked about in Kazakhstan [See the book *Fulfilling Your Highest Spiritual Potential*] where I admonished you to start sharing your own path, your own experiences. Nothing is more inspiring to other people than hearing the kind of testimonies you gave yesterday.

There are many, many people who are not ready to hear what I am saying now, or read it, but they are ready to hear about *your* path, *your* life. Therefore, you can reach people that cannot be reached directly by the teaching that we are giving. They are not quite ready for that but they are ready for *something*, they are longing for *something*.

Changing how people communicate

Look at America again, look at Americans, look at how many people are becoming increasingly stressed and dissatisfied. Look at how many people are taking this into extremes of drug or alcohol abuse because they do not know how to alleviate the stress so they try to find some temporary relief from it. Well, if you have a purpose and a logical path to get there, you do not need relief, you do not need escape. You just need to go further on the path.

The most important thing that you could do for other people is to be willing to share your own path, partly because *they* can lock in to it but also because it is important for *you* to share your path. If more and more people become willing to share openly and honestly, it can actually have the impact of gradually changing how people communicate with each other.

Other masters will speak more about communication but what I want to point out to you is this. Look at the Christians in this nation, look how they talk to each other and to other people. Everything they say to each other or to non-Christians or to those who are outside of their own church is based on what? It is based on a certain judgment of how a human being is supposed to be, specifically how a good Christian is supposed to be. Everything they do is based on them having a standard in their heads of how you are supposed to be and how you are supposed to *not* be. It is a completely black-and-white evaluation and judgment of what it means to be a human being. They evaluate everything based on this.

Now, there may be some Christians who are into humanitarian work and who, at least in their outer actions and speech, have set aside this judgment so that they can supposedly help out everybody. But in their minds they still have the judgment because it is the hallmark of any religion, any thought system, dominated by the fallen beings. We have said it before: What did the fallen beings have to do to really mess things up (as the popular saying goes) on this planet. They only have to do two things: Set up a standard and project that everybody had to live up to the standard, and those who did were *right* and those who did not were *wrong*. That is all they had to do.

Rising above black-and-white judgment

What I came to do 2,000 years ago was to counteract this by giving a path of initiation where you could raise yourself above this black-and-white thinking. When you had reached some measure of Christhood, you would stop judging your brothers and sisters. You would internalize the truth behind the statement "judge not lest ye be judged, for with whatever measure ye meter out to others, it shall be meted out to you."

Christhood – Christ consciousness – is a state where you discern very clearly. At the beginning stages of Christhood you are still affected by black-and-white thinking. In fact, you see many people, including ascended master students, who are beginning to move into discernment and so they very clearly see what is evil in the world and what is wrong with the world. They tend to focus so much on this that sometimes they go into this warring state of mind of thinking they have to go out and combat evil. That is why you see people get sucked into the crusades and the whole spirit (the demon) behind the crusades. You see that in people today as well, but you also see those who can see what is good and evil but they cannot separate evil from the people. When you come to the higher stages of Christhood, you see that evil – you do not even call it that anymore – is all a certain state of consciousness, there are certain spirits.

You can see, of course, that a person might be affected by this state of consciousness, might be identified with a certain outer self. Nevertheless, you also, when you have Christ discernment, see beyond this. Therefore, you are not judging the person and therefore you are not doing what the Christians are doing. You are not relating to that person based on a sense of judgment and therefore based on the sense of superiority that you are above the evil you see in the other person. That is why you see Christians clearly set themselves apart. That is why you see many other spiritual movements clearly set themselves apart. That is why you see previous ascended master dispensations that clearly set themselves apart because they were still in the Piscean mindset and could not rise above it.

What we are calling you to do is to step up to that higher level where you have Christ discernment. You have risen to that level of Christ discernment where you do not judge other people. This is what you had yesterday where many of you felt free to speak out about things you had never felt free to speak about with anybody else. You did not *feel* judged because you *were* not judged. I can assure you, my beloved, that if you can create groups that have that kind of environment, you will attract people who will long to be in a non-judgmental environment and be able to talk about their questions, their feelings, their thinking about spirituality and about life.

What we have attempted to give you, especially in these later years, is the experience that we of the ascended masters love and accept you without conditions. It is because we have that Christ discernment. We see clearly that you have certain external selves and you are somewhat identified with them. We also see that this is not who you are, you are more than this and you have the potential to rise. We see that you are willing to walk the path, you are willing to look at yourselves, as you are able to do at your present level.

What is the need to judge, what is the need to judge other people when you see this? Of course, there are people who are not on the path, but you do not need to judge them. You do not need to interact with them more than necessary. You are not trying to help them because they are not at the level where they can be helped by you. You focus on the people you *can* help and there is no need to judge anyone.

The American sense of superiority

It truly, truly is necessary for aligning America with the mind of Saint Germain that some people become the forerunners for going beyond this state of judgment. What can this lead to in the more long term? Well, of course, you who are among the top 10% can actually set the collective consciousness on a new track. It can lead to the point where you overcome what is one of the subtle and unrecognized elements of the American psyche, and it is the judgment between those who are Americans and those who are not, the distinction between America and all other nations.

This is, as Mother Mary talked about yesterday, where many Americans have taken the sponsorship of Saint Germain and have started taking it for granted. They have felt (even though they were not consciously aware of this) that they must be worthy to live in this great nation and therefore they are entitled to have what they have. Therefore, America is the greatest nation and America is better than all others.

This creates a separation between Americans and other people. It also creates (which is far more devastating for the growth of the nation) a division between groups of people who live in America where there is so much of the inferiority-superiority dynamic going on. Various groups are seeing themselves as being superior to other groups of Americans, therefore seeing themselves as being in an antagonistic struggle with these other groups. Just look at the fact that this nation had to go through a civil war to stop slavery.

Well, what is slavery? Is it not a total division of humans into two separate classes, the property and the owners? People are not property. As the messenger expressed yesterday, you cannot own another human being. It is a complete anti-thesis to the Law of Free Will. It is a complete anti-thesis to the true teachings of Christ. All are created equal, all have been given the same opportunity and there is no value judgment in the mind of Christ and the mind of God.

You see how there was this very deep division, and you can see that there is still this very deep division, not only about the issue of slavery but many other issues. You see, of course, still this very deep division between those who have light skin and those who have darker skin, whatever is the politically correct term for those with darker skin. You see this division today. My beloved, do you really think this division exists in the mind of Christ? Do you really think that I have any kind of judgment, have any kind of opinion, about people with dark skin or red skin or yellow skin or this or that?

America and the defense of the Holy Land

My beloved, I see beyond all of these outer divisions, I see beyond them all. Why did I appear in the Middle East? Because there is hardly a place on the planet that is more divided by these outer differences, more focused on outer differences, than the Middle East. I did not appear there because it is a holy land, as so many Christians in America think. They think America has to defend the modern state of Israel because it is the Holy Land. Do you really think, my beloved, that I want a major war or confrontation because Christians in America feel they have to defend the Holy Land? Do you really think this is what I want? If you do, you are completely out of alignment with the mind of Christ and the mind of Saint Germain.

You see, again, how the fallen beings are quite clever in using the lower aspects, the dualistic consciousness, to set up the scene for conflict. Do you not recognize that thousands of years ago there were certain fallen beings who managed to take a small, not very clearly defined, tribe in the Middle East and give them a sense of superiority that they were God's chosen people, that they had the superior God? Whereas all of the other tribes in the area only had idols, they had the superior, the almighty, God and they were the sons of this God. Do you not see that by creating this state of consciousness, the fallen beings set the Jewish people in an inherent conflict with all others?

Then, by taking other people, such as certain Arab people, and giving them the sense that because they had received the religion of Islam, they were the superior people, they created even more conflict. I came to the Middle East to give people a way beyond this conflict consciousness, namely to walk the path of initiation that leads to Christ discernment. I came there not because it was the *holy* land but because it was the most *unholy* place on earth. It still is because they have not used the teachings and the example I gave to raise their consciousness. They are still rejecting it but so are the Christians in America rejecting it.

That is why the fallen beings have now managed to set up this conflict. The fallen beings used Hitler to create the Holocaust and they used the obvious atrocities against the Jewish people to create the modern state of Israel. They have used the Christians in America to be so fixated on the Holy Land that they are willing to commit the military resources of America into an all-out war to defend the Holy Land. There are Christians, my beloved, in this nation who are willing to create World War III over the State of Israel and who, if it came about, would see it as a sign that this is the Battle of Armageddon. It means the end is near and I am going to appear in the sky and take them and the members of their little church to heaven and send all others to hell. This is how they think in their hearts, even if they are not willing to speak it outwardly.

My beloved, they have people in Congress, in the Senate, in the military, in the media, in the power elite who actually believe this. If there was a threat, they would be willing to commit the military resources of the United States to an all-out war to defend the State of Israel. They have already been instrumental in committing many of the resources (whether hidden or known) to set the State of Israel up as a nuclear power, something that anybody with common sense can see is completely devastating in a densely populated region such as the Middle East. How would Israel be able to use its nuclear weapons without killing itself in the process, its neighbors are too close.

Awakening without being overwhelmed

Does this not show you, when you think about this, that this cannot come from the mind of Christ? If it does not come from the mind of Christ where does it come from: the mind of anti-christ. Does this not show you that the people who are promoting these ideas do not represent Christ in America? They represent anti-christ because, as I said, they are either fallen beings in embodiment or their minds are completely taken over by fallen beings in the higher realms.

My beloved, what can you do about this? You can make the calls. Make the calls for the judgment of these false leaders, as you have done, but also make the calls for radiating this into the collective consciousness so that we can direct the angels to use their cosmic vacuum cleaners to clean up this entire mess. [Reference to vacuum cleaners was due to the hotel staff using a vacuum cleaner right outside the conference room]

My beloved, it is very important that you understand that we are not giving you a teaching in order to make you feel that there is so much opposition that it is overwhelming. We understand very well that many, many people, whether they are ascended master students or not, have been brought up to look at life a certain way and then suddenly something happens.

You make a shift in your mind, you find maybe some teaching, spiritual or otherwise, and people are awakened. You wake up, you realize that things are not the way you were brought up to think they are. You were brought up with a certain illusion and you did not understand how things really are. You see many, many people in America who have gone through this. Some after the election of the last President, other people going back decades where they have awakened to realize that there are certain forces in America that are ruling the country behind the scenes. They have gone into various conspiracy theories and this and that. You see many of these people who go into a phase where, now they see so much more than they saw before. They see so many more problems and it becomes overwhelming to them. They feel almost paralyzed because how can you as an individual do anything about this?

What I am saying to you specifically who are here, those of you who study our teachings on the Internet: Do not go into that reaction, do not feel overwhelmed because what is it that you as an individual can do about even the most overwhelming problems on earth? You can walk the path to Christhood. That is the most efficient way to remove evil. You do not have (as we have said before) to battle the dark forces. If you have not internalized this one concept, then read the *My Lives* book [*My Lives with Lucifer, Satan, Hitler and Jesus*] and internalize it from there so that you do not have to spend, as the protagonist did and as I incidentally did, a million years battling the fallen beings before you see the futility of it. That is not something I wish for any of you.

The masters are not doom sayers

The reality is: You are not powerless. You are all making an invaluable contribution to the raising of the collective consciousness on the planet and in America. Nothing is hopeless, the darkest hour is the hour before dawn. Yet, this is not a particularly dark hour in the history of America. We are not in any way doomsday prophets. I realize that we can come across at certain times as being very sombre, very direct and we are exposing many things that may be shocking to you. Nevertheless, why are we telling you about problems unless we know you can do something about it?

The very fact that we are telling you this should be a cause for optimism because if it was hopeless, what would be the point of telling you—unless we wanted you to go into a negative fear-based state of mind. Then, we would be fallen beings and not ascended masters. We have no desire whatsoever to put you in a state of fear, a state of hopelessness or a state of feeling that nothing you do really matters. *Everything* you do matters—when you are walking the path. Every step up you take on your personal path pulls up on the collective consciousness.

That is what it truly means to be a disciple of Christ where you recognize and realize that you are not doing this just for yourself. You are actually doing it to raise the whole, and you *are* raising the whole, my beloved. You may not always realize this. I can assure you that yesterday, as this messenger was sitting here listening to your personal testimonies of how much it had meant for you to find the teaching he has brought forth, he was realizing that in his normal daily life, he does not quite acknowledge the effect of what he is doing. It is the same with all of you. You are in your daily lives, you are in your daily routine, you are struggling with whatever conditions you are facing and you do not always take time to step back and realize that by the very fact that you have been willing to raise your consciousness, you have made an invaluable contribution to raising the whole.

It is part of Christhood, Christ discernment, that you recognize that you are not a separate being, right? We have said it many times: Duality is the state of separation; Christhood is the state of Oneness. As you walk the path of Christhood, you naturally begin to feel more one with all life—that is why you can stop judging other people. That is also why you can stop judging yourself, and you can realize that because you are one with all life, raising yourself pulls up on everyone else.

I wish you to just take a step back mentally (because you are sitting too close to do it physically) and recognize that you – each one of you – have made major progress on the spiritual path. You are not the same person you were, five, ten or twenty years ago. It is not just after you found the ascended master teachings. You have been making progress all of your life because you have learned from the various experiences you have had.

Acknowledge that by making this progress you have made an invaluable contribution to raising the collective consciousness. You can continue to do so. Yes, you can do outer things, you can make the calls, you can talk to other people, but the most important contribution you are making to the forward progression of this planet is by raising your consciousness and attaining your Christhood. That is, of course, what the leaders of false Christianity will deny and on those fruits, ye can know them.

4 | INVOKING AN EXPOSURE OF THE FALSE LEADERS OF CHRISTIANITY

In the name of the I AM THAT I AM, Jesus Christ, I use the authority that I have as a being in embodiment on earth to call upon Jesus to reinforce my calls and use my chakras to project the statements in this invocation into the collective consciousness and awaken Americans to how the false leaders have perverted Christianity in America. Awaken Americans to the reality that we are spiritual beings and that we can co-create a new future by working with the ascended masters. I especially call for …

[Make your own calls here.]

Part 1

1. I call forth the judgment of Christ upon the leaders of the Christian churches in America who are unwilling to hear the Living Word of the Ascended Master Jesus.

> O Jesus, blessed brother mine,
> I walk the path that you outline,
> a great example to us all,
> I follow now your inner call.
>
> **O Jesus, let the Fire of Joy,**
> **consume the devil's subtle ploy,**
> **transfigured is our planet earth,**
> **the golden age is given birth.**

2. What the Christian leaders are doing today is exactly what the leaders of the Jewish religion did to Jesus when he did appear in the flesh and did not have to speak through a human messenger.

> O Jesus, open inner sight,
> the ego wants to prove it's right,
> but this I will no longer do,
> I want to be all one with you.
>
> **O Jesus, let the Fire of Joy,**
> **consume the devil's subtle ploy,**
> **transfigured is our planet earth,**
> **the golden age is given birth.**

3. I call for the reinforcement of the judgment of Christ upon the false leaders of Christianity.

> O Jesus, I now clearly see,
> the Key of Knowledge given me,
> my Christ self I hereby embrace,
> as you fill up my inner space.
>
> **O Jesus, let the Fire of Joy,**
> **consume the devil's subtle ploy,**
> **transfigured is our planet earth,**
> **the golden age is given birth.**

4. I call for the blind followers to be cut free to see the reality of who Jesus is and who he was and what is and was his true message.

> O Jesus, show me serpent's lie,
> expose the beam in my own eye,
> as Christ discernment you me give,
> in oneness I forever live.
>
> **O Jesus, let the Fire of Joy,**
> **consume the devil's subtle ploy,**
> **transfigured is our planet earth,**
> **the golden age is given birth.**

5. One of the major blocks to aligning America with the mind of Saint Germain is Christianity in America.

> O Jesus, I am truly meek,
> and thus I turn the other cheek,

when the accuser attacks me,
I go within and merge with thee.

O Jesus, let the Fire of Joy,
consume the devil's subtle ploy,
transfigured is our planet earth,
the golden age is given birth.

6. So many people in America say that America is a Christian nation, yet the constitution makes it clear that America is *not* a Christian nation? It is a *secular* nation because it is based on the separation of church and state.

O Jesus, ego I let die,
surrender ev'ry earthly tie,
the dead can bury what is dead,
I choose to walk with you instead.

O Jesus, let the Fire of Joy,
consume the devil's subtle ploy,
transfigured is our planet earth,
the golden age is given birth.

7. The Founding Fathers of America were aware of how things had been in Europe. For over a thousand years the Catholic church had a stranglehold on the nations of Europe and prevented their growth. It was instrumental in restricting the freedom of the people.

O Jesus, help me rise above,
the devil's test through higher love,
show me separate self unreal,
my formless self you do reveal.

**O Jesus, let the Fire of Joy,
consume the devil's subtle ploy,
transfigured is our planet earth,
the golden age is given birth.**

8. The Founding Fathers did not want to create a nation that could be dominated by one religion, like they had seen in Europe, and the Middle East with Islam. They wanted to create a nation where there was freedom *of* religion and freedom *from* religion if that was what people chose.

O Jesus, what is that to me,
I just let go and follow thee,
with this I do pass ev'ry test,
to find with you eternal rest.

**O Jesus, let the Fire of Joy,
consume the devil's subtle ploy,
transfigured is our planet earth,
the golden age is given birth.**

9. The Founding Fathers wanted a nation where the government had freedom from religion and was free to enact laws that were based on the desires and the will of the people and not what some religious authority imposed upon them—as had been done by the Popes throughout the Middle Ages.

O Jesus, fiery master mine,
my heart now melting into thine,
I love with heart and mind and soul,
the God who is my highest goal.

**O Jesus, let the Fire of Joy,
consume the devil's subtle ploy,
transfigured is our planet earth,
the golden age is given birth.**

Part 2

1. The Founding Fathers saw the limitations of the system, they were aware of the need to separate church and state and this is the kind of country we are living in. Therefore, America, if it is true to its own constitution, can never be a Christian nation.

> O Jesus, blessed brother mine,
> I walk the path that you outline,
> a great example to us all,
> I follow now your inner call.

**O Jesus, let the Fire of Joy,
consume the devil's subtle ploy,
transfigured is our planet earth,
the golden age is given birth.**

2. Saint Germain does not want America to be a Christian nation or be dominated by any other religion.

> O Jesus, open inner sight,
> the ego wants to prove it's right,
> but this I will no longer do,
> I want to be all one with you.

**O Jesus, let the Fire of Joy,
consume the devil's subtle ploy,
transfigured is our planet earth,
the golden age is given birth.**

3. The Christian leaders would say that Jesus told them to turn all people into his disciples. Yet, he did not say to make all people members of a Christian religion.

O Jesus, I now clearly see,
the Key of Knowledge given me,
my Christ self I hereby embrace,
as you fill up my inner space.

**O Jesus, let the Fire of Joy,
consume the devil's subtle ploy,
transfigured is our planet earth,
the golden age is given birth.**

4. Those who claim to be representatives of Jesus Christ in America today are not willing to ponder whether there is a difference between the way *they* see Christ and the way Jesus is.

O Jesus, show me serpent's lie,
expose the beam in my own eye,
as Christ discernment you me give,
in oneness I forever live.

**O Jesus, let the Fire of Joy,
consume the devil's subtle ploy,
transfigured is our planet earth,
the golden age is given birth.**

5. They are not willing to consider why Jesus said to Peter: "Get thee behind me Satan."

> O Jesus, I am truly meek,
> and thus I turn the other cheek,
> when the accuser attacks me,
> I go within and merge with thee.
>
> **O Jesus, let the Fire of Joy,**
> **consume the devil's subtle ploy,**
> **transfigured is our planet earth,**
> **the golden age is given birth.**

6. They are not willing to recognize that Peter was superimposing a man-made image upon the Living Christ and Jesus refused to conform to it. They are not willing to see that today, they are superimposing a man-made image upon the Living Christ and Jesus still refuses to conform.

> O Jesus, ego I let die,
> surrender ev'ry earthly tie,
> the dead can bury what is dead,
> I choose to walk with you instead.
>
> **O Jesus, let the Fire of Joy,**
> **consume the devil's subtle ploy,**
> **transfigured is our planet earth,**
> **the golden age is given birth.**

7. Many leaders of the Christian churches think they have contact with Jesus, but are they willing to consider whether they know the real Jesus?

4 | *Invoking an exposure of the false leaders of Christianity*

O Jesus, help me rise above,
the devil's test through higher love,
show me separate self unreal,
my formless self you do reveal.

**O Jesus, let the Fire of Joy,
consume the devil's subtle ploy,
transfigured is our planet earth,
the golden age is given birth.**

8. If we look at the history of the Christian religion, we cannot deny that all modern Christian churches are based on the foundation set by the Catholic church in the year 381.

O Jesus, what is that to me,
I just let go and follow thee,
with this I do pass ev'ry test,
to find with you eternal rest.

**O Jesus, let the Fire of Joy,
consume the devil's subtle ploy,
transfigured is our planet earth,
the golden age is given birth.**

9. Anyone who is willing to apply normal common sense, normal human intelligence, can see that there is a vast gap between what Jesus preached and the image of him created by the Catholic church from the very beginning.

O Jesus, fiery master mine,
my heart now melting into thine,
I love with heart and mind and soul,
the God who is my highest goal.

**O Jesus, let the Fire of Joy,
consume the devil's subtle ploy,
transfigured is our planet earth,
the golden age is given birth.**

Part 3

1. Jesus never claimed to be the *only* son of God. He did not deny that he is a son of God but we are all sons and daughters of God.

> O Jesus, blessed brother mine,
> I walk the path that you outline,
> a great example to us all,
> I follow now your inner call.

> **O Jesus, let the Fire of Joy,
> consume the devil's subtle ploy,
> transfigured is our planet earth,
> the golden age is given birth.**

2. Jesus never set himself apart in a fundamental way because the essence of his message back then and now is that there is a gradual path of initiation that can lead us from our present level of consciousness towards higher stages of consciousness, until we reach the state of consciousness that Jesus demonstrated.

> O Jesus, open inner sight,
> the ego wants to prove it's right,
> but this I will no longer do,
> I want to be all one with you.

> **O Jesus, let the Fire of Joy,**
> **consume the devil's subtle ploy,**
> **transfigured is our planet earth,**
> **the golden age is given birth.**

3. That is why Jesus said: "Those who believe on me, ye can do the works that I did and even greater works." We can do greater works because Jesus started a trend of raising the consciousness.

> O Jesus, I now clearly see,
> the Key of Knowledge given me,
> my Christ self I hereby embrace,
> as you fill up my inner space.

> **O Jesus, let the Fire of Joy,**
> **consume the devil's subtle ploy,**
> **transfigured is our planet earth,**
> **the golden age is given birth.**

4. As the collective consciousness is raised, it becomes easier and easier for people to reach higher levels of consciousness, which is why it is, despite the efforts of all the false preachers and all the dark forces, easier to manifest Christhood today than it was 2,000 years ago.

> O Jesus, show me serpent's lie,
> expose the beam in my own eye,
> as Christ discernment you me give,
> in oneness I forever live.

> **O Jesus, let the Fire of Joy,**
> **consume the devil's subtle ploy,**

**transfigured is our planet earth,
the golden age is given birth.**

5. The Catholic church suppressed any form of religion that diverged from itself, and it removed the idea of a gradual path to higher levels of consciousness, leading to a state of Christ Consciousness. This was done by elevating Jesus to being so above other human beings that we could not follow his footsteps because he was the *exception,* not the *example.*

> O Jesus, I am truly meek,
> and thus I turn the other cheek,
> when the accuser attacks me,
> I go within and merge with thee.

> **O Jesus, let the Fire of Joy,
> consume the devil's subtle ploy,
> transfigured is our planet earth,
> the golden age is given birth.**

6. The Catholic church completely obliterated the path of initiation that had existed for thousands of years before Jesus' appearance in the flesh, and that existed in many other movements at the time throughout the Middle East.

> O Jesus, ego I let die,
> surrender ev'ry earthly tie,
> the dead can bury what is dead,
> I choose to walk with you instead.

> **O Jesus, let the Fire of Joy,
> consume the devil's subtle ploy,**

> transfigured is our planet earth,
> the golden age is given birth.

7. With the formation of the Catholic church, this path was suppressed violently throughout the regions where the Catholic church had influence and it was that way for almost a thousand years.

> O Jesus, help me rise above,
> the devil's test through higher love,
> show me separate self unreal,
> my formless self you do reveal.

> **O Jesus, let the Fire of Joy,**
> **consume the devil's subtle ploy,**
> **transfigured is our planet earth,**
> **the golden age is given birth.**

8. It is still that way in the mainstream, but more and more Americans are rejecting that form of religion, which says we need an outside authority in the form of a church and its priesthood here on earth. It also says we need an external Saviour and the blood of Jesus to wash away our sins.

> O Jesus, what is that to me,
> I just let go and follow thee,
> with this I do pass ev'ry test,
> to find with you eternal rest.

> **O Jesus, let the Fire of Joy,**
> **consume the devil's subtle ploy,**
> **transfigured is our planet earth,**
> **the golden age is given birth.**

9. Our sin is a result of us making choices with our free will, and no matter what choices we have ever made with our free will, we can make more aware choices and thereby free ourselves from the consequences or the sin of our previous choices. We can never make a choice from which we cannot free ourselves by making a more aware choice.

> O Jesus, fiery master mine,
> my heart now melting into thine,
> I love with heart and mind and soul,
> the God who is my highest goal.
>
> **O Jesus, let the Fire of Joy,**
> **consume the devil's subtle ploy,**
> **transfigured is our planet earth,**
> **the golden age is given birth.**

Part 4

1. This is the very essence of free will, and it is exactly what the fallen beings and the dark forces have been attempting to deny and obliterate since they came to this planet.

> O Jesus, blessed brother mine,
> I walk the path that you outline,
> a great example to us all,
> I follow now your inner call.
>
> **O Jesus, let the Fire of Joy,**
> **consume the devil's subtle ploy,**

> transfigured is our planet earth,
> the golden age is given birth.

2. All of the major churches in America, and many of the smaller churches in America, are led by people who are either fallen beings in embodiment or who are well-meaning people whose minds have been completely taken over by demons in the emotional realm or by fallen beings in the mental or identity realm.

> O Jesus, open inner sight,
> the ego wants to prove it's right,
> but this I will no longer do,
> I want to be all one with you.
>
> **O Jesus, let the Fire of Joy,**
> **consume the devil's subtle ploy,**
> **transfigured is our planet earth,**
> **the golden age is given birth.**

3. I call for Christians to be cut free to see what kind of leaders they have and what kind of non-material forces are behind those leaders so they will walk out of their churches.

> O Jesus, I now clearly see,
> the Key of Knowledge given me,
> my Christ self I hereby embrace,
> as you fill up my inner space.
>
> **O Jesus, let the Fire of Joy,**
> **consume the devil's subtle ploy,**
> **transfigured is our planet earth,**
> **the golden age is given birth.**

4. Jesus called the Scribes and Pharisees "sons of the devil" because they also were either fallen beings in embodiment or had their minds taken over by fallen beings.

> O Jesus, show me serpent's lie,
> expose the beam in my own eye,
> as Christ discernment you me give,
> in oneness I forever live.

> **O Jesus, let the Fire of Joy,**
> **consume the devil's subtle ploy,**
> **transfigured is our planet earth,**
> **the golden age is given birth.**

5. I call for the cutting free of those who are hypnotized by these false preachers so they can have a shift that makes them see what they cannot see now.

> O Jesus, I am truly meek,
> and thus I turn the other cheek,
> when the accuser attacks me,
> I go within and merge with thee.

> **O Jesus, let the Fire of Joy,**
> **consume the devil's subtle ploy,**
> **transfigured is our planet earth,**
> **the golden age is given birth.**

6. I am my brother's keepers in the sense that I have seen the limitations and the fallacy of mainstream Christianity. Therefore, I call for my brothers and sisters to be free, as I have become free.

O Jesus, ego I let die,
surrender ev'ry earthly tie,
the dead can bury what is dead,
I choose to walk with you instead.

**O Jesus, let the Fire of Joy,
consume the devil's subtle ploy,
transfigured is our planet earth,
the golden age is given birth.**

7. Making people the disciples of Jesus means that they understand the path of initiation, which can lead us to a higher state of consciousness.

O Jesus, help me rise above,
the devil's test through higher love,
show me separate self unreal,
my formless self you do reveal.

**O Jesus, let the Fire of Joy,
consume the devil's subtle ploy,
transfigured is our planet earth,
the golden age is given birth.**

8. The central message of Jesus is that each human being has an opportunity to raise its awareness and that by raising our awareness, every aspect of our lives will improve. We can be reborn spiritually and psychologically.

O Jesus, what is that to me,
I just let go and follow thee,
with this I do pass ev'ry test,
to find with you eternal rest.

> O Jesus, let the Fire of Joy,
> consume the devil's subtle ploy,
> transfigured is our planet earth,
> the golden age is given birth.

9. More and more Americans are becoming dissatisfied with the state of government and their daily lives. More and more people are feeling a pressure. They do not know what it is but they feel stressed. They feel they cannot stand it—something must change.

> O Jesus, fiery master mine,
> my heart now melting into thine,
> I love with heart and mind and soul,
> the God who is my highest goal.

> O Jesus, let the Fire of Joy,
> consume the devil's subtle ploy,
> transfigured is our planet earth,
> the golden age is given birth.

Part 5

1. If Christianity had not been put on a false track by the fallen beings, if there had been a path of initiation, Americans would have been aware that this nation is the land of opportunity, meaning the opportunity to raise our consciousness.

> O Jesus, blessed brother mine,
> I walk the path that you outline,

a great example to us all,
I follow now your inner call.

**O Jesus, let the Fire of Joy,
consume the devil's subtle ploy,
transfigured is our planet earth,
the golden age is given birth.**

2. Naturally, for the first several centuries of America's history people have been focused on improving the material way of life. If there had been just *some* understanding of a path of initiation, then Americans would have known the purpose for accumulating material wealth.

O Jesus, open inner sight,
the ego wants to prove it's right,
but this I will no longer do,
I want to be all one with you.

**O Jesus, let the Fire of Joy,
consume the devil's subtle ploy,
transfigured is our planet earth,
the golden age is given birth.**

3. A material high standard of living is not an end in itself. The purpose is to give us free time so we can focus on following the path of initiation and raising our awareness.

O Jesus, I now clearly see,
the Key of Knowledge given me,
my Christ self I hereby embrace,
as you fill up my inner space.

**O Jesus, let the Fire of Joy,
consume the devil's subtle ploy,
transfigured is our planet earth,
the golden age is given birth.**

4. I call for the cutting free of the people who are ready to discover the path of initiation so there can be a switch in America.

O Jesus, show me serpent's lie,
expose the beam in my own eye,
as Christ discernment you me give,
in oneness I forever live.

**O Jesus, let the Fire of Joy,
consume the devil's subtle ploy,
transfigured is our planet earth,
the golden age is given birth.**

5. Many of the problems in America could be changed very quickly because when we have a goal for our lives and know where we are going, our entire attitude to life changes.

O Jesus, I am truly meek,
and thus I turn the other cheek,
when the accuser attacks me,
I go within and merge with thee.

**O Jesus, let the Fire of Joy,
consume the devil's subtle ploy,
transfigured is our planet earth,
the golden age is given birth.**

6. Many Americans are becoming increasingly stressed and dissatisfied. Many people are taking this into extremes of drug or alcohol abuse because they do not know how to alleviate the stress so they try to find some temporary relief from it.

> O Jesus, ego I let die,
> surrender ev'ry earthly tie,
> the dead can bury what is dead,
> I choose to walk with you instead.

> **O Jesus, let the Fire of Joy,**
> **consume the devil's subtle ploy,**
> **transfigured is our planet earth,**
> **the golden age is given birth.**

7. If we have a purpose and a logical path to get there, we do not need relief, we do not need escape. We just need to go further on the path.

> O Jesus, help me rise above,
> the devil's test through higher love,
> show me separate self unreal,
> my formless self you do reveal.

> **O Jesus, let the Fire of Joy,**
> **consume the devil's subtle ploy,**
> **transfigured is our planet earth,**
> **the golden age is given birth.**

8. Everything that Christians say to each other or to non-Christians is based on a certain judgment of how a human being is supposed to be, specifically how a good Christian is supposed to be.

O Jesus, what is that to me,
I just let go and follow thee,
with this I do pass ev'ry test,
to find with you eternal rest.

**O Jesus, let the Fire of Joy,
consume the devil's subtle ploy,
transfigured is our planet earth,
the golden age is given birth.**

9. Everything Christians do is based on them having a standard in their heads of how we are supposed to be and how we are supposed to not be. It is a completely black-and-white evaluation and judgment of what it means to be a human being. They evaluate everything based on this.

O Jesus, fiery master mine,
my heart now melting into thine,
I love with heart and mind and soul,
the God who is my highest goal.

**O Jesus, let the Fire of Joy,
consume the devil's subtle ploy,
transfigured is our planet earth,
the golden age is given birth.**

Sealing

In the name of the I AM THAT I AM, I accept that Archangel Michael, Astrea and Shiva form an impenetrable shield around myself and all constructive people in America, sealing us from all fear-based energies in all four octaves. I accept that the Light

of God is consuming and transforming all fear-based energies that make up the dark forces working against America!

5 | INVOKING A SHIFT FROM JUDGMENT TO DISCERNMENT

In the name of the I AM THAT I AM, Jesus Christ, I use the authority that I have as a being in embodiment on earth to call upon Jesus to reinforce my calls and use my chakras to project the statements in this invocation into the collective consciousness and awaken Americans to the difference between human judgment and Christ discernment. Awaken Americans to the reality that we are spiritual beings and that we can co-create a new future by working with the ascended masters. I especially call for …

[Make your own calls here.]

Part 1

1. Even Christians who are into humanitarian work have a black-and-white judgment because it is the

hallmark of any religion, any thought system, dominated by the fallen beings.

> O Jesus, blessed brother mine,
> I walk the path that you outline,
> a great example to us all,
> I follow now your inner call.
>
> **O Jesus, let the Fire of Joy,**
> **consume the devil's subtle ploy,**
> **transfigured is our planet earth,**
> **the golden age is given birth.**

2. All the fallen beings had to do to mess things up on this planet is to set up a standard and project that everybody had to live up to the standard, and those who did were *right* and those who did not were *wrong*.

> O Jesus, open inner sight,
> the ego wants to prove it's right,
> but this I will no longer do,
> I want to be all one with you.
>
> **O Jesus, let the Fire of Joy,**
> **consume the devil's subtle ploy,**
> **transfigured is our planet earth,**
> **the golden age is given birth.**

3. What Jesus came to do 2,000 years ago was to counteract this by giving a path of initiation where we could raise ourselves above this black-and-white thinking.

5 | Invoking a shift from judgment to discernment

O Jesus, I now clearly see,
the Key of Knowledge given me,
my Christ self I hereby embrace,
as you fill up my inner space.

**O Jesus, let the Fire of Joy,
consume the devil's subtle ploy,
transfigured is our planet earth,
the golden age is given birth.**

4. When we reach some measure of Christhood, we will stop judging our brothers and sisters. We will internalize the truth behind the statement: "Judge not lest you be judged, for with whatever measure you meter out to others, it shall be metered out to you."

O Jesus, show me serpent's lie,
expose the beam in my own eye,
as Christ discernment you me give,
in oneness I forever live.

**O Jesus, let the Fire of Joy,
consume the devil's subtle ploy,
transfigured is our planet earth,
the golden age is given birth.**

5. Christ consciousness is a state where we discern very clearly. At the beginning stages of Christhood we are still affected by black-and-white thinking. That is why we can think we have to go out and combat evil.

O Jesus, I am truly meek,
and thus I turn the other cheek,

when the accuser attacks me,
I go within and merge with thee.

**O Jesus, let the Fire of Joy,
consume the devil's subtle ploy,
transfigured is our planet earth,
the golden age is given birth.**

6. When we come to the higher stages of Christhood, we see that evil is a certain state of consciousness and there are certain spirits.

O Jesus, ego I let die,
surrender ev'ry earthly tie,
the dead can bury what is dead,
I choose to walk with you instead.

**O Jesus, let the Fire of Joy,
consume the devil's subtle ploy,
transfigured is our planet earth,
the golden age is given birth.**

7. We see that a person might be affected by this state of consciousness, might be identified with a certain outer self. Nevertheless, we also see beyond this. Therefore, we are not judging the person as the Christians are doing.

O Jesus, help me rise above,
the devil's test through higher love,
show me separate self unreal,
my formless self you do reveal.

**O Jesus, let the Fire of Joy,
consume the devil's subtle ploy,
transfigured is our planet earth,
the golden age is given birth.**

8. We are not relating to people based on a sense of judgment and therefore based on the sense of superiority that we are above the evil we see in the other person.

O Jesus, what is that to me,
I just let go and follow thee,
with this I do pass ev'ry test,
to find with you eternal rest.

**O Jesus, let the Fire of Joy,
consume the devil's subtle ploy,
transfigured is our planet earth,
the golden age is given birth.**

9. Christ discernment is where we do not judge other people, we accept them without conditions. We can do this because we know that the ascended masters accept *us* without conditions.

O Jesus, fiery master mine,
my heart now melting into thine,
I love with heart and mind and soul,
the God who is my highest goal.

**O Jesus, let the Fire of Joy,
consume the devil's subtle ploy,
transfigured is our planet earth,
the golden age is given birth.**

Part 2

1. For the aligning of America with the mind of Saint Germain, some people must become the forerunners for going beyond this state of judgment so we can set the collective consciousness on a new track.

> O Jesus, blessed brother mine,
> I walk the path that you outline,
> a great example to us all,
> I follow now your inner call.
>
> **O Jesus, let the Fire of Joy,**
> **consume the devil's subtle ploy,**
> **transfigured is our planet earth,**
> **the golden age is given birth.**

2. I call for people to be cut free so they can overcome one of the subtle and unrecognized elements of the American psyche, namely the judgment between those who are Americans and those who are not, the distinction between America and all other nations.

> O Jesus, open inner sight,
> the ego wants to prove it's right,
> but this I will no longer do,
> I want to be all one with you.
>
> **O Jesus, let the Fire of Joy,**
> **consume the devil's subtle ploy,**
> **transfigured is our planet earth,**
> **the golden age is given birth.**

5 | Invoking a shift from judgment to discernment

3. Many Americans have taken the sponsorship of Saint Germain for granted. They have felt that they must be worthy to live in this great nation and therefore they are entitled to have what they have. Therefore, America is the greatest nation and America is better than all others.

> O Jesus, I now clearly see,
> the Key of Knowledge given me,
> my Christ self I hereby embrace,
> as you fill up my inner space.
>
> **O Jesus, let the Fire of Joy,**
> **consume the devil's subtle ploy,**
> **transfigured is our planet earth,**
> **the golden age is given birth.**

4. This creates a separation between Americans and other people. It also creates a division between groups of people who live in America where there is so much of the inferiority-superiority dynamic.

> O Jesus, show me serpent's lie,
> expose the beam in my own eye,
> as Christ discernment you me give,
> in oneness I forever live.
>
> **O Jesus, let the Fire of Joy,**
> **consume the devil's subtle ploy,**
> **transfigured is our planet earth,**
> **the golden age is given birth.**

5. Various groups are seeing themselves as being superior to other groups of Americans, therefore seeing themselves as

being in an antagonistic struggle with these other groups. That is why this nation had to go through a civil war to stop slavery.

> O Jesus, I am truly meek,
> and thus I turn the other cheek,
> when the accuser attacks me,
> I go within and merge with thee.
>
> **O Jesus, let the Fire of Joy,**
> **consume the devil's subtle ploy,**
> **transfigured is our planet earth,**
> **the golden age is given birth.**

6. There are many divisions in America, for example between those who have light skin and those who have darker skin. This division does not exists in the mind of Christ. Jesus does not have any kind of judgment of people with dark skin, red skin or yellow skin.

> O Jesus, ego I let die,
> surrender ev'ry earthly tie,
> the dead can bury what is dead,
> I choose to walk with you instead.
>
> **O Jesus, let the Fire of Joy,**
> **consume the devil's subtle ploy,**
> **transfigured is our planet earth,**
> **the golden age is given birth.**

7. Jesus sees beyond all of these outer divisions. Jesus appeared in the Middle East because there is hardly a place on the planet that is more divided by these outer differences than the Middle East.

5 | Invoking a shift from judgment to discernment

O Jesus, help me rise above,
the devil's test through higher love,
show me separate self unreal,
my formless self you do reveal.

**O Jesus, let the Fire of Joy,
consume the devil's subtle ploy,
transfigured is our planet earth,
the golden age is given birth.**

8. Jesus did not appear there because it is a *holy* land, as so many Christians in America think. They think America has to defend the modern state of Israel because it is the Holy Land.

O Jesus, what is that to me,
I just let go and follow thee,
with this I do pass ev'ry test,
to find with you eternal rest.

**O Jesus, let the Fire of Joy,
consume the devil's subtle ploy,
transfigured is our planet earth,
the golden age is given birth.**

9. Jesus does not want a major war or confrontation because Christians in America feel they have to defend the Holy Land. Thinking this is completely out of alignment with the mind of Christ and the mind of Saint Germain.

O Jesus, fiery master mine,
my heart now melting into thine,
I love with heart and mind and soul,
the God who is my highest goal.

**O Jesus, let the Fire of Joy,
consume the devil's subtle ploy,
transfigured is our planet earth,
the golden age is given birth.**

Part 3

1. The fallen beings are very clever in using the lower aspects, the dualistic consciousness, to set the stage for conflict.

> O Jesus, blessed brother mine,
> I walk the path that you outline,
> a great example to us all,
> I follow now your inner call.

> **O Jesus, let the Fire of Joy,
> consume the devil's subtle ploy,
> transfigured is our planet earth,
> the golden age is given birth.**

2. Thousands of years ago certain fallen beings managed to take a small tribe in the Middle East and give them a sense of superiority that they were God's chosen people, that they had the superior God.

> O Jesus, open inner sight,
> the ego wants to prove it's right,
> but this I will no longer do,
> I want to be all one with you.

**O Jesus, let the Fire of Joy,
consume the devil's subtle ploy,
transfigured is our planet earth,
the golden age is given birth.**

3. Whereas all of the other tribes in the area only had idols, they had the superior God and they were the sons of this God. By creating this state of consciousness, the fallen beings set the Jewish people in an inherent conflict with all others.

O Jesus, I now clearly see,
the Key of Knowledge given me,
my Christ self I hereby embrace,
as you fill up my inner space.

**O Jesus, let the Fire of Joy,
consume the devil's subtle ploy,
transfigured is our planet earth,
the golden age is given birth.**

4. By taking certain Arab people and giving them the sense that because they had received the religion of Islam, they were the superior people, they created even more conflict.

O Jesus, show me serpent's lie,
expose the beam in my own eye,
as Christ discernment you me give,
in oneness I forever live.

**O Jesus, let the Fire of Joy,
consume the devil's subtle ploy,
transfigured is our planet earth,
the golden age is given birth.**

5. Jesus came to the Middle East to give people a way beyond this conflict consciousness, namely to walk the path of initiation that leads to Christ discernment.

> O Jesus, I am truly meek,
> and thus I turn the other cheek,
> when the accuser attacks me,
> I go within and merge with thee.
>
> **O Jesus, let the Fire of Joy,**
> **consume the devil's subtle ploy,**
> **transfigured is our planet earth,**
> **the golden age is given birth.**

6. Jesus came there not because it was the *holy* land but because it was the most *unholy* place on earth. It still is because people have not used the teachings and the example Jesus gave to raise their consciousness.

> O Jesus, ego I let die,
> surrender ev'ry earthly tie,
> the dead can bury what is dead,
> I choose to walk with you instead.
>
> **O Jesus, let the Fire of Joy,**
> **consume the devil's subtle ploy,**
> **transfigured is our planet earth,**
> **the golden age is given birth.**

7. The fallen beings used Hitler to create the Holocaust and they used the atrocities against the Jewish people to create the modern state of Israel. They have used the Christians in America to be so fixated on the Holy Land that they are willing to

commit the military resources of America into an all-out war to defend the Holy Land.

> O Jesus, help me rise above,
> the devil's test through higher love,
> show me separate self unreal,
> my formless self you do reveal.

> **O Jesus, let the Fire of Joy,**
> **consume the devil's subtle ploy,**
> **transfigured is our planet earth,**
> **the golden age is given birth.**

8. I call forth the judgment of Christ upon the Christians who are willing to create World War III over the State of Israel and who, if it came about, would see it as a sign that this is the Battle of Armageddon. They would think it means the end is near and Jesus is going to appear in the sky and take them and the members of their little church to heaven and send all others to hell.

> O Jesus, what is that to me,
> I just let go and follow thee,
> with this I do pass ev'ry test,
> to find with you eternal rest.

> **O Jesus, let the Fire of Joy,**
> **consume the devil's subtle ploy,**
> **transfigured is our planet earth,**
> **the golden age is given birth.**

9. I call forth the judgment of Christ upon the people in Congress, in the Senate, in the military, in the media, in the power

elite who would be willing to commit the military resources of the United States to an all-out war to defend the State of Israel.

> O Jesus, fiery master mine,
> my heart now melting into thine,
> I love with heart and mind and soul,
> the God who is my highest goal.
>
> **O Jesus, let the Fire of Joy,**
> **consume the devil's subtle ploy,**
> **transfigured is our planet earth,**
> **the golden age is given birth.**

Part 4

1. They have already been instrumental in committing many of the resources to set up the State of Israel as a nuclear power, something that anybody with common sense can see is completely devastating in a densely populated region such as the Middle East.

> O Jesus, blessed brother mine,
> I walk the path that you outline,
> a great example to us all,
> I follow now your inner call.
>
> **O Jesus, let the Fire of Joy,**
> **consume the devil's subtle ploy,**
> **transfigured is our planet earth,**
> **the golden age is given birth.**

5 | Invoking a shift from judgment to discernment

2. How would Israel be able to use its nuclear weapons without killing itself in the process, its neighbors are too close.

> O Jesus, open inner sight,
> the ego wants to prove it's right,
> but this I will no longer do,
> I want to be all one with you.
>
> **O Jesus, let the Fire of Joy,**
> **consume the devil's subtle ploy,**
> **transfigured is our planet earth,**
> **the golden age is given birth.**

3. This cannot come from the mind of Christ. If it does not come from the mind of Christ, it comes from the mind of anti-christ.

> O Jesus, I now clearly see,
> the Key of Knowledge given me,
> my Christ self I hereby embrace,
> as you fill up my inner space.
>
> **O Jesus, let the Fire of Joy,**
> **consume the devil's subtle ploy,**
> **transfigured is our planet earth,**
> **the golden age is given birth.**

4. The people who are promoting these ideas do not represent Christ in America. They represent anti-christ because they are either fallen beings in embodiment or their minds are completely taken over by fallen beings in the higher realms.

O Jesus, show me serpent's lie,
expose the beam in my own eye,
as Christ discernment you me give,
in oneness I forever live.

**O Jesus, let the Fire of Joy,
consume the devil's subtle ploy,
transfigured is our planet earth,
the golden age is given birth.**

5. I call forth the judgment of Christ upon the false leaders who are radiating this into the collective consciousness. I call for the angels to clean up the entire mess.

O Jesus, I am truly meek,
and thus I turn the other cheek,
when the accuser attacks me,
I go within and merge with thee.

**O Jesus, let the Fire of Joy,
consume the devil's subtle ploy,
transfigured is our planet earth,
the golden age is given birth.**

6. Many Americans have found some teaching, and have awakened to realize that things are not the way we were brought up to think they are. We were brought up with a certain illusion and we did not understand how things really are.

O Jesus, ego I let die,
surrender ev'ry earthly tie,
the dead can bury what is dead,
I choose to walk with you instead.

**O Jesus, let the Fire of Joy,
consume the devil's subtle ploy,
transfigured is our planet earth,
the golden age is given birth.**

7. Many Americans have awakened to realize that there are certain forces in America that are ruling the country behind the scenes.

O Jesus, help me rise above,
the devil's test through higher love,
show me separate self unreal,
my formless self you do reveal.

**O Jesus, let the Fire of Joy,
consume the devil's subtle ploy,
transfigured is our planet earth,
the golden age is given birth.**

8. Many Americans have gone into various conspiracy theories. They see so many more problems and it becomes overwhelming to them. They feel almost paralyzed because how can an individual do anything about this?

O Jesus, what is that to me,
I just let go and follow thee,
with this I do pass ev'ry test,
to find with you eternal rest.

**O Jesus, let the Fire of Joy,
consume the devil's subtle ploy,
transfigured is our planet earth,
the golden age is given birth.**

9. I call for the cutting free of people from this reaction so they will not feel overwhelmed. They will see that we can walk the path to Christhood, and this is the most efficient way to remove evil. We do not have to battle the dark forces.

> O Jesus, fiery master mine,
> my heart now melting into thine,
> I love with heart and mind and soul,
> the God who is my highest goal.
>
> **O Jesus, let the Fire of Joy,**
> **consume the devil's subtle ploy,**
> **transfigured is our planet earth,**
> **the golden age is given birth.**

Part 5

1. We are not powerless. We are all making an invaluable contribution to the raising of the collective consciousness in America. Nothing is hopeless, and this is not a particularly dark hour in the history of America.

> O Jesus, blessed brother mine,
> I walk the path that you outline,
> a great example to us all,
> I follow now your inner call.
>
> **O Jesus, let the Fire of Joy,**
> **consume the devil's subtle ploy,**
> **transfigured is our planet earth,**
> **the golden age is given birth.**

2. The ascended masters are not doomsday prophets. They are only telling us about problems because they know we can do something about them.

> O Jesus, open inner sight,
> the ego wants to prove it's right,
> but this I will no longer do,
> I want to be all one with you.
>
> **O Jesus, let the Fire of Joy,**
> **consume the devil's subtle ploy,**
> **transfigured is our planet earth,**
> **the golden age is given birth.**

3. I call for all Americans to be cut free from the state of fear, the state of hopelessness or the state of feeling that nothing we do really matters. *Everything* we do matters—when we are walking the path. Every step up we take on our personal path pulls up on the collective consciousness.

> O Jesus, I now clearly see,
> the Key of Knowledge given me,
> my Christ self I hereby embrace,
> as you fill up my inner space.
>
> **O Jesus, let the Fire of Joy,**
> **consume the devil's subtle ploy,**
> **transfigured is our planet earth,**
> **the golden age is given birth.**

4. What it truly means to be a disciple of Christ is to realize that we are not doing this just for ourselves. We are doing it to raise the whole, and we *are* raising the whole.

> O Jesus, show me serpent's lie,
> expose the beam in my own eye,
> as Christ discernment you me give,
> in oneness I forever live.
>
> **O Jesus, let the Fire of Joy,**
> **consume the devil's subtle ploy,**
> **transfigured is our planet earth,**
> **the golden age is given birth.**

5. All of the people who have been willing to raise their consciousness, have made an invaluable contribution to raising the whole.

> O Jesus, I am truly meek,
> and thus I turn the other cheek,
> when the accuser attacks me,
> I go within and merge with thee.
>
> **O Jesus, let the Fire of Joy,**
> **consume the devil's subtle ploy,**
> **transfigured is our planet earth,**
> **the golden age is given birth.**

6. It is part of Christ discernment that we recognize that we are not separate beings. Duality is the state of separation; Christhood is the state of Oneness.

> O Jesus, ego I let die,
> surrender ev'ry earthly tie,
> the dead can bury what is dead,
> I choose to walk with you instead.

**O Jesus, let the Fire of Joy,
consume the devil's subtle ploy,
transfigured is our planet earth,
the golden age is given birth.**

7. As we walk the path of Christhood, we naturally begin to feel more one with all life—that is why we can stop judging other people. That is also why we can stop judging ourselves, and we can realize that because we are one with all life, raising ourselves pulls up on everyone else.

O Jesus, help me rise above,
the devil's test through higher love,
show me separate self unreal,
my formless self you do reveal.

**O Jesus, let the Fire of Joy,
consume the devil's subtle ploy,
transfigured is our planet earth,
the golden age is given birth.**

8. All people who have made major progress on the spiritual path have helped raise the collective consciousness. We have been making progress all of our lives because we have learned from the various experiences we have had.

O Jesus, what is that to me,
I just let go and follow thee,
with this I do pass ev'ry test,
to find with you eternal rest.

**O Jesus, let the Fire of Joy,
consume the devil's subtle ploy,**

**transfigured is our planet earth,
the golden age is given birth.**

9. The most important contribution we are making to the forward progression of this planet is by raising our consciousness and attaining Christhood. That is what the leaders of false Christianity will deny and on those fruits, we can know them.

> O Jesus, fiery master mine,
> my heart now melting into thine,
> I love with heart and mind and soul,
> the God who is my highest goal.

> **O Jesus, let the Fire of Joy,
> consume the devil's subtle ploy,
> transfigured is our planet earth,
> the golden age is given birth.**

Sealing

In the name of the I AM THAT I AM, I accept that Archangel Michael, Astrea and Shiva form an impenetrable shield around myself and all constructive people in America, sealing us from all fear-based energies in all four octaves. I accept that the Light of God is consuming and transforming all fear-based energies that make up the dark forces working against America.

6 | FROM THE UNITED STATES OF AMERICA TO THE UNITED PEOPLES OF AMERICA

I AM the Ascended Master Saint Germain. I know that you see me as the Master of Freedom, but is there not a certain joy in freedom? Thus, there is indeed joy on each of the Seven Rays and when you master a particular ray, you begin to feel that joy. Thus, I wish to convey to you the Flame of the Seventh Ray of Joy because I am indeed joyful about being able to be here with you, to interact with your auras and your chakras, to interact with your minds, to hopefully give you an experience that is beyond your normal level of awareness so that you have a frame of reference that you can bring with you as you go out to your place in America or abroad. You can bring that flame with you, and you can have it as a frame of reference for yourself, but you can also convey to others that there is tremendous joy in freedom and there is tremendous freedom in joy.

Americans take themselves too seriously

Thus, I do not wish to in any way be too serious about what it will take to align America with the mind of Saint Germain because you cannot align America or yourself with Saint Germain if you take life too seriously. Obviously, this means that one of the things, one of the changes, that could help align America with the mind of Saint Germain is that people stop taking themselves and this nation so seriously. Truly, when you look at America, there is a certain tendency that Americans take themselves very seriously, whereas you will see that other nations, like Canada, like the Scandinavian countries, have a culture and a tradition where they do not take themselves so seriously. They can make jokes about themselves, about their nation, that Americans sometimes look at and cannot understand why these other people think this is funny.

Of course, we realize that humor is an individual thing but, nevertheless, there is a tendency that Americans in general (not all, of course, but many) take themselves seriously, take their country seriously. You spoke earlier today about this whole consciousness that America has a certain destiny, and this, of course, makes people take themselves very seriously. You see so many of the Christians in this nation who take themselves very, very seriously and feel they have a role to play in making America conform to their vision.

Many Christians are anti-democratic

Building on what Jesus said earlier about the very fact that there is a separation of church and state in America, and that this is absolutely necessary for a functioning democracy, then we can say that those Christians who are attempting to interfere and affect the political process are out of alignment with the mind of Saint Germain, with the Founding Fathers of this nation, with the very principles upon which America is founded.

Truly, it is not wrong as such that religious people are engaged in the political aspect of life. I am not asking religious people to withdraw from society and live in a monastery. Of course, they are free to express their opinions as everyone else, but what I am pointing out is that some Christian churches have found their way to manipulate themselves into the political process and exert an influence that is completely based on their Christian worldview. This view is, as Jesus so eloquently explained, out of alignment with the mind of Christ, the mind of Jesus Christ. Naturally, this is also out of alignment with the mind of Saint Germain. Truly, there are very few Christians who do not take themselves and their faith too seriously.

Truly, we do not wish to start making jokes about Christianity but, nevertheless, it would be helpful if Christians could step back and be a little more humorous about their faith, about themselves, about their path. It would especially be helpful if those of you who are more aware would make the calls for the binding of these very powerful demons that have been created by the major Christian churches in America. These demons take over the minds of some of these pastors and leaders who feel it is their God-given right to interfere with the political process of America. They have been charged by God or Jesus to do this work and it is of epic importance that they impose their vision upon America's leadership.

You have seen certain pastors in the past who have done this, even for several presidents where they have had some advisory position. Well, my beloved, a president of the United States does not need a religious advisor unless he has a board of religious advisors representing every faith in America. *That* I would have no problem with, but taking one particular minister from one particular church and making him the advisor to the president is against the principles of this nation. Thus, I look to you to make the calls for the binding and the judgment of these demons that are behind this phenomenon. Of course, this will enable us to take these demons away over time and this will shift the equation.

Why Saint Germain sponsors America

Now, beyond not taking yourselves so seriously, what would it take for Americans to align themselves with the mind of Saint Germain? Well, I would like to share with you some thoughts on *what* is the mind of Saint Germain, *how* is the mind of Saint Germain. First of all, let us do a reality check. It has been said in ascended master teachings that Saint Germain sponsors America. Now, as Mother Mary said, this is not a blank check, but what I wish to emphasize here is that Saint Germain may sponsor America but this does not mean that Saint Germain works only with America or Saint Germain looks to manifest the Golden Age only in America or first in America. I am the representative of freedom. I am the hierarch for the next 2,000 years of the Age of Aquarius, not just for America but for all people on earth. I work with people in all nations, as I am able, as they are able to tune in, and I have no particular favoritism towards any nation. I sponsored America not because I have any favoritism towards America but because I saw the potential and I am sponsoring that potential.

In a sense, you could say that in my mind I am not concerned about America as a *nation*, I am concerned about America as a *process*, as an experiment in: "How could we manifest a nation with a higher degree of freedom but at the same time manifesting the Golden Age ideals." It has been said, and correctly so, that the Age of Aquarius is the Age of the Holy Spirit and the Age of Community, so community, come-ye-into-unity in these United States.

Community in America

This ties in with what Mother Mary and Jesus talked about, about the individualism, about caring about yourself only, about not feeling you are your brother's keeper, about thinking it is all about raising yourself up, putting America first, making America great again, making America the greatest nation in the world and all of these things. Do I look to sponsor a nation of individuals? Nay, I look to sponsor a community.

What is a nation? A nation is not a collection of individuals, it is a community. Yes, it is made up of individuals and, yes, it is important that there is room for individualism because otherwise how could you, who are ascended master students, have raised your consciousness beyond the collective?

Community is not, in its ideal form, something that pulls everyone down to the lowest common denominator. This is, of course, the way societies have functioned, first of all, communist nations where everybody was forced down to a certain low level in order to make them controllable by the party elite and the party apparatus. This is the one extreme where community has been misused to suppress the people, to lower the consciousness of the people. In America there has been the tendency to go to the other extreme and let individuality, individualism, run wild so that a few people have managed to set themselves up as these billionaire business people, as this privileged elite that is not even openly seen, openly presenting themselves as the elite. Therefore, they still fool so many people into thinking that America does not have an elite that is as repressive as the noble class of medieval society or other elites that you have seen throughout history.

In my mind America is meant to be a community of people who realize: "We are all in this together and we need to take care of each other, help each other grow. We need to therefore look at what is the greatest good for the greatest number of people, not what is the greatest good for those who are willing to take from others without giving anything back."

You realize, do you not, that the only way to become so rich or so powerful is to take from the whole without giving anything back to the whole. A community can function only when a majority of the people, ideally *all* of the people, take from the whole but also give back to the whole. That way, when everybody freely receives, freely gives, then the whole can be multiplied from the ascended realm and *that* is how a society, a community, grows.

America is an ongoing process

Now, my mind is not a fixed mind. There has been a tendency among ascended master students to see us as having been raised to some state of perfection and in perfection there is no need for growth. As we have said, now many times, there *is* growth in the ascended realm. This means that I am not standing here, right now, having a fixed image of where I want America to go in order to manifest the Golden Age. I do not have a fixed image of what the Golden Age will be like in America. Therefore, I do not have in my mind that there will come a certain point where, now America has manifested the Golden Age matrix. Before that, it will not have manifested it and once it has manifested, it will not change for the rest of the 2,000-year period. I very much see this as a dynamic process and that is also why I do not intend to say that America has fallen behind where it could or should have been and that there is some disastrous state and that America is heading for the abyss and terrible things will happen in three and a half hours.

My beloved, I see America as an ongoing process. Certainly, it is true that America could have been further along than where it is right now, no question about that. It is not that America has fallen irreversibly behind or that there is some major disaster or calamity that is impending because America is behind where it ideally could have been. Again, I am not so concerned about the outer characteristics of how we manifest a Golden Age because what is a Golden Age? Is it a period where a civilization has manifested some very high level of sophistication and now it just maintains that level for hundreds or thousands of years? That is not my vision of a Golden Age. My vision of a Golden Age is a period in which people can experience maximum spiritual growth and therefore make major progress towards their Christhood, towards their ascension.

In other words it is a period of growth that makes a Golden Age, not a static state of perfection or sophistication. Is America behind? Well, it depends on whether you look at certain milestones of where *this* could have been manifest, *that* could have been manifest. I am looking at the process of America as a device. America is a device for giving the people that live there (and those who live abroad as well) an opportunity to raise their consciousness. No matter what happens or does not happen in a nation, it still represents an opportunity for people to grow from that point.

How an ascended master maintains sanity

That is why, as an ascended master who has pledged himself to working with a planet like earth for the next 2,000 years, you have to have a certain attitude in order to maintain your sanity. It may sound strange, but even an ascended master can potentially become somewhat discouraged if he fixates his mind on a certain goal and feels that the planet he is working with is not, the people are not, moving towards that goal. There have been examples of ascended masters who have started working with the earth and had to move on to another planet because this one was too difficult. What makes it too difficult is not really the planet as such but more if you, as an ascended master, formulate an opinion, an expectation in your mind of how the unascended people on earth *should* respond to whatever you offer them. That is what can cause even an ascended master to feel some level of discouragement because the goals are not reached. Having observed this, I have determined not to put myself in that situation because that would take away the joy, of course, of working with the earth.

    I do not have this fixed goal, this fixed timetable that this or that should happen at a certain time. I look at the situation as it is now. I accept the situation as it is now and then I say: "How do we move forward from there?" I look at anything that happens, including this latest election that has had an effect on so many people, and I simply say: "Well, this happened, how do we turn it into a positive? How do we move forward from there?"

The latest presidential election

One potential positive is that some people can wake up and realize they now have to engage themselves in the political process. It may be that others will see an outpicturing of a certain state of consciousness, the black-and-white thinking. If you really look at this entire process, you will find that there is an extremely important teaching given by Jesus some time ago where he said that it is actually possible that there are certain people who are not in a particularly high state of consciousness but who nevertheless, at least for a time, can be aligned with the mind of Christ in the sense that they force people to confront something that can bring change. If a society becomes too static, then someone that shakes things up can actually force people to rethink and, therefore, this can be in alignment with the mind of Christ. Even this president serves, to some degree, in that capacity of forcing people to confront certain issues and therefore get out of the apathy that has crept into so many Americans where they feel powerless to do anything about the political process.

This is not to say that I am in agreement with many of the statements made and many of the policies that are an expression of black-and-white thinking. You cannot deny the fact that this President certainly has stirred the pot (and he also smoked pot but that is another issue). The point I want to make is that once the people of a democratic nation have chosen, I accept this and then I say: "How can we move on from here?"

To be honest with you, it has been a very, very long time since there was a President in the White House who was able to have some conscious attunement with me. I do not expect that a President will be able to consciously attune to me, but I do attempt to work with, not only the President but all of his advisors and all of the people who are a part of the government apparatus because, you understand, I do not have these dualistic, black-and-white value judgments.

I am not looking to judge anyone, to find fault with anyone or to put anyone down or to punish anyone. I simply say: "Can I work with this President and this administration? How can I work with them? Are there some ideas I can introduce that will actually help bring America forward?" I cannot allow myself the luxury of feeling that: "Oh, here is a President that I will not work with" because I am committed to helping the American nation and the American people progress. Therefore, I cannot simply withdraw myself completely from the White House for four years or eight years. I need to do whatever I can do to work with the current administration (which, of course, is much more than the President) and see how I can find a way to insert some constructive ideas that will bring some part of America forward. I know that even if the President makes certain decisions that takes America backwards, well, then that can be undone in the future. Nothing is forever so I must take what is there, seek to multiply it and see how we can move forward.

It is the same with Congress and the Senate. I try to work with those that I can work with, and I grant you that that is not so many in a direct capacity. You would still be amazed at how many can, actually, once in a while (without realizing where it comes from) receive an idea from me. It is not a completely hopeless process. Now, of course, this is not to in any way say that things are okay or they are ideal. That is not my intention. My intention is to say that I work with what is there and I seek to improve it. Does that mean I agree with the status quo? Nay, of course not. I would very much like to see improvements in the political system of America.

Changing the public discourse of America

What would I especially like to see? Well, there are many things which I may cover later, but what I desire to bring out here is this. I would truly like to see a change in the public discourse of America, the way people talk about the political situation, the way people talk to each other. This goes to the ordinary American who posts something on Facebook or talks to his neighbor over the hedge. It goes all the way up through the media, through all levels of government and all the way up to how the two parties in Congress discourse with each other.

America has gone through a phase, like most democratic nations, where the advent of the Internet has made it easier and easier for people to express themselves in a public forum, in a public space. Because of the mechanics that you are not talking directly to people when you post on the Internet (and sometimes you are even not posting under your true identity, and you are expressing yourself in words that are written not spoken), because of this mechanic there has been this tendency to a polarization into more and more black-and-white thinking.

This has led to the public forum being taken over by people who are in a black-and-white state of mind, who are in the epic mindset. The most aggressive people are, naturally, the ones who have the epic mindset and believe it is of epic importance that their viewpoint wins the day, that they win the debate, that they convince or destroy the opponent. These are the ones who are the most aggressive in posting in the public space, expressing themselves in the public space. What has this caused? It has caused all of the balanced, moderate Americans to simply give up and withdraw. They do not want to have anything to do with this level of discourse because it is not where they are at in consciousness. We now have a situation in America, and many other democratic nations, where the public discourse has been taken over by these black-and-white thinkers who are always looking for the simple solution, which means forcing some other group of people. It is only degrees away from the willingness to kill those other people, for whom it is so epically important to suppress the viewpoint they have. This has had the effect of turning away all of the people who actually could bring America closer to the Golden Age because they are more balanced, which means they are more on the Middle Way. They are the ones who are more aligned with the mind of Saint Germain and therefore able to receive ideas from me.

There are congressmen and congresswoman, senators who are also more moderate, more balanced, but they have been hijacked by the leaders of the two parties who have also gone into this black-and-white, epic mindset. They are so focused on fighting the other party, winning over the other party, that the concerns about what is actually right for America have faded into the background. That is why they cannot cooperate. Even though there may be a majority in Congress that are for a certain change, that majority can never vote as one block because some of those moderate, balanced people are republicans and some are democrats. They are forced to vote the party line and this is what has created gridlock. It all springs from the fact that the public discourse has become black-and-white and therefore people cannot talk to each other across these divisive, dividing lines.

Look at how many people, ordinary Americans, who cannot talk to people who belong to the other party. They cannot talk to people who are Trump supporters if they are not Trump supporters. Well, my beloved, if you cannot talk to each other, then there is only one outcome: tension will continue to grow until there is some kind of explosion. This is essentially how most wars on earth have started. Tension builds between two groups of people (tribes, religions, nations, political affiliations what have you) until there is a spark that ignites the explosion and then you have war. Well, we are not looking to have a civil war in America but, nevertheless, you have a state of civil war in the minds of many Americans because they have become so attached to winning, to defeating the opposite party that they see as being so epically wrong, so epically bad.

Saint Germain's view on politics

My beloved, if you want to know how I look at the Democratic and the Republican parties, I am completely non-attached to who has a majority in congress. I know that it is not really going to make any difference because neither party is able or willing to take America in a truly new direction. Either party, no matter who runs it, will be politics as usual until there is some major change and that has not happened yet. It is not of epic importance, it is not so that I look at the Democratic Party being absolutely wrong and the Republican Party being absolutely right or the other way around. I look at issues, each issue. What is in my mind for that issue and who is aligned with that? I often see, as I said, that there is actually a majority of people in congress who are aligned with my mind on a particular issue, but they never get to vote as a group because they are split by this black-and-white conflict between the two parties.

There was a time when Republicans and Democrats could cooperate across party lines, could talk to each other. It was not a matter of defeating the other party, it was a matter of coming together in a spirit of cooperation and saying: "What is best for the country? Are we elected by the people to fight the other party or are we elected to do what is best for the country?"

The only way to change this is really to change the public discourse and that is what we look for you to make the calls on. We, of course, look to you also to be the examples of how to have a political discussion that is not based on black-and-white thinking, that is not based on this very simplistic view that one person is the right president and the other is an absolute disaster, that one party will take America in the right direction and the other will destroy it in half an hour. It just is not that way in reality, my beloved. Naturally, I would like to see many other changes in the political system but none of them can actually come about as long as the public discourse is the way it is right now, as long as it is divisive.

Status quo is created by the power elite

The reality is, my beloved – the stark, brutal reality is – that politics as usual, the political status quo that you have in America, is created by the hidden power elite who have never been elected, who have never stood out publicly. They have, over decades, gradually manipulated the political process in America to the point where they have created a situation that allows them to gain more and more privileges by taking it from the people. It is not created just by one party but by elements in both parties. Both parties have been hijacked by these hidden power elites.

Who benefits from politics as usual? Only the power elite. Now, who is going to change the situation in America? Not the power elite. So *who* can change it? Well, the reality is that the two parties that have a monopoly on congress cannot change it. Where can change come from? Only from the people. As I said earlier, when the consciousness of the people changes, then the power elite must give way and the power elite, the fallen beings, they know this. They know that when the people are united, they must give concessions, they must withdraw, they will be forced to give way. They may still think they can maintain some measure of control, but they must give way and, therefore, what is their goal? It is to divide the people into factions so that they cannot come together and speak with one voice and say: "We have had enough of this, we want change."

What is the entire public discourse geared towards? Dividing Americans and keeping them divided! That is the underlying purpose of this divisive public discourse. It is a subtle plot that very, very few people have realized. You can have a major impact by making the calls on this based on these teachings and the invocation that will be created based on this dictation. I can tell you with absolute certainty that there is no way to bring serious changes to America as long as the public discourse is locked in this black-and-white thinking and is taken over and hijacked by these very aggressive, epically-minded people.

There are some of these people, who express themselves in these public forums, who actually believe in what they are doing because they are trapped in the epic mindset. I can assure you that there are those who are paid to do a job by various elite groups who are deliberately polarizing the public discourse in order to divide and conquer. This is an old tactic of the fallen beings, as you see in the Roman Empire, but that goes way, way back to when they first started embodying here. It does not work every time but it works a lot of the time because the people so easily get pulled into thinking that there is such a simple solution to their problems—if only we can defeat the group that is defined as the problem.

As long as you define other people as the problem, you are refusing to take responsibility for your situation. There are enough Americans who have started to take responsibility, who have started to move out of the epic mindset, who have started to see the fallacies of black-and-white thinking that they could make a difference. They have not done so precisely because they do not even want to be exposed to the reaction from these very judgmental, critical, aggressive people. They are standing there, feeling hopeless because they do not see how they could have an impact. I see how they can have an impact and if you, my beloved, make the calls, then they will also begin to see it.

You will see a certain shift where the balanced people will begin to speak out, some having already done so but many more need to follow before it will build that critical mass where it cannot be ignored or put down. Then, you will actually see that you can have a demonstration in Washington, D.C. that is not created by extremists but by the more balanced people who are demonstrating for restoring or creating a public discourse that is focused on: "How do we move America forward?" Not on: "How do we win over those other people."

These were the thoughts I wanted to share with you for today. I have, of course, more to say but I will take it in increments so that it is not too overwhelming for you to deal with. My beloved, I thank you for being here, for your attention. I can assure you that I have taken great joy in seeing how you interact with each other, how you shared yesterday in front of the group but also how freely you talk to each other. Do you not realize, my beloved, that if more Americans could begin to talk so freely, then everything would change? Literally, everything would change if there was free, open, non-judgmental communication.

What is it that is really necessary for the public discourse to change? It is that people connect at the heart level. They connect so that instead of seeing those other people as opponents, they see them as people, as human beings like themselves. They realize we are not actually divided by these outer things because there is something deeper, what we have called the basic humanity, that we all share, that unites us. I would actually like to see that instead of the United States of America, we would have the United Peoples of America. So with that thought, I bid you good night.

7 | INVOKING THE UNIFICATION OF THE PEOPLE OF AMERICA

In the name of the I AM THAT I AM, Jesus Christ, I use the authority that I have as a being in embodiment on earth to call upon Saint Germain to reinforce my calls and use my chakras to project the statements in this invocation into the collective consciousness and awaken Americans to the need to unite. Awaken Americans to the reality that we are spiritual beings and that we can co-create a new future by working with the ascended masters. I especially call for …

[Make your own calls here.]

Part 1

1. Saint Germain, help Americans experience the Flame of the Seventh Ray of Joy so they can have a frame of

reference that there is tremendous joy in freedom and there is tremendous freedom in joy.

> O Saint Germain, you do inspire,
> my vision raised forever higher,
> with you I form a figure-eight,
> your Golden Age I co-create.
>
> **O Saint Germain, what love you bring,**
> **it truly makes all matter sing,**
> **your violet flame does all restore,**
> **with you we are becoming more.**

2. We cannot align America with Saint Germain if we take life too seriously. One of the changes that could help align America with the mind of Saint Germain is that people stop taking themselves and this nation so seriously.

> O Saint Germain, what Freedom Flame,
> released when we recite your name,
> acceleration is your gift,
> our planet it will surely lift.
>
> **O Saint Germain, what love you bring,**
> **it truly makes all matter sing,**
> **your violet flame does all restore,**
> **with you we are becoming more.**

3. There is a tendency that Americans take themselves very seriously, whereas other nations have a culture and a tradition where they do not take themselves so seriously.

O Saint Germain, in love we claim,
our right to bring your violet flame,
from you Above, to us below,
it is an all-transforming flow.

O Saint Germain, what love you bring,
it truly makes all matter sing,
your violet flame does all restore,
with you we are becoming more.

4. There is a consciousness that America has a certain destiny, and this makes people take themselves very seriously. Many of the Christians take themselves very seriously and feel they have a role to play in making America conform to their vision.

O Saint Germain, I love you so,
my aura filled with violet glow,
my chakras filled with violet fire,
I am your cosmic amplifier.

O Saint Germain, what love you bring,
it truly makes all matter sing,
your violet flame does all restore,
with you we are becoming more.

5. Christians who are attempting to interfere and affect the political process are out of alignment with the mind of Saint Germain, with the Founding Fathers, with the very principles upon which America is founded.

O Saint Germain, I am now free,
your violet flame is therapy,

transform all hang-ups in my mind,
as inner peace I surely find.

**O Saint Germain, what love you bring,
it truly makes all matter sing,
your violet flame does all restore,
with you we are becoming more.**

6. Some Christian churches have found a way to manipulate themselves into the political process and exert an influence that is based on their Christian worldview.

O Saint Germain, my body pure,
your violet flame for all is cure,
consume the cause of all disease,
and therefore I am all at ease.

**O Saint Germain, what love you bring,
it truly makes all matter sing,
your violet flame does all restore,
with you we are becoming more.**

7. This view is out of alignment with the mind of Christ, the mind of Jesus Christ. Naturally, this is also out of alignment with the mind of Saint Germain. There are very few Christians who do not take themselves and their faith too seriously.

O Saint Germain, I'm karma-free,
the past no longer burdens me,
a brand new opportunity,
I am in Christic unity.

> O Saint Germain, what love you bring,
> it truly makes all matter sing,
> your violet flame does all restore,
> with you we are becoming more.

8. I call for the binding of the demons that have been created by the major Christian churches in America.

> O Saint Germain, we are now one,
> I am for you a violet sun,
> as we transform this planet earth,
> your Golden Age is given birth.
>
> **O Saint Germain, what love you bring,
> it truly makes all matter sing,
> your violet flame does all restore,
> with you we are becoming more.**

9. I call forth the judgment of Christ upon the pastors and leaders who feel it is their God-given right to interfere with the political process of America, who feel they have been charged by God or Jesus to do this work and it is of epic importance that they impose their vision upon America's leadership.

> O Saint Germain, the earth is free,
> from burden of duality,
> in oneness we bring what is best,
> your Golden Age is manifest.
>
> **O Saint Germain, what love you bring,
> it truly makes all matter sing,
> your violet flame does all restore,
> with you we are becoming more.**

Part 2

1. A president of the United States does not need a religious advisor unless he has a board of religious advisors representing every faith in America.

> O Saint Germain, you do inspire,
> my vision raised forever higher,
> with you I form a figure-eight,
> your Golden Age I co-create.
>
> **O Saint Germain, what love you bring,**
> **it truly makes all matter sing,**
> **your violet flame does all restore,**
> **with you we are becoming more.**

2. Taking one particular minister from one particular church and making him the advisor to the president is against the principles of this nation.

> O Saint Germain, what Freedom Flame,
> released when we recite your name,
> acceleration is your gift,
> our planet it will surely lift.
>
> **O Saint Germain, what love you bring,**
> **it truly makes all matter sing,**
> **your violet flame does all restore,**
> **with you we are becoming more.**

3. I call for the binding and the judgment of the demons that are behind this phenomenon. I call for the demons to be taken away so the equation will shift.

> O Saint Germain, in love we claim,
> our right to bring your violet flame,
> from you Above, to us below,
> it is an all-transforming flow.
>
> **O Saint Germain, what love you bring,**
> **it truly makes all matter sing,**
> **your violet flame does all restore,**
> **with you we are becoming more.**

4. Saint Germain may sponsor America but this does not mean that Saint Germain works only with America or Saint Germain looks to manifest the Golden Age only in America or first in America.

> O Saint Germain, I love you so,
> my aura filled with violet glow,
> my chakras filled with violet fire,
> I am your cosmic amplifier.
>
> **O Saint Germain, what love you bring,**
> **it truly makes all matter sing,**
> **your violet flame does all restore,**
> **with you we are becoming more.**

5. Saint Germain is the representative of freedom, the hierarch for the next 2,000 years, not just for America but for all people on earth.

> O Saint Germain, I am now free,
> your violet flame is therapy,
> transform all hang-ups in my mind,
> as inner peace I surely find.
>
> **O Saint Germain, what love you bring,**
> **it truly makes all matter sing,**
> **your violet flame does all restore,**
> **with you we are becoming more.**

6. Saint Germain works with people in all nations, and he has no particular favoritism towards any nation. He sponsored America not because he has any favoritism towards America but because he saw the potential and he is sponsoring that potential.

> O Saint Germain, my body pure,
> your violet flame for all is cure,
> consume the cause of all disease,
> and therefore I am all at ease.
>
> **O Saint Germain, what love you bring,**
> **it truly makes all matter sing,**
> **your violet flame does all restore,**
> **with you we are becoming more.**

7. Saint Germain is not concerned about America as a *nation*, he is concerned about America as a *process*, as an experiment in: "How could we manifest a nation with a higher degree of freedom but at the same time manifest the Golden Age ideals."

> O Saint Germain, I'm karma-free,
> the past no longer burdens me,

a brand new opportunity,
I am in Christic unity.

**O Saint Germain, what love you bring,
it truly makes all matter sing,
your violet flame does all restore,
with you we are becoming more.**

8. The Age of Aquarius is the Age of the Holy Spirit and the Age of Community, meaning community, come-ye-into-unity in these United States.

O Saint Germain, we are now one,
I am for you a violet sun,
as we transform this planet earth,
your Golden Age is given birth.

**O Saint Germain, what love you bring,
it truly makes all matter sing,
your violet flame does all restore,
with you we are becoming more.**

9. Community is counteracted by individualism, by caring about ourselves only, by not feeling we are our brother's keeper, by thinking it is all about raising ourselves up, putting America first, making America great again, making America the greatest nation in the world.

O Saint Germain, the earth is free,
from burden of duality,
in oneness we bring what is best,
your Golden Age is manifest.

> O Saint Germain, what love you bring,
> it truly makes all matter sing,
> your violet flame does all restore,
> with you we are becoming more.

Part 3

1. Saint Germain does not look to sponsor a nation of individuals. He looks to sponsor a community because a nation is not a collection of individuals, it is a community.

> O Saint Germain, you do inspire,
> my vision raised forever higher,
> with you I form a figure-eight,
> your Golden Age I co-create.

> O Saint Germain, what love you bring,
> it truly makes all matter sing,
> your violet flame does all restore,
> with you we are becoming more.

2. Community is not, in its ideal form, something that pulls everyone down to the lowest common denominator. This is the way some societies have functioned, first of all, communist nations.

> O Saint Germain, what Freedom Flame,
> released when we recite your name,
> acceleration is your gift,
> our planet it will surely lift.

> **O Saint Germain, what love you bring,**
> **it truly makes all matter sing,**
> **your violet flame does all restore,**
> **with you we are becoming more.**

3. In America there has been the tendency to go to the other extreme and let individuality, individualism, run wild so that a few people have managed to set themselves up as these billionaire business people, as this privileged elite that is not even openly seen, openly presenting themselves as the elite.

> O Saint Germain, in love we claim,
> our right to bring your violet flame,
> from you Above, to us below,
> it is an all-transforming flow.

> **O Saint Germain, what love you bring,**
> **it truly makes all matter sing,**
> **your violet flame does all restore,**
> **with you we are becoming more.**

4. They fool so many people into thinking that America does not have an elite that is as repressive as the noble class of medieval society or other elites that we have seen throughout history.

> O Saint Germain, I love you so,
> my aura filled with violet glow,
> my chakras filled with violet fire,
> I am your cosmic amplifier.

> **O Saint Germain, what love you bring,**
> **it truly makes all matter sing,**

> your violet flame does all restore,
> with you we are becoming more.

5. America is meant to be a community of people who realize: "We are all in this together and we need to take care of each other, help each other grow. We need to look at what is the greatest good for the greatest number of people, not what is the greatest good for those who are willing to take from others without giving anything back."

> O Saint Germain, I am now free,
> your violet flame is therapy,
> transform all hang-ups in my mind,
> as inner peace I surely find.

> **O Saint Germain, what love you bring,**
> **it truly makes all matter sing,**
> **your violet flame does all restore,**
> **with you we are becoming more.**

6. The only way to become really rich or powerful is to take from the whole without giving anything back to the whole. A community can function only when a majority of the people take from the whole but also give back to the whole.

> O Saint Germain, my body pure,
> your violet flame for all is cure,
> consume the cause of all disease,
> and therefore I am all at ease.

> **O Saint Germain, what love you bring,**
> **it truly makes all matter sing,**

> your violet flame does all restore,
> with you we are becoming more.

7. When everybody freely receives, freely gives, then the whole can be multiplied from the ascended realm and that is how a community grows.

> O Saint Germain, I'm karma-free,
> the past no longer burdens me,
> a brand new opportunity,
> I am in Christic unity.

> **O Saint Germain, what love you bring,**
> **it truly makes all matter sing,**
> **your violet flame does all restore,**
> **with you we are becoming more.**

8. Saint Germain does not have a fixed image of where he wants America to go in order to manifest the Golden Age. He does not have a fixed image of what the Golden Age will be like in America.

> O Saint Germain, we are now one,
> I am for you a violet sun,
> as we transform this planet earth,
> your Golden Age is given birth.

> **O Saint Germain, what love you bring,**
> **it truly makes all matter sing,**
> **your violet flame does all restore,**
> **with you we are becoming more.**

9. Saint Germain does not have in his mind that there will come a certain point where, now America has manifested the Golden Age matrix. He sees it as a dynamic process, as an ongoing process.

> O Saint Germain, the earth is free,
> from burden of duality,
> in oneness we bring what is best,
> your Golden Age is manifest.
>
> **O Saint Germain, what love you bring,**
> **it truly makes all matter sing,**
> **your violet flame does all restore,**
> **with you we are becoming more.**

Part 4

1. Saint Germain is not so concerned about the outer characteristics of how we manifest a Golden Age because a Golden Age is a period in which people can experience maximum spiritual growth and therefore make major progress towards their Christhood, towards their ascension.

> O Saint Germain, you do inspire,
> my vision raised forever higher,
> with you I form a figure-eight,
> your Golden Age I co-create.
>
> **O Saint Germain, what love you bring,**
> **it truly makes all matter sing,**

> your violet flame does all restore,
> with you we are becoming more.

2. It is a period of growth that makes a Golden Age, not a static state of perfection or sophistication. Saint Germain is looking at the process of America as a device for giving people an opportunity to raise their consciousness.

> O Saint Germain, what Freedom Flame,
> released when we recite your name,
> acceleration is your gift,
> our planet it will surely lift.

> **O Saint Germain, what love you bring,**
> **it truly makes all matter sing,**
> **your violet flame does all restore,**
> **with you we are becoming more.**

3. No matter what happens or does not happen in a nation, it still represents an opportunity for people to grow from that point.

> O Saint Germain, in love we claim,
> our right to bring your violet flame,
> from you Above, to us below,
> it is an all-transforming flow.

> **O Saint Germain, what love you bring,**
> **it truly makes all matter sing,**
> **your violet flame does all restore,**
> **with you we are becoming more.**

4. Saint Germain does not have a fixed goal, a fixed timetable that this or that should happen at a certain time. He looks at the situation as it is now, accepts the situation as it is now and then says: "How do we move forward from here?"

> O Saint Germain, I love you so,
> my aura filled with violet glow,
> my chakras filled with violet fire,
> I am your cosmic amplifier.
>
> **O Saint Germain, what love you bring,**
> **it truly makes all matter sing,**
> **your violet flame does all restore,**
> **with you we are becoming more.**

5. Saint Germain looks at anything that happens and says: "Well, this happened, how do we turn it into a positive? How do we move forward from here?"

> O Saint Germain, I am now free,
> your violet flame is therapy,
> transform all hang-ups in my mind,
> as inner peace I surely find.
>
> **O Saint Germain, what love you bring,**
> **it truly makes all matter sing,**
> **your violet flame does all restore,**
> **with you we are becoming more.**

6. One potential positive of the latest election is that some people can wake up and realize they now have to engage themselves

in the political process. Others might see an outpicturing of a certain state of consciousness, the black-and-white thinking.

> O Saint Germain, my body pure,
> your violet flame for all is cure,
> consume the cause of all disease,
> and therefore I am all at ease.
>
> **O Saint Germain, what love you bring,**
> **it truly makes all matter sing,**
> **your violet flame does all restore,**
> **with you we are becoming more.**

7. If a society becomes too static, then someone that shakes things up can actually force people to rethink, and this can be in alignment with the mind of Christ. Even the president serves in the capacity of forcing people to confront certain issues and therefore get out of the apathy that has crept into so many Americans where they feel powerless to do anything about the political process.

> O Saint Germain, I'm karma-free,
> the past no longer burdens me,
> a brand new opportunity,
> I am in Christic unity.
>
> **O Saint Germain, what love you bring,**
> **it truly makes all matter sing,**
> **your violet flame does all restore,**
> **with you we are becoming more.**

8. Once the people of a democratic nation have chosen, Saint Germain accepts this and says: "How can we move on from

here?" Saint Germain attempts to work with any President, and with the people who are a part of the government apparatus, because he does not have these dualistic, black-and-white value judgments.

> O Saint Germain, we are now one,
> I am for you a violet sun,
> as we transform this planet earth,
> your Golden Age is given birth.

> **O Saint Germain, what love you bring,**
> **it truly makes all matter sing,**
> **your violet flame does all restore,**
> **with you we are becoming more.**

9. Saint Germain is not looking to judge anyone. He simply says: "Can I work with this President and this administration? How can I work with them? Are there some ideas I can introduce that will help bring America forward?"

> O Saint Germain, the earth is free,
> from burden of duality,
> in oneness we bring what is best,
> your Golden Age is manifest.

> **O Saint Germain, what love you bring,**
> **it truly makes all matter sing,**
> **your violet flame does all restore,**
> **with you we are becoming more.**

Sealing

In the name of the I AM THAT I AM, I accept that Archangel Michael, Astrea and Shiva form an impenetrable shield around myself and all constructive people in America, sealing us from all fear-based energies in all four octaves. I accept that the Light of God is consuming and transforming all fear-based energies that make up the dark forces working against America!

8 | INVOKING THE TRANSCENDENCE OF POLARIZATION

In the name of the I AM THAT I AM, Jesus Christ, I use the authority that I have as a being in embodiment on earth to call upon Saint Germain to reinforce my calls and use my chakras to project the statements in this invocation into the collective consciousness and awaken Americans to the need to overcome the polarizations engineered by those who want to destroy America. Awaken Americans to the reality that we are spiritual beings and that we can co-create a new future by working with the ascended masters. I especially call for …

[Make your own calls here.]

Part 1

1. Saint Germain cannot allow himself to reject any president because he is committed to helping the American nation and the American people progress. He cannot withdraw himself from the White House for four years or eight years.

> O Saint Germain, you do inspire,
> my vision raised forever higher,
> with you I form a figure-eight,
> your Golden Age I co-create.
>
> **O Saint Germain, what love you bring,**
> **it truly makes all matter sing,**
> **your violet flame does all restore,**
> **with you we are becoming more.**

2. I call for the cutting free of people in the current administration so they can receive some constructive ideas from Saint Germain that will bring some part of America forward.

> O Saint Germain, what Freedom Flame,
> released when we recite your name,
> acceleration is your gift,
> our planet it will surely lift.
>
> **O Saint Germain, what love you bring,**
> **it truly makes all matter sing,**
> **your violet flame does all restore,**
> **with you we are becoming more.**

3. I call for the cutting free of people in the Congress and the Senate so they can receive ideas from Saint Germain.

> O Saint Germain, in love we claim,
> our right to bring your violet flame,
> from you Above, to us below,
> it is an all-transforming flow.

> **O Saint Germain, what love you bring,**
> **it truly makes all matter sing,**
> **your violet flame does all restore,**
> **with you we are becoming more.**

4. Saint Germain would especially like to see a change in the public discourse of America, the way people talk about the political situation, the way people talk to each other.

> O Saint Germain, I love you so,
> my aura filled with violet glow,
> my chakras filled with violet fire,
> I am your cosmic amplifier.

> **O Saint Germain, what love you bring,**
> **it truly makes all matter sing,**
> **your violet flame does all restore,**
> **with you we are becoming more.**

5. America has gone through a phase where the Internet has made it easier for people to express themselves in a public forum. There has been a tendency to a polarization into more and more black-and-white thinking.

O Saint Germain, I am now free,
your violet flame is therapy,
transform all hang-ups in my mind,
as inner peace I surely find.

**O Saint Germain, what love you bring,
it truly makes all matter sing,
your violet flame does all restore,
with you we are becoming more.**

6. This has led to the public forum being taken over by people who are in a black-and-white state of mind, who are in the epic mindset. The most aggressive people are the ones who have the epic mindset and believe it is of epic importance that they win the debate.

O Saint Germain, my body pure,
your violet flame for all is cure,
consume the cause of all disease,
and therefore I am all at ease.

**O Saint Germain, what love you bring,
it truly makes all matter sing,
your violet flame does all restore,
with you we are becoming more.**

7. This has caused all of the balanced, moderate Americans to give up and withdraw. They do not want to have anything to do with this level of discourse because it is not where they are at in consciousness.

O Saint Germain, I'm karma-free,
the past no longer burdens me,

a brand new opportunity,
I am in Christic unity.

**O Saint Germain, what love you bring,
it truly makes all matter sing,
your violet flame does all restore,
with you we are becoming more.**

8. We now have a situation in America where the public discourse has been taken over by these black-and-white thinkers who are always looking for the simple solution, which means forcing some other group of people.

O Saint Germain, we are now one,
I am for you a violet sun,
as we transform this planet earth,
your Golden Age is given birth.

**O Saint Germain, what love you bring,
it truly makes all matter sing,
your violet flame does all restore,
with you we are becoming more.**

9. This has had the effect of turning away all of the people who could bring America closer to the Golden Age because they are more balanced, which means they are more on the middle way. They are the ones who are more aligned with the mind of Saint Germain and therefore able to receive ideas from him.

O Saint Germain, the earth is free,
from burden of duality,
in oneness we bring what is best,
your Golden Age is manifest.

> O Saint Germain, what love you bring,
> it truly makes all matter sing,
> your violet flame does all restore,
> with you we are becoming more.

Part 2

1. I call for the congressmen and senators who are more moderate to be cut free from being hijacked by the leaders of the two parties who have also gone into this black-and-white, epic mindset.

> O Saint Germain, you do inspire,
> my vision raised forever higher,
> with you I form a figure-eight,
> your Golden Age I co-create.

> O Saint Germain, what love you bring,
> it truly makes all matter sing,
> your violet flame does all restore,
> with you we are becoming more.

2. I call for the judgment of Christ upon the leaders of the Democratic and Republican parties who are so focused on fighting the other party that the concerns about what is actually right for America have faded into the background.

> O Saint Germain, what Freedom Flame,
> released when we recite your name,
> acceleration is your gift,
> our planet it will surely lift.

> O Saint Germain, what love you bring,
> it truly makes all matter sing,
> your violet flame does all restore,
> with you we are becoming more.

3. Even though there may be a majority in Congress that are for a certain change, that majority can never vote as one block because some of those moderate, balanced people are republicans and some are democrats. They are forced to vote the party line and this is what has created gridlock.

O Saint Germain, in love we claim,
our right to bring your violet flame,
from you Above, to us below,
it is an all-transforming flow.

> O Saint Germain, what love you bring,
> it truly makes all matter sing,
> your violet flame does all restore,
> with you we are becoming more.

4. Gridlock springs from the fact that the public discourse has become black-and-white and therefore people cannot talk to each other across these dividing lines.

O Saint Germain, I love you so,
my aura filled with violet glow,
my chakras filled with violet fire,
I am your cosmic amplifier.

> O Saint Germain, what love you bring,
> it truly makes all matter sing,

> your violet flame does all restore,
> with you we are becoming more.

5. If we cannot talk to each other, then there is only one outcome: Tension will continue to grow until there is some kind of explosion. This is essentially how most wars on earth have started.

> O Saint Germain, I am now free,
> your violet flame is therapy,
> transform all hang-ups in my mind,
> as inner peace I surely find.

> **O Saint Germain, what love you bring,
> it truly makes all matter sing,
> your violet flame does all restore,
> with you we are becoming more.**

6. We have a state of civil war in the minds of many Americans because they have become so attached to winning, to defeating the opposite party that they see as being so epically wrong, so epically bad.

> O Saint Germain, my body pure,
> your violet flame for all is cure,
> consume the cause of all disease,
> and therefore I am all at ease.

> **O Saint Germain, what love you bring,
> it truly makes all matter sing,
> your violet flame does all restore,
> with you we are becoming more.**

7. Saint Germain is completely non-attached to who has a majority in congress because it is not going to make any difference. Neither party is able or willing to take America in a truly new direction. Either party, no matter who runs it, will be politics as usual until there is some major change.

> O Saint Germain, I'm karma-free,
> the past no longer burdens me,
> a brand new opportunity,
> I am in Christic unity.

> **O Saint Germain, what love you bring,**
> **it truly makes all matter sing,**
> **your violet flame does all restore,**
> **with you we are becoming more.**

8. Saint Germain does not look at the Democratic Party as being absolutely wrong and the Republican Party as being absolutely right or the other way around. Saint Germain looks at issues.

> O Saint Germain, we are now one,
> I am for you a violet sun,
> as we transform this planet earth,
> your Golden Age is given birth.

> **O Saint Germain, what love you bring,**
> **it truly makes all matter sing,**
> **your violet flame does all restore,**
> **with you we are becoming more.**

9. Saint Germain often sees that there is a majority of people in congress who are aligned with his mind on a particular issue,

but they never get to vote as a group because they are split by this black-and-white conflict between the two parties.

> O Saint Germain, the earth is free,
> from burden of duality,
> in oneness we bring what is best,
> your Golden Age is manifest.
>
> **O Saint Germain, what love you bring,**
> **it truly makes all matter sing,**
> **your violet flame does all restore,**
> **with you we are becoming more.**

Part 3

1. We demand that Republicans and Democrats can cooperate across party lines, can talk to each other. It is not a matter of defeating the other party, it is a matter of coming together in a spirit of cooperation and saying: "What is best for the country? Are we elected by the people to fight the other party or are we elected to do what is best for the country?"

> O Saint Germain, you do inspire,
> my vision raised forever higher,
> with you I form a figure-eight,
> your Golden Age I co-create.
>
> **O Saint Germain, what love you bring,**
> **it truly makes all matter sing,**
> **your violet flame does all restore,**
> **with you we are becoming more.**

2. I call for the cutting free of all Americans who can be examples of how to have a political discussion that is not based on black-and-white thinking, that is not based on the simplistic view that one person is the right president and the other is an absolute disaster, that one party will take America in the right direction and the other will destroy it in half an hour.

> O Saint Germain, what Freedom Flame,
> released when we recite your name,
> acceleration is your gift,
> our planet it will surely lift.
>
> **O Saint Germain, what love you bring,**
> **it truly makes all matter sing,**
> **your violet flame does all restore,**
> **with you we are becoming more.**

3. Saint Germain would like to see many changes in the political system but none of them can come about as long as the public discourse is the way it is right now, as long as it is divisive.

> O Saint Germain, in love we claim,
> our right to bring your violet flame,
> from you Above, to us below,
> it is an all-transforming flow.
>
> **O Saint Germain, what love you bring,**
> **it truly makes all matter sing,**
> **your violet flame does all restore,**
> **with you we are becoming more.**

4. Politics as usual, the political status quo that we have in America, is created by the hidden power elite who have never been elected, who have never stood out publicly.

> O Saint Germain, I love you so,
> my aura filled with violet glow,
> my chakras filled with violet fire,
> I am your cosmic amplifier.

> **O Saint Germain, what love you bring,**
> **it truly makes all matter sing,**
> **your violet flame does all restore,**
> **with you we are becoming more.**

5. The power elite has gradually manipulated the political process in America in order to gain more and more privileges by taking it from the people. It is not created just by one party, but by elements in both parties. Both parties have been hijacked by these hidden power elites.

> O Saint Germain, I am now free,
> your violet flame is therapy,
> transform all hang-ups in my mind,
> as inner peace I surely find.

> **O Saint Germain, what love you bring,**
> **it truly makes all matter sing,**
> **your violet flame does all restore,**
> **with you we are becoming more.**

6. Only the power elite benefits from politics as usual. The elite will not change the situation in America and neither will the two parties that have a monopoly on congress.

8 | Invoking the transcendence of polarization

O Saint Germain, my body pure,
your violet flame for all is cure,
consume the cause of all disease,
and therefore I am all at ease.

**O Saint Germain, what love you bring,
it truly makes all matter sing,
your violet flame does all restore,
with you we are becoming more.**

7. Change can come only from the people. When the consciousness of the people changes, then the power elite must give way and the fallen beings know this.

O Saint Germain, I'm karma-free,
the past no longer burdens me,
a brand new opportunity,
I am in Christic unity.

**O Saint Germain, what love you bring,
it truly makes all matter sing,
your violet flame does all restore,
with you we are becoming more.**

8. They know that when the people are united, they must give concessions, they must withdraw, they will be forced to give way. They may still think they can maintain some measure of control, but they must give way.

O Saint Germain, we are now one,
I am for you a violet sun,
as we transform this planet earth,
your Golden Age is given birth.

> **O Saint Germain, what love you bring,**
> **it truly makes all matter sing,**
> **your violet flame does all restore,**
> **with you we are becoming more.**

9. The goal of the elite is to divide the people into factions so that we cannot come together and speak with one voice and say: "We have had enough of this, we want change."

> O Saint Germain, the earth is free,
> from burden of duality,
> in oneness we bring what is best,
> your Golden Age is manifest.

> **O Saint Germain, what love you bring,**
> **it truly makes all matter sing,**
> **your violet flame does all restore,**
> **with you we are becoming more.**

Part 4

1. The entire public discourse is geared towards dividing Americans and keeping us divided! That is the underlying purpose of this divisive public discourse. It is a subtle plot that very few people have realized.

> O Saint Germain, you do inspire,
> my vision raised forever higher,
> with you I form a figure-eight,
> your Golden Age I co-create.

8 | Invoking the transcendence of polarization

**O Saint Germain, what love you bring,
it truly makes all matter sing,
your violet flame does all restore,
with you we are becoming more.**

2. I call for an exposure of this plot and for the cutting free of all Americans who have the potential to tune in to the mind of Saint Germain.

O Saint Germain, what Freedom Flame,
released when we recite your name,
acceleration is your gift,
our planet it will surely lift.

**O Saint Germain, what love you bring,
it truly makes all matter sing,
your violet flame does all restore,
with you we are becoming more.**

3. There is no way to bring serious changes to America as long as the public discourse is locked in this black-and-white thinking and is taken over and hijacked by these very aggressive, epically-minded people.

O Saint Germain, in love we claim,
our right to bring your violet flame,
from you Above, to us below,
it is an all-transforming flow.

**O Saint Germain, what love you bring,
it truly makes all matter sing,
your violet flame does all restore,
with you we are becoming more.**

4. I call forth the judgment of Christ upon the people who have manipulated the public discourse into black-and-white thinking, both those who are paid to do this and those who are paying them.

> O Saint Germain, I love you so,
> my aura filled with violet glow,
> my chakras filled with violet fire,
> I am your cosmic amplifier.
>
> **O Saint Germain, what love you bring,**
> **it truly makes all matter sing,**
> **your violet flame does all restore,**
> **with you we are becoming more.**

5. I call for the cutting free of Americans from the thinking that there is a simple solution to their problems—if only we can defeat the group that is defined as the problem. As long as we define other people as the problem, we are refusing to take responsibility for our situation.

> O Saint Germain, I am now free,
> your violet flame is therapy,
> transform all hang-ups in my mind,
> as inner peace I surely find.
>
> **O Saint Germain, what love you bring,**
> **it truly makes all matter sing,**
> **your violet flame does all restore,**
> **with you we are becoming more.**

6. I call for the cutting free of Americans who have started to take responsibility and move out of the epic mindset. I call

8 | Invoking the transcendence of polarization

for the cutting free of Americans who could make a difference but have not done so because they do not want to be exposed to the reaction from these very judgmental, critical, aggressive people.

> O Saint Germain, my body pure,
> your violet flame for all is cure,
> consume the cause of all disease,
> and therefore I am all at ease.

> **O Saint Germain, what love you bring,**
> **it truly makes all matter sing,**
> **your violet flame does all restore,**
> **with you we are becoming more.**

7. I call forth a shift where the balanced people will begin to speak out, until it builds that critical mass where it cannot be ignored or put down.

> O Saint Germain, I'm karma-free,
> the past no longer burdens me,
> a brand new opportunity,
> I am in Christic unity.

> **O Saint Germain, what love you bring,**
> **it truly makes all matter sing,**
> **your violet flame does all restore,**
> **with you we are becoming more.**

8. I call forth a demonstration in Washington, D.C. that is not created by extremists but by the more balanced people who are demonstrating for restoring or creating a public discourse that

is focused on: "How do we move America forward?" Not on: "How do we win over those other people."

> O Saint Germain, we are now one,
> I am for you a violet sun,
> as we transform this planet earth,
> your Golden Age is given birth.

> **O Saint Germain, what love you bring,**
> **it truly makes all matter sing,**
> **your violet flame does all restore,**
> **with you we are becoming more.**

9. I call for the cutting free of Americans so we can connect at the heart level to the basic humanity that we all share. I call for Americans to be cut free to see Saint Germain's vision that instead of the United States of America, we have the United Peoples of America.

> O Saint Germain, the earth is free,
> from burden of duality,
> in oneness we bring what is best,
> your Golden Age is manifest.

> **O Saint Germain, what love you bring,**
> **it truly makes all matter sing,**
> **your violet flame does all restore,**
> **with you we are becoming more.**

Sealing

In the name of the I AM THAT I AM, I accept that Archangel Michael, Astrea and Shiva form an impenetrable shield around myself and all constructive people in America, sealing us from all fear-based energies in all four octaves. I accept that the Light of God is consuming and transforming all fear-based energies that make up the dark forces working against America!

9 | WHAT DOES IT MEAN TO BE AN AMERICAN?

I AM the Ascended Master Saint Germain, and I too am freedom. Now, I wish to build on what I gave you yesterday and what Mother Mary and Jesus have given you and talk about the concept of the United Peoples of America. How can we unite the peoples of America? Well, as I said, we need to change the public discourse so that instead of being antagonistic, it becomes open-ended and seeking for a higher solution, a higher understanding. Naturally, when you have a polarized debate, the effect of this is that it seems like there are only two possible solutions to any issue. Not only is this dualistic but it is not difficult for many Americans to realize that this is always a manipulated debate.

Freedom from the power elite

Whenever there is an issue where there seems to be only two options, you can be sure that the debate has been manipulated by the power elite. As Americans, you are dedicated to freedom and what does freedom mean—freedom from what? Why did I sponsor America? What was the vision of the Founding Fathers? Why did so many people leave their lives in Europe and other nations and come to this country with an uncertain future ahead of them? It was because they wanted freedom from the power elite. *That,* my beloved, is the central theme in the creation of America. If you go back to Europe at the time when America was created, you will see that the people were very heavily suppressed and controlled by a small elite, the kings and the noblemen.

Those of you who know about my history, will know that I attempted to work with the kings in order to create a more united, a unified state of Europe. I wanted to create a "United Peoples of Europe" in order to not only take Europe and the world beyond the warfare you had seen in the Middle Ages, but I was also attempting to avoid the first and the second world war. This, of course, did not happen because the power elite was not willing to work on unity because they wanted to have their power, they wanted to set themselves up as being in control. If you were to create a United Peoples or a United States of Europe, then the kings of different countries would feel that they were losing their power as the supreme regent of that country. Naturally, my vision for the United States of Europe was similar to the United States of America where the president was not a dictator and where there were checks and balances that could hopefully prevent the power elite from taking over, as they had always done before.

Dethroning the power elite in America

Now naturally, you can look at America and see that even though there are checks and balances, the power elite has still managed to take over and take control of America. Thus, in order to unite the people of America, they need to understand (and you need to make the calls for this to be radiated into the collective consciousness so that more people become consciously aware of it) that one of the main purposes for the creation of America is precisely to give people freedom from the power elite. Therefore, the people need to be willing to look at what it is that the power elite does in order to control them.

As I said yesterday, one of the primary tools used by the power elite is to create this very polarized public discourse because people cannot talk to each other as human beings and therefore they cannot see what they have in common. If you, again, look at the history of the creation of America, you can see that one of the major purposes for creating America was to bring people together from many different backgrounds. Again, you look at Europe at the time and you see that Europe was divided into separate nations that had often been at war with each other. They were very identified with their national identity. It was very difficult for the Germans and the Frenchmen to get along, and the British as well. You had this very antagonistic situation because people were so identified with their national identity.

What did we create with America? We created a new nation that was in the beginning a blank slate. It was open country, there was nothing there. People were allowed to come from many different backgrounds, many different nations, and when they came here, they were given the opportunity to be free of their old identity, to start anew and say: "Who do I really want to be, what kind of a life do I want to live here in this open space?"

My vision and my highest hope for America was that people would be able to let go of their old animosities, the old consciousness. They would be able to come together in this new physical space, see beyond the old divisions and discover the basic humanity in themselves and in each other so that they could become the United Peoples of America. This was my vision and my highest hope. Naturally, I was realistic in realizing that it would take some time before this could possibly manifest because I was very well aware that birds of a feather flock together. Therefore, people from different nations and backgrounds (partly because they spoke different languages) would tend to congregate together in certain areas. In many cases, they would build on what they had taken with them from the old world instead of freeing themselves from it and adopting something new.

Nevertheless, as you can see from history, it did not take many generations before most of the people who had settled America had adopted at least the English language so they could communicate with each other. They also very quickly started feeling more or less free from the old national identity from Europe so that they adopted an American national identity. You see that despite the fact that they may still have maintained some customs from their old nations, there was still a certain coming together in realizing that as Americans, we are here, were are in the same boat and it is better to cooperate than to work against each other.

What does it mean to be an American?

There have, of course, always been certain groups who clearly set themselves apart. There have been, of course, the difficulties with Native Americans, with African Americans, with Hispanic Americans and so forth and so on, but there has been a certain national identity that has been built. Now, what has happened in recent decades, as I said yesterday, is that people

9 | What does it mean to be an American?

have become less focused on that common national identity and they have become more focused on their differences. It is as if the vision that we are Americans has faded into the background, whereas the divisions have become more important: Republicans, Democrats, Hispanics, this and that division, especially religions, Christians against all others, materialists and atheists against all religious people and so on. Because of what I said about the Internet that has been taken over by, quite frankly, the more hateful people, then this has taken over the public discourse.

How can we, then, change the public discourse? How can we get the more balanced, moderate people to enter the public discourse and make their mark on it? How can we help people move beyond these divisions? Well, we can only realistically do this by raising their sense of identity. This means that we need to talk about what it really means to be an American.

There is a tendency, of course, as Mother Mary said, that people in America take my sponsorship for granted. They think that if you are born in America and you have a birth certificate, then you are automatically an American and you are entitled to enjoy life in America. Well, let me tell you that from a spiritual perspective, a quite substantial number of the people who live in America and have a birth certificate and a passport and a driver's license, I do not consider them Americans because you do not automatically become an American. Being an American is a *choice*. You must make a choice to adopt a certain state of identity, a certain outlook on life and it can only be a conscious, aware choice.

Now, in previous dispensations we have talked about America being a symbol for the "I AM Race." Unfortunately, race is a very divisive word. That is why I do not want to use it. There is no I AM Race that you are born into because being an American is a choice. It is, of course, a play on words: the

I AM, the I AM Presence. You are aware that you are more than a human being, you are more than these outer divisions. I have decided, as a way to help people with this, to release a new American Creed for what it means to be an American. So this is my gift for now.

THE NEW AMERICAN CREED

I AM aware.

I AM aware that I AM aware, meaning I have self-awareness.

I AM able to use my self-awareness to step outside of my current sense of identity, my current state of mind, look at myself and evaluate: "Is this my highest potential or is there *more?*"

I AM willing to step outside of my current sense of identity, my current state of mind and recognize that I do have a higher potential. There is more, there is more awareness that I could attain.

I AM dedicated to raising my awareness.

I AM dedicated to walking a gradual path where I raise my awareness from my current level to succeedingly higher levels of awareness.

I AM aware that as I grew up, a certain world view, a certain perspective on life, was put upon me.

I AM aware that I have the ability to raise my awareness and gain a broader world view, a broader perspective.

I AM dedicating myself to walking the path of raising my awareness of the world, my awareness of life.

I AM aware that as I grew up, a certain view of myself, a certain sense of identity, a certain sense of who I am and what I can and cannot do was put upon me.

I AM aware that I have the ability to raise my sense of identity, to raise my awareness that I can do much more than I was brought up to believe.

I AM dedicated to walking a gradual path of raising my awareness of who I really am and what is indeed possible for me in this world.

I AM aware that as I raise my awareness of who I am, my perspective on everything will change.

I AM aware that the way I look at life right now, the way I look at myself right now, is a product of my current level of awareness, my current level of consciousness.

I AM aware that at my current level, there are things that I cannot see, there are things that I cannot grasp, there are things that I cannot understand, there are things that I cannot experience.

I AM aware that as I raise my awareness, I will begin to see much more than I see now. I will begin to see things that I cannot grasp or understand at my present level.

I AM aware that my present view and understanding of life is inherently limited and that there is a higher understanding available that I will attain as I raise my level of consciousness.

I AM determined to shift my approach to life. I accept the fact that my present understanding and view of life is not the ultimate, is not some absolute truth; is not the only truth.

I AM willing to realize that whatever I know, understand or believe about life, is not the final view or understanding. It is indeed possible to raise myself to a higher level of consciousness where I see what I do not see now.

I AM willing to make the shift where I recognize that since I do not have a final understanding of life right now, I cannot be fully, and I *will* not be fully, identified with my beliefs, with my understanding, with my view of life. Therefore, I will not believe that there is nothing beyond it.

I AM willing to make the shift of realizing that if I do not have the final understanding of life, then it is not of epic importance that I force my current limited understanding upon other people or the nation.

I AM willing to acknowledge that I do not have the right to force a limited understanding upon others and that it will not serve my own interests or the interests of my nation to do so.

I AM aware that the current way I look at life is affected by many external influences that are seeking to manipulate me into a limited state of life, a limited state of consciousness and a state of conflict with other people.

I AM aware that there are certain influences in this world that are seeking to create a division in my own psyche in order to control me.

I AM aware that there are certain influences in this world that are seeking to create a division between myself and other people and that are seeking to create divisions between various groups of people in my nation in order to control all of us.

I AM aware that they can only control me when I have a limited view of life yet believe that it is the final, absolute or only truth.

I AM willing to leave this state of limited awareness behind me and rise to a higher level of awareness where I am constantly reaching for a higher understanding of any issue than what I have right now.

I AM willing to look at the public discourse in America and recognize that it has been taken over by the divisive forces who are seeking to divide Americans into opposing factions in order to control our nation and in order to control ourselves.

I AM aware that these forces are using the divide-and-conquer tactic. I AM aware that this tactic can work only as long as we have a limited awareness but believe it is the final awareness and therefore are not willing to look for a higher understanding.

I AM aware that if we look for a higher understanding, we will find it. I AM aware that when we seek a higher understanding, we will see something that we cannot see when we are so sure that the polarized viewpoints represent some ultimate truth.

I AM aware that the divisive forces will do anything they can to prevent us, to prevent a critical mass of Americans, from becoming aware of this process, this possibility of raising our awareness.

I AM willing to make the shift where I recognize that one of the greatest opportunities I have for raising my own awareness is to interact with other people and hear their perspective on life.

I AM willing to make the shift where I recognize that when I feel threatened by the viewpoints of other people and feel compelled to oppose them, it is because of a certain mechanism in my own psychology that makes me feel insecure.

I AM willing to make the shift where I recognize that this mechanism in my own psychology is deliberately put there by the divisive forces, who are seeking to make me a house divided against myself, so that they can control me from within and not even having to control me through physical means.

I AM aware that I have a desire to be free of these kind of divisive and controlling mechanisms in my own psyche.

I AM dedicating myself to walking a path of freeing myself from all such control mechanisms in my own psychology.

I AM aware that as I free myself from these control mechanisms, I will feel less and less threatened by the fact that other people are different from myself.

I AM aware that as more and more people do this, we will no longer be trapped in these polarized divisions where it seems like every issue has only two possible outcomes, only two possible options we can choose.

I AM aware that in any debate where there is a polarization between two viewpoints, where each claims to be absolutely right, then this is a debate that is artificially created by the divisive forces.

I AM willing to make the shift of dedicating myself to overcoming this division in myself and to overcoming the division between myself and other people.

I AM willing to make the shift of realizing that the differences of other people are not a threat to me, they are my opportunity to raise my awareness and broaden my perspective on life.

I AM willing to make the shift where I stop identifying myself with these outer divisions that have been artificially created.

I AM willing to make the shift of raising my awareness so that the outer sense of identity, based on my nationality, skin color, race, sex, ethnicity and so forth and so on, fall away and I discover a deeper sense of identity in myself.

I AM aware that when I raise my consciousness to see beyond these outer identity factors, I will discover my own essential humanity. I will realize that I am more than a human being. I am a universal being living in a human body.

I AM aware that as I raise my personal awareness to that level of identity, I will see that all other people are my brothers and sisters for they too have that essential humanity, they too are universal beings living in human bodies.

I AM aware that the divisive forces of this world will do anything to prevent us, a critical mass of us, from rising to that level of awareness.

9 | What does it mean to be an American?

I AM aware that nothing scares the divisive forces more than when many people rise to that level of awareness. For when we no longer identify ourselves based on the outer divisions, then the prince of this world has nothing in us whereby he can divide us in ourselves and against each other.

I AM dedicating myself to walking this path of raising my own awareness to the point where I do not feel threatened by other people being different from me.

I AM dedicating myself to attaining the level of awareness where I see the essential humanity in myself and I see the essential humanity in all people I meet.

I AM dedicating myself to seeing beyond the outer divisions, the outer characteristics of the people I meet until I not only see but connect in my heart to their essential humanity.

I AM dedicating myself to seeking first to connect to the essential humanity of other people, and only after I have made that connection do I look at their viewpoints.

I AM dedicating myself to seeking to understand other people based on having connected to their basic, essential humanity.

I AM dedicating myself to freeing myself of all influence of the divisive forces and therefore finding a new way to interact with my brothers and sisters. A way that is not based on division and conflict but on seeing, connecting to the essential humanity in us all.

I AM dedicating myself to shifting the public discourse and the public awareness of America away from all outer divisions and towards a recognition of that essential humanity.

I AM dedicating myself to spreading the awareness that the entire purpose for the creation of America is to create the United Peoples of America.

I AM dedicating myself to spreading the awareness that we can be the United Peoples of America only when we recognize and connect to the essential humanity in ourselves and each other.

I AM aware that this is the highest vision of what it means to be an American.

I AM dedicating myself to raising my awareness to the level where I can truly say: "I AM an American."

Give the people what they want

Thus, my beloved, this is my gift. I trust that as it spreads, as you help spread it, it can indeed reach the hearts of many people. Naturally, this is my *gift*. It is not copyrighted, you are free to do with it whatever you see fit.

My beloved, while this was my essential gift, I will give you an opportunity to step down from the higher awareness you have been willing to go into by making a few other remarks. Naturally, I look to you, who are my direct students, to be forerunners of this shift in awareness. We have given you the teachings and the tools to realize that you are not identified based on these outer divisions, whether it be Republican or Democrat, whether it be nationality, race, ethnicity, religious affiliation, whatever you have. Truly, we look to you to use the tools to connect to that essential humanity in yourselves and to see it in others. You have already demonstrated at this conference that you can do this, that you have reached at least some level of awareness of that humanity. That is why you can interact the way you do, why you can feel free to share without feeling judged.

Truly, my beloved, in the Piscean Age it was, of course, the hope of Jesus that he could create a religious movement, a spiritual movement, that would unite people by giving them the Christ discernment that would help them see that essential humanity in all so that people could be united in Christ. As you see, during the Piscean Age that was a very difficult challenge for people to meet.

You saw what was done to Jesus' teachings to prevent people from uniting in Christ. That is why you saw that the teachings of Jesus were turned into an outer religion that has been one of the most divisive factors in the last 2,000 years. In fact, there is no question that the Catholic church and even later Christian churches have been the single most divisive factor in the Age of Pisces.

This shows you something. It does *not* show you that the fallen beings have more power and therefore can pervert anything we give them. It shows you that the fallen beings are very good at using the psychology of human beings to look at their level of awareness, to see what desires they have and to use those desires to give people the impression that if they follow the fallen beings and accept their system, then the people will get what they want. This is what you saw in the Catholic church where you saw that Jesus taught the inner path but the majority of the people were not ready to follow that inner path. They actually wanted an outer religion that gave them what the scribes and the Pharisees and the Jewish authorities promised people at Jesus' time: "If you adhere to our system, if you obey us, if you follow the rituals that we give you, if you adopt the beliefs that we give you, then you are *guaranteed* to be saved."

People who were not willing to take responsibility for themselves could not grasp the inner path taught by Jesus. That is why they adopted the outer religion created by the fallen beings because in a way it gave them what they wanted. It gave them the belief that by following a few simple outer rules, they could be saved after this lifetime, but aside from going to church on Sunday and following these outer rituals, they could live their lives any way they wanted. This is the essential consciousness that the fallen beings have used to manipulate people throughout the ages.

A new spirituality in America

The reality of the creation of America is that, of course, I was aware of this dynamic. I was very well aware at the time that the people who came from Europe had been so heavily suppressed by the feudal system that they did not long to come to a new nation based on a spiritual foundation. They simply longed to have a piece of land where they could grow enough food to feed their families. *That* was their basic desire at the time. America, in a sense, fulfilled that for at least some of the people who came here, whereas others, of course, ended up in even greater poverty.

What I am giving you now is that America has gradually been raised to the point where, even though the economy is heavily manipulated and even though there is a small power elite that accumulates most of the wealth, there is still a great number of people in America who are able to take care of their material needs and still have some free time, still have free time to follow a path of raising their awareness. This has reached a certain critical mass where there is the potential for a series of shifts—if people can be awakened and reconnect to their higher desires beyond these outer desires, the more immediate desires. There are still many people, of course, who want to live their lives any way they want and then feel they will be saved in the end. That is why they are members of the Christian churches who make that promise. There are many more people in America who have become dissatisfied with Christianity, who have looked into either other religions or some other form of spirituality, and they are the ones who can drive the shift in the collective consciousness.

What you have the potential to do, as ascended master students, is to be the forerunners for these shifts. First of all, by shifting your own consciousness but also by sharing your process of how you have raised your awareness. The shift I am asking you to make (that we have in a sense asked you to make before, but I am attempting to make it more clear, more real to you) is this: The old model that you see in the world, you see it in religious and political contexts, is that some people believe that they have the highest truth or the only truth or the absolute truth. Therefore, they believe that the way to change the world is to convert all other people to their system, to make other people accept their beliefs. The shift I am asking you to make is that this is no longer the highest approach. It never *was* the highest approach, but it is no longer a relevant approach in the Age of Aquarius.

Therefore, I am asking you to shift and say: "It is not a matter of converting people to believe in reincarnation, to believe in ascended masters, to believe in fallen beings or previous spheres or this or that idea that may be beyond their present level. The real issue here is to help people see that there is a path for raising your consciousness and that this path benefits you." This is where I am asking you to look at yourselves and how finding the path benefited you. Perhaps it answered your questions, perhaps it helped you heal your psychology, perhaps it helped you get beyond some limiting psychological condition. Whatever it was for you individually, people who have those same issues, they are the ones that you can reach out to, not with this attitude that you need to convert them to specific beliefs, but that you need to show them that they can raise their awareness.

Uniting people by accepting differences

Do you see, my beloved, before the fallen beings were allowed to come to this planet, there were civilizations that had attempted to create harmony by making everybody the same, making everyone believe in the same. This had put these civilizations in a downward spiral so this is not what I envision for the Golden Age. I do not envision a Golden Age where everybody is an ascended master student and is a member of a particular outer church or religion. I envision a Golden Age where all people can find the concept that there is a path for raising your awareness and that this benefits your life, your daily life. They can find that in various forms, whatever appeals to them. You see: How do we unite people? Not by making them, not by converting them, into all believing the same thing. We unite people by helping them find a path for raising their awareness.

What I am asking you to trust is that when people do raise their awareness, they will at some point discover that essential humanity and *that* is the factor that will unite them, not the outer beliefs. You may say: "Are the teachings we give you beliefs?" Nevertheless, what I am saying is: "Do not attempt to make people believe something. Give them the tools for raising their consciousness until they experience from within. Allow them to have a different experience than you have had, for you are all different."

I am asking you to make the shift that is described in the *My Lives* book [*My Lives with Lucifer, Satan, Hitler and Jesus*] of accepting that you are having a subjective experience and that you are not here to try to make your subjective experience universal by exporting it to other people. Let them have *their* subjective experience but dedicate yourself to raising your awareness so that your experience becomes less and less subjective but still individual.

Give people the path so they can raise their awareness, so that their experience becomes less and less subjective but still individual. Then, rejoice in the fact that when you see the basic humanity in each other, your individuality, your differences are not in competition, are not in opposition. They complement each other for that is why God created individual beings.

10 | INVOKING AN AWARENESS OF OUR BASIC HUMANITY

In the name of the I AM THAT I AM, Jesus Christ, I use the authority that I have as a being in embodiment on earth to call upon Saint Germain to reinforce my calls and use my chakras to project the statements in this invocation into the collective consciousness and awaken Americans to the need to connect to our basic humanity. Awaken Americans to the reality that we are spiritual beings and that we can co-create a new future by working with the ascended masters. I especially call for …

[Make your own calls here.]

Part

1. Saint Germain's goal is to create the United Peoples of America. We can unite the peoples of America only by changing the public discourse so that instead

of being antagonistic, it becomes open-ended and seeking for a higher understanding.

> O Saint Germain, you do inspire,
> my vision raised forever higher,
> with you I form a figure-eight,
> your Golden Age I co-create.

> **O Saint Germain, what love you bring,**
> **it truly makes all matter sing,**
> **your violet flame does all restore,**
> **with you we are becoming more.**

2. When we have a polarized debate, the effect is that it seems like there are only two possible solutions to any issue. This is always a manipulated debate.

> O Saint Germain, what Freedom Flame,
> released when we recite your name,
> acceleration is your gift,
> our planet it will surely lift.

> **O Saint Germain, what love you bring,**
> **it truly makes all matter sing,**
> **your violet flame does all restore,**
> **with you we are becoming more.**

3. Whenever there is an issue where there seems to be only two options, the debate has been manipulated by the power elite.

> O Saint Germain, in love we claim,
> our right to bring your violet flame,

from you Above, to us below,
it is an all-transforming flow.

**O Saint Germain, what love you bring,
it truly makes all matter sing,
your violet flame does all restore,
with you we are becoming more.**

4. As Americans, we are dedicated to freedom and freedom means freedom from the power elite. *That* is the central theme in the creation of America.

O Saint Germain, I love you so,
my aura filled with violet glow,
my chakras filled with violet fire,
I am your cosmic amplifier.

**O Saint Germain, what love you bring,
it truly makes all matter sing,
your violet flame does all restore,
with you we are becoming more.**

5. Even though there are checks and balances, the power elite has still managed to take control of America.

O Saint Germain, I am now free,
your violet flame is therapy,
transform all hang-ups in my mind,
as inner peace I surely find.

**O Saint Germain, what love you bring,
it truly makes all matter sing,**

> your violet flame does all restore,
> with you we are becoming more.

6. In order to unite the people of America, we need to understand that one of the main purposes for the creation of America is to give people freedom from the power elite. Therefore, we need to be willing to look at what the power elite does to control us.

> O Saint Germain, my body pure,
> your violet flame for all is cure,
> consume the cause of all disease,
> and therefore I am all at ease.

> **O Saint Germain, what love you bring,**
> **it truly makes all matter sing,**
> **your violet flame does all restore,**
> **with you we are becoming more.**

7. One of the primary tools used by the power elite is to create this polarized public discourse because people cannot talk to each other as human beings and therefore they cannot see what they have in common.

> O Saint Germain, I'm karma-free,
> the past no longer burdens me,
> a brand new opportunity,
> I am in Christic unity.

> **O Saint Germain, what love you bring,**
> **it truly makes all matter sing,**
> **your violet flame does all restore,**
> **with you we are becoming more.**

8. One of the major purposes for creating America was to bring people together from many different backgrounds. America was a new nation that was in the beginning a blank slate.

> O Saint Germain, we are now one,
> I am for you a violet sun,
> as we transform this planet earth,
> your Golden Age is given birth.
>
> **O Saint Germain, what love you bring,**
> **it truly makes all matter sing,**
> **your violet flame does all restore,**
> **with you we are becoming more.**

9. People were allowed to come from many different backgrounds, many different nations, and when they came here, they were given the opportunity to be free of their old identity, to start anew and say: "Who do I really want to be, what kind of a life do I want to live here in this open space?"

> O Saint Germain, the earth is free,
> from burden of duality,
> in oneness we bring what is best,
> your Golden Age is manifest.
>
> **O Saint Germain, what love you bring,**
> **it truly makes all matter sing,**
> **your violet flame does all restore,**
> **with you we are becoming more.**

Part 2

1. Saint Germain's vision and highest hope for America was that people would be able to let go of their old animosities, the old consciousness.

> O Saint Germain, you do inspire,
> my vision raised forever higher,
> with you I form a figure-eight,
> your Golden Age I co-create.
>
> **O Saint Germain, what love you bring,**
> **it truly makes all matter sing,**
> **your violet flame does all restore,**
> **with you we are becoming more.**

2. Saint Germain hoped that people would be able to come together in this new physical space, see beyond the old divisions and discover the basic humanity in themselves and in each other so that they could become the United Peoples of America.

> O Saint Germain, what Freedom Flame,
> released when we recite your name,
> acceleration is your gift,
> our planet it will surely lift.
>
> **O Saint Germain, what love you bring,**
> **it truly makes all matter sing,**
> **your violet flame does all restore,**
> **with you we are becoming more.**

3. Most Americans have adopted the English language and let go of the old national identity from Europe. Many people realize that as Americans, we are here, we are in the same boat and it is better to cooperate than to work against each other.

> O Saint Germain, in love we claim,
> our right to bring your violet flame,
> from you Above, to us below,
> it is an all-transforming flow.

> **O Saint Germain, what love you bring,**
> **it truly makes all matter sing,**
> **your violet flame does all restore,**
> **with you we are becoming more.**

4. In recent decades, people have become less focused on the common national identity and they have become more focused on their differences. The vision that we are Americans has faded into the background, whereas the divisions have become more important.

> O Saint Germain, I love you so,
> my aura filled with violet glow,
> my chakras filled with violet fire,
> I am your cosmic amplifier.

> **O Saint Germain, what love you bring,**
> **it truly makes all matter sing,**
> **your violet flame does all restore,**
> **with you we are becoming more.**

5. The only way to get the more balanced, moderate people to enter the public discourse and make their mark on it is by

raising their sense of identity, their awareness of what it means to be an American.

> O Saint Germain, I am now free,
> your violet flame is therapy,
> transform all hang-ups in my mind,
> as inner peace I surely find.

> **O Saint Germain, what love you bring,**
> **it truly makes all matter sing,**
> **your violet flame does all restore,**
> **with you we are becoming more.**

6. Many people think that if you are born in America and have a birth certificate, then you are automatically an American and you are entitled to enjoy life in America.

> O Saint Germain, my body pure,
> your violet flame for all is cure,
> consume the cause of all disease,
> and therefore I am all at ease.

> **O Saint Germain, what love you bring,**
> **it truly makes all matter sing,**
> **your violet flame does all restore,**
> **with you we are becoming more.**

7. From a spiritual perspective, a substantial number of the people who live in America and have a birth certificate are not really Americans because we do not automatically become an American.

O Saint Germain, I'm karma-free,
the past no longer burdens me,
a brand new opportunity,
I am in Christic unity.

**O Saint Germain, what love you bring,
it truly makes all matter sing,
your violet flame does all restore,
with you we are becoming more.**

8. Being an American is a *choice*. We must make a choice to adopt a certain state of identity, a certain outlook on life and it can only be a conscious, aware choice.

O Saint Germain, we are now one,
I am for you a violet sun,
as we transform this planet earth,
your Golden Age is given birth.

**O Saint Germain, what love you bring,
it truly makes all matter sing,
your violet flame does all restore,
with you we are becoming more.**

9. The core of being an American is to have some connection to our higher selves, so we know we are more than human beings, more than these outer divisions.

O Saint Germain, the earth is free,
from burden of duality,
in oneness we bring what is best,
your Golden Age is manifest.

**O Saint Germain, what love you bring,
it truly makes all matter sing,
your violet flame does all restore,
with you we are becoming more.**

Part 3

1. As Americans, we are not identified based on these outer divisions, whether it be Republican or Democrat, whether it be nationality, race, ethnicity or religious affiliation.

> O Saint Germain, you do inspire,
> my vision raised forever higher,
> with you I form a figure-eight,
> your Golden Age I co-create.
>
> **O Saint Germain, what love you bring,
> it truly makes all matter sing,
> your violet flame does all restore,
> with you we are becoming more.**

2. As Americans, we connect to the essential humanity in ourselves and we see it in others.

> O Saint Germain, what Freedom Flame,
> released when we recite your name,
> acceleration is your gift,
> our planet it will surely lift.
>
> **O Saint Germain, what love you bring,
> it truly makes all matter sing,**

> your violet flame does all restore,
> with you we are becoming more.

3. It was the hope of Jesus that he could create a spiritual movement that would unite people by giving them the Christ discernment that would help them see that essential humanity in all so that people could be united in Christ.

> O Saint Germain, in love we claim,
> our right to bring your violet flame,
> from you Above, to us below,
> it is an all-transforming flow.

> **O Saint Germain, what love you bring,**
> **it truly makes all matter sing,**
> **your violet flame does all restore,**
> **with you we are becoming more.**

4. In order to prevent people from uniting in Christ, the teachings of Jesus were turned into an outer religion that has been one of the most divisive factors in the last 2,000 years. The Catholic church and even later Christian churches have been the single most divisive factor in the Age of Pisces.

> O Saint Germain, I love you so,
> my aura filled with violet glow,
> my chakras filled with violet fire,
> I am your cosmic amplifier.

> **O Saint Germain, what love you bring,**
> **it truly makes all matter sing,**
> **your violet flame does all restore,**
> **with you we are becoming more.**

5. The fallen beings are very good at using human psychology to see what desires we have and to use those desires to give us the impression that if we follow the fallen beings and accept their system, then we will get what we want.

> O Saint Germain, I am now free,
> your violet flame is therapy,
> transform all hang-ups in my mind,
> as inner peace I surely find.
>
> **O Saint Germain, what love you bring,**
> **it truly makes all matter sing,**
> **your violet flame does all restore,**
> **with you we are becoming more.**

6. Jesus taught the inner path but the majority of the people were not ready to follow that inner path. They wanted an outer religion that gave them what the Jewish authorities promised people at Jesus' time: "If you adhere to our system, if you obey us, if you follow the rituals that we give you, if you adopt the beliefs that we give you, then you are *guaranteed* to be saved."

> O Saint Germain, my body pure,
> your violet flame for all is cure,
> consume the cause of all disease,
> and therefore I am all at ease.
>
> **O Saint Germain, what love you bring,**
> **it truly makes all matter sing,**
> **your violet flame does all restore,**
> **with you we are becoming more.**

7. People who were not willing to take responsibility for themselves could not grasp the inner path taught by Jesus. They adopted the outer religion created by the fallen beings because it gave them what they wanted.

> O Saint Germain, I'm karma-free,
> the past no longer burdens me,
> a brand new opportunity,
> I am in Christic unity.

> **O Saint Germain, what love you bring,**
> **it truly makes all matter sing,**
> **your violet flame does all restore,**
> **with you we are becoming more.**

8. The Catholic church gave people the belief that by following a few outer rules, they could be saved after this lifetime, but aside from going to church on Sunday and following these outer rituals, they could live their lives any way they wanted. This is the essential consciousness that the fallen beings have used to manipulate people throughout the ages.

> O Saint Germain, we are now one,
> I am for you a violet sun,
> as we transform this planet earth,
> your Golden Age is given birth.

> **O Saint Germain, what love you bring,**
> **it truly makes all matter sing,**
> **your violet flame does all restore,**
> **with you we are becoming more.**

9. America has gradually been raised to the point where there is a great number of people in America who are able to take care of their material needs and still have some free time to follow a path of raising their awareness.

> O Saint Germain, the earth is free,
> from burden of duality,
> in oneness we bring what is best,
> your Golden Age is manifest.
>
> **O Saint Germain, what love you bring,**
> **it truly makes all matter sing,**
> **your violet flame does all restore,**
> **with you we are becoming more.**

Part 4

1. I call for Americans to be awakened and reconnect to their higher desires beyond these outer desires.

> O Saint Germain, you do inspire,
> my vision raised forever higher,
> with you I form a figure-eight,
> your Golden Age I co-create.
>
> **O Saint Germain, what love you bring,**
> **it truly makes all matter sing,**
> **your violet flame does all restore,**
> **with you we are becoming more.**

10 | Invoking an awareness of our basic humanity

2. I call for the people who have become dissatisfied with Christianity to be cut free so they can find some other form of spirituality and drive a shift in the collective consciousness.

> O Saint Germain, what Freedom Flame,
> released when we recite your name,
> acceleration is your gift,
> our planet it will surely lift.

> **O Saint Germain, what love you bring,**
> **it truly makes all matter sing,**
> **your violet flame does all restore,**
> **with you we are becoming more.**

3. The old model that we see in religious and political contexts, is that some people believe that they have the highest truth, the only truth or the absolute truth. Therefore, they believe that the way to change the world is to convert all other people to their system.

> O Saint Germain, in love we claim,
> our right to bring your violet flame,
> from you Above, to us below,
> it is an all-transforming flow.

> **O Saint Germain, what love you bring,**
> **it truly makes all matter sing,**
> **your violet flame does all restore,**
> **with you we are becoming more.**

4. I call for Americans to be cut free to make the shift of realizing that this is no longer a relevant approach in this age.

O Saint Germain, I love you so,
my aura filled with violet glow,
my chakras filled with violet fire,
I am your cosmic amplifier.

**O Saint Germain, what love you bring,
it truly makes all matter sing,
your violet flame does all restore,
with you we are becoming more.**

5. It is not a matter of converting people to believe in a specific spiritual philosophy. The real issue is to help people see that there is a path for raising their consciousness and that this path benefits them.

O Saint Germain, I am now free,
your violet flame is therapy,
transform all hang-ups in my mind,
as inner peace I surely find.

**O Saint Germain, what love you bring,
it truly makes all matter sing,
your violet flame does all restore,
with you we are becoming more.**

6. Saint Germain does not envision a Golden Age where everybody is a member of a particular outer church or religion. He envisions a Golden Age where all people can find the concept that there is a path for raising your awareness and that this benefits our daily lives.

O Saint Germain, my body pure,
your violet flame for all is cure,

consume the cause of all disease,
and therefore I am all at ease.

**O Saint Germain, what love you bring,
it truly makes all matter sing,
your violet flame does all restore,
with you we are becoming more.**

7. We do not unite people by making them all believe the same thing. We unite people by helping them find a path for raising their awareness. When people do raise their awareness, they will discover the essential humanity and *that* is the factor that will unite them.

O Saint Germain, I'm karma-free,
the past no longer burdens me,
a brand new opportunity,
I am in Christic unity.

**O Saint Germain, what love you bring,
it truly makes all matter sing,
your violet flame does all restore,
with you we are becoming more.**

8. I accept that I am having a subjective experience and that I am not here to try to make my subjective experience universal by exporting it to other people. I dedicate myself to raising my awareness so that my experience becomes less and less subjective but still individual.

O Saint Germain, we are now one,
I am for you a violet sun,

as we transform this planet earth,
your Golden Age is given birth.

**O Saint Germain, what love you bring,
it truly makes all matter sing,
your violet flame does all restore,
with you we are becoming more.**

9. I call for Americans to be cut free to find the path so they can raise their awareness, so that their experience becomes less and less subjective but still individual. When we see the basic humanity in each other, our differences are not in competition. They complement each other for that is why God created individual beings.

O Saint Germain, the earth is free,
from burden of duality,
in oneness we bring what is best,
your Golden Age is manifest.

**O Saint Germain, what love you bring,
it truly makes all matter sing,
your violet flame does all restore,
with you we are becoming more.**

Sealing

In the name of the I AM THAT I AM, I accept that Archangel Michael, Astrea and Shiva form an impenetrable shield around myself and all constructive people in America, sealing us from all fear-based energies in all four octaves. I accept that the Light

of God is consuming and transforming all fear-based energies that make up the dark forces working against America!

11 | INVOKING THE NEW AMERICAN CREED

In the name of the I AM THAT I AM, Jesus Christ, I use the authority that I have as a being in embodiment on earth to call upon Saint Germain to reinforce my calls and use my chakras to project the statements in this invocation into the collective consciousness and awaken Americans to what it truly means to be an American. Awaken Americans to the reality that we are spiritual beings and that we can co-create a new future by working with the ascended masters. I especially call for …

[Make your own calls here.]

Part 1

1. I AM aware. I AM aware that I AM aware, meaning I have self-awareness.

O Saint Germain, you do inspire,
my vision raised forever higher,
with you I form a figure-eight,
your Golden Age I co-create.

O Saint Germain, what love you bring,
it truly makes all matter sing,
your violet flame does all restore,
with you we are becoming more.

2. I AM able to use my self-awareness to step outside of my current sense of identity, my current state of mind, look at myself and evaluate: "Is this my highest potential or is there *more?*"

O Saint Germain, what Freedom Flame,
released when we recite your name,
acceleration is your gift,
our planet it will surely lift.

O Saint Germain, what love you bring,
it truly makes all matter sing,
your violet flame does all restore,
with you we are becoming more.

3. I AM willing to step outside of my current sense of identity, my current state of mind and recognize that I do have a higher potential. There *is* more, there is more awareness that I could attain.

O Saint Germain, in love we claim,
our right to bring your violet flame,

from you Above, to us below,
it is an all-transforming flow.

**O Saint Germain, what love you bring,
it truly makes all matter sing,
your violet flame does all restore,
with you we are becoming more.**

4. I AM dedicated to raising my awareness. I AM dedicated to walking a gradual path where I raise my awareness from my current level to succeedingly higher levels of awareness.

O Saint Germain, I love you so,
my aura filled with violet glow,
my chakras filled with violet fire,
I am your cosmic amplifier.

**O Saint Germain, what love you bring,
it truly makes all matter sing,
your violet flame does all restore,
with you we are becoming more.**

5. I AM aware that as I grew up, a certain world view, a certain perspective on life, was put upon me. I AM aware that I have the ability to raise my awareness and gain a broader world view, a broader perspective.

O Saint Germain, I am now free,
your violet flame is therapy,
transform all hang-ups in my mind,
as inner peace I surely find.

> **O Saint Germain, what love you bring,**
> **it truly makes all matter sing,**
> **your violet flame does all restore,**
> **with you we are becoming more.**

6. I AM dedicating myself to walking the path of raising my awareness of the world, my awareness of life.

> O Saint Germain, my body pure,
> your violet flame for all is cure,
> consume the cause of all disease,
> and therefore I am all at ease.

> **O Saint Germain, what love you bring,**
> **it truly makes all matter sing,**
> **your violet flame does all restore,**
> **with you we are becoming more.**

7. I AM aware that as I grew up, a certain view of myself, a certain sense of identity, a certain sense of who I am and what I can and cannot do was put upon me.

> O Saint Germain, I'm karma-free,
> the past no longer burdens me,
> a brand new opportunity,
> I am in Christic unity.

> **O Saint Germain, what love you bring,**
> **it truly makes all matter sing,**
> **your violet flame does all restore,**
> **with you we are becoming more.**

8. I AM aware that I have the ability to raise my sense of identity, to raise my awareness that I can do much more than I was brought up to believe.

> O Saint Germain, we are now one,
> I am for you a violet sun,
> as we transform this planet earth,
> your Golden Age is given birth.
>
> **O Saint Germain, what love you bring,**
> **it truly makes all matter sing,**
> **your violet flame does all restore,**
> **with you we are becoming more.**

9. I AM dedicated to walking a gradual path of raising my awareness of who I really am and what is indeed possible for me in this world.

> O Saint Germain, the earth is free,
> from burden of duality,
> in oneness we bring what is best,
> your Golden Age is manifest.
>
> **O Saint Germain, what love you bring,**
> **it truly makes all matter sing,**
> **your violet flame does all restore,**
> **with you we are becoming more.**

Part 2

1. I AM aware that as I raise my awareness of who I am, my perspective on everything will change.

> O Saint Germain, you do inspire,
> my vision raised forever higher,
> with you I form a figure-eight,
> your Golden Age I co-create.
>
> **O Saint Germain, what love you bring,**
> **it truly makes all matter sing,**
> **your violet flame does all restore,**
> **with you we are becoming more.**

2. I AM aware that the way I look at life right now, the way I look at myself right now, is a product of my current level of awareness, my current level of consciousness.

> O Saint Germain, what Freedom Flame,
> released when we recite your name,
> acceleration is your gift,
> our planet it will surely lift.
>
> **O Saint Germain, what love you bring,**
> **it truly makes all matter sing,**
> **your violet flame does all restore,**
> **with you we are becoming more.**

3. I AM aware that at my current level, there are things that I cannot see, there are things that I cannot grasp, there are

things that I cannot understand, there are things that I cannot experience.

> O Saint Germain, in love we claim,
> our right to bring your violet flame,
> from you Above, to us below,
> it is an all-transforming flow.

> **O Saint Germain, what love you bring,**
> **it truly makes all matter sing,**
> **your violet flame does all restore,**
> **with you we are becoming more.**

4. I AM aware that as I raise my awareness, I will begin to see much more than I see now. I will begin to see things that I cannot grasp or understand at my present level.

> O Saint Germain, I love you so,
> my aura filled with violet glow,
> my chakras filled with violet fire,
> I am your cosmic amplifier.

> **O Saint Germain, what love you bring,**
> **it truly makes all matter sing,**
> **your violet flame does all restore,**
> **with you we are becoming more.**

5. I AM aware that my present view and understanding of life is inherently limited and that there is a higher understanding available that I will attain as I raise my level of consciousness.

> O Saint Germain, I am now free,
> your violet flame is therapy,

transform all hang-ups in my mind,
as inner peace I surely find.

**O Saint Germain, what love you bring,
it truly makes all matter sing,
your violet flame does all restore,
with you we are becoming more.**

6. I AM determined to shift my approach to life. I accept the fact that my present understanding and view of life is not the ultimate, is not some absolute truth; is not the *only* truth.

O Saint Germain, my body pure,
your violet flame for all is cure,
consume the cause of all disease,
and therefore I am all at ease.

**O Saint Germain, what love you bring,
it truly makes all matter sing,
your violet flame does all restore,
with you we are becoming more.**

7. I AM willing to realize that whatever I know, understand or believe about life, is not the final view or understanding. It is indeed possible to raise myself to a higher level of consciousness where I see what I do not see now.

O Saint Germain, I'm karma-free,
the past no longer burdens me,
a brand new opportunity,
I am in Christic unity.

**O Saint Germain, what love you bring,
it truly makes all matter sing,
your violet flame does all restore,
with you we are becoming more.**

8. I AM willing to make the shift where I recognize that since I do not have a final understanding of life right now, I cannot be fully, and I *will* not be fully, identified with my beliefs, with my understanding, with my view of life. Therefore, I will not believe that there is nothing beyond it.

O Saint Germain, we are now one,
I am for you a violet sun,
as we transform this planet earth,
your Golden Age is given birth.

**O Saint Germain, what love you bring,
it truly makes all matter sing,
your violet flame does all restore,
with you we are becoming more.**

9. I AM willing to make the shift of realizing that if I do not have the final understanding of life, then it is not of epic importance that I force my current limited understanding upon other people or the nation.

O Saint Germain, the earth is free,
from burden of duality,
in oneness we bring what is best,
your Golden Age is manifest.

**O Saint Germain, what love you bring,
it truly makes all matter sing,**

your violet flame does all restore,
with you we are becoming more.

Part 3

1. I AM willing to acknowledge that I do not have the right to force a limited understanding upon others and that it will not serve my own interests or the interests of my nation to do so.

> O Saint Germain, you do inspire,
> my vision raised forever higher,
> with you I form a figure-eight,
> your Golden Age I co-create.

> **O Saint Germain, what love you bring,
> it truly makes all matter sing,
> your violet flame does all restore,
> with you we are becoming more.**

2. I AM aware that the current way I look at life is affected by many external influences that are seeking to manipulate me into a limited state of life, a limited state of consciousness and a state of conflict with other people.

> O Saint Germain, what Freedom Flame,
> released when we recite your name,
> acceleration is your gift,
> our planet it will surely lift.

> **O Saint Germain, what love you bring,
> it truly makes all matter sing,**

11 | Invoking the New American Creed

> your violet flame does all restore,
> with you we are becoming more.

3. I AM aware that there are certain influences in this world that are seeking to create a division in my own psyche in order to control me.

> O Saint Germain, in love we claim,
> our right to bring your violet flame,
> from you Above, to us below,
> it is an all-transforming flow.

> **O Saint Germain, what love you bring,
> it truly makes all matter sing,
> your violet flame does all restore,
> with you we are becoming more.**

4. I AM aware that there are certain influences in this world that are seeking to create a division between myself and other people and that are seeking to create divisions between various groups of people in my nation in order to control all of us.

> O Saint Germain, I love you so,
> my aura filled with violet glow,
> my chakras filled with violet fire,
> I am your cosmic amplifier.

> **O Saint Germain, what love you bring,
> it truly makes all matter sing,
> your violet flame does all restore,
> with you we are becoming more.**

5. I AM aware that they can only control me when I have a limited view of life yet believe that it is the final, absolute or only truth.

> O Saint Germain, I am now free,
> your violet flame is therapy,
> transform all hang-ups in my mind,
> as inner peace I surely find.
>
> **O Saint Germain, what love you bring,**
> **it truly makes all matter sing,**
> **your violet flame does all restore,**
> **with you we are becoming more.**

6. I AM willing to leave this state of limited awareness behind me and rise to a higher level of awareness where I am constantly reaching for a higher understanding of any issue than what I have right now.

> O Saint Germain, my body pure,
> your violet flame for all is cure,
> consume the cause of all disease,
> and therefore I am all at ease.
>
> **O Saint Germain, what love you bring,**
> **it truly makes all matter sing,**
> **your violet flame does all restore,**
> **with you we are becoming more.**

7. I AM willing to look at the public discourse in America and recognize that it has been taken over by the divisive forces who are seeking to divide Americans into opposing factions in order to control our nation and in order to control ourselves.

O Saint Germain, I'm karma-free,
the past no longer burdens me,
a brand new opportunity,
I am in Christic unity.

**O Saint Germain, what love you bring,
it truly makes all matter sing,
your violet flame does all restore,
with you we are becoming more.**

8. I AM aware that these forces are using the divide-and-conquer tactic. I AM aware that this tactic can work only as long as we have a limited awareness but believe it is the final awareness and therefore are not willing to look for a higher understanding.

O Saint Germain, we are now one,
I am for you a violet sun,
as we transform this planet earth,
your Golden Age is given birth.

**O Saint Germain, what love you bring,
it truly makes all matter sing,
your violet flame does all restore,
with you we are becoming more.**

9. I AM aware that if we look for a higher understanding, we will find it. I AM aware that when we seek a higher understanding, we will see something that we cannot see when we are so sure that the polarized viewpoints represent some ultimate truth.

O Saint Germain, the earth is free,
from burden of duality,

in oneness we bring what is best,
your Golden Age is manifest.

O Saint Germain, what love you bring,
it truly makes all matter sing,
your violet flame does all restore,
with you we are becoming more.

Part 4

1. I AM aware that the divisive forces will do anything they can to prevent us, to prevent a critical mass of Americans, from becoming aware of this process, this possibility of raising our awareness.

O Saint Germain, you do inspire,
my vision raised forever higher,
with you I form a figure-eight,
your Golden Age I co-create.

O Saint Germain, what love you bring,
it truly makes all matter sing,
your violet flame does all restore,
with you we are becoming more.

2. I AM willing to make the shift where I recognize that one of the greatest opportunities I have for raising my own awareness is to interact with other people and hear their perspective on life.

11 | Invoking the New American Creed 243

> O Saint Germain, what Freedom Flame,
> released when we recite your name,
> acceleration is your gift,
> our planet it will surely lift.
>
> **O Saint Germain, what love you bring,**
> **it truly makes all matter sing,**
> **your violet flame does all restore,**
> **with you we are becoming more.**

3. I AM willing to make the shift where I recognize that when I feel threatened by the viewpoints of other people and feel compelled to oppose them, it is because of a certain mechanism in my own psychology that makes me feel insecure.

> O Saint Germain, in love we claim,
> our right to bring your violet flame,
> from you Above, to us below,
> it is an all-transforming flow.
>
> **O Saint Germain, what love you bring,**
> **it truly makes all matter sing,**
> **your violet flame does all restore,**
> **with you we are becoming more.**

4. I AM willing to make the shift where I recognize that this mechanism in my own psychology is deliberately put there by the divisive forces, who are seeking to make me a house divided against myself, so that they can control me from within and not even having to control me through physical means.

> O Saint Germain, I love you so,
> my aura filled with violet glow,

my chakras filled with violet fire,
I am your cosmic amplifier.

**O Saint Germain, what love you bring,
it truly makes all matter sing,
your violet flame does all restore,
with you we are becoming more.**

5. I AM aware that I have a desire to be free of these kind of divisive and controlling mechanisms in my own psyche. I AM dedicating myself to walking a path of freeing myself from all such control mechanisms in my own psychology.

O Saint Germain, I am now free,
your violet flame is therapy,
transform all hang-ups in my mind,
as inner peace I surely find.

**O Saint Germain, what love you bring,
it truly makes all matter sing,
your violet flame does all restore,
with you we are becoming more.**

6. I AM aware that as I free myself from these control mechanisms, I will feel less and less threatened by the fact that other people are different from myself.

O Saint Germain, my body pure,
your violet flame for all is cure,
consume the cause of all disease,
and therefore I am all at ease.

11 | Invoking the New American Creed

**O Saint Germain, what love you bring,
it truly makes all matter sing,
your violet flame does all restore,
with you we are becoming more.**

7. I AM aware that as more and more people do this, we will no longer be trapped in these polarized divisions where it seems like every issue has only two possible outcomes, only two possible options we can choose.

O Saint Germain, I'm karma-free,
the past no longer burdens me,
a brand new opportunity,
I am in Christic unity.

**O Saint Germain, what love you bring,
it truly makes all matter sing,
your violet flame does all restore,
with you we are becoming more.**

8. I AM aware that in any debate where there is a polarization between two viewpoints, where each claims to be absolutely right, then this is a debate that is artificially created by the divisive forces.

O Saint Germain, we are now one,
I am for you a violet sun,
as we transform this planet earth,
your Golden Age is given birth.

**O Saint Germain, what love you bring,
it truly makes all matter sing,**

your violet flame does all restore,
with you we are becoming more.

9. I AM willing to make the shift of dedicating myself to overcoming this division in myself and to overcoming the division between myself and other people.

O Saint Germain, the earth is free,
from burden of duality,
in oneness we bring what is best,
your Golden Age is manifest.

O Saint Germain, what love you bring,
it truly makes all matter sing,
your violet flame does all restore,
with you we are becoming more.

Part 5

1. I AM willing to make the shift of realizing that the differences of other people are not a threat to me, they are my opportunity to raise my awareness and broaden my perspective on life.

O Saint Germain, you do inspire,
my vision raised forever higher,
with you I form a figure-eight,
your Golden Age I co-create.

O Saint Germain, what love you bring,
it truly makes all matter sing,

**your violet flame does all restore,
with you we are becoming more.**

2. I AM willing to make the shift where I stop identifying myself with these outer divisions that have been artificially created.

> O Saint Germain, what Freedom Flame,
> released when we recite your name,
> acceleration is your gift,
> our planet it will surely lift.

> **O Saint Germain, what love you bring,
> it truly makes all matter sing,
> your violet flame does all restore,
> with you we are becoming more.**

3. I AM willing to make the shift of raising my awareness so that the outer sense of identity, based on my nationality, skin color, race, sex, ethnicity and so forth and so on, fall away and I discover a deeper sense of identity in myself.

> O Saint Germain, in love we claim,
> our right to bring your violet flame,
> from you Above, to us below,
> it is an all-transforming flow.

> **O Saint Germain, what love you bring,
> it truly makes all matter sing,
> your violet flame does all restore,
> with you we are becoming more.**

4. I AM aware that when I raise my consciousness to see beyond these outer identity factors, I will discover my own

essential humanity. I will realize that I am more than a human being. I am a universal being living in a human body.

> O Saint Germain, I love you so,
> my aura filled with violet glow,
> my chakras filled with violet fire,
> I am your cosmic amplifier.

> **O Saint Germain, what love you bring,**
> **it truly makes all matter sing,**
> **your violet flame does all restore,**
> **with you we are becoming more.**

5. I AM aware that as I raise my personal awareness to that level of identity, I will see that all other people are my brothers and sisters for they too have that essential humanity, they too are universal beings living in human bodies.

> O Saint Germain, I am now free,
> your violet flame is therapy,
> transform all hang-ups in my mind,
> as inner peace I surely find.

> **O Saint Germain, what love you bring,**
> **it truly makes all matter sing,**
> **your violet flame does all restore,**
> **with you we are becoming more.**

6. I AM aware that the divisive forces of this world will do anything to prevent us, a critical mass of us, from rising to that level of awareness.

11 | Invoking the New American Creed

O Saint Germain, my body pure,
your violet flame for all is cure,
consume the cause of all disease,
and therefore I am all at ease.

**O Saint Germain, what love you bring,
it truly makes all matter sing,
your violet flame does all restore,
with you we are becoming more.**

7. I AM aware that nothing scares the divisive forces more than when many people rise to that level of awareness. For when we no longer identify ourselves based on the outer divisions, then the prince of this world has nothing in us whereby he can divide us in ourselves and against each other.

O Saint Germain, I'm karma-free,
the past no longer burdens me,
a brand new opportunity,
I am in Christic unity.

**O Saint Germain, what love you bring,
it truly makes all matter sing,
your violet flame does all restore,
with you we are becoming more.**

8. I AM dedicating myself to walking this path of raising my own awareness to the point where I do not feel threatened by other people being different from me.

O Saint Germain, we are now one,
I am for you a violet sun,

as we transform this planet earth,
your Golden Age is given birth.

**O Saint Germain, what love you bring,
it truly makes all matter sing,
your violet flame does all restore,
with you we are becoming more.**

9. I AM dedicating myself to attaining the level of awareness where I see the essential humanity in myself and I see the essential humanity in all people I meet.

O Saint Germain, the earth is free,
from burden of duality,
in oneness we bring what is best,
your Golden Age is manifest.

**O Saint Germain, what love you bring,
it truly makes all matter sing,
your violet flame does all restore,
with you we are becoming more.**

Part 6

1. I AM dedicating myself to seeing beyond the outer divisions, the outer characteristics of the people I meet until I not only see but connect in my heart to their essential humanity.

O Saint Germain, you do inspire,
my vision raised forever higher,

with you I form a figure-eight,
your Golden Age I co-create.

**O Saint Germain, what love you bring,
it truly makes all matter sing,
your violet flame does all restore,
with you we are becoming more.**

2. I AM dedicating myself to seeking first to connect to the essential humanity of other people, and only after I have made that connection do I look at their viewpoints.

O Saint Germain, what Freedom Flame,
released when we recite your name,
acceleration is your gift,
our planet it will surely lift.

**O Saint Germain, what love you bring,
it truly makes all matter sing,
your violet flame does all restore,
with you we are becoming more.**

3. I AM dedicating myself to seeking to understand other people based on having connected to their basic, essential humanity.

O Saint Germain, in love we claim,
our right to bring your violet flame,
from you Above, to us below,
it is an all-transforming flow.

**O Saint Germain, what love you bring,
it truly makes all matter sing,**

> your violet flame does all restore,
> with you we are becoming more.

4. I AM dedicating myself to freeing myself of all influence of the divisive forces and therefore finding a new way to interact with my brothers and sisters. A way that is not based on division and conflict but on seeing, connecting to the essential humanity in us all.

> O Saint Germain, I love you so,
> my aura filled with violet glow,
> my chakras filled with violet fire,
> I am your cosmic amplifier.

> **O Saint Germain, what love you bring,**
> **it truly makes all matter sing,**
> **your violet flame does all restore,**
> **with you we are becoming more.**

5. I AM dedicating myself to shifting the public discourse and the public awareness of America away from all outer divisions and towards a recognition of that essential humanity.

> O Saint Germain, I am now free,
> your violet flame is therapy,
> transform all hang-ups in my mind,
> as inner peace I surely find.

> **O Saint Germain, what love you bring,**
> **it truly makes all matter sing,**
> **your violet flame does all restore,**
> **with you we are becoming more.**

6. I AM dedicating myself to spreading the awareness that the entire purpose for the creation of America is to create the United Peoples of America.

> O Saint Germain, my body pure,
> your violet flame for all is cure,
> consume the cause of all disease,
> and therefore I am all at ease.
>
> **O Saint Germain, what love you bring,
> it truly makes all matter sing,
> your violet flame does all restore,
> with you we are becoming more.**

7. I AM dedicating myself to spreading the awareness that we can be the United Peoples of America only when we recognize and connect to the essential humanity in ourselves and each other.

> O Saint Germain, I'm karma-free,
> the past no longer burdens me,
> a brand new opportunity,
> I am in Christic unity.
>
> **O Saint Germain, what love you bring,
> it truly makes all matter sing,
> your violet flame does all restore,
> with you we are becoming more.**

8. I AM aware that this is the highest vision of what it means to be an American.

O Saint Germain, we are now one,
I am for you a violet sun,
as we transform this planet earth,
your Golden Age is given birth.

**O Saint Germain, what love you bring,
it truly makes all matter sing,
your violet flame does all restore,
with you we are becoming more.**

9. I AM dedicating myself to raising my awareness to the level where I can truly say: "I AM an American."

O Saint Germain, the earth is free,
from burden of duality,
in oneness we bring what is best,
your Golden Age is manifest.

**O Saint Germain, what love you bring,
it truly makes all matter sing,
your violet flame does all restore,
with you we are becoming more.**

Sealing

In the name of the I AM THAT I AM, I accept that Archangel Michael, Astrea and Shiva form an impenetrable shield around myself and all constructive people in America, sealing us from all fear-based energies in all four octaves. I accept that the Light of God is consuming and transforming all fear-based energies that make up the dark forces working against America!

12 | WINNING THE POLITICAL GAME IN THE GOLDEN AGE

I AM the Ascended Master Saint Germain. I desire you to understand that when we talk about aligning America with the mind of Saint Germain, and when we point out certain conditions that have to change, it does not mean that I am imposing conditions upon whether or not I will share my ideas for manifesting a Golden Age in America. I have no conditions. I am perfectly willing to release these ideas to anyone who is able to receive them. In other words, I am *not* saying that before I will release my ideas to America, America has to live up to certain conditions. I am radiating those ideas constantly, so the real question is not whether the ideas are released but whether people can receive them.

What we are talking about is: What will it take for at least some Americans to be able to receive these ideas? What will it take for a critical mass of Americans to be able to accept these ideas so that they can actually be manifest in the nation instead of remaining ideas only? We are not in any way criticizing or condemning America or the American people. We are simply making clear to you what it will take for you to receive the ideas that will set you free from the limitations and suffering you see in this nation right now.

Winning over the obsession with winning

The next thing I want to bring up here is that if America is to become aligned with the mind of Saint Germain, America needs to, and Americans need to, overcome the obsession with winning. America as a nation, in the national psyche, has an obsession with winning. How many nations on earth have in their collective consciousness the concept that they are the greatest nation on earth? But America has it. Look at American sports, look at how competitive Americans are, look at how they always want to win. For example, not so long ago when there was a world soccer championship and a very small nation called Croatia beat some of the biggest soccer nations in the world, they made it to the finals. They did not win the final game but they did not think they had lost the world championship. They thought they had won second place in the entire world, but if Americans had been in that position: "Oh, that team, they were so bad, they lost, they didn't become world champions."

This is the essence of that obsession with winning: It is win or lose, winners take all. You see it even in the political process, you see it in people's mindset. You see that America is obsessed with being the best, always being ahead, and this creates a strange dichotomy in the American psyche. On one hand, Americans are always comparing themselves to other nations but they are only doing this to show how America is better than other nations. They are not comparing themselves to other nations and saying: "Do these nations have something

12 | *Winning the political game in the Golden Age*

we could learn from?" Again, I am talking in general terms, not about everyone, but there is that tendency to look at how Americans can exceed and get ahead of other nations, not being so willing to look at whether there are other nations that are ahead in certain areas.

The obsession with not losing

You see this, for example, in the history of America. There is the concept that America won the Second World War, America won the Cold War, the Gulf war, the war in Iraq. "Yeah, there was that hiccup with the Vietnam War. We didn't quite win that war but you know, we won so many other wars, it doesn't really matter."

If you go back and look at this honestly, you will see what a trauma it was for America after the Vietnam War. America could not deal with this, and why was it? Because America is so obsessed with winning that it cannot face *not* winning. It cannot deal with not winning in a neutral, objective way. America does not have the ability to say: "We made a mistake. Let's learn from it and move on." If you made a mistake, not only did you not win, but you actually *lost*. It is either you win and you are the good guy and you are right, or you lose and you are absolutely wrong. It is the all-or-nothing, the black-and-white thinking.

This, my beloved, is something that you who are ascended master students have already moved beyond, or at least you can very quickly move beyond it. You can make the calls because I assure you that there are many Americans who are very, very close to also breaking through and realizing this entire game of always wanting to be the winner and always wanting to interpret any event as if America came out on top. "We didn't really make a mistake because, after all, we are the greatest nation on earth and we are the good guys. Even if we did go out to some other country and we did sort of create some situation that wasn't really good, after all, we are Americans. We have to spread freedom and democracy around the world, that's what we are here for."

What this obsession with winning creates is an opposite polarity, the obsession with not losing. When you have an obsession with not losing, what you cannot do is say: "We made a mistake, let's learn from it and then we move on." You cannot acknowledge that you made a mistake.

The game of pretending in American politics

We have, of course, given many teachings on overcoming the sense that you made a mistake. There is no need to think in terms of right and wrong, mistakes or not mistakes. It is simply a matter of going into a neutral state of mind, looking at a situation and saying: "Was the outcome really what we wanted?" If it was not what you wanted, then you ask: "How can we then improve so we get what we want?" You see how this dynamic – the obsession with winning, the obsession with not losing – prevents people from going into that neutral state of mind.

Instead of thinking: "How could we improve things?" they go into this very contrived, artificial state of mind of pretending they did not actually lose: "Ah, maybe we didn't win but we certainly didn't lose because it wasn't so bad after all." Instead of just looking at a situation and saying: "We don't want to repeat that. How do we avoid repeating it so we can do better the next time?" This state of consciousness permeates the collective psyche of America. It has many ramifications. You can see the ridiculousness of it in sports but now look at the political arena.

There may be some people in America who have not read the fairy tale by Hans Christian Andersen where an emperor has invited a team of very, supposedly, advanced tailors to make a new dress for him for a major event. These tailors come in and pretend to be sewing this dress but they are not making a real dress. They are so good at pretending that everybody, from the emperor to all of the people in his court, actually see this dress. The emperor appears before the people in his new dress and nobody will come out and say that they do not see it until a little boy cries out: "But the emperor has nothing on!"

This is what needs to happen in the political arena of America. What you have right now is a political situation where the senators, the representatives in the House and all other levels of American politics have used this obsession with winning, the obsession with not losing, to create a situation where the politicians are not doing the job that they were charged to do by the U.S. Constitution. They are not doing the job that the American people elected them to do. But everybody is pretending that they are doing their jobs. They are trying to pretend that they are doing the right thing, that they could not be doing anything else or that there are certain problems that just cannot be solved but it is not their fault. Nobody wants to come out and say: "The emperor has nothing on!"

Washington, D.C., is just one big game of pretending to look out for the interests of the American people. In reality, as a whole (again, individual differences but as a whole) Congress, the President, the Supreme Court, are not looking out for the interests of the American people. They are looking out for the interests of a small power elite. *That* is the naked reality of politics in America.

Very few people dare to come out and say it because in order to say it, you have to free yourself from the mentality of wanting to win, not wanting to lose, therefore not wanting to be neutral and simply say: "Are the politicians doing their job? Are they taking care of what is in the best interests of the people of America?" If they are not, it is not a matter of saying: "Oh, they're wrong, they're so bad, they're this, they're that." The question is: "How can we move forward? How can we do better? How can we avoid repeating a situation that we realize isn't what we really want?"

The gap between public and hidden politics

If you read how the media is treating the political situation and if you see how the politicians are talking about it, it is truly amazing that everybody can ignore the elephant in the room. I am not talking about a particular person, whether in or out of the White House. I am talking about the very fact that the political system, the political apparatus, in America is not looking out for the interests of the people. They are all pretending that they are. Some of them honestly believe that they are, but they are blinded. They are blinded by a consciousness that has been created in Washington, D.C. over many decades and simply comes down as a cloak over the minds of the elected politicians.

There are some of the newly elected politicians that do not have it, but it usually does not take that many years before a politician is blinded by this state of consciousness. Suddenly, the ideals that caused that person to run for office have faded into the background. This is partly based on the stark reality that a newly elected congressman or senator has to spend most of his or her time fundraising for the re-election campaign.

12 | Winning the political game in the Golden Age

It also has to do with the fact that the ideals have to fall by the wayside so that the representatives can walk the party line because if they do not, they will not even be able to run for re-election.

There is a certain sense of apathy that has crept into this mindset, namely that there are certain things that they just cannot do anything about. Some problems are too big, some are so complex or they cannot do anything about it because the opposing party will not agree and therefore nothing can get done. In other words, you are talking about voter apathy but there is also a politician apathy that has very much engulfed Washington, D.C. as a black cloud. In the vocabulary we use with our direct students, a huge beast, a huge demon has been created and it is very, very aggressive in attacking the minds of newly elected representatives. You, of course, can make the calls for this.

It needs to be recognized by the people (and by some of the politicians themselves who are open to this) that there is this cloud that takes over the minds of most politicians in Washington. You can especially see it in those who have been there for a long time. You can go to any kind of debate or any kind of hearing, like this recent hearing for the Supreme Court judge, and you can just see that these people all have a certain look on their faces. They all have a certain way of talking. They have a certain way of reasoning.

If you can read the vibration, you can see that they have all aligned themselves with a certain mindset. Most of them would deny this consciously but what the seasoned politicians in Washington, D.C. have realized is that politics in America is a game of pretending—nothing else. You say what you think you need to say, what the public wants to hear in order to get elected. You vote the way your party wants you to, but the seasoned politicians all know that there is a facade that you show to the public and there is a reality of what you are doing when you think nobody is watching you. There is a huge gap between the public front that you put on and the reality of what goes on in the corridors of power when they think nobody is watching.

Why nobody can go against the status quo

Just as Mother Mary mentioned in the movie industry, where the insiders have for decades known about the sexual abuse but nobody from the inside will speak out, the insiders in Washington – the politicians, the bureaucrats – they all know about this huge gap between the public front and the political reality. The daily hidden discourse of what goes on and how politics is done and how there is wheeling and dealing and how there are special interests and how there is lobbying and how this person is bought by this special interest group and the other person is bought by that. Therefore, it is not at all about what is best for the people. It is only what is best for the elite and the special interest groups that have bought their way into the political system.

Everyone who is an insider in D.C. knows this. Why has nobody cried out that the emperor has nothing on? Because the moment you cry out, you are no longer an insider. You will be frozen out instantly and they will attempt to destroy you, as you see how the politicians and the media are attempting to destroy anyone who is, to use that good old American expression, a whistle-blower.

Those who go against the status quo will be attacked. In fact, if we again step back and take a look at the political process and step up from the public discourse (not only how the public is talking but also how the political system is working), you can see something very interesting. Ask yourself this simple

12 | Winning the political game in the Golden Age

question: What does it take to be an elected representative in the United States and survive psychologically? Look at what those who are running for office or those who are elected, have to go through: the scrutiny in the media, the blatant criticism, that good old American word "mud-slinging" that takes place all of the time. Look at the hate mail that anyone running for office gets from unbalanced people of every persuasion.

You realize that running for public office in the United States of America is very similar to a method of torture that they had centuries ago, called the gauntlet. You have two rows of people that are standing, forming a tunnel. They have various kinds of weapons and somebody has to run through it and the people on both sides are trying to harm them or kill them or cut their limbs off to the best of their ability. Running for public office in the United States today is like running a gauntlet.

Ask yourself: What kind of a person is willing to endure this in order to win public office? You will see that it takes a rather special psychological profile to be able to run, to be able to win and then to be able to find your bearings in the stark political reality that takes place behind the scenes. I can assure you that a balanced, harmonious, non-aggressive person is very unlikely to be willing to endure this. I am not saying there are no exceptions but there are too few of them to make a real difference in terms of changing what I am talking about, this cloud that is hanging over D.C.

There are too few because the majority of them have that psychological profile, the obsession with winning. They will do anything to win, and they can get themselves into a state of mind where anybody who attacks them can be ignored or pushed aside—or even affirms their view that they are against those other people. You know this very, very well. Many people have that psychological profile where anybody who opposes them actually affirms how right they are and how wrong those other people are: "Because that's why they are opposing me, they are automatically wrong if they are opposing me."

Going along in order to get along

What you basically see is that those who can win and those who can survive psychologically once they have won, have one simple ability: the willingness to compromise and the willingness to go along in order to get along. They are all willing to do whatever it takes to get into office and to stay in office. They are willing to play the game as the game is currently being played. Now, of course, you can say to yourself: "Well, how did we get to the point where the political game has become the way it is? Is that because there's some evil conspiracy that consciously created this political climate?" Well, on the one hand, there *is* an evil conspiracy, namely the fallen beings in the identity, mental and emotional realms, but there is not a conspiracy in the physical.

There was no physical person who deliberately attempted to distort the political process. This all happened very gradually over time, without anyone realizing what was happening. It happened so gradually that those who had been there a long time had become used to it. Of course, those who are newly elected and are not compromisers but have idealism, come in and they are shocked at how things are done. There is usually some older politician that comes up to this newly elected person, puts his arm around him or her, and says: "You know, I understand why you are a little disturbed by how things are done but let me just explain a few things to you." What happens is that either the person is persuaded by the elders to play the game or says: "I will have nothing to do with this" and withdraws. This is why you have a situation where, from a purely realistic viewpoint, you can say the vast majority of the politicians and the bureaucrats in Washington are literally hypnotized by this state of consciousness. They know there is a huge gap between the public appearance and the reality in the hidden corridors, but none of them will speak out about it because most of them have resigned themselves to thinking: "Well, that's just the way it is. That's just the way politics is done in America. Nothing we can do about it. We just have to go along and then hopefully it will all work out."

There are even those who enjoy the way politics is being done in America because what does it allow them to do? It allows them to look out for their own interests and enrich themselves by being in office. My beloved, we look to you to make the calls for the shattering of this beast, this demon that is hanging over D.C., for the clearing of it, so that there can be a growing awareness where people can begin to wake up.

How scapegoating ruins the political climate

Many, many people are already so dissatisfied with the political system that the awakening I am looking for is that people, again, get over this consciousness that there has to be a winner and a loser. What is the obsession with winning? How do you win? Well, it is a relative, dualistic concept because, in order for *you* to win, *someone* has to lose—at least if there are two opposing polarities.

What you see is that many people are today very dissatisfied with the political process but because they do not understand what is going on and because they are trapped in the win-lose mindset, what do they do? They look for someone to blame. They look for a scapegoat and they say: "That person or that group of people, that's the bad guy. That's the problem." They are looking to blame, rather than looking for a higher understanding so that they can move forward.

I am not looking for these people who are close to waking up to start blaming the politicians. It is not a matter of blaming the politicians. It is simply a matter of recognizing that: "For reasons we don't even need to fully understand and expose, we have a situation where politics in America has slid into a place that doesn't serve the people. We have had enough of it and we want politics to be the way it should be, namely that everybody in Washington is cooperating in order to do what is in the best interests of the people."

It is not a matter of finding out who is to blame because neither the Republicans nor the Democrats are to blame. There is, in fact, no single senator or congressman who is to blame. There is no group who is to blame. Of course, those who have been there the longest are the most blinded by the consciousness but it is not a matter of blaming anybody. It is simply a matter of crying out that the emperor has nothing on so there suddenly is that shift in awareness where everybody can see what they cannot see today. Everybody can see how far from the ideal politics has gone, how polarized it has become, how it has become a total game of pretending. If we could have that shift, it would have a major impact on the political arena in America.

Taking money out of politics

There are, of course, many others things that could happen and that I envision happening as we move towards the Golden Age. You must recognize that when I sponsored the creation of the United States, I did not have total control over the process.

12 | Winning the political game in the Golden Age

I was not enabled to dictate the Declaration of Independence or the Constitution. It was something that had to be created by working with the people who were there at the time. Their consciousness was, of course, an expression of the collective consciousness and the entire state of the world then. I never envisioned that the Constitution of the United States was a fully ideal, perfect matrix for democratic nations and would never have to change. I have always seen that what could be brought forth then was the highest for that distant time, but as the world moves forward and the collective consciousness is raised, naturally we need to revise and create a new platform based on the way the consciousness is today.

When I look to the Golden Age, I look to certain changes to happen and here are some of them. First of all, in the Golden Age, money will be taken out of politics. This means, for one thing, that a person running for public office in America will not have to do fundraising in order to afford a campaign. You will not need to raise hundreds of thousands or millions of dollars in order to run for public office. You will, as is already implemented in some nations in Europe, be able to get equal media coverage with everyone else. You will be able to participate in debates and, of course, with the Internet you will be able to promote your viewpoints.

There will actually come a point where it will be illegal for politicians and political parties to buy advertising because it favors those who have money over those who do not. Laws will be enacted that will, so to speak, level the playing field so that the success of those running for office will not depend on how much money they can raise but only on their idealism, their enthusiasm, their ability to relate to the people and give the people the impression that they are sincere and honest and will do what they promised. Money will be eliminated from the election process completely.

You know, if you look at this, that those running for office have to spend most of their time raising money for their campaigns. What many of you do not realize is that even those who are elected spend the majority of their time fundraising for their re-election campaigns. Which means what? Which means they do not even have time to read the texts of the laws that they have to vote on. You may say: "Why do they even have to read the text of those laws because it doesn't matter whether they understand them or agree with them? They have to hold the party line anyway." Nevertheless, if you spend most of your time raising money, what attention and time do you have left to actually engage yourself in the political process, to make your mark?

Eliminating lobbying

The other thing that will happen in the Golden Age is, of course, that money will be taken out of politics in the sense that lobbying will be completely eliminated. It will be absolutely illegal for lobbying groups to seek to buy influence as they are doing today. Quite frankly, what is the entire lobbying phenomenon? It is a form of legalized, visible corruption—nothing else. It is corruption that has become legalized and accepted and it should be seen for what it is and eliminated.

It obviously favors those who have lots of money and who has the money? The power elite. It is well known and has been exposed for decades that the top 10% control the majority of the wealth and that the top 2% control the vast majority of the wealth in America. This fact, which has been exposed by statistics now for decades, is the most obvious demonstration of the fact that the American political system has gone completely away from the intention behind the Constitution.

12 | Winning the political game in the Golden Age

This is not a land that functions to enrich the few by taking from the many. It is a country, as I said, that is meant to be a community of equals where each person has equal opportunity to make an effort and reap the rewards of those efforts. This has been aborted, not only by the political process but also by another aspect of American society that I will comment on later. For now, I want to remain with the political changes that I envision happening in the Golden Age.

Eliminating the two-party system

One of the more immediate changes that I see happening before too long is that the electoral college with be eliminated. It had, perhaps, some practical validity when it was created, but certainly with modern communication it is completely obsolete. In the Golden Age, the President will be elected by popular vote. Whichever candidate gets the most votes in the entire country goes to the White House because the electoral college will be gone.

What I also envision is that in the short term there needs to be a challenge to the two-party system and the gridlock of having only two parties. I envision several interim stages that could happen. One is that a third party or even more than one, could begin to gain seats in the House of Representatives so that people would see that they actually have something to vote for besides the Democrats and Republicans.

Voter apathy comes primarily from the fact that there are so many people who feel that neither the Democrats nor the Republicans represent them or that it does not really matter which party has the majority because it is all politics as usual. As an interim stage, a new party could come in, be part of the debate and perhaps even create a situation where either the

Republicans or the Democrats would have to cooperate with this third party in order to get a majority. I know some will cry out that this would split the vote, and I say: "So what! Do you think the current gridlock is a good situation?"

If a third party came in, what would happen? Well, in some situations the Democrats might cooperate with this third party in order to get a majority. But the third party would not agree with the Democrats on everything so there would be other situations where the Republicans would cooperate with the third party in order to get a majority on some issue. That would mean that there is the possibility, as I said, that the moderates, the more balanced people, could now suddenly begin to get their policy through and take it away from the extremists on both sides.

Another possible scenario would be to revisit why we even created two political parties and whether political parties really have any validity anymore. Have they outlived their usefulness? Should we simply say that all representatives run based on their own merit, not based on party affiliation? Once they are in, they can vote their conscience and there are no party lines that divide the house into two opposing factions. The reality is that most representatives are not really voting based on their conviction but because they have come to realize that they have to play the game so they play it and vote the party line. If there was a situation where they were free to vote their conviction, and they were directly responsible to their voters instead of being responsible to the party, then you would see how the political process would change and things would be done that cannot be done today.

12 | Winning the political game in the Golden Age

The hidden power elite

I also foresee that there will be a process whereby it will be exposed that there is a small power elite that exercises completely disproportionate influence on the political process. This is not because these people buy influence, it is because they have what has been called an "old boys' network" where they know people who know people. They have, over generations, formed this network of people who see themselves as the elite that runs America. They think they are doing it for the good of the country but since they have accumulated more wealth than they could possibly spend, and since this is limiting the growth of the U.S. economy, then, if they were honest, they would be able to see that they are not doing it for the good of the country. You can ask about these people – the old wealth in the Northeast, for example – are they really evil or are they, as I said about the representatives in Washington, blinded by a dark cloud, a certain beast that has taken over their minds? Of course, they are blinded by this. Many of them are not evil people. I am not saying they are all fallen beings, although certainly a majority of them are. In the Golden Age I see that this will be exposed, people will be aware of this, they will see the power elite for what it is.

They will realize that you cannot have a functioning democracy if you allow a small power elite to exercise influence by buying it or by persuading or by favoritism where: "You do me a favor, I do you a favor." It can even happen through pressure where you will be ostracized from the inner circle if you do not follow the line, and thereby your family will be embarrassed and shamed. You can see that as Europe had these noble class families, you have a "noble class" of families in the United States who all follow the lines so they can remain part of that inner circle that is not even in Washington but exists elsewhere and has formed this network of influential people.

These are just some of the visions I have about how the political process will change in the Golden Age. There are, of course, others. If you think these ideas are somewhat radical, some of my other ideas are far more radical than most Americans will be able to handle today. Therefore, I will not put them out in the collective consciousness at this point. I can assure you that, along with health care and the drug companies that I said earlier will disappear in the Golden Age, well, there are companies and political institutions that you today take for granted in America that will simply disappear too. They will be replaced by something else that is based on the awareness of togetherness and wanting to raise up the whole rather than wanting to raise up one individual or one group.

What is behind this obsession with winning? Well, there can only be a small group of winners, right? Because what happens when you win? Well, at least for a moment you are superior to all those who did not win. This is the game played by the noble class of America. They think they are superior and they have been hidden for so long, been rich for so long, been powerful for so long, that they think this is a permanent state. They think they are completely superior to the people but it can only happen in comparison to those who are inferior, and in the Golden Age that consciousness will fade away.

There will be a widespread acceptance that all men and women are created equal, that they are endowed by their Creator with certain inalienable rights and among those is the right to improve your consciousness, to raise your awareness to increasingly higher levels. You especially are endowed by your Creator with the right to raise your consciousness beyond the epic mindset, beyond duality, beyond the consciousness of the power elite. *That* is your most sacred right.

13 | INVOKING AN END TO THE OBSESSION WITH WINNING

In the name of the I AM THAT I AM, Jesus Christ, I use the authority that I have as a being in embodiment on earth to call upon Saint Germain to reinforce my calls and use my chakras to project the statements in this invocation into the collective consciousness and awaken Americans from the obsession with winning. Awaken Americans to the reality that we are spiritual beings and that we can co-create a new future by working with the ascended masters. I especially call for …

[Make your own calls here.]

Part 1

1. Saint Germain is willing to share his ideas for manifesting a Golden Age in America with anyone who is able to receive them.

> O Saint Germain, you do inspire,
> my vision raised forever higher,
> with you I form a figure-eight,
> your Golden Age I co-create.
>
> **O Saint Germain, what love you bring,**
> **it truly makes all matter sing,**
> **your violet flame does all restore,**
> **with you we are becoming more.**

2. Saint Germain is not saying that before he will release his ideas to America, America has to live up to certain conditions. Saint Germain is radiating those ideas constantly, so the real question is whether we can receive them.

> O Saint Germain, what Freedom Flame,
> released when we recite your name,
> acceleration is your gift,
> our planet it will surely lift.
>
> **O Saint Germain, what love you bring,**
> **it truly makes all matter sing,**
> **your violet flame does all restore,**
> **with you we are becoming more.**

3. If America is to become aligned with the mind of Saint Germain, Americans need to overcome the obsession with winning. In the national psyche, America has an obsession with winning.

> O Saint Germain, in love we claim,
> our right to bring your violet flame,

13 | Invoking an end to the obsession with winning

from you Above, to us below,
it is an all-transforming flow.

O Saint Germain, what love you bring,
it truly makes all matter sing,
your violet flame does all restore,
with you we are becoming more.

4. Not many nations on earth have in their collective consciousness the concept that they are the greatest nation on earth. America has it.

O Saint Germain, I love you so,
my aura filled with violet glow,
my chakras filled with violet fire,
I am your cosmic amplifier.

O Saint Germain, what love you bring,
it truly makes all matter sing,
your violet flame does all restore,
with you we are becoming more.

5. The obsession with winning means it is win or lose, winners take all. America is obsessed with being the best, always being ahead, and this creates a strange dichotomy in the American psyche.

O Saint Germain, I am now free,
your violet flame is therapy,
transform all hang-ups in my mind,
as inner peace I surely find.

> **O Saint Germain, what love you bring,**
> **it truly makes all matter sing,**
> **your violet flame does all restore,**
> **with you we are becoming more.**

6. On one hand, Americans are always comparing themselves to other nations but they are only doing this to show how America is better than other nations. They are not comparing themselves to other nations and saying: "Do these nations have something we could learn from?"

> O Saint Germain, my body pure,
> your violet flame for all is cure,
> consume the cause of all disease,
> and therefore I am all at ease.

> **O Saint Germain, what love you bring,**
> **it truly makes all matter sing,**
> **your violet flame does all restore,**
> **with you we are becoming more.**

7. Americans have a tendency to look at how they can exceed and get ahead of other nations, not being so willing to look at whether other nations are ahead in certain areas.

> O Saint Germain, I'm karma-free,
> the past no longer burdens me,
> a brand new opportunity,
> I am in Christic unity.

> **O Saint Germain, what love you bring,**
> **it truly makes all matter sing,**

> your violet flame does all restore,
> with you we are becoming more.

8. It was a trauma for America after the Vietnam War. America could not deal with this because America is so obsessed with winning that it cannot face *not* winning. It cannot deal with not winning in a neutral, objective way.

O Saint Germain, we are now one,
I am for you a violet sun,
as we transform this planet earth,
your Golden Age is given birth.

> O Saint Germain, what love you bring,
> it truly makes all matter sing,
> your violet flame does all restore,
> with you we are becoming more.

9. America does not have the ability to say: "We made a mistake. Let's learn from it and move on," If we made a mistake, not only did we not win, but we actually lost. It is either we win and we are the good guys, or we lose and we are absolutely wrong. It is all-or-nothing, black-and-white thinking.

O Saint Germain, the earth is free,
from burden of duality,
in oneness we bring what is best,
your Golden Age is manifest.

> O Saint Germain, what love you bring,
> it truly makes all matter sing,
> your violet flame does all restore,
> with you we are becoming more.

Part 2

1. I call for the cutting free of the Americans who are close to breaking through and being free from the entire game of always wanting to be the winner and always wanting to interpret any event as if America came out on top.

> O Saint Germain, you do inspire,
> my vision raised forever higher,
> with you I form a figure-eight,
> your Golden Age I co-create.
>
> **O Saint Germain, what love you bring,**
> **it truly makes all matter sing,**
> **your violet flame does all restore,**
> **with you we are becoming more.**

2. The obsession with winning creates an opposite polarity, the obsession with not losing. When we have an obsession with not losing, we cannot say: "We made a mistake, let's learn from it and then we move on." We cannot acknowledge that we made a mistake.

> O Saint Germain, what Freedom Flame,
> released when we recite your name,
> acceleration is your gift,
> our planet it will surely lift.
>
> **O Saint Germain, what love you bring,**
> **it truly makes all matter sing,**
> **your violet flame does all restore,**
> **with you we are becoming more.**

3. There is no need to think in terms of right and wrong, mistakes or not mistakes. It is a matter of going into a neutral state of mind, looking at a situation and saying: "If the outcome was not what we wanted, how can we improve so we get what we want?"

> O Saint Germain, in love we claim,
> our right to bring your violet flame,
> from you Above, to us below,
> it is an all-transforming flow.

> **O Saint Germain, what love you bring,**
> **it truly makes all matter sing,**
> **your violet flame does all restore,**
> **with you we are becoming more.**

4. This dynamic – the obsession with winning, the obsession with not losing – prevents us from going into a neutral state of mind.

> O Saint Germain, I love you so,
> my aura filled with violet glow,
> my chakras filled with violet fire,
> I am your cosmic amplifier.

> **O Saint Germain, what love you bring,**
> **it truly makes all matter sing,**
> **your violet flame does all restore,**
> **with you we are becoming more.**

5. Instead of thinking: "How could we improve things," we go into an artificial state of mind of pretending we did not actually lose.

> O Saint Germain, I am now free,
> your violet flame is therapy,
> transform all hang-ups in my mind,
> as inner peace I surely find.
>
> **O Saint Germain, what love you bring,
> it truly makes all matter sing,
> your violet flame does all restore,
> with you we are becoming more.**

6. Instead of looking at a situation and saying: "We don't want to repeat that. How do we avoid repeating it so we can do better the next time," we go into denial, a state of pretending that things are not what they are. This state of consciousness permeates the collective psyche of America.

> O Saint Germain, my body pure,
> your violet flame for all is cure,
> consume the cause of all disease,
> and therefore I am all at ease.
>
> **O Saint Germain, what love you bring,
> it truly makes all matter sing,
> your violet flame does all restore,
> with you we are becoming more.**

7. We have a political situation where the senators, the representatives in the house and all other levels of American politics have used this obsession with winning, the obsession with not losing, to create a situation where the politicians are not doing the job that they were charged to do by the U.S. Constitution.

13 | Invoking an end to the obsession with winning

> O Saint Germain, I'm karma-free,
> the past no longer burdens me,
> a brand new opportunity,
> I am in Christic unity.
>
> **O Saint Germain, what love you bring,
> it truly makes all matter sing,
> your violet flame does all restore,
> with you we are becoming more.**

8. The politicians are not doing the job that the American people elected them to do, but everybody is pretending that they are doing their jobs. They are either trying to pretend that they are doing the right thing, that they could not be doing anything else or that there are certain problems that just cannot be solved but it is not their fault.

> O Saint Germain, we are now one,
> I am for you a violet sun,
> as we transform this planet earth,
> your Golden Age is given birth.
>
> **O Saint Germain, what love you bring,
> it truly makes all matter sing,
> your violet flame does all restore,
> with you we are becoming more.**

9. Washington, D.C., is one big game of pretending to look out for the interests of the American people. In reality, as a whole Congress, the President, the Supreme Court, are not looking out for the interests of the American people. They are looking out for the interests of a small power elite. *That* is the naked reality of politics in America.

O Saint Germain, the earth is free,
from burden of duality,
in oneness we bring what is best,
your Golden Age is manifest.

**O Saint Germain, what love you bring,
it truly makes all matter sing,
your violet flame does all restore,
with you we are becoming more.**

Part 3

1. Very few people dare to come out and say this because in order to say it, we have to free ourselves from the mentality of wanting to win, not wanting to lose, therefore not wanting to be neutral and simply say: "Are the politicians doing their job? Are they taking care of what is in the best interests of the American people?"

O Saint Germain, you do inspire,
my vision raised forever higher,
with you I form a figure-eight,
your Golden Age I co-create.

**O Saint Germain, what love you bring,
it truly makes all matter sing,
your violet flame does all restore,
with you we are becoming more.**

2. If the politicians are not doing their job, it is not a matter of saying they are wrong or bad, but the question is: "How can

we move forward? How can we do better? How can we avoid repeating a situation that we realize isn't what we really want?"

> O Saint Germain, what Freedom Flame,
> released when we recite your name,
> acceleration is your gift,
> our planet it will surely lift.

> **O Saint Germain, what love you bring,**
> **it truly makes all matter sing,**
> **your violet flame does all restore,**
> **with you we are becoming more.**

3. When we read how the media is treating the political situation and see how the politicians are talking about it, it is amazing that everybody can ignore the elephant in the room, namely that the political apparatus is not looking out for the interests of the people.

> O Saint Germain, in love we claim,
> our right to bring your violet flame,
> from you Above, to us below,
> it is an all-transforming flow.

> **O Saint Germain, what love you bring,**
> **it truly makes all matter sing,**
> **your violet flame does all restore,**
> **with you we are becoming more.**

4. They are all pretending that they are. Some of them honestly believe that they are, but they are blinded by a consciousness that has been created in Washington, D.C. over many decades

and comes down as a cloak over the minds of the elected politicians.

> O Saint Germain, I love you so,
> my aura filled with violet glow,
> my chakras filled with violet fire,
> I am your cosmic amplifier.
>
> **O Saint Germain, what love you bring,**
> **it truly makes all matter sing,**
> **your violet flame does all restore,**
> **with you we are becoming more.**

5. Some newly elected politicians do not have it, but it usually does not take many years before a politician is blinded by this state of consciousness. Suddenly, the ideals that caused that person to run for office have faded into the background.

> O Saint Germain, I am now free,
> your violet flame is therapy,
> transform all hang-ups in my mind,
> as inner peace I surely find.
>
> **O Saint Germain, what love you bring,**
> **it truly makes all matter sing,**
> **your violet flame does all restore,**
> **with you we are becoming more.**

6. It is not constructive that a newly elected congressman or senator has to spend most of his or her time fundraising for the re-election campaign.

13 | Invoking an end to the obsession with winning

> O Saint Germain, my body pure,
> your violet flame for all is cure,
> consume the cause of all disease,
> and therefore I am all at ease.
>
> **O Saint Germain, what love you bring,**
> **it truly makes all matter sing,**
> **your violet flame does all restore,**
> **with you we are becoming more.**

7. The ideals have to fall by the wayside so that the representatives can walk the party line because if they do not, they will not be able to run for re-election.

> O Saint Germain, I'm karma-free,
> the past no longer burdens me,
> a brand new opportunity,
> I am in Christic unity.
>
> **O Saint Germain, what love you bring,**
> **it truly makes all matter sing,**
> **your violet flame does all restore,**
> **with you we are becoming more.**

8. A certain sense of apathy has crept into the political mindset, namely that there are certain things that they just cannot do anything about. Some problems are too big, some are too complex, or they cannot do anything about it because the opposing party will not agree and therefore nothing can get done.

> O Saint Germain, we are now one,
> I am for you a violet sun,

as we transform this planet earth,
your Golden Age is given birth.

O Saint Germain, what love you bring,
it truly makes all matter sing,
your violet flame does all restore,
with you we are becoming more.

9. This apathy is like a black cloud. I call for the binding and consuming of the demon that is attacking the minds of newly elected representatives.

O Saint Germain, the earth is free,
from burden of duality,
in oneness we bring what is best,
your Golden Age is manifest.

O Saint Germain, what love you bring,
it truly makes all matter sing,
your violet flame does all restore,
with you we are becoming more.

Part 4

1. I call for the cutting free of the people and the politicians who can come to see that there is this cloud that takes over the minds of most politicians in Washington, especially those who have been there for a long time.

O Saint Germain, you do inspire,
my vision raised forever higher,

13 | Invoking an end to the obsession with winning

> with you I form a figure-eight,
> your Golden Age I co-create.
>
> **O Saint Germain, what love you bring,**
> **it truly makes all matter sing,**
> **your violet flame does all restore,**
> **with you we are becoming more.**

2. The older politicians all have a certain look on their faces, they all have a certain way of talking. They have a certain way of reasoning. They have all aligned themselves with a certain mindset.

> O Saint Germain, what Freedom Flame,
> released when we recite your name,
> acceleration is your gift,
> our planet it will surely lift.
>
> **O Saint Germain, what love you bring,**
> **it truly makes all matter sing,**
> **your violet flame does all restore,**
> **with you we are becoming more.**

3. The seasoned politicians in Washington, D.C. have realized that politics in America is a game of pretending—nothing else. You say what you think you need to say, what the public wants to hear in order to get elected. Then, you vote the way your party wants you to.

> O Saint Germain, in love we claim,
> our right to bring your violet flame,
> from you Above, to us below,
> it is an all-transforming flow.

> **O Saint Germain, what love you bring,**
> **it truly makes all matter sing,**
> **your violet flame does all restore,**
> **with you we are becoming more.**

4. The seasoned politicians all know that there is a facade that you show to the public and there is a reality of what you are doing when you think nobody is watching you. There is a huge gap between the public front that you put on and the reality of what goes on in the corridors of power when they think nobody is watching.

> O Saint Germain, I love you so,
> my aura filled with violet glow,
> my chakras filled with violet fire,
> I am your cosmic amplifier.

> **O Saint Germain, what love you bring,**
> **it truly makes all matter sing,**
> **your violet flame does all restore,**
> **with you we are becoming more.**

5. The insiders in Washington – the politicians, the bureaucrats – all know about this huge gap between the public front and the political reality, the daily hidden discourse of what goes on and how politics is done through wheeling and dealing, special interests and lobbying.

> O Saint Germain, I am now free,
> your violet flame is therapy,
> transform all hang-ups in my mind,
> as inner peace I surely find.

13 | Invoking an end to the obsession with winning

> **O Saint Germain, what love you bring,**
> **it truly makes all matter sing,**
> **your violet flame does all restore,**
> **with you we are becoming more.**

6. The political game is not at all about what is best for the people. It is only what is best for the elite and the special interest groups that have bought their way into the political system.

> O Saint Germain, my body pure,
> your violet flame for all is cure,
> consume the cause of all disease,
> and therefore I am all at ease.

> **O Saint Germain, what love you bring,**
> **it truly makes all matter sing,**
> **your violet flame does all restore,**
> **with you we are becoming more.**

7. Everyone who is an insider in D.C. knows this. Nobody has cried out that the emperor has nothing on because the moment you cry out, you are no longer an insider. You will be frozen out instantly and they will attempt to destroy you.

> O Saint Germain, I'm karma-free,
> the past no longer burdens me,
> a brand new opportunity,
> I am in Christic unity.

> **O Saint Germain, what love you bring,**
> **it truly makes all matter sing,**
> **your violet flame does all restore,**
> **with you we are becoming more.**

8. The politicians and the media will attempt to destroy anyone who is a whistle-blower. Those who go against the status quo will be attacked.

> O Saint Germain, we are now one,
> I am for you a violet sun,
> as we transform this planet earth,
> your Golden Age is given birth.
>
> **O Saint Germain, what love you bring,**
> **it truly makes all matter sing,**
> **your violet flame does all restore,**
> **with you we are becoming more.**

9. Running for public office in the United States of America is very similar to a method of torture, called the gauntlet. What kind of a person is willing to endure this in order to win public office?

> O Saint Germain, the earth is free,
> from burden of duality,
> in oneness we bring what is best,
> your Golden Age is manifest.
>
> **O Saint Germain, what love you bring,**
> **it truly makes all matter sing,**
> **your violet flame does all restore,**
> **with you we are becoming more.**

Part 5

1. It takes a special psychological profile to be able to run, to be able to win and then to be able to find your bearings in the stark political reality that takes place behind the scenes.

> O Saint Germain, you do inspire,
> my vision raised forever higher,
> with you I form a figure-eight,
> your Golden Age I co-create.
>
> **O Saint Germain, what love you bring,**
> **it truly makes all matter sing,**
> **your violet flame does all restore,**
> **with you we are becoming more.**

2. A balanced, harmonious, non-aggressive person is very unlikely to be willing to endure this. The majority of politicians have a psychological profile that is obsessed with winning.

> O Saint Germain, what Freedom Flame,
> released when we recite your name,
> acceleration is your gift,
> our planet it will surely lift.
>
> **O Saint Germain, what love you bring,**
> **it truly makes all matter sing,**
> **your violet flame does all restore,**
> **with you we are becoming more.**

3. Many politicians will do anything to win, and they can get themselves into a state of mind where anybody who attacks

them can be ignored or pushed aside—or even affirms their view that they are against those other people.

> O Saint Germain, in love we claim,
> our right to bring your violet flame,
> from you Above, to us below,
> it is an all-transforming flow.
>
> **O Saint Germain, what love you bring,**
> **it truly makes all matter sing,**
> **your violet flame does all restore,**
> **with you we are becoming more.**

4. The politicians who can win and those who can survive psychologically once they have won, have one simple ability: the willingness to compromise and the willingness to *go* along in order to *get* along.

> O Saint Germain, I love you so,
> my aura filled with violet glow,
> my chakras filled with violet fire,
> I am your cosmic amplifier.
>
> **O Saint Germain, what love you bring,**
> **it truly makes all matter sing,**
> **your violet flame does all restore,**
> **with you we are becoming more.**

5. The politicians are willing to do whatever it takes to get into office and to stay in office. They are willing to play the game as the game is currently being played.

13 | Invoking an end to the obsession with winning

O Saint Germain, I am now free,
your violet flame is therapy,
transform all hang-ups in my mind,
as inner peace I surely find.

**O Saint Germain, what love you bring,
it truly makes all matter sing,
your violet flame does all restore,
with you we are becoming more.**

6. I call forth the judgment of Christ upon the fallen beings in the identity, mental and emotional realms who are influencing the American political process at all levels.

O Saint Germain, my body pure,
your violet flame for all is cure,
consume the cause of all disease,
and therefore I am all at ease.

**O Saint Germain, what love you bring,
it truly makes all matter sing,
your violet flame does all restore,
with you we are becoming more.**

7. At the physical level, the distortion happened very gradually, without anyone realizing what was happening. Those who had been there a long time became used to it.

O Saint Germain, I'm karma-free,
the past no longer burdens me,
a brand new opportunity,
I am in Christic unity.

> **O Saint Germain, what love you bring,**
> **it truly makes all matter sing,**
> **your violet flame does all restore,**
> **with you we are becoming more.**

8. The vast majority of the politicians and the bureaucrats in Washington are hypnotized by this state of consciousness. They know there is a huge gap between the public appearance and the reality in the hidden corridors.

> O Saint Germain, we are now one,
> I am for you a violet sun,
> as we transform this planet earth,
> your Golden Age is given birth.

> **O Saint Germain, what love you bring,**
> **it truly makes all matter sing,**
> **your violet flame does all restore,**
> **with you we are becoming more.**

9. I call forth the judgment of Christ upon those who will not speak out because they have resigned themselves to thinking: "Well, that's just the way it is. That's just the way politics is done in America. Nothing we can do about it. We just have to go along and then hopefully it will all work out."

> O Saint Germain, the earth is free,
> from burden of duality,
> in oneness we bring what is best,
> your Golden Age is manifest.

> **O Saint Germain, what love you bring,**
> **it truly makes all matter sing,**

**your violet flame does all restore,
with you we are becoming more.**

Sealing

In the name of the I AM THAT I AM, I accept that Archangel Michael, Astrea and Shiva form an impenetrable shield around myself and all constructive people in America, sealing us from all fear-based energies in all four octaves. I accept that the Light of God is consuming and transforming all fear-based energies that make up the dark forces working against America!

14 | INVOKING THE POLITICAL CHANGES OF THE GOLDEN AGE

In the name of the I AM THAT I AM, Jesus Christ, I use the authority that I have as a being in embodiment on earth to call upon Saint Germain to reinforce my calls and use my chakras to project the statements in this invocation into the collective consciousness and awaken Americans to the vision of what political changes are needed in order to bring forth your Golden Age. Awaken Americans to the reality that we are spiritual beings and that we can co-create a new future by working with the ascended masters. I especially call for …

[Make your own calls here.]

Part 1

1. I call forth the judgment of Christ upon those who enjoy the way politics is being done in America because it allows them to look out for their own interests and enrich themselves by being in office.

> O Saint Germain, you do inspire,
> my vision raised forever higher,
> with you I form a figure-eight,
> your Golden Age I co-create.
>
> **O Saint Germain, what love you bring,**
> **it truly makes all matter sing,**
> **your violet flame does all restore,**
> **with you we are becoming more.**

2. I call for the shattering of this beast, this demon that is hanging over Washington, D.C., for the clearing of it so that there can be a growing awareness where people can begin to wake up.

> O Saint Germain, what Freedom Flame,
> released when we recite your name,
> acceleration is your gift,
> our planet it will surely lift.
>
> **O Saint Germain, what love you bring,**
> **it truly makes all matter sing,**
> **your violet flame does all restore,**
> **with you we are becoming more.**

3. The awakening that Saint Germain is looking for is that people get over this consciousness that there has to be a winner and a loser. Winning is a relative, dualistic concept because, in order for *you* to win, *someone* has to lose—at least if there are two opposing polarities.

> O Saint Germain, in love we claim,
> our right to bring your violet flame,
> from you Above, to us below,
> it is an all-transforming flow.
>
> **O Saint Germain, what love you bring,**
> **it truly makes all matter sing,**
> **your violet flame does all restore,**
> **with you we are becoming more.**

4. Many Americans are very dissatisfied with the political process but because they do not understand what is going on and because they are trapped in the win-lose mindset, they look for someone to blame. They look for a scapegoat and they say: "That person or that group of people, that's the bad guy. That's the problem."

> O Saint Germain, I love you so,
> my aura filled with violet glow,
> my chakras filled with violet fire,
> I am your cosmic amplifier.
>
> **O Saint Germain, what love you bring,**
> **it truly makes all matter sing,**
> **your violet flame does all restore,**
> **with you we are becoming more.**

5. Saint Germain is not looking for people to start blaming the politicians. It is not a matter of blaming the politicians. It is a matter of recognizing that: "We have a situation where politics in America doesn't serve the people. We have had enough of it and we want politics to be the way it should be, namely that everybody in Washington is cooperating in order to do what is in the best interests of the people."

> O Saint Germain, I am now free,
> your violet flame is therapy,
> transform all hang-ups in my mind,
> as inner peace I surely find.
>
> **O Saint Germain, what love you bring,**
> **it truly makes all matter sing,**
> **your violet flame does all restore,**
> **with you we are becoming more.**

6. It is not a matter of finding out who is to blame because neither the Republicans nor the Democrats are to blame. There is no single senator or congressman who is to blame. There is no group who is to blame.

> O Saint Germain, my body pure,
> your violet flame for all is cure,
> consume the cause of all disease,
> and therefore I am all at ease.
>
> **O Saint Germain, what love you bring,**
> **it truly makes all matter sing,**
> **your violet flame does all restore,**
> **with you we are becoming more.**

7. It is not a matter of blaming anybody. It is a matter of crying out that the emperor has nothing on so there suddenly is that shift in awareness where everybody can see what they cannot see today. Everybody can see how far from the ideal politics has gone, how polarized it has become, how it has become a total game of pretending.

> O Saint Germain, I'm karma-free,
> the past no longer burdens me,
> a brand new opportunity,
> I am in Christic unity.
>
> **O Saint Germain, what love you bring,**
> **it truly makes all matter sing,**
> **your violet flame does all restore,**
> **with you we are becoming more.**

8. When Saint Germain sponsored the creation of the United States, he did not have total control over the process. The Constitution had to be created by working with the people who were there at the time. Their consciousness was an expression of the collective consciousness and the entire state of the world then.

> O Saint Germain, we are now one,
> I am for you a violet sun,
> as we transform this planet earth,
> your Golden Age is given birth.
>
> **O Saint Germain, what love you bring,**
> **it truly makes all matter sing,**
> **your violet flame does all restore,**
> **with you we are becoming more.**

9. Saint Germain never envisioned that the Constitution was an ideal, perfect matrix for democratic nations and would never have to change. As the world moves forward and the collective consciousness is raised, naturally we need to revise and create a new platform based on the way the consciousness is today.

> O Saint Germain, the earth is free,
> from burden of duality,
> in oneness we bring what is best,
> your Golden Age is manifest.
>
> **O Saint Germain, what love you bring,**
> **it truly makes all matter sing,**
> **your violet flame does all restore,**
> **with you we are becoming more.**

Part 2

1. In the Golden Age, money will be taken out of politics. A person running for public office in America will not have to do fundraising in order to afford a campaign. You will not need to raise millions of dollars in order to run for public office.

> O Saint Germain, you do inspire,
> my vision raised forever higher,
> with you I form a figure-eight,
> your Golden Age I co-create.
>
> **O Saint Germain, what love you bring,**
> **it truly makes all matter sing,**

**your violet flame does all restore,
with you we are becoming more.**

2. You will be able to get equal media coverage with everyone else. You will be able to participate in debates, and with the Internet you will be able to promote your viewpoints.

O Saint Germain, what Freedom Flame,
released when we recite your name,
acceleration is your gift,
our planet it will surely lift.

**O Saint Germain, what love you bring,
it truly makes all matter sing,
your violet flame does all restore,
with you we are becoming more.**

3. I call for it to be illegal for politicians and political parties to buy advertising because it favors those who have money over those who do not. I call forth the enactment of laws that will level the playing field so that the success of those running for office will not depend on how much money they can raise.

O Saint Germain, in love we claim,
our right to bring your violet flame,
from you Above, to us below,
it is an all-transforming flow.

**O Saint Germain, what love you bring,
it truly makes all matter sing,
your violet flame does all restore,
with you we are becoming more.**

4. The success of political candidates will depend only on their idealism, their enthusiasm, their ability to relate to the people and give the people the impression that they are sincere and honest and will do what they promised. Money shall be eliminated from the election process.

> O Saint Germain, I love you so,
> my aura filled with violet glow,
> my chakras filled with violet fire,
> I am your cosmic amplifier.
>
> **O Saint Germain, what love you bring,**
> **it truly makes all matter sing,**
> **your violet flame does all restore,**
> **with you we are becoming more.**

5. In the Golden Age, money will be taken out of politics in the sense that lobbying will be completely eliminated. It will be absolutely illegal for lobbying groups to seek to buy influence as they are doing today.

> O Saint Germain, I am now free,
> your violet flame is therapy,
> transform all hang-ups in my mind,
> as inner peace I surely find.
>
> **O Saint Germain, what love you bring,**
> **it truly makes all matter sing,**
> **your violet flame does all restore,**
> **with you we are becoming more.**

6. The lobbying phenomenon is a form of legalized, visible corruption—nothing else. It is corruption that has become

legalized and accepted and it should be seen for what it is and eliminated.

> O Saint Germain, my body pure,
> your violet flame for all is cure,
> consume the cause of all disease,
> and therefore I am all at ease.

> **O Saint Germain, what love you bring,**
> **it truly makes all matter sing,**
> **your violet flame does all restore,**
> **with you we are becoming more.**

7. Lobbying favors those who have lots of money, namely the power elite. The top 10% control the majority of the wealth in America.

> O Saint Germain, I'm karma-free,
> the past no longer burdens me,
> a brand new opportunity,
> I am in Christic unity.

> **O Saint Germain, what love you bring,**
> **it truly makes all matter sing,**
> **your violet flame does all restore,**
> **with you we are becoming more.**

8. This unequal distribution of wealth is the most obvious demonstration of the fact that the American political system has gone completely away from the intention behind the Constitution.

O Saint Germain, we are now one,
I am for you a violet sun,
as we transform this planet earth,
your Golden Age is given birth.

**O Saint Germain, what love you bring,
it truly makes all matter sing,
your violet flame does all restore,
with you we are becoming more.**

9. This is not meant to be a land that functions to enrich the few by taking from the many. It is a country that is meant to be a community of equals where each person has equal opportunity to make an effort and reap the rewards of those efforts.

O Saint Germain, the earth is free,
from burden of duality,
in oneness we bring what is best,
your Golden Age is manifest.

**O Saint Germain, what love you bring,
it truly makes all matter sing,
your violet flame does all restore,
with you we are becoming more.**

Part 3

1. Saint Germain wants the electoral college to be eliminated because with modern communication, it is obsolete. In the Golden Age, the President will be elected by popular vote.

14 | Invoking the political changes of the Golden Age

> O Saint Germain, you do inspire,
> my vision raised forever higher,
> with you I form a figure-eight,
> your Golden Age I co-create.
>
> **O Saint Germain, what love you bring,**
> **it truly makes all matter sing,**
> **your violet flame does all restore,**
> **with you we are becoming more.**

2. Saint Germain envisions a challenge to the two-party system and the gridlock of having only two parties. As an interim stage, other parties could gain seats in the House of Representatives so that people would see that they have something to vote for besides the Democrats and Republicans.

> O Saint Germain, what Freedom Flame,
> released when we recite your name,
> acceleration is your gift,
> our planet it will surely lift.
>
> **O Saint Germain, what love you bring,**
> **it truly makes all matter sing,**
> **your violet flame does all restore,**
> **with you we are becoming more.**

3. Voter apathy comes primarily from the fact that there are so many people who feel that neither the Democrats nor the Republicans represent them or that it does not really matter which party has the majority because it is all politics as usual.

> O Saint Germain, in love we claim,
> our right to bring your violet flame,

> from you Above, to us below,
> it is an all-transforming flow.
>
> **O Saint Germain, what love you bring,**
> **it truly makes all matter sing,**
> **your violet flame does all restore,**
> **with you we are becoming more.**

4. As an interim stage, a new party could be part of the debate and perhaps create a situation where either the Republicans or the Democrats would have to cooperate with this third party in order to get a majority.

> O Saint Germain, I love you so,
> my aura filled with violet glow,
> my chakras filled with violet fire,
> I am your cosmic amplifier.
>
> **O Saint Germain, what love you bring,**
> **it truly makes all matter sing,**
> **your violet flame does all restore,**
> **with you we are becoming more.**

5. A third party brings the possibility that the moderates, the more balanced people, could begin to get their policy through and take it away from the extremists on both sides.

> O Saint Germain, I am now free,
> your violet flame is therapy,
> transform all hang-ups in my mind,
> as inner peace I surely find.

> **O Saint Germain, what love you bring,**
> **it truly makes all matter sing,**
> **your violet flame does all restore,**
> **with you we are becoming more.**

6. Another possible scenario is to let all representatives run based on their own merit, not based on party affiliation. Once they are in, they can vote their conscience and there are no party lines that divide the house into two opposing factions.

> O Saint Germain, my body pure,
> your violet flame for all is cure,
> consume the cause of all disease,
> and therefore I am all at ease.

> **O Saint Germain, what love you bring,**
> **it truly makes all matter sing,**
> **your violet flame does all restore,**
> **with you we are becoming more.**

7. Today, most representatives are not voting based on their conviction but because they have to play the game so they vote according to the party line.

> O Saint Germain, I'm karma-free,
> the past no longer burdens me,
> a brand new opportunity,
> I am in Christic unity.

> **O Saint Germain, what love you bring,**
> **it truly makes all matter sing,**
> **your violet flame does all restore,**
> **with you we are becoming more.**

8. If representatives were free to vote their conviction, and they were directly responsible to their voters instead of being responsible to the party, then the political process would change and things would be done that cannot be done today.

> O Saint Germain, we are now one,
> I am for you a violet sun,
> as we transform this planet earth,
> your Golden Age is given birth.
>
> **O Saint Germain, what love you bring,**
> **it truly makes all matter sing,**
> **your violet flame does all restore,**
> **with you we are becoming more.**

9. I call for the exposure of the fact that there is a small power elite that exercises a disproportionate influence on the political process.

> O Saint Germain, the earth is free,
> from burden of duality,
> in oneness we bring what is best,
> your Golden Age is manifest.
>
> **O Saint Germain, what love you bring,**
> **it truly makes all matter sing,**
> **your violet flame does all restore,**
> **with you we are becoming more.**

Part 4

1. This is not because these people buy influence, it is because they have an "old boys' network" where they know people who know people. They have, over generations, formed this network of people who see themselves as the elite that runs America.

> O Saint Germain, you do inspire,
> my vision raised forever higher,
> with you I form a figure-eight,
> your Golden Age I co-create.
>
> **O Saint Germain, what love you bring,**
> **it truly makes all matter sing,**
> **your violet flame does all restore,**
> **with you we are becoming more.**

2. These people think they are doing it for the good of the country but since they have accumulated more wealth than they could possibly spend, and since this is limiting the growth of the U.S. economy, they are not doing it for the good of the country.

> O Saint Germain, what Freedom Flame,
> released when we recite your name,
> acceleration is your gift,
> our planet it will surely lift.
>
> **O Saint Germain, what love you bring,**
> **it truly makes all matter sing,**

> your violet flame does all restore,
> with you we are becoming more.

3. These people are not necessarily evil because many are blinded by a dark cloud, a certain beast that has taken over their minds. I call for Archangel Michael to bind and consume this beast so the people will see the power elite for what it is.

> O Saint Germain, in love we claim,
> our right to bring your violet flame,
> from you Above, to us below,
> it is an all-transforming flow.

> **O Saint Germain, what love you bring,**
> **it truly makes all matter sing,**
> **your violet flame does all restore,**
> **with you we are becoming more.**

4. We cannot have a functioning democracy if we allow a small power elite to exercise influence by buying it, by persuasion or by favoritism where: "You do me a favor, I do you a favor."

> O Saint Germain, I love you so,
> my aura filled with violet glow,
> my chakras filled with violet fire,
> I am your cosmic amplifier.

> **O Saint Germain, what love you bring,**
> **it truly makes all matter sing,**
> **your violet flame does all restore,**
> **with you we are becoming more.**

5. I call forth the judgment of Christ upon the "noble class" of families in the United States who all follow the lines so they can remain part of that inner circle that is not even in Washington but exists elsewhere and has formed this network of influential people.

> O Saint Germain, I am now free,
> your violet flame is therapy,
> transform all hang-ups in my mind,
> as inner peace I surely find.

> **O Saint Germain, what love you bring,**
> **it truly makes all matter sing,**
> **your violet flame does all restore,**
> **with you we are becoming more.**

6. There are companies and political institutions that we today take for granted in America, but they will disappear in the Golden Age. They will be replaced by something else that is based on the awareness of togetherness and wanting to raise up the whole rather than wanting to raise up one individual or one group.

> O Saint Germain, my body pure,
> your violet flame for all is cure,
> consume the cause of all disease,
> and therefore I am all at ease.

> **O Saint Germain, what love you bring,**
> **it truly makes all matter sing,**
> **your violet flame does all restore,**
> **with you we are becoming more.**

7. What is behind the obsession with winning is that when you win, you are superior to all those who did not win. This is the game played by the noble class of America. They think they are superior and they have been hidden for so long, been rich for so long, been powerful for so long, that they think this is a permanent state.

> O Saint Germain, I'm karma-free,
> the past no longer burdens me,
> a brand new opportunity,
> I am in Christic unity.

> **O Saint Germain, what love you bring,**
> **it truly makes all matter sing,**
> **your violet flame does all restore,**
> **with you we are becoming more.**

8. The noble class think they are completely superior to the people but it can only happen in comparison to those who are inferior, and in the Golden Age that consciousness will fade away. There will be a widespread acceptance that all men and women are created equal and that we are endowed by our Creator with certain inalienable rights.

> O Saint Germain, we are now one,
> I am for you a violet sun,
> as we transform this planet earth,
> your Golden Age is given birth.

> **O Saint Germain, what love you bring,**
> **it truly makes all matter sing,**
> **your violet flame does all restore,**
> **with you we are becoming more.**

9. We have the right to improve our consciousness, to raise our awareness to increasingly higher levels. We are endowed by our Creator with the right to raise our consciousness beyond the epic mindset, beyond duality, beyond the consciousness of the power elite. That is our most sacred right.

> O Saint Germain, the earth is free,
> from burden of duality,
> in oneness we bring what is best,
> your Golden Age is manifest.
>
> **O Saint Germain, what love you bring,**
> **it truly makes all matter sing,**
> **your violet flame does all restore,**
> **with you we are becoming more.**

Sealing

In the name of the I AM THAT I AM, I accept that Archangel Michael, Astrea and Shiva form an impenetrable shield around myself and all constructive people in America, sealing us from all fear-based energies in all four octaves. I accept that the Light of God is consuming and transforming all fear-based energies that make up the dark forces working against America!

15 | TOTAL TRANSPARENCY IN GOVERNMENT

As the messenger said before you went to break: "At a quarter to four, come back for more" so here I am, the Ascended Master MORE. I wish to build on what Saint Germain has given you and take it in a slightly different direction, not because I am in competition with Saint Germain but because I am one with Saint Germain. As all ascended masters working with the earth are one with Saint Germain and his goal for manifesting the Golden Age on earth and in America as well.

There is a sentence that has always been a guiding light, not only for America but for democracy in general. It is that there is a government "with the consent of the governed." In other words, the people who are being governed are in agreement with the government and how it functions. This also means that in a truly democratic nation, whether a republic or another form of democracy, a government only has legitimacy when it has the consent of the governed.

My beloved, what does it take for a government to have the consent of the governed? Is it enough that every four years the governed go to a little booth and put a mark on a piece of paper and vote in representatives? Then, in those four years, the representatives can do whatever they want and, come four years, they will either be voted back in or they will be voted out. Is that the consent of the governed? Surely, you all realize it is not!

So what does it take to have a government that has the consent of the governed? Well my beloved, in order to describe this, I will use a word but I will explain a few things before I use the word because this word is what scares the power elite more than any other word on earth. Nothing scares the fallen beings or the power elite, the hidden power elite that attempts to run any country, more than this word that I will use now. What is the word? "Transparency."

How can a government have legitimacy unless it has the consent of the governed? How can it have the consent of the governed unless those governed know what is going on in government? Thus, for there truly to be the consent of the governed, there must be total, absolute, undiluted, unrestricted transparency in the government.

A society where nothing is hidden

I can assure you that in the Golden Age there will be, at some point, total transparency in all levels of government. There will, in fact, be total transparency in all levels of society. The reason for this is, of course, that there will come a point where Saint Germain will release the technology to read the Akashic records. Those of you who are ascended master students know that there is a certain level of energy, a certain level of vibration, that serves as a recording device. You can consider that it is as if there were a billion camcorders or video cameras spread throughout the earth and they are constantly recording everything that is going on. What they are recording is being stored on a massive server complex somewhere. I am just using the images you have, I am not implying that the Akashic records work that way.

Imagine that everything that happens in the hidden corridors of power, everything that is said, how decisions are made, how deals are made, all of this is recorded in these Akashic records. In that point in the future when Saint Germain determines the time is right, the technology will be released whereby you can go into the Akashic records, go back to a certain date, a certain situation and play back what happened in that location, almost as if you were the proverbial fly on the wall.

Who killed JFK? Oh let us go in and play back what actually happened. I am not really wanting to tell you that information right now, even though it is awfully tempting. [Pause] Well, it was the power elite, of course.

Just imagine what the release of this technology will do, what ramifications, what reverberations it will have throughout society when it begins to dawn on people that they cannot hide anything anymore. Now, go down to the present situation and see how many things are hidden all over the planet. Crime! Could there really be crime on earth if the criminals would always be caught? Corruption! Could there be corruption if they would always be caught in the act or at least would be caught after the act? Now apply this to the political process of the United States, based on what Saint Germain said. There is a vast distance, a vast gap, between the public appearance of the political apparatus and what is actually going on in the corridors of power. Imagine you could remove that gap and imagine what that would do?

Now my beloved, in a sense you could say that if the American government functioned the way it was meant to function, it should not matter because then there would not be the gap. Because there would be such integrity among those who are part of the government apparatus that they would never naturally do anything that could not stand the light of day.

Those who think they can get away with anything

We are not in the ideal situation, and as Saint Germain said: A cloud has enveloped Washington, D.C. that makes the people in government, both the elected representatives and those in the bureaucracy, those in the lobbying groups, those in the power elite groups and the networks and the "old boys" networks;" they all think, they all take for granted, that they can do these things and keep them hidden. In other words, they think they can do what they know the people would not accept and get away with it.

It is exactly like Harvey Weinstein who thought he could continue to abuse women and if someone spoke up, he could just pull out his checkbook and buy their silence. These power brokers think they can do the same. They think they have gotten away with it for so long that they can continue to get away with it. There will, as I said, come a day where the access to the Akashic records will be released. But we do not have to wait for that day because we have ascended master students who can make the calls for the exposure of these hidden dealings.

You can make the calls for the shattering of that energy veil that is clouding the minds of those in Washington, but that is also preventing those from the outside, those who are not part of the inner circle, from seeing and then exposing what is going on. You will see, if you read the book or watch the movie about the Watergate scandal, how two journalists kept digging and digging and how there eventually was someone who gave them more and more information, some insider who decided to expose what was going on.

You can make the calls for this to happen in many fields. You can make the calls that there will be a raising of the collective consciousness where suddenly it is as if the scales fall from people's eyes and they look around and say: "But isn't it obvious that there should be transparency in government? How can we have a democratic nation if we don't have transparency? How can we give our consent to those who govern us if we don't know what they do and say in the corridors of power? Why have we never thought about this before? Isn't it obvious?"

When you make these calls, things will begin to be exposed. Look at what happened in Korea when the students started making the calls. It is not hopeless, it is not so that there is nothing you can do. *That* my beloved, is another cloud that envelops America in its entirety. It has pacified the people where they think, as the saying goes: "You can't fight city hall," and, of course, much less can you fight Congress.

Truly, we are very optimistic because the fallen beings, the power elite, they think they can get away with what they have gotten away with for so long. We know that they cannot even fathom the power of ascended master students making the calls for the exposure of these hidden wheelings and dealings.

The situation is not hopeless

Truly, things are not really as hopeless as you might think they are. I encourage you who are our students to look at yourselves and see if you have allowed yourself to be affected by this cloud of hopelessness, this cloud of despair, this cloud of unknowing that has enveloped the American people. Then, free yourself from it. Tune in to our vibration, whichever master you are close to, tune in to the mind of Saint Germain and realize that we are optimists. Now, I know very well, my beloved, that this does not say that much because the earth is a rather low planet. I can assure you that those ascended masters who have vowed to stay with earth have done so because we are optimists or we would not be here. Nevertheless, we are still optimistic because we see the hidden potential of how it is possible to awaken the American people and to make them stand up.

Quite frankly, my beloved, imagine that there was a million-man march in Washington demanding transparency in government. Who could object to this? You see my beloved, one way to outmaneuver the fallen beings is to put them in a situation, as they are so good at doing to you, where they have really no way out. Because if you demand transparency in government, who in the government can oppose this without exposing that they are not committed to democratic principles and the constitution?

I know very well what they will attempt to hide behind national security. "I could tell you but then I'd have to kill you." Nevertheless, my beloved, we may allow certain things to remain hidden for the sake of national security (as artificial of a concept as that it is, or at least has become). Yet, certainly, you cannot say that the old boy's network, who are making wheeling's and dealings in the Senate or the House, that this is covered by national security, at least when it has nothing to do with military secrets or any such things. Surely, there will be things that cannot be pushed under the rug upon which it says "national security."

This can be a real awakening, a galvanizing of people, where they realize that: "We actually have a right to demand transparency." This can have many ramifications. My beloved, Saint Germain was talking about the gauntlet of running for office. It is, of course, true that people should not have to be selected through such an aggressive process. Nevertheless, it has also had the effect of making people realize that if you have skeletons in the closet, it may not be the best idea to run for public office in the current situation. As it has selected certain people (of the balanced people) who have withdrawn from the process, there are also some very corrupt people who have decided to withdraw from the process because they were afraid that certain things would be exposed in their past that they did not really want exposed.

When you make the calls, then you can have a situation where this will be reinforced so that those who are corrupt will not dare to run for office, those who are the compromisers will not dare to run for office. You can get into a situation where those who have something to hide cannot run. Only those who have nothing to hide can run. Who are those who have nothing to hide? Those who are honest, those who have integrity.

Hiding something is not human nature

I know very well that when we are talking about transparency and exposing everything, we are going against what we might call one of the characteristics of quote-unquote "human nature." I say quote-unquote because it is not truly human nature, but it is the dualistic, separate self, the nature of that self. The separate self has something to hide and always wants to hide because it wants to have special privileges, it wants to get away with things, it wants to do something that it thinks is for its own good and then hide how it actually harms others.

This is the essence of the power elite. They want to establish a privileged position for themselves by taking away the wealth of the people but they do not want the people to know about it. You will also find among many, many normal people that there is that certain element of wanting to hide something. There is a certain resistance in the collective psychology towards total transparency.

You already have this concept of the surveillance society, "Big Brother is watching you," and the fallen beings are very clever at using this. They will actually attempt to use this to say that: "Well, if you the people are demanding transparency in government, you should also be subjected to have total transparency so that you can't hide anything." Many people will actually then withdraw and say: "Ah well, we'll just let the politicians hide something so we can continue to hide what we don't want out."

Transparency and privacy

My beloved, what will happen as we move towards the Golden Age is that this will begin to fade away. There will be a realization that the majority of the people may have certain things to hide but they do not have nearly as much to hide as those in the power elite, those in the governing elite, those who are in the political apparatus. They have much more to hide so they have much more to lose from transparency than you do.

There will (and you can make the calls for this as well) come a point where you will recognize that (where people will recognize that) of course you have a right to privacy. We are not talking about using the Akashic records to go back and spy on what you are doing in your home. That is not how the Akashic records would be used. You realize, my beloved, that you have a right to set a standard for those who govern you and it is not a matter of exposing their private lives, not

15 | Total transparency in government

even their youthful sexual improprieties that many people have indulged in as they were young. It is a matter of exposing that which is clearly corrupt, that which is clearly the "old boys network" and it is a matter that you have a right to demand that this gap between what they say and what they do is removed because they cannot hide what they do.

You who are ascended master students can become forerunners for this by coming to the point where there is nothing you feel you need to hide. Some of you have done this in this conference, when you stood up on the first day and told your personal story, even some of you telling things in front of a group that you had never been able to say before to anyone else.

You realize, of course, that you have the concept, going back decades in ascended master teachings, of invoking spiritual protection. You invoke the light of Archangel Michael that forms a wall around you that certain dark forces cannot penetrate. You also realize, when you look at our later teachings, that the reason the fallen beings and dark forces, have an inroad into your consciousness is that you have some unresolved psychology. In order to get a reprieve, so you can work on that psychology, you invoke protection so that you are not overwhelmed by the dark energies.

You also realize that when you resolve that psychology (overcome the primal self and all these separate selves) you come to the point that Jesus described as: "The prince of this world cometh and hath nothing in me." Therefore, you realize that the ultimate form of protection is transparency. Whatever the dark forces direct at you, goes right through because there is nothing in you that can create a reaction, there is nothing in you that they can stir up. You know very well that the rays of the sun will make things get hot but only that which has mass can become hot. The unresolved psychology, the misqualified energies in your four lower bodies, is something that has mass and the fallen beings can direct energy at it and stir it up and agitate you. When it is not there, there is nothing that these lower fear-based energies can hit and stir up. There comes that point where you actually do not need spiritual protection because you are transparent and that, of course, is the ultimate defense.

Shaking the foundations of the power elite

I realize that this is not something you can make the American public see in the near future, but you can certainly be instrumental in helping people see that the further you go back in time, you see that it was easier and easier for people to hide something. You can also help people see that in any dictatorship, the dictator has always been able to hide certain things. You may say that the German people supported Hitler but the German people did not have the full understanding of what was going on with the Holocaust, because they certainly would not have supported that.

You can see how, during the thousand years where the Catholic church had a stranglehold on the minds of Europe, it was because they had excluded all competing knowledge and teachings, such as the Greek philosophers. They were actively suppressing anyone who questioned their authority, and any dictatorship has to do this in order to stay in power because even a dictator needs the consent of the governed. It is a limited consent because it is based on the people not fully understanding what is going on.

In a democratic nation with the Constitution of the United States and your inalienable rights, you can see that you cannot allow yourself to have the government hide from you in the

15 | Total transparency in government

same way as a dictatorial government is hiding things from the people. If your government has as much secrecy and as much hidden wheelings and dealings as they have in China or Russia, what makes you think your government is any better? You have a right to demand that higher level of transparency—if your government claims to be more legitimate than the governments of Putin or China. Of course, they all do, do they not? Do they not all take pride in: "Oh, America is a free nation, we are not like Russia or China." Well, then walk your talk.

Give people the transparency because the real difference between a free nation and a dictatorship is simply the level of transparency. The more transparency in government, the more freedom in that nation. The less transparency, the less freedom. It can be no other way. This is not rocket science. It is what should be common sense and common knowledge and common awareness.

You, of course, realize that when you resolve your psychology, you have no need to hide anything. There are many among the American people, my beloved, who also really have nothing to hide in their private lives. They have never done anything in their lives that they would be ashamed of admitting publicly. They have integrity. They have honesty. These people can be galvanized to realize that they do not care that you have greater transparency because they have nothing to hide.

Only those who have something to hide will oppose transparency. This is where you can make the calls to project into the collective consciousness until there is that awakening. As I said, people suddenly look around and say: "This is obvious. Why haven't we demanded this before? Let's go to Washington. Let's print up the banners. Let's go there and demand : TRANS-PA-REN-CY, TRANS-PA-REN-CY, TRANS-PA-REN-CY."

When a million people do that, you will shake the foundations of the power elite in America, as I have generated an impulse that, at the spiritual level, will shake the foundations of the power elite in America. When you ratify it, when the people stand up and bring it into the physical, it *will* make a difference.

16 | INVOKING TRANSPARENCY IN GOVERNMENT

In the name of the I AM THAT I AM, Jesus Christ, I use the authority that I have as a being in embodiment on earth to call upon Master MORE to reinforce my calls and use my chakras to project the statements in this invocation into the collective consciousness and awaken Americans to the need for absolute transparency in government. Awaken Americans to the reality that we are spiritual beings and that we can co-create a new future by working with the ascended masters. I especially call for …

[Make your own calls here.]

Part 1

1. In a truly democratic nation, whether a republic or another form of democracy, a government only has legitimacy when it has the consent of the governed.

> Master MORE, come to the fore,
> we will absorb your flame of MORE.
> Master MORE, our will so strong,
> our power centers cleared by song.
>
> **Master MORE, your Sacred Heart,**
> **from this we will no more depart,**
> **we are forever in your flow,**
> **of Diamond Will that you bestow.**

2. What does it take for a government to have the consent of the governed? Is it enough that every four years the governed vote in representatives? Then, in those four years, the representatives can do whatever they want.

> Master MORE, your wisdom flows,
> as our attunement ever grows.
> Master MORE, we have a tie,
> that helps us see through Serpent's lie.
>
> **Master MORE, your Sacred Heart,**
> **from this we will no more depart,**
> **we are forever in your flow,**
> **of Diamond Will that you bestow.**

3. There is a word that scares the power elite more than any other word on earth. Nothing scares the fallen beings or the hidden power elite that attempts to run any country, more than this word and it is: "transparency."

> Master MORE, your love so pink,
> there is no purer love, we think.

16 | Invoking transparency in government

> Master MORE, you set us free,
> from all conditionality.
>
> **Master MORE, your Sacred Heart,**
> **from this we will no more depart,**
> **we are forever in your flow,**
> **of Diamond Will that you bestow.**

4. How can a government have legitimacy unless it has the consent of the governed? How can it have the consent of the governed unless those governed know what is going on in government? For there to be the consent of the governed, there must be total, absolute, undiluted, unrestricted transparency in the government.

> Master MORE, we will endure,
> your discipline that makes us pure.
> Master MORE, intentions true,
> as we are always one with you.
>
> **Master MORE, your Sacred Heart,**
> **from this we will no more depart,**
> **we are forever in your flow,**
> **of Diamond Will that you bestow.**

5. In the Golden Age there will be total transparency in all levels of government and in all levels of society. Saint Germain will release the technology to read the Akashic records.

> Master MORE, our vision raised,
> the will of God is always praised.
> Master MORE, creative will,
> raising all life higher still.

> Master MORE, your Sacred Heart,
> from this we will no more depart,
> we are forever in your flow,
> of Diamond Will that you bestow.

6. Everything that happens in the hidden corridors of power, everything that is said, how decisions are made, how deals are made, all of this is recorded in the Akashic records.

> Master MORE, your peace is power,
> the demons of war it will devour.
> Master MORE, we serve all life,
> our flames consuming war and strife.

> Master MORE, your Sacred Heart,
> from this we will no more depart,
> we are forever in your flow,
> of Diamond Will that you bestow.

7. The release of this technology will have ramifications throughout society when it begins to dawn on people that they cannot hide anything anymore.

> Master MORE, we are so free,
> eternal bond from you we see.
> Master MORE, we find rebirth,
> in flow of your eternal mirth.

> Master MORE, your Sacred Heart,
> from this we will no more depart,
> we are forever in your flow,
> of Diamond Will that you bestow.

16 | Invoking transparency in government

8. Could there really be crime on earth if the criminals would always be caught? Could there be corruption if they would always be caught?

> Master MORE, you balance all,
> the seven rays upon our call.
> Master MORE, forever MORE,
> we are the Spirit's open door.
>
> **Master MORE, your Sacred Heart,**
> **from this we will no more depart,**
> **we are forever in your flow,**
> **of Diamond Will that you bestow.**

9. In the political process of the United States, there is a vast gap between the public appearance of the political apparatus and what is actually going on in the corridors of power. Imagine we could remove that gap and what that would do.

> Master MORE, your Presence here,
> filling up the inner sphere.
> Life is now a sacred flow,
> God Power we on all bestow.
>
> **Master MORE, your Sacred Heart,**
> **from this we will no more depart,**
> **we are forever in your flow,**
> **of Diamond Will that you bestow.**

Part 2

1. A cloud has enveloped Washington, D.C. that makes the people in government, both the elected representatives and those in the bureaucracy, those in the lobbying groups, the power elite groups and the "old boys" networks" think that they can do things and keep them hidden.

> Master MORE, come to the fore,
> we will absorb your flame of MORE.
> Master MORE, our will so strong,
> our power centers cleared by song.
>
> **Master MORE, your Sacred Heart,**
> **from this we will no more depart,**
> **we are forever in your flow,**
> **of Diamond Will that you bestow.**

2. These people think they can do what they know the people would not accept and get away with it. These power brokers think they have gotten away with it for so long that they can continue to get away with it.

> Master MORE, your wisdom flows,
> as our attunement ever grows.
> Master MORE, we have a tie,
> that helps us see through Serpent's lie.
>
> **Master MORE, your Sacred Heart,**
> **from this we will no more depart,**
> **we are forever in your flow,**
> **of Diamond Will that you bestow.**

3. I hereby call for the exposure of these hidden dealings. I call for the shattering of the energy veil that is clouding the minds of those in Washington but is also preventing those from the outside, those who are not part of the inner circle, from seeing and then exposing what is going on.

> Master MORE, your love so pink,
> there is no purer love, we think.
> Master MORE, you set us free,
> from all conditionality.
>
> **Master MORE, your Sacred Heart,**
> **from this we will no more depart,**
> **we are forever in your flow,**
> **of Diamond Will that you bestow.**

4. I call for the cutting free of the journalists who will keep digging and the insiders who will expose what is going on. I call for this exposure to happen in many fields.

> Master MORE, we will endure,
> your discipline that makes us pure.
> Master MORE, intentions true,
> as we are always one with you.
>
> **Master MORE, your Sacred Heart,**
> **from this we will no more depart,**
> **we are forever in your flow,**
> **of Diamond Will that you bestow.**

5. I call for a raising of the collective consciousness where people will suddenly look around and say: "But isn't it obvious that there should be transparency in government? How can we

have a democratic nation if we don't have transparency? How can we give our consent to those who govern us, if we don't know what they do and say in the corridors of power? Why have we never thought about this before? Isn't it obvious?"

> Master MORE, our vision raised,
> the will of God is always praised.
> Master MORE, creative will,
> raising all life higher still.
>
> **Master MORE, your Sacred Heart,**
> **from this we will no more depart,**
> **we are forever in your flow,**
> **of Diamond Will that you bestow.**

6. Things are not hopeless, it is not so that there is nothing we can do. There is another cloud that envelops America in its entirety, and it has pacified the people where they think that we can't fight city hall, much less Congress.

> Master MORE, your peace is power,
> the demons of war it will devour.
> Master MORE, we serve all life,
> our flames consuming war and strife.
>
> **Master MORE, your Sacred Heart,**
> **from this we will no more depart,**
> **we are forever in your flow,**
> **of Diamond Will that you bestow.**

7. The ascended masters are very optimistic because the fallen beings, the power elite, think they can get away with what they have gotten away with for so long. They cannot even fathom

the power of ascended master students making the calls for the exposure of these hidden wheelings and dealings.

> Master MORE, we are so free,
> eternal bond from you we see.
> Master MORE, we find rebirth,
> in flow of your eternal mirth.
>
> **Master MORE, your Sacred Heart,**
> **from this we will no more depart,**
> **we are forever in your flow,**
> **of Diamond Will that you bestow.**

8. I call for the most aware Americans to be cut free from this cloud of hopelessness, this cloud of despair, this cloud of unknowing that has enveloped the American people.

> Master MORE, you balance all,
> the seven rays upon our call.
> Master MORE, forever MORE,
> we are the Spirit's open door.
>
> **Master MORE, your Sacred Heart,**
> **from this we will no more depart,**
> **we are forever in your flow,**
> **of Diamond Will that you bestow.**

9. I call for the most aware Americans to be cut free to tune in to the mind of Saint Germain and realize that he is an optimist. He is optimistic because he sees the hidden potential of how it is possible to awaken the American people and make them stand up.

Master MORE, your Presence here,
filling up the inner sphere.
Life is now a sacred flow,
God Power we on all bestow.

**Master MORE, your Sacred Heart,
from this we will no more depart,
we are forever in your flow,
of Diamond Will that you bestow.**

Part 3

1. Who can object to the demand for transparency in government? We can outmaneuver the fallen beings by putting them in a situation where they have no way out.

Master MORE, come to the fore,
we will absorb your flame of MORE.
Master MORE, our will so strong,
our power centers cleared by song.

**Master MORE, your Sacred Heart,
from this we will no more depart,
we are forever in your flow,
of Diamond Will that you bestow.**

2. If we demand transparency in government, who in the government can oppose this without exposing that they are not committed to democratic principles and the constitution?

16 | Invoking transparency in government

> Master MORE, your wisdom flows,
> as our attunement ever grows.
> Master MORE, we have a tie,
> that helps us see through Serpent's lie.
>
> **Master MORE, your Sacred Heart,**
> **from this we will no more depart,**
> **we are forever in your flow,**
> **of Diamond Will that you bestow.**

3. They will attempt to hide behind national security, but the old boy's network, who are making wheeling's and dealings in the Senate or the House, this is not covered by national security.

> Master MORE, your love so pink,
> there is no purer love, we think.
> Master MORE, you set us free,
> from all conditionality.
>
> **Master MORE, your Sacred Heart,**
> **from this we will no more depart,**
> **we are forever in your flow,**
> **of Diamond Will that you bestow.**

4. I call for an awakening and galvanizing of people where they realize that we actually have a right to demand transparency.

> Master MORE, we will endure,
> your discipline that makes us pure.
> Master MORE, intentions true,
> as we are always one with you.

> **Master MORE, your Sacred Heart,**
> **from this we will no more depart,**
> **we are forever in your flow,**
> **of Diamond Will that you bestow.**

5. I call forth the exposure so that those who are corrupt will not dare to run for office, those who are the compromisers will not dare to run, those who have something to hide cannot run.

> Master MORE, our vision raised,
> the will of God is always praised.
> Master MORE, creative will,
> raising all life higher still.

> **Master MORE, your Sacred Heart,**
> **from this we will no more depart,**
> **we are forever in your flow,**
> **of Diamond Will that you bestow.**

6. I call forth a situation where only those who have nothing to hide can run, those who are honest, those who have integrity.

> Master MORE, your peace is power,
> the demons of war it will devour.
> Master MORE, we serve all life,
> our flames consuming war and strife.

> **Master MORE, your Sacred Heart,**
> **from this we will no more depart,**
> **we are forever in your flow,**
> **of Diamond Will that you bestow.**

16 | Invoking transparency in government

7. It is not human nature to hide something, it is the nature of the dualistic self. The separate self has something to hide and always wants to hide because it wants to have special privileges, it wants to get away with things, it wants to do something that it thinks is for its own good and then hide how it actually harms others.

> Master MORE, we are so free,
> eternal bond from you we see.
> Master MORE, we find rebirth,
> in flow of your eternal mirth.

> **Master MORE, your Sacred Heart,**
> **from this we will no more depart,**
> **we are forever in your flow,**
> **of Diamond Will that you bestow.**

8. The essence of the power elite is that they want to establish a privileged position for themselves by taking away the wealth of the people but they do not want the people to know about it.

> Master MORE, you balance all,
> the seven rays upon our call.
> Master MORE, forever MORE,
> we are the Spirit's open door.

> **Master MORE, your Sacred Heart,**
> **from this we will no more depart,**
> **we are forever in your flow,**
> **of Diamond Will that you bestow.**

9. I call forth the judgment of Christ upon those who will attempt to use the concept of a surveillance society to get the

people to stop demanding transparency in government because they themselves feel they have something to hide.

> Master MORE, your Presence here,
> filling up the inner sphere.
> Life is now a sacred flow,
> God Power we on all bestow.
>
> **Master MORE, your Sacred Heart,**
> **from this we will no more depart,**
> **we are forever in your flow,**
> **of Diamond Will that you bestow.**

Part 4

1. I call forth the realization that the majority of the people may have certain things to hide but they do not have nearly as much to hide as those in the power elite, those in the governing elite, those who are in the political apparatus. They have much more to hide so they have much more to lose from transparency.

> Master MORE, come to the fore,
> we will absorb your flame of MORE.
> Master MORE, our will so strong,
> our power centers cleared by song.
>
> **Master MORE, your Sacred Heart,**
> **from this we will no more depart,**
> **we are forever in your flow,**
> **of Diamond Will that you bestow.**

2. Of course people have a right to privacy. We have a right to set a standard for those who govern us, and it is not a matter of exposing their private lives. It is a matter of exposing that which is clearly corrupt, that which is clearly the "old boys network."

> Master MORE, your wisdom flows,
> as our attunement ever grows.
> Master MORE, we have a tie,
> that helps us see through Serpent's lie.
>
> **Master MORE, your Sacred Heart,**
> **from this we will no more depart,**
> **we are forever in your flow,**
> **of Diamond Will that you bestow.**

3. We have a right to demand, that the gap between what politicians say and what they do is removed because they cannot hide what they say and do.

> Master MORE, your love so pink,
> there is no purer love, we think.
> Master MORE, you set us free,
> from all conditionality.
>
> **Master MORE, your Sacred Heart,**
> **from this we will no more depart,**
> **we are forever in your flow,**
> **of Diamond Will that you bestow.**

4. The further we go back in time, the easier it was for people to hide something. In any dictatorship, the dictator has always been able to hide certain things.

> Master MORE, we will endure,
> your discipline that makes us pure.
> Master MORE, intentions true,
> as we are always one with you.
>
> **Master MORE, your Sacred Heart,**
> **from this we will no more depart,**
> **we are forever in your flow,**
> **of Diamond Will that you bestow.**

5. Any dictatorship has to hide something in order to stay in power because even a dictator needs the consent of the governed. It is a limited consent because it is based on the people not fully understanding what is going on.

> Master MORE, our vision raised,
> the will of God is always praised.
> Master MORE, creative will,
> raising all life higher still.
>
> **Master MORE, your Sacred Heart,**
> **from this we will no more depart,**
> **we are forever in your flow,**
> **of Diamond Will that you bestow.**

6. In a democratic nation with the Constitution of the United States and our inalienable rights, we cannot allow the government to hide from us in the same way as a dictatorial government is hiding things from the people.

> Master MORE, your peace is power,
> the demons of war it will devour.

Master MORE, we serve all life,
our flames consuming war and strife.

**Master MORE, your Sacred Heart,
from this we will no more depart,
we are forever in your flow,
of Diamond Will that you bestow.**

7. If our government has as much secrecy and as much hidden wheelings and dealings as they have in China or Russia, what makes us think our government is any better? We have a right to demand a higher level of transparency—if our government claims to be more legitimate than the governments of Putin or China.

Master MORE, we are so free,
eternal bond from you we see.
Master MORE, we find rebirth,
in flow of your eternal mirth.

**Master MORE, your Sacred Heart,
from this we will no more depart,
we are forever in your flow,
of Diamond Will that you bestow.**

8. The real difference between a free nation and a dictatorship is the level of transparency. The more transparency in government, the more freedom in that nation. The less transparency, the less freedom. It can be no other way. This is not rocket science. It should be common sense, common knowledge and common awareness.

Master MORE, you balance all,
the seven rays upon our call.
Master MORE, forever MORE,
we are the Spirit's open door.

**Master MORE, your Sacred Heart,
from this we will no more depart,
we are forever in your flow,
of Diamond Will that you bestow.**

9. I call forth an awakening so a million Americans will march on Washington, D.C. and demand transparency in government. I call forth the shaking of the foundations of the power elite in America, and I ratify the impulse of Master MORE. We, the people, stand up and bring it into the physical, and it *will* make a difference.

Master MORE, your Presence here,
filling up the inner sphere.
Life is now a sacred flow,
God Power we on all bestow.

**Master MORE, your Sacred Heart,
from this we will no more depart,
we are forever in your flow,
of Diamond Will that you bestow.**

Sealing

In the name of the I AM THAT I AM, I accept that Archangel Michael, Astrea and Shiva form an impenetrable shield around myself and all constructive people in America, sealing us from

all fear-based energies in all four octaves. I accept that the Light of God is consuming and transforming all fear-based energies that make up the dark forces working against America!

17 | FREEING AMERICA FROM THE SLAVERY OF CAPITALISM

I AM the Ascended Master Saint Germain, and I thank you for your patience, for your willingness to listen to me so many times, instead of following that human tendency of wanting something different. You will indeed get something different every time because the topic is, of course, different.

What I wish to do here is to build upon the concept of this compulsive desire for winning that you see in the American national psyche. One outcome of this is that many Americans think that America won the Cold War because the Soviet Union was dissolved and communism had to retreat and the people were freed from the communist yoke. This is, of course, correct in the sense that people in the former Soviet Union or those in the Warsaw Pact have been freed from the yoke of communism, at least to a larger or smaller extent, smaller in Russia than in most of the other former Soviet Republics or Warsaw countries.

Have Americans been freed from capitalism?

However, before Americans become too overexcited about having won the Cold War, we might look the other way and ask ourselves: "Have Americans been freed from capitalism?" The fact of the matter is that capitalism and communism formed the archetypal example of a dualistic polarity. Totally created by the fallen beings, totally set up to be in a never-ending, irresolvable, irreconcilable struggle and conflict. Of course, you can say the struggle ended in the sense that communism collapsed but has it ended in the sense that has the other dualistic polarity ended, has capitalism ended? There are, of course, many Americans who would say: "No, and we don't want capitalism to end because capitalism is the greatest economic system and it is a free economy of free enterprise." It is one of the greatest illusions in America that people think a capitalist economy is the same as free enterprise. There is nothing free about a capitalist economy—except that the power elite have total freedom to exploit the people. Of course, the freedom to exploit is not really a freedom, at least not a freedom that is found in the Seventh Ray of Freedom and the vision of Saint Germain.

Capitalism is a form of slavery

A great breakthrough would be to radiate into the collective consciousness this awareness that capitalism has only one purpose, and that is to enslave the people under a small power elite. We can look to the communist system and see that it was a system controlled by a small party elite who had the physical means to control the people. This was brought about by an unrestricted willingness to kill those who opposed the

17 | Freeing America from the slavery of capitalism

system. In the Soviet Union, this was initiated by Stalin who was willing to kill any amount of people that either opposed him or whom he thought opposed him. In China you saw the "great" Chairman Mao being likewise willing to kill any number of Chinese that he thought opposed him.

We see that this is one way that the fallen beings like to set themselves up in control of the people. By creating the physical control, the physical power apparatus whereby they can kill anyone who opposes the system and therefore forces people to go into this state where they basically have a choice: "Do I want to stay in embodiment or don't I?" If I do, I must submit to the system because if I object, I will instantly be killed and possibly my entire family will be killed as well. There is no blame here that so many people submitted to this system. There was not really that much else they could do unless they wanted to go out of embodiment.

It is, of course, relatively easy to see for many Americans that there was a power elite, that there were a certain type of beings who had this total insensitivity to life. What is much harder for Americans to see – but what needs to be seen – is that the capitalist system is not free, it is not a free economy. It is a system created by another group of fallen beings who also have the desire to control but who have a different approach as to how they accomplish this. These fallen beings are, one might say, more subtle, more clever in a way than the fallen beings who created the Soviet Union. They have realized that as the collective consciousness has been raised, there has come a point where people have become aware of certain of the more obvious forms of suppression and the people have become willing to revolt against this.

They, of course, saw that this was what actually led to the birth of the American nation, as out-pictured in the saying of Thomas Paine: "Give me liberty or give me death!" You see that in the Soviet system where they were totally willing to kill, it attracted people who wanted to stay in embodiment and did not want to be killed. In America you have seen a certain amount of people who have the attitude: "Give me liberty or give me death," and the fallen beings saw that it would be impossible (or at least very, very difficult) to control America in the same overt way through physical means as it was done in the Soviet Union. This did not mean they gave up. They simply said: "Well how can we, then, control people, how can we gain control of the American nation?"

How the elite perverts freedom

What the fallen beings will always do is they will seek to take something that is given for the benefit of the people and make use of it. What can they do in America? Well, they can take the concept of freedom and make full use of it so that they can do absolutely anything they want, because they have set themselves up as an untouchable elite that is not even seen by the people, or at least not seen for what they are. You might say that the fallen beings who controlled the Soviet Union were also, in a sense, a hidden elite. Even though people knew there was a party elite who was running the system, they were still not really seen for who they were. They exercised control by restricting the freedom of the people in a very obvious manner. At the same time, they had to pay a price for that in the sense that they themselves also had to, at least to some degree, follow the system.

It is clear, for example, that even though the party elite could take to themselves certain privileges, there was a limit to what they could take. For example, they might have a bigger apartment than most of the people in the nation but it was not

17 | Freeing America from the slavery of capitalism

a mansion. They might have a dacha in the country, a summer house in the country, but it was not a palace because there simply was not the money in the economy to support that. What you saw in the Soviet Union was, in a sense, that it attracted a certain kind of fallen beings who were more concerned about having power than about having money or privileges. They were more concerned about restricting the freedom of the people and less concerned about being able to do anything they wanted.

What America attracted was another group of fallen beings, who do not need or do not want that absolute physical power and control. They want a more hidden form of power, they want money but they first of all want the freedom to do anything they want, regardless of the consequences that it has for the people.

They were driven by this desire to set themselves up as people who have so much money that they could use this to gain privileges that were far, far beyond the population. At the same time, they were untouchable because they were not elected. Even though it was publicly known that they had lots of money, it was not really understood how much money they had, how they were able to use this to influence the political process and how they could do whatever they wanted personally with that money.

You simply see that with communism, it is obvious for most Americans that this was a repressive system. Capitalism is simply another form of oppression where the people are oppressed by a small elite. Most Americans have not yet awakened to see this but they certainly can, especially when they are supported by your calls.

It is quite possible to have another paradigm shift where Americans wake up and suddenly see that it is obvious that there is a power elite running America behind the scenes and that we cannot allow this to go on. What you see is that the fallen beings in America said: "We have a country here who gives a certain amount of personal freedom but also economic freedom. So let's make use of this economic freedom to accumulate wealth and use that wealth to exert influence on the nation and use that wealth for our own gratification." In other words, they were determined to take the freedom of opportunity that was given in the early days of America and use it for their own gratification.

American businesses are inhumane

Therefore, if you apply the psychological models that have been created, you have to say that these people were the archetype of a narcissist. They did not care whatsoever about the consequences of their actions for other people, they were willing to do anything for their own gratification and they *did* anything. They used the economic freedom to seek to create monopolies, to destroy other businesses, to create unfair competition. This is really the hallmark of a capitalist economy, it is dog-eat-dog. It is everyone against everyone else. It is do whatever it takes to get ahead, no matter what consequences this has for other people.

This, then, leads to a consideration of the state of American business, and especially the large corporations who are not even truly American corporations because they have now gone multinational and therefore are not truly American businesses any more. You cannot even say that they have any loyalty to America whatsoever or any dedication to preserving the American way of life. What was created during the 1800s by these early industrialists (the financiers and those who attempted to create monopoly capitalism) was that they set American

17 | Freeing America from the slavery of capitalism

businesses on this track where business has become a fiercely competitive sport, where the only way to get ahead is to be more ruthless than the competition.

This has, of course, created a system that is so typical for the fallen beings (and that you see in the feudal systems of Europe) where the elite has absolutely no concern for how their actions affect the people. They do not care about the people whatsoever, they just look at them as tools, as a kind of property that can be exploited to an almost ultimate degree. It needs to be stated that American business, the American business climate and especially the large corporations are completely and utterly inhumane.

It is based on a complete denial of the essential humanity of the American people. They are seen only as worker bees to be exploited until they have worked themselves to death and then be discarded. There is absolutely no way to express this in diplomatic terms. It is a completely inhumane system and you see so many people who have been sucked into this system, who have been bought off with a bit larger salary than those other people, who have then spent 60-80 hours a week for 30 or 40 years until they are burned out and do not even know what to do with themselves after they retire. So many of them die within a year or two after retirement simply because they were worked to death in an inhumane system that did not care whatsoever about people but only cared about profit that then can be used to exert power and to buy privilege.

Capitalism is by nature against a free economy

Therefore, it needs to be seen that capitalism is by its very nature against a free economy. It is based on destroying the freedom of the economy by destroying the freedom of the people, destroying the opportunity of the people to come up and challenge these larger businesses. It is based on destroying the competition and, of course, destroying people in the process. You see so many examples of this where businesses have used illegal, inhumane, unfair tactics to destroy the competition. You see the concept of hostile takeovers, you see how a large corporation will close a factory and fire 10,000 workers in order to boost their stock price by 10% and therefore give larger dividends to their shareholders.

You see how, just as politics has become a game, business has become a game where it is only a matter of getting ahead, and it does not matter what is the human cost of you getting ahead. This is seen so clearly, or at least can be seen so clearly, in the 2008 financial crisis. You can even see some of the popular movies that have been made that actually, at least to some degree, portrayed the mind-set of these leaders of the investment banks and the regular banks and their attitude and how they reacted afterwards.

What is not portrayed in these popular movies is what is going on behind the scenes, how these people actually talk amongst themselves, how they plot and plan and how they look at the people and talk about the people. I can assure you that if you could hear how some of these high level financiers talk about the people of America, talk about America's political system and talk about America as a country, you would be shocked. Americans would simply say: "Why on earth are we allowing these people to even do business in America? Why haven't we run them out of town tarred and feathered?"

The reality here is that if America is to become aligned with the mind of Saint Germain, more Americans, a critical mass of Americans, need to acknowledge the existence of a power elite who all suffer from narcissistic personality disorder, having absolutely no concerns whatsoever for the population. It is necessary that the people say: "How can we possibly maintain freedom in America as long as we allow these people freedom to do whatever they want and to exploit the freedom of America, to exploit the system and to exploit the people?"

Why on earth, my beloved, should the majority of a population in a country allow a small elite to exploit them? Why—when you have a system where the majority have the power to vote in a new form of government that will challenge this elite and restrict their ability to exploit the people. Why should this be allowed? Again, this needs to be one of those realizations that come to a critical mass of people where they wake up and see that the emperors of business, the emperors of finance, have nothing on.

You cannot allow people to make money on money

Naturally, I have already talked about money and the money system. I want to briefly touch on it here by saying that in the Golden Age it will be very, very clear (and it will at some point be instituted by law as well) that in a free nation you cannot allow people to make money on money. You cannot allow them to use money to make more money. Therefore, I can assure you that in the Golden Age the large financial banks, the investment banks and other financial institutions that you have today will simply go the way of the dinosaurs.

They have already become so large, and you can see in 2008 what happened. No human being could foresee or calculate the risk of these sub-prime mortgages and how they were sold off so the whole system was in danger of collapsing. It should also be possible for Americans to see that what the government did was to use the people's money to buy off, to bail out, the elite. They had created the situation that was threatening a collapse of the system and the government bailed them out.

I can assure you that in the Golden Age there will be no concept of "too big to fail." What you see in this very concept "too big to fail" is exactly how the power elite have set themselves up so that they have created the impression that the people could not do without them. If these big investment banks were allowed to fail, then it would have such devastating effects on the economy that the people would suffer.

Well, if you go back to the feudal system of Europe, you would see that for a long time, until that system started falling apart, many among the people actually believed that they could not exist without the feudal lords. They thought that the feudal lords were the knights who could raise an army and defend them against invasion from this or that force. Who were the feudal lords of one country defending the people against? The feudal lords of another country.

Again, this is the power elite setting themselves up so that the people have to submit to one group of fallen beings in order to protect them from another group of fallen beings. What was the dynamic that the fallen beings used when the Soviet Union was created? Well, Americans needed to be protected from communism and therefore they needed to submit to the elite that was running this country. What you see is that they have managed to create this belief that the people cannot do without the elite and the institutions they have created.

The noble class families of America

This is what we have talked about as the old boys network in politics where you have this group of old families that are like the noble class of America. They have managed to put themselves in a position where they have formed a network of families who all believe that they are absolutely necessary for the survival of America, the economy and the people. They believe that the people could not do without them. They have managed to create such a network, that branches out into so many aspects of American society, that many, many people who are not part of those few families have actually come to believe the lie. They have drunk the Kool-Aid. They also believe that America and the American people could not do without the financial elite, the power elite. That is why they managed to sell the politicians (who were elected to look after the interests of the people) the lie that these investment banks were too big to fail.

The irony is, of course, that when they are not in trouble, these very same people will hail the capitalist system and claim that the system can regulate itself! You see, when you look at the history of this, that in previous decades there were laws enacted that restricted all of these financial instruments. The dominant families then managed to gain influence over the Federal Reserve and its chairman, over presidents from Regan forward. They managed to make them believe that it was not necessary for the government to interfere with the financial markets because capitalism was such a wonderful system that the market mechanism would regulate itself and weed out those who could not make it in the system.

This is what they say when they themselves are not in trouble. They say: "Oh, the system will just regulate itself," but how does it regulate itself? By some businesses failing. Then, the minute their own business is in danger of failing, they say: "Oh no, now we don't need to let the market take care of itself because our business is too big to fail." So now the government needs to step in and do something and bail them out. Well, if capitalism is such a wonderful system, let the system work, let them fail—that is what you say: "We'll regulate the system and it will all be for the benefit of all."

You see the hypocrisy, you see the contradiction, you see how utterly ridiculous it is to let people who are in such a state of (what do you call that state, my beloved: blindness, inability to see) to let them run the economy, the financial system of this nation. All of these financial instruments that they have created are created to enrich the elite.

Those who keep accumulating money

Now, my beloved, ask yourself this: "What creates value? What creates something that increases the economy, adds to the wealth?" Well, you either have to bring forth an idea or an invention, you have to manufacture a product or you have to provide a service. These financial instruments created by the elite, they are not bringing forth a new idea, they are not manufacturing a product, they are not providing a service—unless you consider enriching the elite a service but certainly not a service to the people. They are not adding value to the overall economy.

It is the labor of the people that is adding value. What are the financial instruments designed to do? To take the value that has been created by the people's labor and concentrate it in the control of a small group of people. They are literally siphoning off the wealth created by the people and bringing it under their control. The effect of this is very simple. As we have said before, there is a limit to how many mansions, how many yachts, how many Rolls Royce, how many private jets you can buy. There comes a point where these people have so much money that they could not possibly spend it. That is when they go into this obsessive-compulsive reaction of wanting to accumulate more and more money. For when can you actually feel secure?

This messenger not so long ago watched a program on television that portrayed the lives of billionaires and the conclusion he came to was that if you believed what was said on this program, we should all feel sorry for the billionaires for their lives were just so stressful. It was consumed by trying to protect their money and trying to accumulate so much money that they could feel secure, and these poor people were just so stressed out that we should all have pity on them. It is true that some people do get sucked into this obsessive-compulsive disorder of feeling fundamentally insecure no matter how much money they have. It is partly (it comes with the territory) because you realize you have stolen that money by manipulating the system. You know that there is somebody else out there who is also willing to manipulate the system, and you know that there is a risk that instead of seeking to steal money from the people, they will come after you.

It is a dog-eat-dog world and nobody can ever feel really secure when they are in that state of mind. They get to this point where they accumulate more and more money and what does it do? It takes the money out of circulation. If the money is accumulating in accounts overseas, most of them not even American accounts, then it is not being spent. If it is not being spent, then it is not being used to buy the goods and services that other people produce. That means it actually lowers the overall economy, the wealth of the economy.

An economy that goes from crisis to crises

Whenever there is a crisis in the economy, the commentators on TV always talk about consumer spending driving the economy. Just ask yourself this: If the financial elite are taking money away from the consumers, is it not just a matter of time before we have the next crisis? That is why you see that the American economy, instead of being on a steady growth path, has gone from crisis to crisis now for a long time. You can look at the history and you can see that every time the government allows certain financial instruments, such as selling mortgages (instead of a bank holding the mortgage until it is paid back), it has resulted in a financial crisis within a few years. How many times do we need to repeat the same mistake before we realize that it just does not work, at least not for the people?

For every time, of course, the elite have made a huge profit before the crisis manifests. If you step even further back, you understand that behind this there is a small group of fallen beings, most of whom are not even in embodiment, and they are not even concerned about the elite that is in embodiment. The fallen beings in the identity realm are just using them as tools and they have (as we explained in the *My Lives* book and other books) only one goal: to create chaos and destruction. They want an economy that goes from crisis to crisis but is that what the American people want? Is that what the Founding Fathers wanted? Is that what I want?

My beloved, if you had a truly free economy in America, then you could look at the fact that the American people are quite willing to work, they are willing to work hard. This means that they are increasing productivity, and you can see that productivity has been increased dramatically for the past decades. If a people are willing to work and increase productivity, they are multiplying their talents. This means that the economy in that nation should be steadily growing without ever having a crisis. If you have a free economy, then the people who make money on their work and save it for their pensions, for example, they should never have to fear losing that money in a crisis.

They should never, ever have to fear losing their life savings due to some financial crisis. If you have a free economy, you have a freedom from the risk of crisis. It is simply child's logic, it is not rocket science. Anyone who is willing to take a look, can see this. Therefore, you can look back at the last several decades and beyond and see that the American economy has gone from one crisis to another and therefore it is not a free economy. This just simply demonstrates what I have been saying, namely that capitalism is not a free economy, it is not an economy that benefits the people. It is the dualistic polarity that survived the struggle with communism but America did not win, the people of America did not win, only the power elite won.

This is what I look to you to make the calls on, to educate yourself on the money system and to spread this awareness. You can make the calls and again take what I have said about the public discourse. You are not talking to other people in order to prove them wrong. In many cases you can benefit from studying that old Greek philosopher Socrates who never actually made statements but merely asked questions.

You can take the teachings we have given and you can present them, not as the statements we give but as a series of questions. You can ask people: "Well what do you think about this? Do you really think the economy is free when we have one crisis after another?" By doing this, you can help raise awareness and get people to think, instead of creating this antagonistic dialogue where other people feel you are trying to prove them wrong and they go into a defensive reaction and try to prove you wrong and we get into this there always has to be winners and losers.

The economy of the Golden Age

My vision for the Golden Age is to create a society where there are no losers because the people of America have a free economy, a steadily growing economy. That means that the value of their labor will not be degraded by inflation, they cannot lose their life savings. They do not have to spend 30 years paying off their mortgage on the house so that they end up spending three times as much on interest payments as the price of the house.

You have an economy where the wealth stays with the people who are using it to enjoy life and therefore are contributing to the overall growth of the economy. Of course, I also envision that there will come a point where the vast majority of Americans have such financial freedom, they have a steady job, they have a steady income, they have their house, they have their pensions taken care of, and now they find they actually have money that they can use to help people in other countries or even help people in America.

They can then use this money no longer to raise themselves but to raise the whole because, my beloved, the power elite have narcissistic personality disorder but the American people do not. Therefore, you find that if you look at ordinary (so to speak) Americans, they are very much willing to help. This has also been manipulated by the fallen beings but in the Golden Age I look very much to Americans to overcome the focus on self and be willing to help others. This, of course, cannot happen until Americans are free from this manipulation of the financial capitalist elite.

The economists who can receive new ideas

Now my beloved, I know I have given you a mouthful but I have a little more. There is a movie about the financial crisis that portrays how the government reacted to it and how the secretaries involved with this were attempting to deal with the crisis. By looking at this, you can see very clearly demonstrated how the leaders of the government, the elected representatives of the government, had a very, very limited vision of what they could do about a situation like this. This is caused by the fact, as I said, that you have this small group of people who have such an influence that they have managed to make so many people buy into their basic philosophy. This is something you need to make the calls on. You need to make the calls for the shattering of this because this is another black cloud that is not only hanging over Washington, D.C., but also over Wall Street and the financial district in New York and elsewhere.

It is, for that matter, a worldwide phenomenon where those who are in that system are so blinded by a certain state of consciousness that they cannot really see. First of all, they could not see that the system was about to collapse, but they have very limited vision for seeing what could be done about this. It is, of course, fine that the leaders of investment banks have a limited vision because it can only lead to their banks collapsing. It is not good when those in government also have that limited vision and simply cannot see how to create a system that is *of* the people, *by* the people and *for* the people.

You can make the calls for the creation of a new awareness, for the stepping forward of people who are able to tune in to my ideas and who have the expertise to formulate them and to implement them. There can, in the beginning, be a vision of a new type of economy that is not based on the exploitation of the people and therefore has the potential to become a truly free economy. This is important for you to make the calls on so that these people who have the potential to receive the ideas for the Golden Age economy are cut free to tune in to my mind, to align themselves with the mind of Saint Germain and to receive these ideas and have the courage to implement them.

Naturally, there is a way out, there is a way to bring the economy forward. There is more than one way, of course, and I am ready to release this to those who are in positions to do something about it. You are also in a position to do something about it by making the calls. You do not all need to have that expertise on how the system works because you are not in position, you are not part of the system. If you were part of the system, you probably would not be as open as you are to ascended master teachings. That is why, again, from a totally realistic assessment, you cannot expect these people who are in the system to suddenly become open to ascended master teachings.

What you can envision is that they become open to certain ideas from me that they can receive without knowing where it comes from. It is not a problem for me that some economist takes credit for an idea that I have formulated and becomes a famous economist. I am not seeking fame or fortune or anything else from earth. I am only seeking to set the people free.

On that note, I will set you free to go to my retreat tonight so that I can give you further things that you may not be quite ready for in your conscious minds. With this, you have my gratitude for being willing to be here and set this platform that has allowed me to release these teachings into the collective consciousness of America.

18 | INVOKING FREEDOM FROM THE SLAVERY OF CAPITALISM

In the name of the I AM THAT I AM, Jesus Christ, I use the authority that I have as a being in embodiment on earth to call upon Saint Germain to reinforce my calls and use my chakras to project the statements in this invocation into the collective consciousness and awaken Americans to the need to transcend capitalism. Awaken Americans to the reality that we are spiritual beings and that we can co-create a new future by working with the ascended masters. I especially call for …

[Make your own calls here.]

Part 1

1. Many Americans think that America won the Cold War because the Soviet Union was dissolved,

communism had to retreat and the people were freed from the communist yoke.

> O Saint Germain, you do inspire,
> my vision raised forever higher,
> with you I form a figure-eight,
> your Golden Age I co-create.

> **O Saint Germain, what love you bring,**
> **it truly makes all matter sing,**
> **your violet flame does all restore,**
> **with you we are becoming more.**

2. Have Americans been freed from capitalism? Capitalism and communism formed the archetypal example of a dualistic polarity, created by the fallen beings and set up to be in a never-ending, irresolvable, irreconcilable struggle.

> O Saint Germain, what Freedom Flame,
> released when we recite your name,
> acceleration is your gift,
> our planet it will surely lift.

> **O Saint Germain, what love you bring,**
> **it truly makes all matter sing,**
> **your violet flame does all restore,**
> **with you we are becoming more.**

3. Many Americans would say they don't want capitalism to end because capitalism is the greatest economic system and it is a free economy of free enterprise.

18 | Invoking freedom from the slavery of capitalism

O Saint Germain, in love we claim,
our right to bring your violet flame,
from you Above, to us below,
it is an all-transforming flow.

**O Saint Germain, what love you bring,
it truly makes all matter sing,
your violet flame does all restore,
with you we are becoming more.**

4. It is one of the greatest illusions in America that people think a capitalist economy is the same as free enterprise. There is nothing free about a capitalist economy—except that the power elite have total freedom to exploit the people.

O Saint Germain, I love you so,
my aura filled with violet glow,
my chakras filled with violet fire,
I am your cosmic amplifier.

**O Saint Germain, what love you bring,
it truly makes all matter sing,
your violet flame does all restore,
with you we are becoming more.**

5. The freedom to exploit is not a freedom, at least not a freedom that is found in the Seventh Ray of Freedom and the vision of Saint Germain.

O Saint Germain, I am now free,
your violet flame is therapy,
transform all hang-ups in my mind,
as inner peace I surely find.

> **O Saint Germain, what love you bring,**
> **it truly makes all matter sing,**
> **your violet flame does all restore,**
> **with you we are becoming more.**

6. Capitalism has only one purpose, and that is to enslave the people under a small power elite.

> O Saint Germain, my body pure,
> your violet flame for all is cure,
> consume the cause of all disease,
> and therefore I am all at ease.

> **O Saint Germain, what love you bring,**
> **it truly makes all matter sing,**
> **your violet flame does all restore,**
> **with you we are becoming more.**

7. The communist system was a system controlled by a small party elite who had the physical means to control the people. They had an unrestricted willingness to kill those who opposed the system.

> O Saint Germain, I'm karma-free,
> the past no longer burdens me,
> a brand new opportunity,
> I am in Christic unity.

> **O Saint Germain, what love you bring,**
> **it truly makes all matter sing,**
> **your violet flame does all restore,**
> **with you we are becoming more.**

8. One way that the fallen beings like to set themselves up in control of the people, is by creating the physical power apparatus whereby they can kill anyone who opposes the system. They can therefore force people to submit to the system.

> O Saint Germain, we are now one,
> I am for you a violet sun,
> as we transform this planet earth,
> your Golden Age is given birth.

> **O Saint Germain, what love you bring,**
> **it truly makes all matter sing,**
> **your violet flame does all restore,**
> **with you we are becoming more.**

9. I call for the awakening of Americans to see that the capitalist system is not a free economy. It is a system created by another group of fallen beings who also have the desire to control but who have a more subtle approach.

> O Saint Germain, the earth is free,
> from burden of duality,
> in oneness we bring what is best,
> your Golden Age is manifest.

> **O Saint Germain, what love you bring,**
> **it truly makes all matter sing,**
> **your violet flame does all restore,**
> **with you we are becoming more.**

Part 2

1. In America more people are willing to die for freedom, and the fallen beings saw that it would be very difficult to control America through physical means as it was done in the Soviet Union.

> O Saint Germain, you do inspire,
> my vision raised forever higher,
> with you I form a figure-eight,
> your Golden Age I co-create.
>
> **O Saint Germain, what love you bring,**
> **it truly makes all matter sing,**
> **your violet flame does all restore,**
> **with you we are becoming more.**

2. The fallen beings will seek to take something that is given for the benefit of the people and make use of it. In America, they took the concept of freedom and made full use of it so that they could do anything they wanted, because they had set themselves up as an untouchable elite that was not seen by the people.

> O Saint Germain, what Freedom Flame,
> released when we recite your name,
> acceleration is your gift,
> our planet it will surely lift.
>
> **O Saint Germain, what love you bring,**
> **it truly makes all matter sing,**

**your violet flame does all restore,
with you we are becoming more.**

3. The Soviet Union attracted a certain kind of fallen beings who were more concerned about having power than about having money or privileges. They were more concerned about restricting the freedom of the people and less concerned about being able to do anything they wanted.

> O Saint Germain, in love we claim,
> our right to bring your violet flame,
> from you Above, to us below,
> it is an all-transforming flow.

**O Saint Germain, what love you bring,
it truly makes all matter sing,
your violet flame does all restore,
with you we are becoming more.**

4. America attracted another group of fallen beings who do not need absolute physical power and control. They want a more hidden form of power, they want money, but they first of all want the freedom to do anything they want, regardless of the consequences it has for the people.

> O Saint Germain, I love you so,
> my aura filled with violet glow,
> my chakras filled with violet fire,
> I am your cosmic amplifier.

**O Saint Germain, what love you bring,
it truly makes all matter sing,**

> your violet flame does all restore,
> with you we are becoming more.

5. They are driven by the desire to set themselves up as people who have so much money that they can use this to gain privileges that are far beyond the population. At the same time, they are untouchable because they are not elected.

> O Saint Germain, I am now free,
> your violet flame is therapy,
> transform all hang-ups in my mind,
> as inner peace I surely find.

> **O Saint Germain, what love you bring,**
> **it truly makes all matter sing,**
> **your violet flame does all restore,**
> **with you we are becoming more.**

6. Even though it is publicly known that they have lots of money, it is not really understood how much money they have, how they are able to use this to influence the political process and how they can do whatever they want personally with that money.

> O Saint Germain, my body pure,
> your violet flame for all is cure,
> consume the cause of all disease,
> and therefore I am all at ease.

> **O Saint Germain, what love you bring,**
> **it truly makes all matter sing,**
> **your violet flame does all restore,**
> **with you we are becoming more.**

18 | Invoking freedom from the slavery of capitalism

7. It is obvious for most Americans that communism was a repressive system. Capitalism is another form of oppression where the people are oppressed by a small elite. I call for Americans to be awakened to see this.

> O Saint Germain, I'm karma-free,
> the past no longer burdens me,
> a brand new opportunity,
> I am in Christic unity.

> **O Saint Germain, what love you bring,**
> **it truly makes all matter sing,**
> **your violet flame does all restore,**
> **with you we are becoming more.**

8. I call forth a paradigm shift where Americans wake up and see that it is obvious that there is a power elite running America behind the scenes and that we cannot allow this to go on.

> O Saint Germain, we are now one,
> I am for you a violet sun,
> as we transform this planet earth,
> your Golden Age is given birth.

> **O Saint Germain, what love you bring,**
> **it truly makes all matter sing,**
> **your violet flame does all restore,**
> **with you we are becoming more.**

9. The fallen beings in America said: "We have a country that gives a certain amount of personal freedom but also economic freedom. So let's make use of this economic freedom

to accumulate wealth and use that wealth to exert influence on the nation for our own gratification."

> O Saint Germain, the earth is free,
> from burden of duality,
> in oneness we bring what is best,
> your Golden Age is manifest.

> **O Saint Germain, what love you bring,**
> **it truly makes all matter sing,**
> **your violet flame does all restore,**
> **with you we are becoming more.**

Part 3

1. If we apply the psychological models, the capitalists are the archetype of a narcissist. They do not care whatsoever about the consequences of their actions for other people, and they are willing to do anything for their own gratification.

> O Saint Germain, you do inspire,
> my vision raised forever higher,
> with you I form a figure-eight,
> your Golden Age I co-create.

> **O Saint Germain, what love you bring,**
> **it truly makes all matter sing,**
> **your violet flame does all restore,**
> **with you we are becoming more.**

18 | Invoking freedom from the slavery of capitalism

2. They have used the economic freedom to seek to create monopolies, to destroy other businesses, to create unfair competition. This is the hallmark of a capitalist economy, it is dog-eat-dog. It is everyone against everyone else. It is do whatever it takes to get ahead, no matter what consequences this has for other people.

> O Saint Germain, what Freedom Flame,
> released when we recite your name,
> acceleration is your gift,
> our planet it will surely lift.
>
> **O Saint Germain, what love you bring,**
> **it truly makes all matter sing,**
> **your violet flame does all restore,**
> **with you we are becoming more.**

3. The large corporations are not truly American corporations because they have gone multinational and have no loyalty to America or any dedication to preserving the American way of life.

> O Saint Germain, in love we claim,
> our right to bring your violet flame,
> from you Above, to us below,
> it is an all-transforming flow.
>
> **O Saint Germain, what love you bring,**
> **it truly makes all matter sing,**
> **your violet flame does all restore,**
> **with you we are becoming more.**

4. During the 1800s, the early industrialists and financiers attempted to create monopoly capitalism. This set American businesses on a track where business has become a fiercely competitive sport, where the only way to get ahead is to be more ruthless than the competition.

> O Saint Germain, I love you so,
> my aura filled with violet glow,
> my chakras filled with violet fire,
> I am your cosmic amplifier.
>
> **O Saint Germain, what love you bring,**
> **it truly makes all matter sing,**
> **your violet flame does all restore,**
> **with you we are becoming more.**

5. Capitalism has created a system that is typical for the fallen beings, where the elite has absolutely no concern for how their actions affect the people. They do not care about the people whatsoever, they just look at us as tools, as a kind of property that can be exploited to an almost ultimate degree.

> O Saint Germain, I am now free,
> your violet flame is therapy,
> transform all hang-ups in my mind,
> as inner peace I surely find.
>
> **O Saint Germain, what love you bring,**
> **it truly makes all matter sing,**
> **your violet flame does all restore,**
> **with you we are becoming more.**

18 | Invoking freedom from the slavery of capitalism

6. I call forth an awareness that American business, the American business climate and especially the large corporations are completely and utterly inhumane.

> O Saint Germain, my body pure,
> your violet flame for all is cure,
> consume the cause of all disease,
> and therefore I am all at ease.
>
> **O Saint Germain, what love you bring,**
> **it truly makes all matter sing,**
> **your violet flame does all restore,**
> **with you we are becoming more.**

7. American business is based on a complete denial of the essential humanity of the American people. We are seen only as worker bees to be exploited until we have worked ourselves to death, and then we are discarded.

> O Saint Germain, I'm karma-free,
> the past no longer burdens me,
> a brand new opportunity,
> I am in Christic unity.
>
> **O Saint Germain, what love you bring,**
> **it truly makes all matter sing,**
> **your violet flame does all restore,**
> **with you we are becoming more.**

8. Capitalism is a completely inhumane system and many Americans have worked themselves to death in a corporate machine that did not care whatsoever about people, but only

cared about profit that can be used to exert power and buy privilege.

> O Saint Germain, we are now one,
> I am for you a violet sun,
> as we transform this planet earth,
> your Golden Age is given birth.

> **O Saint Germain, what love you bring,**
> **it truly makes all matter sing,**
> **your violet flame does all restore,**
> **with you we are becoming more.**

9. Capitalism is by its very nature against a free economy. It is based on destroying the freedom of the economy by destroying the freedom of the people, destroying the opportunity of the people to come up and challenge these larger businesses.

> O Saint Germain, the earth is free,
> from burden of duality,
> in oneness we bring what is best,
> your Golden Age is manifest.

> **O Saint Germain, what love you bring,**
> **it truly makes all matter sing,**
> **your violet flame does all restore,**
> **with you we are becoming more.**

Part 4

1. Capitalism is based on destroying the competition and destroying people in the process. Businesses often use illegal, inhumane, unfair tactics to destroy the competition.

> O Saint Germain, you do inspire,
> my vision raised forever higher,
> with you I form a figure-eight,
> your Golden Age I co-create.
>
> **O Saint Germain, what love you bring,**
> **it truly makes all matter sing,**
> **your violet flame does all restore,**
> **with you we are becoming more.**

2. A large corporation will close a factory and fire 10,000 workers in order to boost their stock price by 10% and therefore give larger dividends to their shareholders.

> O Saint Germain, what Freedom Flame,
> released when we recite your name,
> acceleration is your gift,
> our planet it will surely lift.
>
> **O Saint Germain, what love you bring,**
> **it truly makes all matter sing,**
> **your violet flame does all restore,**
> **with you we are becoming more.**

3. As politics has become a game, business has become a game where it is only a matter of getting ahead, and it does not matter what is the human cost of you getting ahead.

> O Saint Germain, in love we claim,
> our right to bring your violet flame,
> from you Above, to us below,
> it is an all-transforming flow.
>
> **O Saint Germain, what love you bring,**
> **it truly makes all matter sing,**
> **your violet flame does all restore,**
> **with you we are becoming more.**

4. This can be seen so clearly in the 2008 financial crisis. If Americans could hear how some of the high-level financiers talk about the people of America, talk about America's political system and talk about America as a country, we would be shocked.

> O Saint Germain, I love you so,
> my aura filled with violet glow,
> my chakras filled with violet fire,
> I am your cosmic amplifier.
>
> **O Saint Germain, what love you bring,**
> **it truly makes all matter sing,**
> **your violet flame does all restore,**
> **with you we are becoming more.**

5. I call forth an awakening so Americans will say: "Why on earth are we allowing these people to even do business in

America? Why haven't we run them out of town tarred and feathered?"

> O Saint Germain, I am now free,
> your violet flame is therapy,
> transform all hang-ups in my mind,
> as inner peace I surely find.
>
> **O Saint Germain, what love you bring,**
> **it truly makes all matter sing,**
> **your violet flame does all restore,**
> **with you we are becoming more.**

6. If America is to become aligned with the mind of Saint Germain, a critical mass of Americans need to acknowledge the existence of a power elite who all suffer from narcissistic personality disorder, having absolutely no concerns whatsoever for the population.

> O Saint Germain, my body pure,
> your violet flame for all is cure,
> consume the cause of all disease,
> and therefore I am all at ease.
>
> **O Saint Germain, what love you bring,**
> **it truly makes all matter sing,**
> **your violet flame does all restore,**
> **with you we are becoming more.**

7. I call forth an awakening so the American people will say: "How can we possibly maintain freedom in America as long as we allow these people freedom to do whatever they want and

to exploit the freedom of America, to exploit the system and to exploit the people?"

> O Saint Germain, I'm karma-free,
> the past no longer burdens me,
> a brand new opportunity,
> I am in Christic unity.
>
> **O Saint Germain, what love you bring,**
> **it truly makes all matter sing,**
> **your violet flame does all restore,**
> **with you we are becoming more.**

8. Why should the majority of a population in a country allow a small elite to exploit them? When the majority have the power to vote in a new form of government that will challenge this elite and restrict their ability to exploit the people, why should this be allowed?

> O Saint Germain, we are now one,
> I am for you a violet sun,
> as we transform this planet earth,
> your Golden Age is given birth.
>
> **O Saint Germain, what love you bring,**
> **it truly makes all matter sing,**
> **your violet flame does all restore,**
> **with you we are becoming more.**

9. I call forth an awakening so a critical mass of Americans will wake up and see that the emperors of business, the emperors of finance, have nothing on.

O Saint Germain, the earth is free,
from burden of duality,
in oneness we bring what is best,
your Golden Age is manifest.

**O Saint Germain, what love you bring,
it truly makes all matter sing,
your violet flame does all restore,
with you we are becoming more.**

Sealing

In the name of the I AM THAT I AM, I accept that Archangel Michael, Astrea and Shiva form an impenetrable shield around myself and all constructive people in America, sealing us from all fear-based energies in all four octaves. I accept that the Light of God is consuming and transforming all fear-based energies that make up the dark forces working against America!

19 | INVOKING A POST-CAPITALIST ECONOMY

In the name of the I AM THAT I AM, Jesus Christ, I use the authority that I have as a being in embodiment on earth to call upon Saint Germain to reinforce my calls and use my chakras to project the statements in this invocation into the collective consciousness and awaken Americans to the need for a new approach to the economy. Awaken Americans to the reality that we are spiritual beings and that we can co-create a new future by working with the ascended masters. I especially call for …

[Make your own calls here.]

Part 1

1. In the Golden Age it will be clear that in a free nation, we cannot allow people to make money on money. We cannot allow them to use money to make more money.

> O Saint Germain, you do inspire,
> my vision raised forever higher,
> with you I form a figure-eight,
> your Golden Age I co-create.
>
> **O Saint Germain, what love you bring,
> it truly makes all matter sing,
> your violet flame does all restore,
> with you we are becoming more.**

2. In the Golden Age the large financial banks, the investment banks and other financial institutions that we have today will go the way of the dinosaurs.

> O Saint Germain, what Freedom Flame,
> released when we recite your name,
> acceleration is your gift,
> our planet it will surely lift.
>
> **O Saint Germain, what love you bring,
> it truly makes all matter sing,
> your violet flame does all restore,
> with you we are becoming more.**

3. In 2008 the government used the people's money to bail out the elite. The elite had created the situation that was threatening a collapse of the system and the government bailed them out.

> O Saint Germain, in love we claim,
> our right to bring your violet flame,
> from you Above, to us below,
> it is an all-transforming flow.

> **O Saint Germain, what love you bring,**
> **it truly makes all matter sing,**
> **your violet flame does all restore,**
> **with you we are becoming more.**

4. In the Golden Age there will be no concept of "too big to fail." This concept shows how the power elite have set themselves up so that they have created the impression that the people could not do without them. If these big investment banks were allowed to fail, then it would have such devastating effects on the economy that the people would suffer.

> O Saint Germain, I love you so,
> my aura filled with violet glow,
> my chakras filled with violet fire,
> I am your cosmic amplifier.

> **O Saint Germain, what love you bring,**
> **it truly makes all matter sing,**
> **your violet flame does all restore,**
> **with you we are becoming more.**

5. The power elite will attempt to set themselves up so that the people have to submit to one group of fallen beings in order to protect them from another group of fallen beings.

> O Saint Germain, I am now free,
> your violet flame is therapy,
> transform all hang-ups in my mind,
> as inner peace I surely find.

> **O Saint Germain, what love you bring,**
> **it truly makes all matter sing,**

> your violet flame does all restore,
> with you we are becoming more.

6. It was this dynamic that the fallen beings used when the Soviet Union was created. They said that Americans needed to be protected from communism and therefore they needed to submit to the elite that was running this country. They have created this belief that the people cannot do without the elite and the institutions they have created.

> O Saint Germain, my body pure,
> your violet flame for all is cure,
> consume the cause of all disease,
> and therefore I am all at ease.
>
> **O Saint Germain, what love you bring,
> it truly makes all matter sing,
> your violet flame does all restore,
> with you we are becoming more.**

7. I call forth the exposure of the group of old families that are like the noble class of America. They have managed to put themselves in a position where they have formed a network of families who all believe that they are absolutely necessary for the survival of America, the economy and the people.

> O Saint Germain, I'm karma-free,
> the past no longer burdens me,
> a brand new opportunity,
> I am in Christic unity.
>
> **O Saint Germain, what love you bring,
> it truly makes all matter sing,**

> **your violet flame does all restore,**
> **with you we are becoming more.**

8. I call forth the judgment of Christ upon those who have created a network that branches out into so many aspects of American society that many people who are not part of those few families have actually come to believe the lie. They have drunk the Kool-Aid.

> O Saint Germain, we are now one,
> I am for you a violet sun,
> as we transform this planet earth,
> your Golden Age is given birth.
>
> **O Saint Germain, what love you bring,**
> **it truly makes all matter sing,**
> **your violet flame does all restore,**
> **with you we are becoming more.**

9. I call forth an awakening of a critical mass of Americans from the lie that America and the American people could not do without the financial elite, the power elite or that their investment banks are too big to fail.

> O Saint Germain, the earth is free,
> from burden of duality,
> in oneness we bring what is best,
> your Golden Age is manifest.
>
> **O Saint Germain, what love you bring,**
> **it truly makes all matter sing,**
> **your violet flame does all restore,**
> **with you we are becoming more.**

Part 2

1. The dominant families managed to gain influence over the Federal Reserve and over presidents, making them believe that it was not necessary for the government to interfere with the financial markets because capitalism was such a wonderful system that the market mechanism would regulate itself and weed out those who could not make it in the system.

> O Saint Germain, you do inspire,
> my vision raised forever higher,
> with you I form a figure-eight,
> your Golden Age I co-create.
>
> **O Saint Germain, what love you bring,
> it truly makes all matter sing,
> your violet flame does all restore,
> with you we are becoming more.**

2. When they themselves are not in trouble, they say: "Oh, the system will just regulate itself," but how does it regulate itself? By some businesses failing. Then, the minute their own business is in danger of failing, they say: "Oh no, now we don't need to let the market take care of itself because our business is too big to fail."

> O Saint Germain, what Freedom Flame,
> released when we recite your name,
> acceleration is your gift,
> our planet it will surely lift.

**O Saint Germain, what love you bring,
it truly makes all matter sing,
your violet flame does all restore,
with you we are becoming more.**

3. If capitalism is such a wonderful system, let the system work, let them fail. This is hypocrisy, and it is ridiculous to let people in this state of mind run the financial system of this nation. All of these financial instruments that they have created are created to enrich the elite.

O Saint Germain, in love we claim,
our right to bring your violet flame,
from you Above, to us below,
it is an all-transforming flow.

**O Saint Germain, what love you bring,
it truly makes all matter sing,
your violet flame does all restore,
with you we are becoming more.**

4. What creates value is to bring forth an idea or an invention, to manufacture a product or to provide a service. The financial instruments created by the elite are not bringing forth a new idea, not manufacturing a product or providing a service. They are not adding value to the overall economy.

O Saint Germain, I love you so,
my aura filled with violet glow,
my chakras filled with violet fire,
I am your cosmic amplifier.

> O Saint Germain, what love you bring,
> it truly makes all matter sing,
> your violet flame does all restore,
> with you we are becoming more.

5. It is the labor of the people that is adding value. The financial instruments are designed to take the value that has been created by the people's labor and concentrate it under the control of a small group of people.

> O Saint Germain, I am now free,
> your violet flame is therapy,
> transform all hang-ups in my mind,
> as inner peace I surely find.

> O Saint Germain, what love you bring,
> it truly makes all matter sing,
> your violet flame does all restore,
> with you we are becoming more.

6. The elites are siphoning off the wealth created by the people and bringing it under their control. There comes a point where these people have so much money that they could not possibly spend it. That is when they go into this obsessive-compulsive reaction of wanting to accumulate more and more money.

> O Saint Germain, my body pure,
> your violet flame for all is cure,
> consume the cause of all disease,
> and therefore I am all at ease.

> O Saint Germain, what love you bring,
> it truly makes all matter sing,

19 | Invoking a post-capitalist economy

**your violet flame does all restore,
with you we are becoming more.**

7. Many among the elite have an obsessive-compulsive disorder of feeling fundamentally insecure no matter how much money they have. They realize they have stolen that money by manipulating the system. They know there is somebody else who is also willing to manipulate the system, and there is a risk that instead of seeking to steal money from the people, they will come after the elite.

O Saint Germain, I'm karma-free,
the past no longer burdens me,
a brand new opportunity,
I am in Christic unity.

**O Saint Germain, what love you bring,
it truly makes all matter sing,
your violet flame does all restore,
with you we are becoming more.**

8. The obsessive-compulsive accumulation of money takes the money out of circulation. If the money is accumulating in accounts overseas, then it is not being spent. If it is not being spent, then it is not being used to buy the goods and services that other people produce. That means it actually lowers the overall economy.

O Saint Germain, we are now one,
I am for you a violet sun,
as we transform this planet earth,
your Golden Age is given birth.

**O Saint Germain, what love you bring,
it truly makes all matter sing,
your violet flame does all restore,
with you we are becoming more.**

9. If the financial elite are taking money away from the consumers, it is just a matter of time before we have the next crisis. That is why the American economy, instead of being on a steady growth path, has gone from crisis to crisis for a long time.

O Saint Germain, the earth is free,
from burden of duality,
in oneness we bring what is best,
your Golden Age is manifest.

**O Saint Germain, what love you bring,
it truly makes all matter sing,
your violet flame does all restore,
with you we are becoming more.**

Part 3

1. Every time the government allows certain financial instruments, such as selling mortgages, it has resulted in a financial crisis within a few years. How many times do we need to repeat the same mistake before we realize that it just does not work, at least not for the people?

O Saint Germain, you do inspire,
my vision raised forever higher,

with you I form a figure-eight,
your Golden Age I co-create.

**O Saint Germain, what love you bring,
it truly makes all matter sing,
your violet flame does all restore,
with you we are becoming more.**

2. Of course, the elite have made a huge profit before the crisis manifests. Behind this there is a small group of fallen beings, most of whom are not even in embodiment, and they are not even concerned about the elite that is in embodiment.

O Saint Germain, what Freedom Flame,
released when we recite your name,
acceleration is your gift,
our planet it will surely lift.

**O Saint Germain, what love you bring,
it truly makes all matter sing,
your violet flame does all restore,
with you we are becoming more.**

3. The fallen beings in the identity realm are just using the physical elite as tools and they have one goal: to create chaos and destruction. They want an economy that goes from crisis to crisis but is that what the American people want? Is that what the Founding Fathers wanted? Is that what Saint Germain wants?

O Saint Germain, in love we claim,
our right to bring your violet flame,

from you Above, to us below,
it is an all-transforming flow.

**O Saint Germain, what love you bring,
it truly makes all matter sing,
your violet flame does all restore,
with you we are becoming more.**

4. The American people are quite willing to work, they are willing to increase productivity. If people are willing to work and increase productivity, they are multiplying their talents. This means that the economy in that nation should be steadily growing without ever having a crisis.

O Saint Germain, I love you so,
my aura filled with violet glow,
my chakras filled with violet fire,
I am your cosmic amplifier.

**O Saint Germain, what love you bring,
it truly makes all matter sing,
your violet flame does all restore,
with you we are becoming more.**

5. If we have a free economy, then the people who make money on their work and save it for their pensions should never have to fear losing that money in a crisis. They should never have to fear losing their life savings due to some financial crisis.

O Saint Germain, I am now free,
your violet flame is therapy,
transform all hang-ups in my mind,
as inner peace I surely find.

> O Saint Germain, what love you bring,
> it truly makes all matter sing,
> your violet flame does all restore,
> with you we are becoming more.

6. If we have a free economy, we have freedom from the risk of crisis. Since the American economy has gone from one crisis to another, it cannot be a free economy.

> O Saint Germain, my body pure,
> your violet flame for all is cure,
> consume the cause of all disease,
> and therefore I am all at ease.

> O Saint Germain, what love you bring,
> it truly makes all matter sing,
> your violet flame does all restore,
> with you we are becoming more.

7. Capitalism is not a free economy, it is not an economy that benefits the people. It is the dualistic polarity that survived the struggle with communism but America did not win, the people of America did not win, only the power elite won.

> O Saint Germain, I'm karma-free,
> the past no longer burdens me,
> a brand new opportunity,
> I am in Christic unity.

> O Saint Germain, what love you bring,
> it truly makes all matter sing,
> your violet flame does all restore,
> with you we are becoming more.

8. Saint Germain's vision for the Golden Age is to create a society where there are no losers because the people of America have a free economy, a steadily growing economy.

> O Saint Germain, we are now one,
> I am for you a violet sun,
> as we transform this planet earth,
> your Golden Age is given birth.
>
> **O Saint Germain, what love you bring,**
> **it truly makes all matter sing,**
> **your violet flame does all restore,**
> **with you we are becoming more.**

9. Saint Germain's vision is that the value of our labor will not be degraded by inflation, we cannot lose our life savings. We do not have to spend 30 years paying off our mortgage on our houses so that we end up spending three times as much on interest payments as the price of the house.

> O Saint Germain, the earth is free,
> from burden of duality,
> in oneness we bring what is best,
> your Golden Age is manifest.
>
> **O Saint Germain, what love you bring,**
> **it truly makes all matter sing,**
> **your violet flame does all restore,**
> **with you we are becoming more.**

Part 4

1. In Saint Germain's vision we have an economy where the wealth stays with the people who are contributing to the overall growth of the economy. Saint Germain envisions that the vast majority of Americans have such financial freedom that they can help people in other countries or even help people in America.

> O Saint Germain, you do inspire,
> my vision raised forever higher,
> with you I form a figure-eight,
> your Golden Age I co-create.
>
> **O Saint Germain, what love you bring,**
> **it truly makes all matter sing,**
> **your violet flame does all restore,**
> **with you we are becoming more.**

2. We can use this money to no longer raise ourselves but to raise the whole. The power elite have narcissistic personality disorder but the American people do not. Most Americans are very much willing to help.

> O Saint Germain, what Freedom Flame,
> released when we recite your name,
> acceleration is your gift,
> our planet it will surely lift.
>
> **O Saint Germain, what love you bring,**
> **it truly makes all matter sing,**

> your violet flame does all restore,
> with you we are becoming more.

3. In the Golden Age, Saint Germain looks to Americans to overcome the focus on self and be willing to help others. This cannot happen until Americans are free from this manipulation of the financial, capitalist elite.

> O Saint Germain, in love we claim,
> our right to bring your violet flame,
> from you Above, to us below,
> it is an all-transforming flow.

> **O Saint Germain, what love you bring,**
> **it truly makes all matter sing,**
> **your violet flame does all restore,**
> **with you we are becoming more.**

4. I call for the shattering of the limited vision of the leaders of the government concerning how to align the American economy with the mind of Saint Germain.

> O Saint Germain, I love you so,
> my aura filled with violet glow,
> my chakras filled with violet fire,
> I am your cosmic amplifier.

> **O Saint Germain, what love you bring,**
> **it truly makes all matter sing,**
> **your violet flame does all restore,**
> **with you we are becoming more.**

5. I call for the shattering of the black cloud that is not only hanging over Washington, D.C., but also over Wall Street and the financial district in New York.

> O Saint Germain, I am now free,
> your violet flame is therapy,
> transform all hang-ups in my mind,
> as inner peace I surely find.

> **O Saint Germain, what love you bring,**
> **it truly makes all matter sing,**
> **your violet flame does all restore,**
> **with you we are becoming more.**

6. I call for the shattering of the black cloud that is a worldwide phenomenon, where those who are in the economic system are so blinded by a certain state of consciousness that they cannot see that the system is about to collapse, and they cannot see what could be done about this.

> O Saint Germain, my body pure,
> your violet flame for all is cure,
> consume the cause of all disease,
> and therefore I am all at ease.

> **O Saint Germain, what love you bring,**
> **it truly makes all matter sing,**
> **your violet flame does all restore,**
> **with you we are becoming more.**

7. I call for the cutting free of the economists and other people who can tune in to Saint Germain's mind and receive the ideas and have the expertise to formulate them and to implement

them. I call for the cutting free of the people in government who can receive Saint Germain's vision for how to create an economy that is *of* the people, *by* the people and *for* the people.

> O Saint Germain, I'm karma-free,
> the past no longer burdens me,
> a brand new opportunity,
> I am in Christic unity.

> **O Saint Germain, what love you bring,**
> **it truly makes all matter sing,**
> **your violet flame does all restore,**
> **with you we are becoming more.**

8. I call forth a new awareness of Saint Germain's vision of a new type of economy that is not based on the exploitation of the people and therefore has the potential to become a truly free economy.

> O Saint Germain, we are now one,
> I am for you a violet sun,
> as we transform this planet earth,
> your Golden Age is given birth.

> **O Saint Germain, what love you bring,**
> **it truly makes all matter sing,**
> **your violet flame does all restore,**
> **with you we are becoming more.**

9. I call for the cutting free of the people who have the potential to receive the ideas for the Golden Age economy, so they can align themselves with the mind of Saint Germain and receive these ideas and have the courage to implement them.

O Saint Germain, the earth is free,
from burden of duality,
in oneness we bring what is best,
your Golden Age is manifest.

**O Saint Germain, what love you bring,
it truly makes all matter sing,
your violet flame does all restore,
with you we are becoming more.**

Sealing

In the name of the I AM THAT I AM, I accept that Archangel Michael, Astrea and Shiva form an impenetrable shield around myself and all constructive people in America, sealing us from all fear-based energies in all four octaves. I accept that the Light of God is consuming and transforming all fear-based energies that make up the dark forces working against America!

20 | WHY AMERICANS DO NOT DEMAND BETTER LEADERSHIP

I AM the Ascended Master Elohim Cyclopea. I come bearing gifts in the sense that I pledge that whatever invocations are created based on the dictations at this conference, I will multiply your calls by a considerable factor. Numbers do not really matter but you need to know that any call you give will be multiplied by me. I will do this multiplication specifically for the exposure of anything that is hidden in American society and that would not be acceptable to the American people. Therefore, my aim is to shatter this energy-veil that the fallen beings, the dark forces, the power-elite have put over America and which blinds not only the people but also the leaders so that these things can continue to go on decade after decade.

As we said with the movie industry and Washington, DC, the insiders know but very few people from the outside ever realize what is going on. Naturally, one of the consequences of this can be that more of the insiders begin to leak information, as you have already seen in several cases. You can see what an impact this has had. It has an impact that is not even seen because it goes into shifting certain people's attitude and making them realize that they cannot get away with it. The sad fact is that at the current level of consciousness on earth there are many, many people who simply need to be faced with this reality check that they cannot continue to hide what they know is wrong. It is the only way they are going to reform their actions at their level of consciousness.

How the fallen beings use the concept of sin

Now, yesterday Master MORE talked a little about the attitude that Americans have to their government and their reluctance to stand up and demand a better government. I wish to expound upon this because there is a very, very subtle dynamic that has been created by the fallen beings over a very long time. It goes much further back than even recorded history. In order to explain it, I want to start by referring to the Catholic church, who (with the help of St. Augustine who was working with fallen beings in the identity realm) introduced the concept of original sin. This is a concept that has been introduced in previous ages as well.

When you consider the fact that many, many Americans look at America as a Christian nation and look upon themselves as Christians, you can begin to see that they are very, very deeply affected by this concept of original sin. It, of course, affects people in many ways.

What I am concerned about explaining here is how the fallen beings have used this to create this very, very subtle attitude in many people that because they see themselves as sinners and therefore not being perfect, they cannot really demand that their leaders should be perfect or should live up to a higher standard than they feel they themselves can live up to. This is a dynamic that is deliberately created by the fallen beings to prevent the people from challenging the power elite in embodiment. This is not something you will even pick up, hardly at all, in written sources, books or the press.

You will hardly ever hear it in the public discourse because it is something that takes place in the minds of individuals. For many people, it even happens at subconscious levels or at barely conscious levels. They have been brought up with this idea that they are sinners. Without being aware of it, they have been programmed to think that whenever they see something that their leaders are doing that is not right, they are not allowed to speak out and demand a higher standard from their leaders because they themselves are not perfect. "I'm a sinner, so what right do I have to demand something from the politicians in Washington?"

It is this very subtle attitude that in order to criticize (and I mean this in a neutral way), in order to point out the flaws of what the fallen beings are doing, you should first be perfect because if you are not and you stand up publicly, you will be attacked. You can see this (as it happens in political circles) how, if somebody blows the whistle, what is the media and what are those affected going to do?

They are going to say: "Let's turn this man's life over and find anything we can use to blame him and discredit him. Because, if we can discredit him personally, then we have automatically (or at least they think) discredited what he is saying." How many times do you see this going on in the American media? The subtle effect of this in people's minds is that they are very reluctant to stand up and demand a better leadership. This is a consciousness that probably has more far-ranging effects than any other single characteristic that you can point out.

The pacifying mechanism

It is amazing as you look at it from my perspective. I can see, of course, from my perspective what you cannot see in the physical. I see how everything, of course, starts in the three higher realms: the identity, mental and emotional. I see how there is a physical event that takes place. It can be anything that goes on in politics that is not right. Something is exposed or somebody makes a decision that most people do not agree with and you see how there is a certain emotional reaction to this. This goes up into people's mental bodies and then it goes up into their identity bodies, and in their identity bodies there is a reaction.

Now, let us imagine that people have seen something that is not right and they are not necessarily angry about it, they are determined, clear in their minds, that this is not right and this should not be going on. This creates an emotional reaction, goes up into the mental body and then into the identity. In the identity they have a mechanism, because they identify themselves as sinners and as basically unworthy because they are not perfect in the eyes of God.

Part of this whole consciousness is, of course, the idea of the angry judgmental God that requires you to be perfect before you can go to heaven. In the identity body it is almost like this impetus that comes up is reversed where the people say: "But wait a minute, I know this isn't right but since I am a sinner and I'm not perfect either, what right do I have to demand that these people change. What right do I have to speak out?"

Now, the impulse goes back down through the mental, into the emotional and at the conscious level (without necessarily realizing what has happened), people just kind of shrug their shoulders, resign and say: "Oh well! Maybe I just shouldn't even say anything about this."

Of course, even though America is a Christian nation, not all Americans are Christians. The majority of them are and certainly the majority of them are brought up in a Christian tradition. A large majority of Americans have this very mechanism that prevents them from having that righteous indignation which is more of a clarity, a determination, to stand up and say: "This is not acceptable to us. No more of this, we have had enough of this form of leadership." That is why Americans cannot come together in a large enough group to demand changes even though there is a vast majority in America who clearly want certain changes. They are clearly experiencing that the Congress is not enacting these changes, the President is not enacting these changes. They are dissatisfied with that situation but they cannot come together precisely because so many of them feel that: "Who am I to speak out, who am I to tell the politicians what to do, I'm just a sinner." Again, for most of them it is not even conscious, it has been programmed into them, not only since childhood in this embodiment but in many previous embodiments where they have also embodied in a Christian culture. It is not my intent to say that this is the only problem that the Catholic church has created, but it is certainly one of the most severe problems that the Catholic church has created.

You all know, of course, that Jesus never talked about original sin. You must ask yourself: Why have not at least the Lutheran, protestant churches gone back and said: "This was clearly put in by the Catholic church, let us take it out." Well, they have not, my beloved, because many of the leaders of those churches are either blinded by this heavy cloud of the sinner consciousness or their minds are taken over by fallen beings in the mental or identity realm who want people to feel like sinners because that allows them to control the people.

The power elite and the abuse of the people

Do you realize how efficient of a control mechanism this is? There is no need for physical control here, people are controlling themselves. It allows the power elite in embodiment and it allows the fallen beings in higher realms to continue, not only to control the people but to continue to abuse the people.

What Saint Germain talked about (about the financial elite), this is a form of abuse. Let us not mince words about this. Taking the wealth from the people is abuse, but they get away with it time and time again because the people cannot reach that point of determination to speak out and demand better leadership.

You see, my beloved, it is necessary to make the calls that Americans are awakened to this dynamic and they are awakened to the realization that if America is to function as it was intended to function by the Constitution, by the Founding Fathers, by Saint Germain, then they have to accept that they have a right to demand that their leaders live up to a certain (I know "standard" is a difficult word to use but for practical purposes let us use it here), a certain standard of integrity and honesty and willingness to do what is in the best interest of the people rather than the best interest of the elite. These are not unreasonable demands by the American people. They are natural demands given what America has the potential to be. It is not unreasonable that the American people look at the potential for what America could be, look at what it is today and identify that there is a gap, a very large gap.

Demanding better leadership in America

This is another one of these shifts where people can wake up and say: "The emperor has nothing on." Suddenly, they see how obvious it is. They see the potential of what America *can* be, given its constitution, given its whole history of why it was created. Then, they see how far it has fallen below that potential today and they suddenly realize this is utterly and completely unacceptable. Therefore, they then have that determination to demand that their leaders either start working to close the gap or get out of the way. This is not an unreasonable reaction by the American people but they have been lulled to sleep by many things, of course, but especially by this mechanism of feeling that in order to make demands on other people, you have to be perfect yourself. If you are not, then perhaps you should hold your tongue. This is something you can make calls for.

You can make calls, of course, for the exposure of anything that is hidden, especially for the exposure of the power elite, including what is going on in the financial system, the money system. Again, we face a situation that the American economy is run by the Federal Reserve, which despite the name is not a federal institution but a collection of private banks. Still, a very large portion of Americans do not know this, do not realize this. So many Americans do not know how money is created as debt, how this creates inflation and so forth and so on. You can make the calls that people wake up and again see this, look at America's potential, look at the idea that this should be a government *of* the people, *by* the people, *for* the people, then recognize the reality that it has become a government and a financial system that is *of* the elite, *by* the elite and *for* the elite. Then, they reach that determination to say: "This cannot go on. This is enough, we have to do something about this; we have to demand something better."

The middle class has been bought

You can also make the calls that the people in America who belong to what is normally called the "middle class," will wake up and realize that they have been bought. Their silence, their consent, has been bought. Now, Master MORE talked about the consent of the governed. You actually have a rather large group of so-called middle class Americans who have, without fully realizing what they have been doing, given their consent to the current state of the economy. The reason they have done this is that they are still in that level of awareness where they are primarily focused on themselves, on their own immediate lives and they feel they have a good life. They have lived their life, they have played the corporate game or they have been in government. They have had a stable income, they have bought their houses, they have paid off their houses, they have seen their houses triple or quadruple in value, they have two cars in the garage, they have stocks, they have bonds, they have their retirement plans and they know they are taken care of with a comfortable standard of living for the rest of their lives.

They do not want to rock the boat, they do not want to lose what they have, their comfortable lifestyle. They do not want to risk anything by upsetting the financial system. They are not really concerned about the fact that the number of poor people in America is growing, that the number of homeless is growing, that those in the lower parts of the middle class are seeing their incomes reduced. They are not even noticing that their wealth has been reduced because they have enough that they are not worried about it. They feel they can be comfortable for the rest of their lives. This is, in a way, consent of the governed to status quo but is it true consent? Is it enlightened consent? Are they aware of what they are consenting to? They are not. You can make the calls that this will shift and that they will become more and more aware of what is going on.

Retirement plans guarantee the stock market

Perhaps you do not realize this, my beloved, but there was a time when people paid into a retirement plan. That plan was used to make some investments that could give people a greater return on their money. Now, why, when you think about this, do people need to have an increase in their savings so that they have enough money for when they retire? Well, the only reason for this is inflation because if there was no inflation, then the money you put into your retirement plan could buy the same in thirty years as they are buying now.

Because of inflation (and the rise in house prices is part of inflation) people cannot just put money in the bank for retirement. They are forced to go into some kind of investment scheme where they can get a higher return on their money than inflation, so that inflation does not eat up their savings. However, there were many, many years where people's retirement was only invested in so-called "safe" investments, primarily government bonds where there was a guaranteed return on the investment and there was no risk. Even if the stock market collapsed, well it would not affect the return on government bonds.

There happened a shift where now it was allowed that people's retirement money could be invested in the stock market. This has been going on for some time, to the point where many people have a considerable part (some even have all) of their retirement money invested in stocks. Well, my beloved, what happens if the stock market crashes and goes to 10,000, that the Dow Jones goes to 10,000 which is less than half of its current value? Well, those people who have their retirement money invested in the stock market will lose big, will they not?

What is the scheme behind this? Why did the fallen beings manage to get this idea through government so this was allowed? Well, you have heard the saying "too big to fail." What they want to create is an environment where, if there is a threat that they themselves could lose money, the government must step in.

You know very well that the very big investors, they make money whether the stock market goes up or down. They manipulate the market so that it goes up and then it goes down, then it goes up. You will see that they only do this within a certain range. You will see in the financial crisis of 2008 how the economy got away from them. The sub-prime mortgages, these investments and other investment schemes, they ran away from them and suddenly they faced a collapse of the entire system.

Now, they know that this could also happen with the stock market, as it happened in 1929. There could be a point where the market is in threat of total collapse. What is their plan? Their plan is that they can say to the government: "Look, this is too big to fail. Look how many millions of Americans have their retirement money invested in the stock market. You can't let this fail. You have to step in and use taxpayer money to prop up the system just like you did in 2008, otherwise the entire economy will go." In other words, the entire reason for letting the middle class invest their retirement money in the stock market is to bail out the elite, if the elite needs to be bailed out. In the meantime, they will hail the wonders of the capitalist system and say: "It's all great and the market will take care of itself." But then when the market starts to take care of *them,* they are going to say: "Bail us out!"

This cannot be allowed to stand, my beloved. It requires the middle class Americans to wake up and say: "Wait a minute, now. Do I really want my retirement plan to be dependent on something as volatile as the stock market, especially when I realize that it is manipulated by the elite and only serves to enrich the elite? Do I want to be tied to that?" They do not understand karma, I realize that, but the reality here is that the upper middle class in America are tied into the power elite even though they are not part of the power elite. I can assure you that the power elite do not give a dime about the upper middle class Americans, they would sacrifice them any day to make a profit. Unfortunately, the upper middle class Americans are beginning to feel that: "We are somebody, we are part of the elite, we matter." In reality, to the real elite, you do not matter at all. They could not care less about you losing your retirement money.

These are things that you can make calls on. It can, over time, lead to a shift, lead to an exposure. Of course, my beloved, you are not the only people who know this. There are people in the financial system, there are people in the media, there are people in universities, economists, there are people in government who realize this. What you so often see is that there is a situation where there is this cloud of energy that is blinding most people. One person here, one person there begins to see through the veil, the energy veil, and see that something is not right. But it takes time before there are so many people who see it that they finally begin to speak out. Then, when they begin to speak out, it still takes time before enough people see it that they say: "We have to do something about this."

You can, again, make the calls that these people, who are in the right position and who have the knowledge, will be willing to speak out and that more will be able to see what is actually going on so that there can be that shift in awareness. Not only will the people start demanding change, but also those who are in position to bring forth new ideas will speak out and say: "This cannot go on, we are heading for another crisis and we have to stop it before it goes too far."

How we limit our vision of what can happen

My beloved, again we are giving you some very heavy concepts to deal with. We are giving them to you because we know that when you make the calls, the call compels the answer. Again, look at Korea (but do not forget to look at the past actions of ascended master students) because I can assure you, as Mother Mary said, that without the decrees given at those many Saint Germain services, the Soviet Union would not have collapsed. Did anybody expect this? Not very many people. This shows you how, when enough people make the calls to shatter the energy veil, suddenly a change happens that very few people could even imagine.

I will ask you, as the Elohim of the Fifth Ray who deals with vision, to take a little time to ponder how you might be limiting your own vision. How you might have been brought up with certain ideas, not only in this lifetime but in many lifetimes, about what can or cannot happen. I am asking you to ponder this, ask for my guidance so you can come to see how you are limiting yourself and what you can do and what you cannot do. What you can overcome, what you can heal but also that you can actually help other people.

As was demonstrated clearly the first day when you shared your stories, many of you have gone through a process and have reached a level of awareness that is way beyond what most people have gone through. Therefore, you have something that can inspire and help other people but many times you limit yourselves in various ways by thinking that other people will not be interested, that it really is not that important. Many times you do this because again: "Who am I to speak out, I am not perfect, right?"

The Fifth Ray, the Ray of Vision, has by many people been seen as tied to perfection. The reality is that there is no state of perfection anywhere in the universe. It is the fallen beings who have created the concept of perfection as a static state that cannot change. We have said there is growth in the ascended realm. We have said that the Creator grows by all of us who are extensions of the Creator growing. There is no state of perfection to be reached, there is ongoing growth.

Ponder this in yourselves, listen to what the messenger said, that for years he had struggled with this consciousness that a spiritual teacher should be in some state of perfection. He had finally realized that what he actually wanted to do as a spiritual teacher was come out and say: "Look, I am a human being walking a path of gradually raising my consciousness. If I can teach you anything, it's not because I am perfect, it's because I have overcome some of the things that you might not yet have overcome and I can demonstrate to you how to walk that path."

All of you are capable of being teachers in the same way, regardless of your level of consciousness because it is still higher than most of the people out there or you would not be sitting here. Look at this in yourselves. Be willing to overcome it. Be willing to identify that there was a time where the fallen beings did exactly what I have described. They accused you of not being perfect and they projected, they programmed into you, that if you were not perfect, you did not have a right to speak out.

Be willing to come to the point where you identify this as a separate self. For most of you it will not be your primal self, it will be one that was created later. Come to the point where you identify it as a separate self, and in identifying it as a separate self, you have separated yourself from it. You can look at it. You can say: "You are not me, I do not want you in my life, I am letting you die." Then, when you keep working on this, you can come to (as the messenger described) that release where you feel: "Now, it's gone."

Then, you can be at peace with being who you are, being where you are on the path, not always comparing to some state of what the "perfect chela" is supposed to be like. Instead, accepting where you are and then speaking out and helping other people from that level while continuing to grow. This is all we have ever asked of our students, regardless of what culture might have existed in previous dispensations where they also had a certain obsession with this state of perfection that nobody could really define. It is so difficult to reach a goal that you cannot define, my beloved. The real goal is just to take the next step on the path. That is the hallmark of a true chela. You are always focused on taking the next step and not worrying about what lies several steps ahead.

With this, my gratitude for you setting the platform. Again, I have radiated this into the collective consciousness by magnifying it through your chakras and your attention, and for this you have my gratitude.

21 | INVOKING BETTER LEADERSHIP IN AMERICA

In the name of the I AM THAT I AM, Jesus Christ, I use the authority that I have as a being in embodiment on earth to call upon Elohim Cyclopea to reinforce my calls and use my chakras to project the statements in this invocation into the collective consciousness and awaken Americans to the determination to demand better leadership. Awaken Americans to the reality that we are spiritual beings and that we can co-create a new future by working with the ascended masters. I especially call for ...

[Make your own calls here.]

Part 1

1. I call for the exposure of anything that is hidden in American society and that would not be acceptable to the American people.

> Cyclopea so dear, the truth you reveal,
> the truth that duality's ailments will heal,
> your Emerald Light is like a great balm,
> our emotional bodies are perfectly calm.
>
> **Cyclopea so dear, in Emerald Sphere,**
> **in raising perception we shall persevere,**
> **as deep in our hearts your truth we revere,**
> **to immaculate vision the earth does adhere.**

2. I call for the shattering of the energy-veil that the fallen beings, the dark forces, the power-elite have put over America and which blinds not only the people but also the leaders so that these things can continue to go on decade after decade.

> Cyclopea so dear, with you we unwind,
> all negative spirals clouding the mind,
> we know pure awareness is truly our core,
> the key to becoming the wide-open door.
>
> **Cyclopea so dear, in Emerald Sphere,**
> **in raising perception we shall persevere,**
> **as deep in our hearts your truth we revere,**
> **to immaculate vision the earth does adhere.**

3. I call for a shattering of the deadlock where the insiders know but very few people from the outside ever realize what is going on.

> Cyclopea so dear, clear our inner sight,
> empowered, we pierce the soul's fearful night,
> we now see our life through your single eye,
> beyond all disease we're ready to fly.

**Cyclopea so dear, in Emerald Sphere,
in raising perception we shall persevere,
as deep in our hearts your truth we revere,
to immaculate vision the earth does adhere.**

4. I call forth a shift so that more of the insiders begin to leak information, causing a shift in certain people's attitude and making them realize that they cannot get away with it.

Cyclopea so dear, life can only reflect,
the images that the mind does project,
the key to our healing is clearing the mind,
from the images the ego is hiding behind.

**Cyclopea so dear, in Emerald Sphere,
in raising perception we shall persevere,
as deep in our hearts your truth we revere,
to immaculate vision the earth does adhere.**

5. I call for certain people to be faced with the reality check that they cannot continue to hide what they know is wrong.

Cyclopea so dear, we want to aim high,
to your healing flame we ever draw nigh,
through veils of duality we now take flight,
bathed in your penetrating Emerald Light.

**Cyclopea so dear, in Emerald Sphere,
in raising perception we shall persevere,
as deep in our hearts your truth we revere,
to immaculate vision the earth does adhere.**

6. I call forth an exposure of the dynamic that has been created by the fallen beings over a very long time, based on the concept of original sin.

> Cyclopea so dear, your Emerald Flame,
> exposes every subtle, dualistic power game,
> including the game of wanting to say,
> that truth is defined in only one way.
>
> **Cyclopea so dear, in Emerald Sphere,**
> **in raising perception we shall persevere,**
> **as deep in our hearts your truth we revere,**
> **to immaculate vision the earth does adhere.**

7. Many Americans are deeply affected by the concept of original sin. The fallen beings have used this to create a subtle attitude that because people see themselves as sinners, they cannot demand that their leaders should be perfect or should live up to a higher standard than they feel they themselves can live up to.

> Cyclopea so dear, we're feeling the flow,
> as your Living Truth upon us you bestow,
> from all dual vision we are now set free,
> planet earth in immaculate matrix will be.
>
> **Cyclopea so dear, in Emerald Sphere,**
> **in raising perception we shall persevere,**
> **as deep in our hearts your truth we revere,**
> **to immaculate vision the earth does adhere.**

8. This is a dynamic that is deliberately created by the fallen beings to prevent the people from challenging the power elite in embodiment.

> Cyclopea so dear, the truth is now clear,
> we see higher purpose for which we are here
> we know truth transcends all systems below,
> immersed in your light, we continue to grow.
>
> **Cyclopea so dear, in Emerald Sphere,**
> **in raising perception we shall persevere,**
> **as deep in our hearts your truth we revere,**
> **to immaculate vision the earth does adhere.**

9. For many people, this happens at subconscious levels or at barely conscious levels. They have been brought up with this idea that they are sinners, and they have been programmed to think that whenever their leaders are doing something that is not right, they are not allowed to speak out and demand a higher standard from their leaders because they themselves are not perfect.

> Cyclopea so dear, we're feeling your joy,
> as creative vision we now do employ,
> in lifting earth out of serpentine cage,
> to manifest Saint Germain's Golden Age.
>
> **Cyclopea so dear, in Emerald Sphere,**
> **in raising perception we shall persevere,**
> **as deep in our hearts your truth we revere,**
> **to immaculate vision the earth does adhere.**

Part 2

1. I call for the shattering of the attitude that in order to point out the flaws of what the fallen beings are doing, we should first be perfect because if we are not and we stand up publicly, we will be attacked.

> Cyclopea so dear, the truth you reveal,
> the truth that duality's ailments will heal,
> your Emerald Light is like a great balm,
> our emotional bodies are perfectly calm.

> **Cyclopea so dear, in Emerald Sphere,**
> **in raising perception we shall persevere,**
> **as deep in our hearts your truth we revere,**
> **to immaculate vision the earth does adhere.**

2. I call for the binding of the demons that are behind the phenomenon where any individual that exposes the elite will be scrutinized and psychologically or physically killed by the system.

> Cyclopea so dear, with you we unwind,
> all negative spirals clouding the mind,
> we know pure awareness is truly our core,
> the key to becoming the wide-open door.

> **Cyclopea so dear, in Emerald Sphere,**
> **in raising perception we shall persevere,**
> **as deep in our hearts your truth we revere,**
> **to immaculate vision the earth does adhere.**

3. I call for the shattering of the mechanism that makes Americans reluctant to stand up and demand better leadership. I call for the exposure of the far-ranging effects of this consciousness.

> Cyclopea so dear, clear our inner sight,
> empowered, we pierce the soul's fearful night,
> we now see our life through your single eye,
> beyond all disease we're ready to fly.
>
> **Cyclopea so dear, in Emerald Sphere,**
> **in raising perception we shall persevere,**
> **as deep in our hearts your truth we revere,**
> **to immaculate vision the earth does adhere.**

4. I call for the shattering of the mechanism in the identity bodies of Americans that causes them to identify themselves as sinners or as not being perfect, making them reluctant to speak out when their leaders do something that is not right.

> Cyclopea so dear, life can only reflect,
> the images that the mind does project,
> the key to our healing is clearing the mind,
> from the images the ego is hiding behind.
>
> **Cyclopea so dear, in Emerald Sphere,**
> **in raising perception we shall persevere,**
> **as deep in our hearts your truth we revere,**
> **to immaculate vision the earth does adhere.**

5. I call for the shattering of the consciousness of the angry judgmental God that requires us to be perfect before we can go to heaven.

Cyclopea so dear, we want to aim high,
to your healing flame we ever draw nigh,
through veils of duality we now take flight,
bathed in your penetrating Emerald Light.

**Cyclopea so dear, in Emerald Sphere,
in raising perception we shall persevere,
as deep in our hearts your truth we revere,
to immaculate vision the earth does adhere.**

6. I call for Americans to be cut free from the mechanism that prevents us from having a righteous indignation, the clarity, and determination to stand up and say: "This is not acceptable to us. No more of this, we have had enough of this form of leadership."

Cyclopea so dear, your Emerald Flame,
exposes every subtle, dualistic power game,
including the game of wanting to say,
that truth is defined in only one way.

**Cyclopea so dear, in Emerald Sphere,
in raising perception we shall persevere,
as deep in our hearts your truth we revere,
to immaculate vision the earth does adhere.**

7. A majority in America want certain changes. They are experiencing that the Congress and the President are not enacting these changes. They are dissatisfied with that situation but they cannot come together precisely because so many of us feel that: "Who am I to speak out, who am I to tell the politicians what to do, I'm just a sinner."

Cyclopea so dear, we're feeling the flow,
as your Living Truth upon us you bestow,
from all dual vision we are now set free,
planet earth in immaculate matrix will be.

**Cyclopea so dear, in Emerald Sphere,
in raising perception we shall persevere,
as deep in our hearts your truth we revere,
to immaculate vision the earth does adhere.**

8. I call forth the judgment of Christ upon this mechanism that has been programmed into Americans by a Christian culture. I call forth the judgment of Christ upon the Catholic church for creating, spreading and upholding this consciousness.

Cyclopea so dear, the truth is now clear,
we see higher purpose for which we are here
we know truth transcends all systems below,
immersed in your light, we continue to grow.

**Cyclopea so dear, in Emerald Sphere,
in raising perception we shall persevere,
as deep in our hearts your truth we revere,
to immaculate vision the earth does adhere.**

9. I call for the judgment of Christ upon the Christian leaders who are either blinded by this heavy cloud of the sinner consciousness or whose minds are taken over by fallen beings in the mental or identity realms who want people to feel like sinners because that allows them to control the people.

Cyclopea so dear, we're feeling your joy,
as creative vision we now do employ,

in lifting earth out of serpentine cage,
to manifest Saint Germain's Golden Age.

**Cyclopea so dear, in Emerald Sphere,
in raising perception we shall persevere,
as deep in our hearts your truth we revere,
to immaculate vision the earth does adhere.**

Part 3

1. This is a very efficient control mechanism. There is no need for physical control, people are controlling themselves. It allows the power elite in embodiment and it allows the fallen beings in higher realms to continue to control the people and to abuse the people.

Cyclopea so dear, the truth you reveal,
the truth that duality's ailments will heal,
your Emerald Light is like a great balm,
our emotional bodies are perfectly calm.

**Cyclopea so dear, in Emerald Sphere,
in raising perception we shall persevere,
as deep in our hearts your truth we revere,
to immaculate vision the earth does adhere.**

2. The financial elite are exposing people to a form of abuse. Taking the wealth from the people is abuse, but they get away with it time and time again because the people cannot reach that point of determination to speak out and demand better leadership.

21 | Invoking better leadership in America

Cyclopea so dear, with you we unwind,
all negative spirals clouding the mind,
we know pure awareness is truly our core,
the key to becoming the wide-open door.

**Cyclopea so dear, in Emerald Sphere,
in raising perception we shall persevere,
as deep in our hearts your truth we revere,
to immaculate vision the earth does adhere.**

3. I call for Americans to be awakened to this dynamic and the realization that if America is to function as it was intended to function by the Constitution, by the Founding Fathers, by Saint Germain, then we have to demand that our leaders live up to a certain standard of integrity and honesty.

Cyclopea so dear, clear our inner sight,
empowered, we pierce the soul's fearful night,
we now see our life through your single eye,
beyond all disease we're ready to fly.

**Cyclopea so dear, in Emerald Sphere,
in raising perception we shall persevere,
as deep in our hearts your truth we revere,
to immaculate vision the earth does adhere.**

4. The American people have a right to demand that our leaders have a willingness to do what is in the best interest of the people rather than the best interest of the elite.

Cyclopea so dear, life can only reflect,
the images that the mind does project,

the key to our healing is clearing the mind,
from the images the ego is hiding behind.

**Cyclopea so dear, in Emerald Sphere,
in raising perception we shall persevere,
as deep in our hearts your truth we revere,
to immaculate vision the earth does adhere.**

5. These are not unreasonable demands by the American people. They are natural demands given what America has the potential to be. It is not unreasonable that the American people look at the potential for what America could be, look at what it is today and identify that there is a very large gap.

Cyclopea so dear, we want to aim high,
to your healing flame we ever draw nigh,
through veils of duality we now take flight,
bathed in your penetrating Emerald Light.

**Cyclopea so dear, in Emerald Sphere,
in raising perception we shall persevere,
as deep in our hearts your truth we revere,
to immaculate vision the earth does adhere.**

6. I call forth a shift where people can wake up and see the potential of what America *can* be, given its constitution, given its history of why it was created. Then, we see how far it has fallen below that potential today and we realize this is utterly and completely unacceptable.

Cyclopea so dear, your Emerald Flame,
exposes every subtle, dualistic power game,

including the game of wanting to say,
that truth is defined in only one way.

**Cyclopea so dear, in Emerald Sphere,
in raising perception we shall persevere,
as deep in our hearts your truth we revere,
to immaculate vision the earth does adhere.**

7. I call for Americans to have the determination to demand that our leaders either start working to close the gap or get out of the way. This is not an unreasonable reaction by the American people but we have been lulled to sleep by this mechanism of feeling that in order to make demands on other people, we have to be perfect ourselves.

Cyclopea so dear, we're feeling the flow,
as your Living Truth upon us you bestow,
from all dual vision we are now set free,
planet earth in immaculate matrix will be.

**Cyclopea so dear, in Emerald Sphere,
in raising perception we shall persevere,
as deep in our hearts your truth we revere,
to immaculate vision the earth does adhere.**

8. I call for the exposure of anything that is hidden, especially for the exposure of the power elite, including what is going on in the financial system, the money system. I call for the exposure of the fact that the American economy is run by the Federal Reserve, which is not a federal institution but a collection of private banks.

Cyclopea so dear, the truth is now clear,
we see higher purpose for which we are here
we know truth transcends all systems below,
immersed in your light, we continue to grow.

**Cyclopea so dear, in Emerald Sphere,
in raising perception we shall persevere,
as deep in our hearts your truth we revere,
to immaculate vision the earth does adhere.**

9. I call for an awakening of Americans to how money is created as debt and how this creates inflation.

Cyclopea so dear, we're feeling your joy,
as creative vision we now do employ,
in lifting earth out of serpentine cage,
to manifest Saint Germain's Golden Age.

**Cyclopea so dear, in Emerald Sphere,
in raising perception we shall persevere,
as deep in our hearts your truth we revere,
to immaculate vision the earth does adhere.**

Part 4

1. I call for Americans to be awakened to the reality that we have a government and a financial system that is *of* the elite, *by* the elite and *for* the elite. I call for people to reach the determination: "This cannot go on. This is enough, we have to do something about this; we have to demand something better."

21 | Invoking better leadership in America

> Cyclopea so dear, the truth you reveal,
> the truth that duality's ailments will heal,
> your Emerald Light is like a great balm,
> our emotional bodies are perfectly calm.

> **Cyclopea so dear, in Emerald Sphere,**
> **in raising perception we shall persevere,**
> **as deep in our hearts your truth we revere,**
> **to immaculate vision the earth does adhere.**

2. I call for those Americans who belong to the "middle class" to wake up and realize that we have been bought. Our silence, our consent, has been bought.

> Cyclopea so dear, with you we unwind,
> all negative spirals clouding the mind,
> we know pure awareness is truly our core,
> the key to becoming the wide-open door.

> **Cyclopea so dear, in Emerald Sphere,**
> **in raising perception we shall persevere,**
> **as deep in our hearts your truth we revere,**
> **to immaculate vision the earth does adhere.**

3. We have a large group of so-called middle class Americans who have given their consent to the current state of the economy. The reason they have done this is that they are still in that level of awareness where they are primarily focused on themselves, on their own immediate lives.

> Cyclopea so dear, clear our inner sight,
> empowered, we pierce the soul's fearful night,

we now see our life through your single eye,
beyond all disease we're ready to fly.

**Cyclopea so dear, in Emerald Sphere,
in raising perception we shall persevere,
as deep in our hearts your truth we revere,
to immaculate vision the earth does adhere.**

4. I call for the awakening of those who have lived their lives, they have played the corporate game or they have been in government. They have had a stable income, they have bought their houses, they have paid off their houses, they have seen their houses triple or quadruple in value, they have stocks and bonds, they have their retirement plans.

Cyclopea so dear, life can only reflect,
the images that the mind does project,
the key to our healing is clearing the mind,
from the images the ego is hiding behind.

**Cyclopea so dear, in Emerald Sphere,
in raising perception we shall persevere,
as deep in our hearts your truth we revere,
to immaculate vision the earth does adhere.**

5. I call for an awakening of those who are comfortable and do not want to rock the boat, do not want to risk anything by upsetting the financial system. Yet they are not noticing that their wealth has been reduced because they have enough that they are not worried about it.

Cyclopea so dear, we want to aim high,
to your healing flame we ever draw nigh,

through veils of duality we now take flight,
bathed in your penetrating Emerald Light.

**Cyclopea so dear, in Emerald Sphere,
in raising perception we shall persevere,
as deep in our hearts your truth we revere,
to immaculate vision the earth does adhere.**

6. From the middle class, there is consent of the governed to status quo but is it true consent? Is it enlightened consent? Are they aware of what they are consenting to? I call forth a shift so they will become aware of what is going on.

Cyclopea so dear, your Emerald Flame,
exposes every subtle, dualistic power game,
including the game of wanting to say,
that truth is defined in only one way.

**Cyclopea so dear, in Emerald Sphere,
in raising perception we shall persevere,
as deep in our hearts your truth we revere,
to immaculate vision the earth does adhere.**

7. I call forth an awakening to the fact that the only reason people need to invest in retirement plans is because of inflation. If there was no inflation, then the money we put into our retirement plan could buy the same in thirty years as they are buying now.

Cyclopea so dear, we're feeling the flow,
as your Living Truth upon us you bestow,
from all dual vision we are now set free,
planet earth in immaculate matrix will be.

> **Cyclopea so dear, in Emerald Sphere,**
> **in raising perception we shall persevere,**
> **as deep in our hearts your truth we revere,**
> **to immaculate vision the earth does adhere.**

8. Because of inflation (and the rise in house prices is part of inflation) people cannot just put money in the bank for retirement. We are forced to go into some kind of investment scheme where we can get a higher return on our money than inflation.

> Cyclopea so dear, the truth is now clear,
> we see higher purpose for which we are here
> we know truth transcends all systems below,
> immersed in your light, we continue to grow.

> **Cyclopea so dear, in Emerald Sphere,**
> **in raising perception we shall persevere,**
> **as deep in our hearts your truth we revere,**
> **to immaculate vision the earth does adhere.**

9. I call forth an awakening to the fact that if the stock market collapsed, those people who have their retirement money invested in the stock market will lose big. The fallen beings managed to get the government to accept this form of investment because they want to create an environment where, if there is a threat that they themselves could lose money, the government must step in.

> Cyclopea so dear, we're feeling your joy,
> as creative vision we now do employ,
> in lifting earth out of serpentine cage,
> to manifest Saint Germain's Golden Age.

**Cyclopea so dear, in Emerald Sphere,
in raising perception we shall persevere,
as deep in our hearts your truth we revere,
to immaculate vision the earth does adhere.**

Part 5

1. If there is a situation where the market is in threat of total collapse, the big investors will say to the government: "This is too big to fail. Look how many millions of Americans have their retirement money invested in the stock market. You must use taxpayer money to prop up the system, otherwise the entire economy will go."

Raphael Archangel, your light so intense,
raise us beyond all human pretense.
Mother Mary and you have a vision so bold,
to see that our highest potential unfold.

**Raphael Archangel, for vision we pray,
Raphael Archangel, show us the way,
Raphael Archangel, your emerald ray,
Raphael Archangel, our lives a new day.**

2. The entire reason for letting the middle class invest their retirement money in the stock market is to bail out the elite, if the elite needs to be bailed out. In the meantime, they will hail the wonders of the capitalist system and say: "It's all great and the market will take care of itself."

Raphael Archangel, in emerald sphere,
to immaculate vision we always adhere.
Mother Mary enfolds us in her Sacred Heart,
from Mother's true love, we're never apart.

Raphael Archangel, for vision we pray,
Raphael Archangel, show us the way,
Raphael Archangel, your emerald ray,
Raphael Archangel, our lives a new day.

3. When the market starts to take care of *them*, they are going to say: "Bail us out!" I call for the middle class Americans to wake up and say: "Do I really want my retirement plan to be dependent on something as volatile as the stock market, especially when I realize that it is manipulated by the elite and only serves to enrich the elite?"

Raphael Archangel, all ailments you heal,
each cell in our bodies in light now you seal.
Mother Mary's immaculate concept we see,
perfection of health our new reality.

Raphael Archangel, for vision we pray,
Raphael Archangel, show us the way,
Raphael Archangel, your emerald ray,
Raphael Archangel, our lives a new day.

4. The upper middle class in America are tied into the power elite even though they are not part of the power elite. The power elite do not give a dime about the upper middle class Americans, they would sacrifice them any day to make a profit.

> Raphael Archangel, your light is so real,
> the vision of Christ in us you reveal.
> Mother Mary now helps us to truly transcend,
> in emerald light with you we ascend.
>
> **Raphael Archangel, for vision we pray,**
> **Raphael Archangel, show us the way,**
> **Raphael Archangel, your emerald ray,**
> **Raphael Archangel, our lives a new day.**

5. The upper middle class Americans are beginning to feel that: "We are somebody, we are part of the elite, we matter." In reality, to the real elite, they do not matter at all. The elite could not care less about people losing their retirement money.

> Raphael Archangel, diseases are done,
> as you help us see that all life is One,
> we no longer do your true love reject,
> immaculate vision on all we project.
>
> **Raphael Archangel, for vision we pray,**
> **Raphael Archangel, show us the way,**
> **Raphael Archangel, your emerald ray,**
> **Raphael Archangel, our lives a new day.**

6. I call for the people in the financial system, in the media, in universities and in government to be cut free from this cloud of energy that is blinding most people.

> Raphael Archangel, we're healing the earth,
> in immaculate vision we give her rebirth,
> a new era has on this day begun,
> your emerald light now shines like a sun.

**Raphael Archangel, for vision we pray,
Raphael Archangel, show us the way,
Raphael Archangel, your emerald ray,
Raphael Archangel, our lives a new day.**

7. I call for the cutting free of the people who can see through the energy veil, and see that something is not right. I call for them to be cut free to speak out. I call for a critical mass of Americans to see this and decide: "We have to do something about this."

Raphael Archangel, the fall is behind,
as all of earth's people the Christ path do find,
we call now to you all people to heal,
as four lower bodies in love you do seal.

**Raphael Archangel, for vision we pray,
Raphael Archangel, show us the way,
Raphael Archangel, your emerald ray,
Raphael Archangel, our lives a new day.**

8. I call for the people who are in the right positions and who have the knowledge, to be willing to speak out so that more will be able to see what is actually going on and bring about a shift in awareness.

Raphael Archangel, as you bring the light,
the forces of darkness swiftly take flight,
their day is now done as we claim the earth,
spreading to all an innocent mirth.

**Raphael Archangel, for vision we pray,
Raphael Archangel, show us the way,**

**Raphael Archangel, your emerald ray,
Raphael Archangel, our lives a new day.**

9. I call for the cutting free of Americans to demand change. I call for the cutting free of those who are in positions to bring forth new ideas to speak out and say: "This cannot go on, we are heading for another crisis and we have to stop it before it goes too far."

Raphael Archangel, our vision set free,
as we can now see God's reality,
as Saint Germain's vision is manifest here,
the earth is now sealed in immaculate sphere.

**Raphael Archangel, for vision we pray,
Raphael Archangel, show us the way,
Raphael Archangel, your emerald ray,
Raphael Archangel, our lives a new day.**

Part 6

1. I call for the cutting free of all who have been brought up with certain ideas, not only in this lifetime but in many lifetimes, about what can or cannot happen.

Raphael Archangel, your light so intense,
raise us beyond all human pretense.
Mother Mary and you have a vision so bold,
to see that our highest potential unfold.

**Raphael Archangel, for vision we pray,
Raphael Archangel, show us the way,
Raphael Archangel, your emerald ray,
Raphael Archangel, our lives a new day.**

2. Cyclopea, I call for you to help all Americans see how we are limiting ourselves. Help us see what we can do and what we cannot do, what we can overcome, what we can heal and how we can help other people.

Raphael Archangel, in emerald sphere,
to immaculate vision we always adhere.
Mother Mary enfolds us in her Sacred Heart,
from Mother's true love, we're never apart.

**Raphael Archangel, for vision we pray,
Raphael Archangel, show us the way,
Raphael Archangel, your emerald ray,
Raphael Archangel, our lives a new day.**

3. The reality is that there is no state of perfection anywhere in the universe. It is the fallen beings who have created the concept of perfection as a static state that cannot change. There is no state of perfection to be reached, there is ongoing growth.

Raphael Archangel, all ailments you heal,
each cell in our bodies in light now you seal.
Mother Mary's immaculate concept we see,
perfection of health our new reality.

**Raphael Archangel, for vision we pray,
Raphael Archangel, show us the way,**

**Raphael Archangel, your emerald ray,
Raphael Archangel, our lives a new day.**

4. I call for the cutting free of all those who are capable of being teachers in any field of life and help raise the awareness of Americans.

Raphael Archangel, your light is so real,
the vision of Christ in us you reveal.
Mother Mary now helps us to truly transcend,
in emerald light with you we ascend.

**Raphael Archangel, for vision we pray,
Raphael Archangel, show us the way,
Raphael Archangel, your emerald ray,
Raphael Archangel, our lives a new day.**

5. I call for all potential teachers to be cut free from the programming that if we are not perfect, we do not have a right to speak out.

Raphael Archangel, diseases are done,
as you help us see that all life is One,
we no longer do your true love reject,
immaculate vision on all we project.

**Raphael Archangel, for vision we pray,
Raphael Archangel, show us the way,
Raphael Archangel, your emerald ray,
Raphael Archangel, our lives a new day.**

6. Cyclopea, help all potential teachers identify this as a separate self and see that they can just let it die. They do not have

to live up to any standard of perfection before they can speak out about how to improve America.

> Raphael Archangel, we're healing the earth,
> in immaculate vision we give her rebirth,
> a new era has on this day begun,
> your emerald light now shines like a sun.
>
> **Raphael Archangel, for vision we pray,**
> **Raphael Archangel, show us the way,**
> **Raphael Archangel, your emerald ray,**
> **Raphael Archangel, our lives a new day.**

7. Cyclopea, help all potential teachers be at peace with being who they are, being where they are on the path, not always comparing to some state of what the "perfect person" is supposed to be like.

> Raphael Archangel, the fall is behind,
> as all of earth's people the Christ path do find,
> we call now to you all people to heal,
> as four lower bodies in love you do seal.
>
> **Raphael Archangel, for vision we pray,**
> **Raphael Archangel, show us the way,**
> **Raphael Archangel, your emerald ray,**
> **Raphael Archangel, our lives a new day.**

8. Cyclopea, help all potential teachers accept where they are on the path, and then speaking out and helping other people from that level while continuing to grow.

> Raphael Archangel, as you bring the light,
> the forces of darkness swiftly take flight,
> their day is now done as we claim the earth,
> spreading to all an innocent mirth.
>
> **Raphael Archangel, for vision we pray,**
> **Raphael Archangel, show us the way,**
> **Raphael Archangel, your emerald ray,**
> **Raphael Archangel, our lives a new day.**

9. Cyclopea, help all potential teachers overcome all obsession with this state of perfection that nobody can define. Therefore, we have a right to demand better leadership in America, even thought we are not perfect or at the highest level of awareness. For our level of awareness is still higher than that of the power elite.

> Raphael Archangel, our vision set free,
> as we can now see God's reality,
> as Saint Germain's vision is manifest here,
> the earth is now sealed in immaculate sphere.
>
> **Raphael Archangel, for vision we pray,**
> **Raphael Archangel, show us the way,**
> **Raphael Archangel, your emerald ray,**
> **Raphael Archangel, our lives a new day.**

Sealing

In the name of the I AM THAT I AM, I accept that Archangel Michael, Astrea and Shiva form an impenetrable shield around myself and all constructive people in America, sealing us from

all fear-based energies in all four octaves. I accept that the Light of God is consuming and transforming all fear-based energies that make up the dark forces working against America!

22 | THE POWER ELITE AND AMERICAN FOREIGN POLICY

I AM the Ascended Master Saint Germain, and I wish to give you one more discourse because we have talked about the internal state of America, but naturally we also need to talk about America's role in the world.

The fallen beings are clever. They always manage to find something that appeals to the people and they use it for their own ends. What appeals to Americans? Freedom! It is one of the themes for the founding of this nation, and many Americans have a freedom flame they carry with them, a sense of what freedom is and this is very strong in Americans. We have talked a little bit about the difference between a communist society and America. In a communist society, the people who survived did not have a strong freedom flame or they would not have survived. I am not saying this to blame anybody but just to show the contrast.

Capitalism and communism have the same goal

What you have in America is that you have many people who have a strong dedication to freedom and how do the fallen beings pervert this? They pervert it (in a sense) from the very beginning of the creed: "Give me liberty or give me death." They are saying: "Are you willing to die for the cause of freedom?"

Over the centuries that America has existed, many people have been willing to die for what they thought was the cause of freedom. We need to recognize the very fact that the power elite, and the fallen beings behind them, have an agenda, they have a very clear agenda. We have said it before, but I will repeat it here (so it can be part of the calls in the invocation made) that capitalism and communism are simply two different ways of achieving the same goal, namely a society that is completely controlled by the fallen beings through a power elite in embodiment. In a communist system, from the very beginning there is one entity that owns all property and all means of production, namely the state.

In a capitalist system, it seems as if there are many different owners of the means of production and there is the illusion that anybody can start a new business. The reality is that if you take capitalism to its ultimate conclusion, you will see, what you are already seeing now, that instead of a multitude of small independent businesses run by one person (maybe employing a few people but staying at a human scale where the individual matters), what you see is the emergence of corporations that very quickly become so big that they lose that human scale. They lose humanity because suddenly the workers do not matter anymore. It is only the leaders, and in many cases those leaders are not even involved with the business. They are stockholders, shareholders, they are board members that are not directly doing the work. What you have seen is the emergence of these corporations that are based on a completely narcissistic philosophy and attitude. They have no allegiance whatsoever to the people who are doing the actual work, not even to those who are the leaders but only to those who are the owners and the hidden power elite behind them.

Multinational corporations and foreign policy

There came a point when these corporations had become so large in America that they started looking outside of America to find new markets. They went international and multinational, if you will. Ever since that happened, you have seen these corporations try to extend their reach further and further around the globe. You have seen them become larger and larger, you have seen them fight with each other but you have also seen them merge into larger and larger entities. If you take capitalism to its logical conclusion, there will come a point where one corporation has now destroyed all competition and therefore we have a situation just like in a communist system where one entity owns or controls all means of production. It may not technically be the state, but if one corporation owns all means of production, it will also own the state, de facto. Capitalism and communism are two systems defined by the fallen beings to, in different ways, reach the same end, with a completely centralized system controlled by the fallen beings.

What does this have to do with American foreign policy? If you look at the constitution, it is very, very clear that the government is supposed to maintain an army for the common defense. In other words, the American armed forces constitutionally have only one role: to defend the *people* of America. What have you instead seen? You have seen that to an increasing degree, America's armed forces have been used to fight battles and wars in foreign countries. This is not according to the constitution. What has been the reason, the justification given for why you send American soldiers to foreign lands, to shed their blood there when it is not what is defined in the constitution as the purpose of the American armed forces? Well, the excuse has always been "to defend freedom."

The excuse for sacrificing American soldiers

For many years it was communism, but if communism is a system created by the fallen beings and it stands to reason that they are good at using the dualistic consciousness, so this was simply an excuse for getting American soldiers to give their lives. It was getting America built up to a point where it was starting to use its armed forces to extend power beyond American borders, something the constitution does not actually allow for. The reality here is that the fallen beings have used communism as an excuse for putting America in the mindset that the American people are willing to accept that their sons primarily, now also daughters, go abroad and give their lives for a seemingly just cause.

Now, I know you can argue that communism, the Soviet Union especially, was a real threat to the freedom of the rest of the world. It is reasonable to say that there was a point where the fallen beings had created these two systems, communism and capitalism, and they did not know which of the two would win dominion over the planet. They did not care because either way they would have been in control. For them it was simply a matter of creating the two systems, pitting them against each other and then saying: "Which one is going to win?" I know that many Americans will say: "But certainly, communism was the worst possible system" and why do they say this? Because they have the strong freedom flame. I very well understand this. I am in no way criticizing this or putting it down. I am simply pointing out the mechanism. Communism was a system that in a very obvious way repressed freedom. Therefore, those who have the freedom flame say: "It was certainly better that communism didn't take over the world and therefore it was necessary that America fought communism, to prevent them from taking over the world."

We have given teachings, Jesus has given some very, very profound teachings, on the fact that there can be times where there is such an unbalanced condition in the world that even something that is clearly unbalanced can still help bring the world forward. Yes, there was a time where it was the lesser of two evils that communism did not take over the world. What Americans fail to realize, and what you can make the calls to help them see, is that the fact that communism collapsed does not mean that we are now in the clear and now we have freedom in America or throughout the world. What Americans need to see – and they need to use their freedom flame to see this – is that capitalism is not a system that gives freedom to the people. It just takes that freedom away in a more subtle, hidden way than did communism.

Capitalism also takes away freedom

It is critically important that Americans begin to see this because otherwise they will not be able to shed the yoke that the power elite has brought upon this nation. Therefore, it is also necessary to make the calls for the exposure of the very fact that America's armed forces – America's soldiers – have in many cases not fought for the cause of freedom, they have fought for the power elite, they have fought for the cause of the power elite. It is necessary to call for the exposure of all of these incidents where, either the armed forces in an overt way or the CIA or other secret forces in a covert way, have extended influence, tried to overthrow governments in other nations. This was not done for the cause of freedom, it was done for the cause of allowing these multinational corporations to extend their reach, to capture new markets, to put themselves in monopoly positions in those markets.

It is necessary to recognize that there are people in other nations who have criticized America precisely for this point. It is necessary to recognize that although they sometimes come from an unbalanced perspective and do not have the best interests of America at heart, there is a point to their criticism. It is by no means according to the Constitution nor is it according to the freedom flame that many Americans have, that American sons and daughters are shedding their blood to extend the reach of multinational corporations that have no loyalty to America or to the American people. It is simply an outrage that has been going on for far too long. Once again, those inside the system know very well what is going on but nobody is talking, and that is why there is this cloud of silence again, this cloud of darkness, this energy veil that prevents the American people from reaching that awareness where they can say: "This is unacceptable and we will no longer stand for it."

Do you see what I am saying here? The fallen beings have taken the primary characteristics of the American people – the freedom flame – they have created the illusion that it is America's role in the world to spread, as a former president said, "freedom and democracy." They have used Americans' freedom flame to get Americans to be willing to sacrifice their lives or the lives of their children for this cause, but it is not the cause of freedom and democracy and certainly not in all cases. It is in many cases the cause of the power elite wanting to extend their power, wanting to spread the capitalist system, which is a system set up only *by* the elite, *for* the elite.

Again, I look for you to make the calls, to educate yourselves and to hold the vision. Again, I am not telling you this – I know it is a heavy topic – but I am not telling you this to make you feel depressed or powerless or hopeless. I am telling you this because I know that by making the calls and raising your own consciousness, you can pull up the collective and work towards this shift where, again, it just becomes obvious to people that this has been going on and this cannot be allowed to go on.

In other words, it is, again, a matter of realizing that there is a huge gap between the public perception that has been created about America's role in the world and what is actually going on in the hidden corridors of power. The people who are in those corridors of power have a completely different way of looking at it. They have a completely different agenda than what you see in the public facade. When Americans begin to see this gap, they will have that freedom flame that says: "This isn't right, we will not accept it anymore" and therefore it is necessary to call for the exposure of this.

Loyalty to the power elite is not patriotism

My beloved, we need to talk about a topic here that hardly anyone has ever even considered. Americans have been brought up – and this is another perversion of the freedom flame – with this sense of loyalty to America, which they see as patriotism. This has been used very cleverly by the fallen beings to make many Americans feel that you cannot really criticize America. You heard Cyclopea talk about this mechanism of where you feel like a sinner and therefore you cannot criticize the elite. Another perversion of this is this sense of patriotism where many people feel that in order to be a patriot and be loyal to the country, you cannot criticize America. You especially cannot criticize the foreign policy and especially not the military policy.

In other words, when a President says: "We are going to war in Iraq," a true patriot cannot object to this. This prevents Americans from seeing what I am talking about, what is going on behind the scenes. It prevents them from seeing the hidden agenda. Many people, many Americans, also feel that other countries are overly critical of America.

In order to be loyal to America, they cannot take a neutral, objective look at this criticism and say: "Wait a minute, do they have a point? When they say that America is interfering with their domestic policy, is it actually true? Are we actually doing that? Are we actually seeking to control other governments?" You have the outrage about Russia seeking to interfere with American elections, but is America doing something similar in a covert manner and have they been doing this for decades? "Have we actively overthrown governments?"

You have the concept of a banana republic and you all know what the CIA has been doing in some of these banana republics. Take that to an even greater scale and see that America – behind the scenes – has created an entire task force that is not known to the public, that is dedicated to controlling governments in other countries, totally against the free will of the people. Some of these countries are democracies but America wants to make sure that the people vote the way that they see as being in America's interests. Is this really what the Constitution is all about? Is this really what the freedom flame supports? You may say: "Oh, it's in the best interests of these people," but what I am saying is: "Consider whether it really is in the best interests of the people or the best interests of the elite."

What I am trying to point out here is that Americans need to step back and ask the question: "Is American foreign policy always in alignment with the freedom flame we have in our hearts?" Is the American foreign policy motivated by (dedicated to) the cause of freedom? "Are we really fighting for the cause of freedom or are we actually being abused by the power elite to fight for the cause of anti-freedom, the cause of the elite?" This is why we need to talk about this topic, as I said, hardly anybody talks about.

Acknowledging problems is not unpatriotic

Is there a mechanism in the American psyche that actually prevents America from becoming a truly free country? The mechanism is that the American people, through this indoctrination about being patriots, have been blocked from taking an objective, neutral look at America, American institutions, American foreign policy. They have been indoctrinated that it is unpatriotic to criticize America. Therefore, there are many, many Americans who are actually resisting the exposure of how the power elite is manipulating them. They feel they have to be loyal to the nation and in order to be loyal to the nation, they feel they have to uphold the image that America is the greatest nation on earth and that America is always dedicated to the cause of freedom.

My beloved, if America is driven by a hidden agenda that is the antithesis to the cause of freedom, how can it be wrong to acknowledge that and therefore correct the situation and bring America and America's foreign policy back in alignment with the cause of freedom, which is also bringing it into alignment with the mind of Saint Germain? In other words, what are you truly loyal to? Are you loyal to the outer facade, the illusion created by the power elite? Or are you loyal to the freedom flame and the cause of freedom? What does it mean to be an American, what does it mean to be a patriot? It does not – in my view, in my mind – mean to be loyal to the power elite and the illusions they have created.

It is far better to acknowledge that America has gone off track in a certain area, to openly acknowledge it. This is not a criticism of America. It is a criticism of the power elite that is manipulating America and *that* is not unpatriotic in my book, neither is it unamerican in my book. It is not unamerican to say: "We are off course, we need to come back on the right course." Openly acknowledging the problems and course correcting, that is in my book truly American, truly patriotic and a true expression of the freedom flame that people have in their hearts. Allowing the power elite to manipulate you into this false loyalty is in fact unamerican, unpatriotic and anti-freedom. That, my beloved, was a message that many Americans do not want to hear. When you make the calls for a shift in the collective consciousness, there will, I do not say there *can,* I am saying that there *will* come that point where there is a shift and more and more Americans begin to see the reality of what I have just spoken in the physical for the first time in the history of this nation.

Therefore, my gratitude for you being willing to be the electrodes for the broadcast of this message. My gratitude for you being willing to come here for this entire conference, for you being willing to walk the path, overcome the issues in your own psychology so that you can come to that point of having attained that neutral state of mind where you are the open doors, nothing less, nothing more, just the open door because you have no agenda. There is nothing, as the messenger has said, that you *have* to do on this planet other than being the open doors for your I AM Presence and the ascended masters and also allowing yourself to enjoy life on earth.

It is not a sin to enjoy life

It is, as you just talked about, not a sin to be in a physical body, to be in physical embodiment and to enjoy the enjoyable aspects of life on earth. In fact, we might say that for the raising of the collective consciousness, it is necessary that there are some spiritual people who allow themselves to enjoy life on earth. Not in a hedonistic way but actually by making peace with being on earth, a topic we will talk about at our next conference.

You see that one thing leads to another because whereas you might from your perspective see that: "Oh now we have released one book and we had one conference," we of course have a broader perspective where we see how everything fits together and one thing leads to the next. Allow yourselves to feel that you are part of that chain of events, you are part of that flow of the River of Life. Perhaps, even make a little effort to look at the teachings we have given and allow yourselves to accept that you are flowing with the River of Life when you are walking the path, taking one step at a time.

It is not, my beloved, so much (and this is an illusion held by many spiritual people) that you are taking outer measures, walking step-by-step towards this humongous breakthrough where you will suddenly be enlightened and see everything in a different light. The breakthrough that really happens is when you come to the point of accepting yourself at your present level. You know that this will not make you stop growing, you will still continue to take one step at a time but you are no longer waiting for the breakthrough. You are accepting your present position in the River of Life, enjoying that and enjoying knowing that you will flow on. You are not in that deficit mode of waiting for something in the future. You are accepting the now and flowing with that.

This is what we desire to see for you, and it will happen only when you deal with the birth trauma, the primal self and these other selves that keep you from enjoying life, from being at peace with being on a planet as dense as earth. It is important that there are spiritual people who can demonstrate that even on a planet as dense as earth, one can be at peace and one can flow with the River of Life because you know you are not human beings. You are not trapped on this earth, you are extensions of the mind of God, of the ascended masters. You are not apart from us, you are one with us, you are extensions of us. You are extensions of your I AM Presence and therefore you know you are *in* the world but not *of* the world.

You are at peace with being in the world now, making the most of it, realizing that one day you will make your ascension. You will no longer be on earth and that is the time when you can experience all of these other things, but while you are on earth, you are accepting that you are here and making the best of it. Certainly, my beloved, you have made the best of the time you have had together at this conference. For this, I applaud you.

23 | INVOKING THE EXPOSURE OF AMERICAN FOREIGN POLICY

In the name of the I AM THAT I AM, Jesus Christ, I use the authority that I have as a being in embodiment on earth to call upon Saint Germain to reinforce my calls and use my chakras to project the statements in this invocation into the collective consciousness and awaken Americans to the influence of the power elite on American foreign policy. Awaken Americans to the reality that we are spiritual beings and that we can co-create a new future by working with the ascended masters. I especially call for …

[Make your own calls here.]

Part 1

1. The fallen beings seek to find something that appeals to the people and they use it for their own ends. Freedom is one of the themes for the founding of this nation, and many Americans have a freedom flame they carry with them.

> O Saint Germain, you do inspire,
> my vision raised forever higher,
> with you I form a figure-eight,
> your Golden Age I co-create.
>
> **O Saint Germain, what love you bring,**
> **it truly makes all matter sing,**
> **your violet flame does all restore,**
> **with you we are becoming more.**

2. Many Americans have a strong dedication to freedom and the fallen beings pervert this in the creed: "Give me liberty or give me death." They are saying: "Are you willing to die for the cause of freedom?"

> O Saint Germain, what Freedom Flame,
> released when we recite your name,
> acceleration is your gift,
> our planet it will surely lift.
>
> **O Saint Germain, what love you bring,**
> **it truly makes all matter sing,**
> **your violet flame does all restore,**
> **with you we are becoming more.**

3. Many Americans have been willing to die for what they thought was the cause of freedom. The power elite and the fallen beings behind them have an agenda that is unknown to the people.

> O Saint Germain, in love we claim,
> our right to bring your violet flame,
> from you Above, to us below,
> it is an all-transforming flow.
>
> **O Saint Germain, what love you bring,**
> **it truly makes all matter sing,**
> **your violet flame does all restore,**
> **with you we are becoming more.**

4. Capitalism and communism are simply two different ways of achieving the same goal, namely a society that is completely controlled by the fallen beings through a power elite in embodiment.

> O Saint Germain, I love you so,
> my aura filled with violet glow,
> my chakras filled with violet fire,
> I am your cosmic amplifier.
>
> **O Saint Germain, what love you bring,**
> **it truly makes all matter sing,**
> **your violet flame does all restore,**
> **with you we are becoming more.**

5. If we take capitalism to its ultimate conclusion, we see the emergence of corporations that very quickly become so big

that they lose the human scale. They lose humanity because the workers do not matter anymore.

> O Saint Germain, I am now free,
> your violet flame is therapy,
> transform all hang-ups in my mind,
> as inner peace I surely find.
>
> **O Saint Germain, what love you bring,**
> **it truly makes all matter sing,**
> **your violet flame does all restore,**
> **with you we are becoming more.**

6. All that matters in a corporation are the leaders, and in many cases those leaders are not even involved with the business. They are stockholders, shareholders and board members that are not directly doing the work.

> O Saint Germain, my body pure,
> your violet flame for all is cure,
> consume the cause of all disease,
> and therefore I am all at ease.
>
> **O Saint Germain, what love you bring,**
> **it truly makes all matter sing,**
> **your violet flame does all restore,**
> **with you we are becoming more.**

7. We see the emergence of these corporations that are based on a completely narcissistic philosophy and attitude. They have no allegiance whatsoever to the people who are doing the actual work, not even to those who are the leaders but only to

those who are the owners and the hidden power elite behind them.

> O Saint Germain, I'm karma-free,
> the past no longer burdens me,
> a brand new opportunity,
> I am in Christic unity.

> **O Saint Germain, what love you bring,**
> **it truly makes all matter sing,**
> **your violet flame does all restore,**
> **with you we are becoming more.**

8. There came a point when these corporations had become so large in America that they started looking outside of America to find new markets. They went international and multinational, trying to extend their reach further and further around the globe.

> O Saint Germain, we are now one,
> I am for you a violet sun,
> as we transform this planet earth,
> your Golden Age is given birth.

> **O Saint Germain, what love you bring,**
> **it truly makes all matter sing,**
> **your violet flame does all restore,**
> **with you we are becoming more.**

9. If we take capitalism to its logical conclusion, one corporation will have destroyed all competition, and therefore we have a situation just like in a communist system where one entity owns or controls all means of production.

> O Saint Germain, the earth is free,
> from burden of duality,
> in oneness we bring what is best,
> your Golden Age is manifest.

> **O Saint Germain, what love you bring,**
> **it truly makes all matter sing,**
> **your violet flame does all restore,**
> **with you we are becoming more.**

Part 2

1. If one corporation owns all means of production, it will also own the state. Capitalism and communism are two systems defined by the fallen beings to reach the same end, with a completely centralized system controlled by the fallen beings.

> O Saint Germain, you do inspire,
> my vision raised forever higher,
> with you I form a figure-eight,
> your Golden Age I co-create.

> **O Saint Germain, what love you bring,**
> **it truly makes all matter sing,**
> **your violet flame does all restore,**
> **with you we are becoming more.**

2. According to the American Constitution, the government is supposed to maintain an army for the common defense. The American armed forces constitutionally have only one role, namely to defend the *people* of America.

23 | Invoking the exposure of American foreign policy

> O Saint Germain, what Freedom Flame,
> released when we recite your name,
> acceleration is your gift,
> our planet it will surely lift.

> **O Saint Germain, what love you bring,**
> **it truly makes all matter sing,**
> **your violet flame does all restore,**
> **with you we are becoming more.**

3. To an increasing degree, America's armed forces have been used to fight battles and wars in foreign countries. This is not according to the constitution.

> O Saint Germain, in love we claim,
> our right to bring your violet flame,
> from you Above, to us below,
> it is an all-transforming flow.

> **O Saint Germain, what love you bring,**
> **it truly makes all matter sing,**
> **your violet flame does all restore,**
> **with you we are becoming more.**

4. The justification for sending American soldiers to foreign lands, to shed their blood there when it is not what is defined in the constitution as the purpose of the American armed forces, has always been "to defend freedom."

> O Saint Germain, I love you so,
> my aura filled with violet glow,
> my chakras filled with violet fire,
> I am your cosmic amplifier.

**O Saint Germain, what love you bring,
it truly makes all matter sing,
your violet flame does all restore,
with you we are becoming more.**

5. For many years it was the fight against communism, but since communism is a system created by the fallen beings, this was simply an excuse for getting American soldiers to give their lives. It was getting America built up to a point where it was starting to use its armed forces to extend power beyond American borders, something the constitution does not actually allow.

O Saint Germain, I am now free,
your violet flame is therapy,
transform all hang-ups in my mind,
as inner peace I surely find.

**O Saint Germain, what love you bring,
it truly makes all matter sing,
your violet flame does all restore,
with you we are becoming more.**

6. The fallen beings have used communism as an excuse for putting America in the mindset where the American people are willing to accept that their sons and daughters go abroad and give their lives for a seemingly just cause.

O Saint Germain, my body pure,
your violet flame for all is cure,
consume the cause of all disease,
and therefore I am all at ease.

**O Saint Germain, what love you bring,
it truly makes all matter sing,
your violet flame does all restore,
with you we are becoming more.**

7. Communism was a system that in a very obvious way repressed freedom. Therefore, those who have the freedom flame say: "It was certainly better that communism didn't take over the world and therefore it was necessary that America fought communism to prevent them from taking over the world."

O Saint Germain, I'm karma-free,
the past no longer burdens me,
a brand new opportunity,
I am in Christic unity.

**O Saint Germain, what love you bring,
it truly makes all matter sing,
your violet flame does all restore,
with you we are becoming more.**

8. There was a time where it was the lesser of two evils that communism did not take over the world. I call for Americans to realize that the fact that communism collapsed does not mean that we now have freedom in America or throughout the world.

O Saint Germain, we are now one,
I am for you a violet sun,
as we transform this planet earth,
your Golden Age is given birth.

> **O Saint Germain, what love you bring,**
> **it truly makes all matter sing,**
> **your violet flame does all restore,**
> **with you we are becoming more.**

9. I call for Americans to be awakened so they can use their freedom flame to see that capitalism is not a system that gives freedom to the people. It just takes that freedom away in a more subtle way than did communism.

> O Saint Germain, the earth is free,
> from burden of duality,
> in oneness we bring what is best,
> your Golden Age is manifest.

> **O Saint Germain, what love you bring,**
> **it truly makes all matter sing,**
> **your violet flame does all restore,**
> **with you we are becoming more.**

Part 3

1. I call for Americans to be cut free to see this so they can shed the yoke that the power elite has brought upon this nation. I call for the exposure of the very fact that America's armed forces – America's soldiers – have in many cases not fought for the cause of freedom, they have fought for the power elite, they have fought for the cause of the power elite.

> O Saint Germain, you do inspire,
> my vision raised forever higher,

23 | Invoking the exposure of American foreign policy

with you I form a figure-eight,
your Golden Age I co-create.

**O Saint Germain, what love you bring,
it truly makes all matter sing,
your violet flame does all restore,
with you we are becoming more.**

2. I call for the exposure of all of these incidents where, either the armed forces in an overt way or the CIA or other secret forces in a covert way, have extended influence or tried to overthrow governments in other nations.

O Saint Germain, what Freedom Flame,
released when we recite your name,
acceleration is your gift,
our planet it will surely lift.

**O Saint Germain, what love you bring,
it truly makes all matter sing,
your violet flame does all restore,
with you we are becoming more.**

3. I demand the exposure that this was not done for the cause of freedom, it was done for the cause of allowing these multinational corporations to extend their reach, to capture new markets, to put themselves in monopoly positions in those markets.

O Saint Germain, in love we claim,
our right to bring your violet flame,
from you Above, to us below,
it is an all-transforming flow.

> O Saint Germain, what love you bring,
> it truly makes all matter sing,
> your violet flame does all restore,
> with you we are becoming more.

4. It is necessary to recognize that there are people in other nations who have criticized America precisely for this point. It is necessary to recognize that although they sometimes come from an unbalanced perspective and do not have the best interests of America at heart, there is a point to their criticism.

> O Saint Germain, I love you so,
> my aura filled with violet glow,
> my chakras filled with violet fire,
> I am your cosmic amplifier.

> **O Saint Germain, what love you bring,**
> **it truly makes all matter sing,**
> **your violet flame does all restore,**
> **with you we are becoming more.**

5. It is by no means according to the Constitution nor is it according to the freedom flame that many Americans have, that American sons and daughters are shedding their blood to extend the reach of multinational corporations that have no loyalty to America or to the American people.

> O Saint Germain, I am now free,
> your violet flame is therapy,
> transform all hang-ups in my mind,
> as inner peace I surely find.

**O Saint Germain, what love you bring,
it truly makes all matter sing,
your violet flame does all restore,
with you we are becoming more.**

6. It is an outrage that has been going on for far too long. I call for the judgment of Christ upon those inside the system who know what is going on but are not talking.

O Saint Germain, my body pure,
your violet flame for all is cure,
consume the cause of all disease,
and therefore I am all at ease.

**O Saint Germain, what love you bring,
it truly makes all matter sing,
your violet flame does all restore,
with you we are becoming more.**

7. I call for the shattering of the cloud of silence, the cloud of darkness, the energy veil that prevents the American people from reaching the awareness where we can say: "This is unacceptable and we will no longer stand for it."

O Saint Germain, I'm karma-free,
the past no longer burdens me,
a brand new opportunity,
I am in Christic unity.

**O Saint Germain, what love you bring,
it truly makes all matter sing,
your violet flame does all restore,
with you we are becoming more.**

8. The fallen beings have taken the primary characteristics of the American people – the freedom flame – they have created the illusion that it is America's role in the world to spread "freedom and democracy."

> O Saint Germain, we are now one,
> I am for you a violet sun,
> as we transform this planet earth,
> your Golden Age is given birth.
>
> **O Saint Germain, what love you bring,**
> **it truly makes all matter sing,**
> **your violet flame does all restore,**
> **with you we are becoming more.**

9. The fallen beings have used the freedom flame to get Americans to be willing to sacrifice their lives for this cause, but it is not the cause of freedom and democracy. It is in many cases the cause of the power elite wanting to extend their power, wanting to spread the capitalist system, which is a system set up only *by* the elite, *for* the elite.

> O Saint Germain, the earth is free,
> from burden of duality,
> in oneness we bring what is best,
> your Golden Age is manifest.
>
> **O Saint Germain, what love you bring,**
> **it truly makes all matter sing,**
> **your violet flame does all restore,**
> **with you we are becoming more.**

23 | Invoking the exposure of American foreign policy

Part 4

1. I call for the raising of the collective consciousness and a shift where it becomes obvious to Americans that this has been going on and this cannot be allowed to go on.

> O Saint Germain, you do inspire,
> my vision raised forever higher,
> with you I form a figure-eight,
> your Golden Age I co-create.

> **O Saint Germain, what love you bring,**
> **it truly makes all matter sing,**
> **your violet flame does all restore,**
> **with you we are becoming more.**

2. There is a huge gap between the public perception that has been created about America's role in the world and what is actually going on in the hidden corridors of power.

> O Saint Germain, what Freedom Flame,
> released when we recite your name,
> acceleration is your gift,
> our planet it will surely lift.

> **O Saint Germain, what love you bring,**
> **it truly makes all matter sing,**
> **your violet flame does all restore,**
> **with you we are becoming more.**

3. I call forth the judgment of Christ upon the people who are in those corridors of power and who have a completely

different way of looking at the world. They have a completely different agenda than what we see in the public facade.

> O Saint Germain, in love we claim,
> our right to bring your violet flame,
> from you Above, to us below,
> it is an all-transforming flow.
>
> **O Saint Germain, what love you bring,**
> **it truly makes all matter sing,**
> **your violet flame does all restore,**
> **with you we are becoming more.**

4. I call for Americans to see this gap, and then use our freedom flame to say: "This isn't right, we will not accept it anymore."

> O Saint Germain, I love you so,
> my aura filled with violet glow,
> my chakras filled with violet fire,
> I am your cosmic amplifier.
>
> **O Saint Germain, what love you bring,**
> **it truly makes all matter sing,**
> **your violet flame does all restore,**
> **with you we are becoming more.**

5. Another perversion of the freedom flame is that Americans have been brought up with this sense of loyalty to America, which they see as patriotism. This has been used by the fallen beings to make many Americans feel that we cannot criticize America.

*O Saint Germain, I am now free,
your violet flame is therapy,
transform all hang-ups in my mind,
as inner peace I surely find.*

**O Saint Germain, what love you bring,
it truly makes all matter sing,
your violet flame does all restore,
with you we are becoming more.**

6. It is a perversion when people have a sense of patriotism where they feel that in order to be a patriot and be loyal to the country, you cannot criticize America. You especially cannot criticize the foreign policy and especially not the military policy.

*O Saint Germain, my body pure,
your violet flame for all is cure,
consume the cause of all disease,
and therefore I am all at ease.*

**O Saint Germain, what love you bring,
it truly makes all matter sing,
your violet flame does all restore,
with you we are becoming more.**

7. When a President says: "We are going to war in Iraq," people think a true patriot cannot object to this. This prevents Americans from seeing what is going on behind the scenes. It prevents us from seeing the hidden agenda.

*O Saint Germain, I'm karma-free,
the past no longer burdens me,*

a brand new opportunity,
I am in Christic unity.

O Saint Germain, what love you bring,
it truly makes all matter sing,
your violet flame does all restore,
with you we are becoming more.

8. In order to be truly loyal to America, we must take a neutral, objective look at foreign criticism and say: "Do they have a point? When they say that America is interfering with their domestic policy, is it actually true? Are we actually doing that? Are we actually seeking to control other governments?"

O Saint Germain, we are now one,
I am for you a violet sun,
as we transform this planet earth,
your Golden Age is given birth.

O Saint Germain, what love you bring,
it truly makes all matter sing,
your violet flame does all restore,
with you we are becoming more.

9. We have the outrage about Russia seeking to interfere with American elections, but is America doing something similar in a covert manner and have they been doing this for decades? Has America actively overthrown governments?

O Saint Germain, the earth is free,
from burden of duality,
in oneness we bring what is best,
your Golden Age is manifest.

**O Saint Germain, what love you bring,
it truly makes all matter sing,
your violet flame does all restore,
with you we are becoming more.**

Part 5

1. I call forth the exposure of what the CIA has been doing in so-called banana republics and elsewhere. I call forth the exposure that America has created an entire task force that is not known to the public, but that is dedicated to controlling governments in other countries, totally against the free will of the people.

O Saint Germain, you do inspire,
my vision raised forever higher,
with you I form a figure-eight,
your Golden Age I co-create.

**O Saint Germain, what love you bring,
it truly makes all matter sing,
your violet flame does all restore,
with you we are becoming more.**

2. Some of these countries are democracies but America wants to make sure that the people vote the way that they see as being in America's interests. Is this really what the Constitution is all about? Is this really what the freedom flame supports?

O Saint Germain, what Freedom Flame,
released when we recite your name,

acceleration is your gift,
our planet it will surely lift.

**O Saint Germain, what love you bring,
it truly makes all matter sing,
your violet flame does all restore,
with you we are becoming more.**

3. Americans need to step back and ask the question: "Is American foreign policy always in alignment with the freedom flame we have in our hearts?" Is the American foreign policy motivated by the cause of freedom?

O Saint Germain, in love we claim,
our right to bring your violet flame,
from you Above, to us below,
it is an all-transforming flow.

**O Saint Germain, what love you bring,
it truly makes all matter sing,
your violet flame does all restore,
with you we are becoming more.**

4. Are we really fighting for the cause of freedom or are we actually being abused by the power elite to fight for the cause of anti-freedom, the cause of the elite?

O Saint Germain, I love you so,
my aura filled with violet glow,
my chakras filled with violet fire,
I am your cosmic amplifier.

23 | Invoking the exposure of American foreign policy

**O Saint Germain, what love you bring,
it truly makes all matter sing,
your violet flame does all restore,
with you we are becoming more.**

5. There is a mechanism in the American psyche that prevents America from becoming a truly free country. The mechanism is that the American people, through this indoctrination about being patriots, have been blocked from taking an objective, neutral look at America, American institutions, American foreign policy.

O Saint Germain, I am now free,
your violet flame is therapy,
transform all hang-ups in my mind,
as inner peace I surely find.

**O Saint Germain, what love you bring,
it truly makes all matter sing,
your violet flame does all restore,
with you we are becoming more.**

6. We have been indoctrinated that it is unpatriotic to criticize America. Many Americans are actually resisting the exposure of how the power elite is manipulating us.

O Saint Germain, my body pure,
your violet flame for all is cure,
consume the cause of all disease,
and therefore I am all at ease.

**O Saint Germain, what love you bring,
it truly makes all matter sing,**

> your violet flame does all restore,
> with you we are becoming more.

7. Many Americans feel we have to be loyal to the nation and in order to be loyal to the nation, we have to uphold the image that America is the greatest nation on earth and that America is always dedicated to the cause of freedom.

> O Saint Germain, I'm karma-free,
> the past no longer burdens me,
> a brand new opportunity,
> I am in Christic unity.

> **O Saint Germain, what love you bring,**
> **it truly makes all matter sing,**
> **your violet flame does all restore,**
> **with you we are becoming more.**

8. If America is driven by a hidden agenda that is the antithesis to the cause of freedom, how can it be wrong to acknowledge that and therefore correct the situation and bring America's foreign policy back in alignment with the cause of freedom, which is also bringing it into alignment with the mind of Saint Germain?

> O Saint Germain, we are now one,
> I am for you a violet sun,
> as we transform this planet earth,
> your Golden Age is given birth.

> **O Saint Germain, what love you bring,**
> **it truly makes all matter sing,**

your violet flame does all restore,
with you we are becoming more.

9. What are we truly loyal to? Are we loyal to the outer facade, the illusion created by the power elite? Or are we loyal to the freedom flame and the cause of freedom?

O Saint Germain, the earth is free,
from burden of duality,
in oneness we bring what is best,
your Golden Age is manifest.

**O Saint Germain, what love you bring,
it truly makes all matter sing,
your violet flame does all restore,
with you we are becoming more.**

Part 6

1. What does it mean to be an American, what does it mean to be a patriot? It does not mean to be loyal to the power elite and the illusions they have created.

O Saint Germain, you do inspire,
my vision raised forever higher,
with you I form a figure-eight,
your Golden Age I co-create.

**O Saint Germain, what love you bring,
it truly makes all matter sing,**

> your violet flame does all restore,
> with you we are becoming more.

2. Acknowledging that America has gone off track in a certain area, is not a criticism of America. It is a criticism of the power elite that is manipulating America and *that* is not unpatriotic, neither is it unamerican.

> O Saint Germain, what Freedom Flame,
> released when we recite your name,
> acceleration is your gift,
> our planet it will surely lift.
>
> **O Saint Germain, what love you bring,
> it truly makes all matter sing,
> your violet flame does all restore,
> with you we are becoming more.**

3. It is not unamerican to say: "We are off course, we need to come back on the right course."

> O Saint Germain, in love we claim,
> our right to bring your violet flame,
> from you Above, to us below,
> it is an all-transforming flow.
>
> **O Saint Germain, what love you bring,
> it truly makes all matter sing,
> your violet flame does all restore,
> with you we are becoming more.**

23 | Invoking the exposure of American foreign policy

4. Openly acknowledging the problems and course correcting, that is truly American, truly patriotic and a true expression of the freedom flame that we have in our hearts.

> O Saint Germain, I love you so,
> my aura filled with violet glow,
> my chakras filled with violet fire,
> I am your cosmic amplifier.

> **O Saint Germain, what love you bring,**
> **it truly makes all matter sing,**
> **your violet flame does all restore,**
> **with you we are becoming more.**

5. Allowing the power elite to manipulate us into this false loyalty is unamerican, unpatriotic and anti-freedom.

> O Saint Germain, I am now free,
> your violet flame is therapy,
> transform all hang-ups in my mind,
> as inner peace I surely find.

> **O Saint Germain, what love you bring,**
> **it truly makes all matter sing,**
> **your violet flame does all restore,**
> **with you we are becoming more.**

6. I call for a shift in the collective consciousness, so that more and more Americans begin to see the reality of how manipulated is the foreign policy of America.

> O Saint Germain, my body pure,
> your violet flame for all is cure,

consume the cause of all disease,
and therefore I am all at ease.

**O Saint Germain, what love you bring,
it truly makes all matter sing,
your violet flame does all restore,
with you we are becoming more.**

7. I call for Americans to be cut free from the beast of false loyalty that has enabled the power elite to create wars at times when the American people demanded a domestic change.

O Saint Germain, I'm karma-free,
the past no longer burdens me,
a brand new opportunity,
I am in Christic unity.

**O Saint Germain, what love you bring,
it truly makes all matter sing,
your violet flame does all restore,
with you we are becoming more.**

8. I call for the exposure of how war has been used as a weapon to silence the people and prevent an exposure or overthrow of the power elite.

O Saint Germain, we are now one,
I am for you a violet sun,
as we transform this planet earth,
your Golden Age is given birth.

**O Saint Germain, what love you bring,
it truly makes all matter sing,**

**your violet flame does all restore,
with you we are becoming more.**

9. I call for Americans to be cut free to see that waging war is never in alignment with the mind of Saint Germain, for Saint Germain is not a dualistic being but an ascended master. Saint Germain has the vision of how to manifest the Golden Age without war.

> O Saint Germain, the earth is free,
> from burden of duality,
> in oneness we bring what is best,
> your Golden Age is manifest.

**O Saint Germain, what love you bring,
it truly makes all matter sing,
your violet flame does all restore,
with you we are becoming more.**

Sealing

In the name of the I AM THAT I AM, I accept that Archangel Michael, Astrea and Shiva form an impenetrable shield around myself and all constructive people in America, sealing us from all fear-based energies in all four octaves. I accept that the Light of God is consuming and transforming all fear-based energies that make up the dark forces working against America!

24 | AMERICANS HAVE A RIGHT TO DEMAND BETTER LEADERS

I AM the Ascended Master Gautama Buddha. It has been my privilege to seal many of these ascended master conferences, and it is always a great joy for me because I get to see how much progress you have made in such a short time span. I have a few remarks on the topic of how to align America with the mind of Saint Germain. First, I want to build upon what Saint Germain talked about, about those who have been fooled into fighting for the cause of freedom. I simply want to put out the question in the collective consciousness of America: "How can killing another human being ever advance the cause of freedom?"

When you contemplate this, you recognize, at least if you know the teachings we have given on the fallen beings and the duality consciousness, that one of the primary things that people need to be free from on earth is the manipulation of the fallen beings where people have been manipulated into killing each other for some epic cause. A cause that was defined by the fallen beings and had either the purpose of creating chaos and destruction or the purpose of getting people to misuse their free will in order to seemingly prove God wrong.

You see that anytime, literally *anytime,* where people have been manipulated into killing each other for some cause, that cause was defined by the fallen beings, the entire situation was manipulated by the fallen beings. Therefore, truly, you never can advance the true cause of freedom if you are killing other people. As long as you think that it is necessary to kill other people, perhaps even justified in order to advance some cause, then you are not in alignment with the mind of Saint Germain or the mind of Christ or the mind of the Buddha.

Would Jesus abuse children?

I also want to comment on this consciousness exposed by Cyclopea where, because people feel like sinners, they are not willing to speak out. They think that they are not worthy to speak out and therefore they remain silent in the face of abuse, manipulation and lies.

As someone pointed out to this messenger during lunch, you also have the statement made by Jesus in the situation where a woman was caught in adultery and the crowd wanted to stone her, and Jesus said: "Let he who is without sin among you cast the first stone." This statement has, of course, been used to reinforce the consciousness that unless you are without sin or perfect, you should not criticize anyone else. The reality is, however, that Jesus made that statement in a specific situation where these men were willing to kill another human being.

If you want to take it literally, you could say: "Only those who are without sin should consider killing another human being." In other words, if you recognize that you are not without sin, do not ever consider killing another human being. Of course, if you are without sin, you would never even consider killing another human being.

Of course, it is also an example of the fact that (and I have certainly seen this with the teachings I gave so long ago) whatever statement you make as a spiritual teacher in the dense environment of earth, the fallen beings can find a way to pervert it or make use of it to further their own ends. They have certainly made use of this statement, especially after they came up with the idea of original sin. You will see, for example, how they have used this in the Catholic church where there was hardly anyone for a thousand years who dared to criticize the leadership of the church. Even today, you see how this very consciousness of not thinking you can criticize if you are not free from sin, if you are not perfect, is one of the main reasons why it has taken so long before Catholics have exposed the sexual abuse by priests.

There is still this concept, this consciousness, that the people are ordinary sinners, that the leaders of the church although still human beings are in a higher class than the ordinary people because they are leaders of the church. Therefore, those below them should not criticize or point out any flaws. Do you see how perverted this consciousness is?

Let us just take at face value what the Catholic church claims that it is the true church representing Jesus Christ. Well, in that case, if the leaders of the church are representing Christ, they obviously should never do anything that Christ would not do. Certainly, I am sure that very few people would imagine to think that Jesus would have abused children. You see, if they really represent Christ, they should be in a higher state of mind. Therefore, if they are not, then they are not representing Christ. Therefore, it is not only legitimate but necessary that the people speak out and stop the abuse. Again, if the church has any legitimacy as representing Christ, then if there are actions taken by people in the church that are off course, if they are not pointed out, how can the church ever get back on course?

How the fallen beings use ritual

You see that there is this very heavy consciousness of not thinking that people have a right to criticize those above them. There is this heavy consciousness that people are sinners but the fallen beings are clever enough to know that not everyone is going to completely subscribe to this. Even if they do believe in this, there is a certain inbuilt drive in human psychology that people want to improve their position. It is very difficult to make human beings accept something as permanent. You can see this outplayed when people, as they so often do in America, sit in front of their televisions and flip channels.

The mind finds it difficult to stay on one topic for a long time but wants to shift into something else. You can see it in how many people struggle with meditation where it is so difficult to make the mind focus on one thing for any length of time. This is, in a sense, a saving grace. When the fallen beings come up with a concept of original sin, it seems to be a permanent state and there are people who will long for some way out of this permanent state.

The fallen beings have come up with a way to try to divert that longing. First of all, they have done it by the whole concept that you will be saved by the external savior after you die. Jesus will come and save you and take you to heaven if you have been a good Christian. They also do something else, which is perhaps even more subtle. They create a certain culture where, on the one hand, you are made to feel that you are a sinner, you are imperfect, you are not good enough. But then the fallen beings define a set of rules and rituals, and then they project that those who follow the rules and rituals, they are now better than those who do not. As a diversionary tactic to get people to look critically at the belief that you are sinners, they give you this diversion of saying that by following all the rules, by following all the rituals, then you are better than you were before, you are better than those who are not doing it.

You see this in the Catholic tradition, for example, where some people literally are afraid of not going to mass. They feel it is disastrous if their family members do not go to mass. You see it also, my beloved, in spiritual movements where, for example, you can see in Tibet how they have created these elaborate rituals, even the prayer wheels where they believe that by performing this (rather mechanical) ritual over and over and over again, they will actually make progress towards whatever they see as their goal.

Look at even several previous ascended master dispensations where there were strict rules and where people became obsessed with following the rules. It was truly an obsessive-compulsive disorder that not only drove people to follow the rules, but it also created this very judgmental culture towards those who did not follow the rules. This was especially dysfunctional because it prevented the people from being united in Christ.

You have the story of Pentecost where the disciples received the Holy Spirit because they were of one accord in one place. Well, we have seen ascended master students be in one place but be so divided by this judgmental attitude that the Spirit could not descend. Naturally, we are calling you to come to a higher level and you are already at that higher level but you can, of course, progress even higher by using these teachings about the birth trauma and the separate selves. For when you come to that point of being in the neutral state of mind, you have no need to follow rules and you have no need to judge others based on whether they are following the rules. Rules fade away in Christhood and Buddhahood.

Being in a neutral state of mind

What is Buddhahood? Well, an important component of it is to be in that neutral state of mind, being non-attached because there is nothing that compels you to do anything. I am not saying this is all there is to Buddhahood, as there are stages of Buddhahood but it is certainly one component of it. When I sat under the Bo tree and was tempted by the demons of Mara, I could avoid reacting to their temptations only by remaining in that neutral state of mind. You cannot be in a neutral state of mind as long as you have the primal self and these other separate selves that are pulling you, compelling you, to do this, do that, do the next thing. More than that, these selves are telling you that you are not good enough, that there is something you have not done on earth, that you are supposed to do something on earth but you have not done it yet, you have not accomplished it.

As this messenger realized, an important component of this is that most of you came here because you wanted to improve things on earth but the only way to really improve things and produce tangible results is to change other people. As long as you think you have to change other people, you cannot be at peace. You are in this constant push-pull of being compelled to do something that is impossible to achieve because of the free will of other people. This can cause some avatars to go into wanting to use force, even though they, of course, never use force to the degree that the fallen beings are using force. There can be this desire to use force in order to free people from suffering.

This is, of course, one of the primary challenges for an avatar: to take a look at what it was for you individually that brought you to earth. What were your desires, your vision, your understanding? What was the goal you had that you wanted to accomplish? Then, take a look at this and realize that this was based on your consciousness at the time. In reality you did not come here to change other people but to free yourself from that consciousness that you had when you came here, however it was for you individually. In a sense what have the other masters talked about? Improving the public discourse, connecting to the essential humanity, finding a different way to talk to each other, these are all aspects of attaining that neutral state of mind.

Looking at how America fits into the whole

I am, of course, not looking to convert all Americans to become Buddhists, as the Buddhist religion has little relevance for the West in the modern age. However, it was never my intention to get people who considered themselves my followers to join a particular outer religion. I wanted people to walk the path towards Buddhahood, and certainly Saint Germain has attained Buddhahood and, as he has demonstrated in his dictations, he seeks to raise all life. The most important shift that could happen for aligning America or rather Americans with the mind of Saint Germain is that they begin to look beyond themselves, to look at the whole. How can we use the privileges and the freedoms we have to help others? My beloved, you take Saint Germain's discourse about American foreign policy being an extension of the fallen beings and the power elite. You can see that there may be some trepidation about how America would be able to actually help the whole rather than serving the cause of the power elite. Nevertheless, there are enough Americans who either have begun to shift, or who could quickly begin to shift based on your calls, that they could be willing to come to that state where they can look neutrally at what is happening in America. Therefore, they can speak out about what is not right and demand change without going into an angry, dualistic reaction. There are enough Americans who can be neutral enough about looking at how they can help others without perpetuating the cause of the power elite.

Why Americans cannot fight the power elite

An important shift would also be, of course, to make the calls that Americans will understand the way that the fallen beings are setting up these artificial conflicts. People need to come to this understanding that there are many Americans who are dissatisfied with their government. There are many Americans who believe something is wrong, something is hidden, something is going on behind the scenes. There are many Americans who subscribe to various conspiracy theories but it is very important to make the calls that people begin to see that when the fallen beings can no longer hide from the people (when the fallen beings are beginning to be exposed, the people are beginning to see that there is a power elite and see how they are manipulating) this does not mean that the fallen beings will just give up. They have one last-ditch attempt at staying in control of the situation and it is to try to get the people to fight them.

All of the things we have given you (and I know that you who are here know this but it needs to be stated into the collective consciousness), all of the things we have given you about the fallen beings and the power elite are, of course, not given in order to get you or anybody else in a state of mind where you go and fight the power elite. It is not efficient to fight the power elite. It is, in fact, not possible to defeat the power elite by fighting them.

This is one of the themes demonstrated in the *My Lives* book [*My Lives with Lucifer, Satan, Hitler and Jesus*] and this is something that you need to make calls on because it will be very difficult for many Americans to get this point. They are, as was said, so inflamed with fighting for the cause of freedom, they are so ready to fight. They have been so indoctrinated by movies that the ultimate solution to any problem is to whip out the machine gun and start blasting away at anything that moves until you are the last man standing.

You need to make the calls for this so that people begin to realize that many times in history, the dark forces, the power elite, have pulled the people into this antagonistic reaction where the people are willing to use violence to fight the elite. Whenever that happens, it only opens the door so that an aspiring power elite can use the dissatisfaction of the people to defeat the established power elite and the people end up being under the control of this new aspiring elite that now becomes the established elite. We go from one elite to another and it is time to break this deadlock.

Removing the elite without a violent revolution

It is time that the people rise above this and realize that it is actually possible to remove the power elite from America without having a violent revolution but what is the key to doing this? Well, knowledge is power. You need to bring knowledge but in order for this knowledge to be received and have an impact, it has to be brought from a neutral state of mind. In other words, a state of mind that is not seeking to inflame, not seeking to get people to fight, not seeking to appoint a scapegoat, not seeking to put other people down. It simply states things as you see them to the best of your vision. You state things from a neutral state of mind and when enough people do this, it will shift the equation.

There are enough Americans who are at a level of consciousness where they can respond to this kind of neutral exposure of what is happening. As more and more people begin to accept these ideas, as more and more exposures come forward, then gradually the consciousness will begin to shift as other masters have talked about. People suddenly see something, see how obvious it is and then they are ready to make a change. Again, not through a violent revolution, not through criticizing, condemning, putting down, not through mudslinging or any of the other American pastimes, but simply by being determined and by realizing that as Americans we have a right to demand a better form of leadership.

You take the Americans Creed given by Saint Germain where you see yourself as being on the path towards raising your consciousness. When enough Americans are willing to commit to this, they have a right to demand a leadership who is also on that path of raising awareness. They have a right to demand a leadership that realizes that they can only govern based on their vision, based on their state of awareness. Therefore, a good leader is constantly seeking to raise his or her awareness.

You have a right to demand a leadership that does not at any point claim to have the absolute truth or the only truth. In fact, you have a right to demand a leadership that does not claim to have a dualistic truth where they say: "Our party will make America great and the other party will destroy America." You have a right to demand a leadership that is not divided along these dualistic polarities but is able and willing to come together and neutrally look at what is best for America, what is best for the American people, at least the greatest possible number of them. You have a right to demand a leadership that is not bought or controlled or blinded or persuaded by a small power elite, seeking to take advantage of America's freedoms for themselves while denying those freedoms to the people.

These are reasonable demands for Americans who have pledged themselves to the process of raising their awareness. You who are here, some of you can say you are American citizens, others are not, but you can all say that you are true Americans for you have pledged yourself to that path of raising awareness. Therefore, you have a right to demand a higher form of leadership in America and I would like you to join me in saying this: "I am a true American. I demand a higher, more aware leadership in America and I accept that my call compels the answer. Therefore, I accept that America is from this moment set on a new course."

With this, my beloved, I seal this statement and we all multiply your statements. I seal you, I seal this conference and I extend to you the gratitude of all of us, for we truly are grateful when you come together like this and achieve this state of harmony, non-judgmentalness and unity that you have achieved in this gathering. This is truly the sangha of the Buddha.

25 | INVOKING NON-DUALISTIC LEADERSHIP IN AMERICA

In the name of the I AM THAT I AM, Jesus Christ, I use the authority that I have as a being in embodiment on earth to call upon Gautama Buddha to reinforce my calls and use my chakras to project the statements in this invocation into the collective consciousness and awaken Americans to our right to demand leaders who have transcended duality. Awaken Americans to the reality that we are spiritual beings and that we can co-create a new future by working with the ascended masters. I especially call for …

[Make your own calls here.]

Part 1

1. How can killing another human being ever advance the cause of freedom?

> Gautama, show my mental state
> that does give rise to love and hate,
> your exposé I do endure,
> so my perception will be pure.
>
> **Gautama, Flame of Cosmic Peace,**
> **unruly thoughts do hereby cease,**
> **we radiate from you and me**
> **the peace to still Samsara's Sea.**

2. One of the primary things that people need to be free from on earth is the manipulation of the fallen beings, where people have been manipulated into killing each other for some epic cause.

> Gautama, in your Flame of Peace,
> the struggling self I now release,
> the Buddha Nature I now see,
> it is the core of you and me.
>
> **Gautama, Flame of Cosmic Peace,**
> **unruly thoughts do hereby cease,**
> **we radiate from you and me**
> **the peace to still Samsara's Sea.**

3. The fallen beings have defined the cause, and it had either the purpose of creating chaos and destruction or the purpose

of getting people to misuse their free will in order to seemingly prove God wrong.

> Gautama, I am one with thee,
> Mara's demons do now flee,
> your Presence like a soothing balm,
> my mind and senses ever calm.

> **Gautama, Flame of Cosmic Peace,**
> **unruly thoughts do hereby cease,**
> **we radiate from you and me**
> **the peace to still Samsara's Sea.**

4. Anytime, literally *anytime,* where people have been manipulated into killing each other for some cause, that cause was defined by the fallen beings, the entire situation was manipulated by the fallen beings.

> Gautama, I now take the vow,
> to live in the eternal now,
> with you I do transcend all time,
> to live in present so sublime.

> **Gautama, Flame of Cosmic Peace,**
> **unruly thoughts do hereby cease,**
> **we radiate from you and me**
> **the peace to still Samsara's Sea.**

5. We never can advance the true cause of freedom if we are killing other people.

> Gautama, I have no desire,
> to nothing earthly I aspire,

in non-attachment I now rest,
passing Mara's subtle test.

**Gautama, Flame of Cosmic Peace,
unruly thoughts do hereby cease,
we radiate from you and me
the peace to still Samsara's Sea.**

6. As long as we think it is necessary to kill other people, perhaps even justified in order to advance some cause, then we are not in alignment with the mind of Saint Germain, the mind of Christ or the mind of the Buddha.

Gautama, I melt into you,
my mind is one, no longer two,
immersed in your resplendent glow,
Nirvana is all that I know.

**Gautama, Flame of Cosmic Peace,
unruly thoughts do hereby cease,
we radiate from you and me
the peace to still Samsara's Sea.**

7. Jesus' statement: "Let he who is without sin among you cast the first stone" has been used to reinforce the consciousness that unless we are without sin or perfect, we should not criticize anyone else.

Gautama, in your timeless space,
I am immersed in Cosmic Grace,
I know the God beyond all form,
to world I will no more conform.

> Gautama, Flame of Cosmic Peace,
> unruly thoughts do hereby cease,
> we radiate from you and me
> the peace to still Samsara's Sea.

8. The reality is that Jesus made that statement in order to stop people from killing each other, not in order to stop them from criticizing their leaders.

> Gautama, I am now awake,
> I clearly see what is at stake,
> and thus I claim my sacred right
> to be on earth the Buddhic Light.

> Gautama, Flame of Cosmic Peace,
> unruly thoughts do hereby cease,
> we radiate from you and me
> the peace to still Samsara's Sea.

9. Whatever statement is made by a spiritual teacher, the fallen beings can find a way to pervert it or make use of it to further their own ends. They have made use of this statement to stop people from criticizing the leadership of the Catholic church.

> Gautama, with your thunderbolt,
> we give the earth a mighty jolt,
> I know that some will understand,
> and join the Buddha's timeless band.

> Gautama, Flame of Cosmic Peace,
> unruly thoughts do hereby cease,
> we radiate from you and me
> the peace to still Samsara's Sea.

Part 2

1. This very consciousness of not thinking we can criticize if we are not free from sin, is one of the main reasons it has taken so long before Catholics have exposed the sexual abuse by priests.

> Gautama, show my mental state
> that does give rise to love and hate,
> your exposé I do endure,
> so my perception will be pure.

> **Gautama, Flame of Cosmic Peace,**
> **unruly thoughts do hereby cease,**
> **we radiate from you and me**
> **the peace to still Samsara's Sea.**

2. There is this consciousness that the people are ordinary sinners, and that the leaders of the church are in a higher class than ordinary people because they are leaders of the church. Therefore, those below them should not criticize or point out any flaws.

> Gautama, in your Flame of Peace,
> the struggling self I now release,
> the Buddha Nature I now see,
> it is the core of you and me.

> **Gautama, Flame of Cosmic Peace,**
> **unruly thoughts do hereby cease,**
> **we radiate from you and me**
> **the peace to still Samsara's Sea.**

3. The Catholic church claims that it is the true church representing Jesus Christ. In that case, if the leaders of the church are representing Christ, they obviously should never do anything that Christ would not do. Yet how many people would imagine that Jesus would have abused children?

> Gautama, I am one with thee,
> Mara's demons do now flee,
> your Presence like a soothing balm,
> my mind and senses ever calm.

> **Gautama, Flame of Cosmic Peace,**
> **unruly thoughts do hereby cease,**
> **we radiate from you and me**
> **the peace to still Samsara's Sea.**

4. If they really represent Christ, they should be in a higher state of mind. If they are not, then they are not representing Christ. Therefore, it is not only legitimate but necessary that the people speak out and stop the abuse.

> Gautama, I now take the vow,
> to live in the eternal now,
> with you I do transcend all time,
> to live in present so sublime.

> **Gautama, Flame of Cosmic Peace,**
> **unruly thoughts do hereby cease,**
> **we radiate from you and me**
> **the peace to still Samsara's Sea.**

5. If the church has any legitimacy as representing Christ, then if there are actions taken by people in the church that are off

course, if they are not pointed out, how can the church ever get back on course?

> Gautama, I have no desire,
> to nothing earthly I aspire,
> in non-attachment I now rest,
> passing Mara's subtle test.

> **Gautama, Flame of Cosmic Peace,**
> **unruly thoughts do hereby cease,**
> **we radiate from you and me**
> **the peace to still Samsara's Sea.**

6. I call forth the judgment of Christ upon the consciousness of thinking that people do not have a right to criticize those above them.

> Gautama, I melt into you,
> my mind is one, no longer two,
> immersed in your resplendent glow,
> Nirvana is all that I know.

> **Gautama, Flame of Cosmic Peace,**
> **unruly thoughts do hereby cease,**
> **we radiate from you and me**
> **the peace to still Samsara's Sea.**

7. When the fallen beings come up with a concept of original sin, it seems to be a permanent state and there are people who will long for some way out of this permanent state.

> Gautama, in your timeless space,
> I am immersed in Cosmic Grace,

I know the God beyond all form,
to world I will no more conform.

**Gautama, Flame of Cosmic Peace,
unruly thoughts do hereby cease,
we radiate from you and me
the peace to still Samsara's Sea.**

8. The fallen beings have come up with a way to divert that longing. They have done this by the whole concept that we will be saved by the external savior after we die.

Gautama, I am now awake,
I clearly see what is at stake,
and thus I claim my sacred right
to be on earth the Buddhic Light.

**Gautama, Flame of Cosmic Peace,
unruly thoughts do hereby cease,
we radiate from you and me
the peace to still Samsara's Sea.**

9. The fallen beings have created a culture where, on the one hand we are made to feel that we are sinners, but then the fallen beings define a set of rules and rituals and project that those who follow them are now better than those who do not.

Gautama, with your thunderbolt,
we give the earth a mighty jolt,
I know that some will understand,
and join the Buddha's timeless band.

> **Gautama, Flame of Cosmic Peace,**
> **unruly thoughts do hereby cease,**
> **we radiate from you and me**
> **the peace to still Samsara's Sea.**

Part 3

1. The most important shift that could happen for aligning Americans with the mind of Saint Germain is that we begin to look beyond ourselves, to look at the whole.

> Gautama, show my mental state
> that does give rise to love and hate,
> your exposé I do endure,
> so my perception will be pure.
>
> **Gautama, Flame of Cosmic Peace,**
> **unruly thoughts do hereby cease,**
> **we radiate from you and me**
> **the peace to still Samsara's Sea.**

2. Americans need to ask: "How can we use the privileges and the freedoms we have to help others?

> Gautama, in your Flame of Peace,
> the struggling self I now release,
> the Buddha Nature I now see,
> it is the core of you and me.
>
> **Gautama, Flame of Cosmic Peace,**
> **unruly thoughts do hereby cease,**

**we radiate from you and me
the peace to still Samsara's Sea.**

3. I call for a critical mass of Americans to be cut free so we can make the shift of where we can look neutrally at what is happening in America. Therefore, we can speak out about what is not right and demand change without going into an angry, dualistic reaction.

> Gautama, I am one with thee,
> Mara's demons do now flee,
> your Presence like a soothing balm,
> my mind and senses ever calm.

> **Gautama, Flame of Cosmic Peace,
> unruly thoughts do hereby cease,
> we radiate from you and me
> the peace to still Samsara's Sea.**

4. I call for the cutting free of the Americans who can be neutral enough about looking at how we can help others without perpetuating the cause of the power elite.

> Gautama, I now take the vow,
> to live in the eternal now,
> with you I do transcend all time,
> to live in present so sublime.

> **Gautama, Flame of Cosmic Peace,
> unruly thoughts do hereby cease,
> we radiate from you and me
> the peace to still Samsara's Sea.**

5. I call for Americans to be cut free to understand the way that the fallen beings are setting up these artificial conflicts.

> Gautama, I have no desire,
> to nothing earthly I aspire,
> in non-attachment I now rest,
> passing Mara's subtle test.

> **Gautama, Flame of Cosmic Peace,**
> **unruly thoughts do hereby cease,**
> **we radiate from you and me**
> **the peace to still Samsara's Sea.**

6. Many Americans are dissatisfied with the government. They believe something is wrong, something is hidden, something is going on behind the scenes. Many Americans subscribe to various conspiracy theories.

> Gautama, I melt into you,
> my mind is one, no longer two,
> immersed in your resplendent glow,
> Nirvana is all that I know.

> **Gautama, Flame of Cosmic Peace,**
> **unruly thoughts do hereby cease,**
> **we radiate from you and me**
> **the peace to still Samsara's Sea.**

7. I call for Americans to be cut free to see that when the fallen beings can no longer hide from the people, this does not mean that the fallen beings will just give up. They have one last-ditch attempt at staying in control of the situation and it is to try to get the people to fight them.

25 | Invoking non-dualistic leadership in America

Gautama, in your timeless space,
I am immersed in Cosmic Grace,
I know the God beyond all form,
to world I will no more conform.

**Gautama, Flame of Cosmic Peace,
unruly thoughts do hereby cease,
we radiate from you and me
the peace to still Samsara's Sea.**

8. I call for Americans to be cut free from the mindset where they want to fight the power elite. It is not efficient to fight the power elite. It is not possible to defeat the power elite by fighting them.

Gautama, I am now awake,
I clearly see what is at stake,
and thus I claim my sacred right
to be on earth the Buddhic Light.

**Gautama, Flame of Cosmic Peace,
unruly thoughts do hereby cease,
we radiate from you and me
the peace to still Samsara's Sea.**

9. I call for Americans to be cut free from being inflamed with fighting for the cause of freedom, from being indoctrinated by movies that the ultimate solution to any problem is to whip out the machine gun and start blasting away at anything that moves until you are the last man standing.

Gautama, with your thunderbolt,
we give the earth a mighty jolt,

I know that some will understand,
and join the Buddha's timeless band.

**Gautama, Flame of Cosmic Peace,
unruly thoughts do hereby cease,
we radiate from you and me
the peace to still Samsara's Sea.**

Part 4

1. I call for Americans to realize that the dark forces, the power elite, have pulled the people into this antagonistic reaction where the people are willing to use violence to fight the elite.

Gautama, show my mental state
that does give rise to love and hate,
your exposé I do endure,
so my perception will be pure.

**Gautama, Flame of Cosmic Peace,
unruly thoughts do hereby cease,
we radiate from you and me
the peace to still Samsara's Sea.**

2. Whenever that happens, it only opens the door so that an aspiring power elite can use the dissatisfaction of the people to defeat the established power elite. The people end up being under the control of this new elite that now becomes the established elite.

Gautama, in your Flame of Peace,
the struggling self I now release,
the Buddha Nature I now see,
it is the core of you and me.

**Gautama, Flame of Cosmic Peace,
unruly thoughts do hereby cease,
we radiate from you and me
the peace to still Samsara's Sea.**

3. It is time to break this deadlock and realize that it is possible to remove the power elite from America without having a violent revolution. The key to doing this is that knowledge is power.

Gautama, I am one with thee,
Mara's demons do now flee,
your Presence like a soothing balm,
my mind and senses ever calm.

**Gautama, Flame of Cosmic Peace,
unruly thoughts do hereby cease,
we radiate from you and me
the peace to still Samsara's Sea.**

4. I call for the cutting free of those who can bring this knowledge from a neutral state of mind, a state of mind that is not seeking to inflame, not seeking to get people to fight, not seeking to appoint a scapegoat, not seeking to put other people down.

Gautama, I now take the vow,
to live in the eternal now,

with you I do transcend all time,
to live in present so sublime.

**Gautama, Flame of Cosmic Peace,
unruly thoughts do hereby cease,
we radiate from you and me
the peace to still Samsara's Sea.**

5. I call for Americans to be cut free to see the obvious and make a change. Not through a violent revolution, not through criticizing, but by being determined and by realizing that as Americans, we are seeking to raise our awareness, and this gives us the right to demand a better form of leadership.

Gautama, I have no desire,
to nothing earthly I aspire,
in non-attachment I now rest,
passing Mara's subtle test.

**Gautama, Flame of Cosmic Peace,
unruly thoughts do hereby cease,
we radiate from you and me
the peace to still Samsara's Sea.**

6. As true Americans, we have a right to demand a leadership who is on the path of raising awareness. We have a right to demand a leadership that realizes that they can only govern based on their vision, based on their state of awareness. Therefore, a good leader is constantly seeking to raise his or her awareness.

Gautama, I melt into you,
my mind is one, no longer two,

immersed in your resplendent glow,
Nirvana is all that I know.

**Gautama, Flame of Cosmic Peace,
unruly thoughts do hereby cease,
we radiate from you and me
the peace to still Samsara's Sea.**

7. As true Americans, we have a right to demand a leadership that does not claim to have the absolute truth, that is not divided along dualistic polarities but is able and willing to come together and neutrally look at what is best for America, what is best for the American people.

Gautama, in your timeless space,
I am immersed in Cosmic Grace,
I know the God beyond all form,
to world I will no more conform.

**Gautama, Flame of Cosmic Peace,
unruly thoughts do hereby cease,
we radiate from you and me
the peace to still Samsara's Sea.**

8. As true Americans, we have a right to demand a leadership that is not bought, controlled, blinded or persuaded by a small power elite, seeking to take advantage of America's freedoms for themselves while denying those freedoms to the people.

Gautama, I am now awake,
I clearly see what is at stake,
and thus I claim my sacred right
to be on earth the Buddhic Light.

**Gautama, Flame of Cosmic Peace,
unruly thoughts do hereby cease,
we radiate from you and me
the peace to still Samsara's Sea.**

9. I am a true American. I demand a higher, more aware leadership in America and I accept that my call compels the answer. Therefore, I accept that America is from this moment set on a new course.

Gautama, with your thunderbolt,
we give the earth a mighty jolt,
I know that some will understand,
and join the Buddha's timeless band.

**Gautama, Flame of Cosmic Peace,
unruly thoughts do hereby cease,
we radiate from you and me
the peace to still Samsara's Sea.**

Sealing

In the name of the I AM THAT I AM, I accept that Archangel Michael, Astrea and Shiva form an impenetrable shield around myself and all constructive people in America, sealing us from all fear-based energies in all four octaves. I accept that the Light of God is consuming and transforming all fear-based energies that make up the dark forces working against America!

PART 2 FREEING AMERICA FROM BLACK-AND-WHITE THINKING

The dictations in Part 2 were given at a conference held in Los Angeles in July 2015. The invocations that follow each dictation were made based on the dictation. The last four invocations were made for the conference and given by the participants during the conference. The primary theme for the conference was to help people overcome prejudice and intolerance.

26 | A HIGHER FORM OF DEMOCRACY IN AMERICA

I AM FREEDOM! And I AM the Ascended Master Saint Germain, the primary sponsor of this nation of the United States of America.

Of course, the nation that you see today is not the one I sponsored so long ago, but then again, what I sponsored so long ago was what could be manifested at the time. Therefore, it was never meant to be the final solution, for there is, of course, no final matrix for America. America is a process, it is not a result, it is not a static state. It is an ever-self-transcending state, a mindset of wanting to go beyond boundaries, wanting to find greater and greater freedom and manifest a higher and higher level of the Golden Age matrix of Saint Germain that I am.

A greater release of the Freedom Flame

I bring it to this planet, not only for America but for all nations on earth that are willing to transcend themselves and the former mindset that shall not stand in the light of Saint Germain in the Aquarian Age. I am here to manifest, this moment and forward, my Presence in a greater manifestation than before. Therefore, I am releasing a greater intensity of the Freedom Flame than has ever been released on this planet before and drawing a line in the sand that is saying: "Thus far and no farther." These manifestations of intolerance that you have made the call for [By using the last four invocations in Part 2] shall be consumed this moment in a greater manifestation than has ever been possible before.

America, the United States of America, the *United* States of America, is meant to be a country united: one nation under God whereby the people of America all see themselves as the sons and daughters of God. How can there be unity, how can there be one nation under God, when there is such intolerance against those who are different from oneself? Whatever the outer excuse is for creating intolerance and manifesting this state, this mindset of intolerance, it is directly un-American. If you want to call it unpatriotic, it is certainly unpatriotic, which means that most of those who call themselves patriots are greatly unpatriotic, for they are more intolerant than almost any other people in America.

I tell you, my beloved, they do not capture the Freedom Flame of Saint Germain by their hollow rhetoric and their hoarding of their guns and ammunition. For this nation may have been built by the use of guns, but it will not enter the Golden Age by the use of guns, bombs or any other kind of force-based device. The Golden Age, even though I may sound forceful, is not going to be manifest by force. It is going to be manifest by the power of God that is beyond force, and I am indeed beyond force, but I am not beyond power. How can you be free unless you have the power of God flowing through you to consume the forces of anti-love and anti-freedom,

26 | A higher form of democracy in America

which would tie you down in a certain matrix and therefore seek to maintain their illusions over time? They shall not stand!

A release of the violet flame

I, Saint Germain, have come to clean up this nation in a greater release of the violet flame than ever before. I ask you to visualize now the continent of North America where you know there are four flyways where the birds migrate North and South in spring and fall. You know that some of these birds migrate through Central America into South America, so I ask you to visualize these lines going from the North Pole along these flyways down to the North American continent, through Central America, through South America, where they spread out again, and then to the South Pole. Then, I ask you to visualize that I am standing on the North Pole and Portia is standing on the South Pole. Therefore, there is a figure-eight flow between us, flowing along these four flyways, these four energy currents, that have been created over thousands of years by the migrations of the birds, which are truly in many ways a more pure expression of the light of God than many other things manifest by man.

I ask you to visualize this push-pull, this figure-eight flow of the violet flame. I ask you, if you are willing, to open your chakras to the release of this into the physical octave right here, not only in California, but on the entire North American continent, the entire American continent, and flowing around the globe in this release of violet flame that truly brings out joy. What do you hear when the birds are singing in the spring? Do you not hear the pure joy of the birds rejoicing at the rising of the sun in the morning and the release of prana in the air? They start singing out of pure joy, as you have been singing out of pure joy when you gave this invocation and this decree. Truly, the word of God, the spoken word, released in joy, makes all matter sing. So let it sing, let it sing, let it sing. Let it sing with the Freedom Flame of Saint Germain.

Intolerance as a tool for fallen beings

Truly, intolerance started with the fallen beings, which were intolerant of God the Creator. Since they fell into an unascended sphere, and therefore realized they could not truly reach God, they then turned their intolerance to the sons and daughters of God. Anyone who had light, more light than they had, was subjected to and became the target of their intolerance. It is truly not that they are intolerant of the outer groups. The fallen beings are not intolerant of people with dark skin, red skin or yellow skin. They are intolerant of those who embody light. Therefore, they attempt to create division and put down certain groups of people that can be set apart by outer characteristics. They are not trying to put down black Americans. They are trying to put down those lifestreams that embody in a body with dark skin and who have the potential to manifest Christhood.

They, of course, are also, in a certain sense, putting down white people because white people have come from certain nationalities so they attempt to put down those. Or they attempt to put down women, or they attempt to put down poor people, those who do not have an education, who do not belong to a particular religion. You see, my beloved, once you allow the mindset of intolerance in a nation, there is no one who is free from being the target of intolerance. When you allow a nation to be taken over by this mindset of intolerance, you all become the targets of it, even those who think they are superior or exempt because they belong to this or that elite group. They are still, in a certain sense, the target of intolerance by someone.

Do you not see that this has created a downward spiral in this nation? It was meant to be the gathering place of people from all around the globe, from all kinds of backgrounds, in order to demonstrate—what? That outer differences do not matter when you have the recognition in your hearts that you are the sons and daughters of God.

The fallen beings are always divided within themselves and amongst themselves. Why do you think they have not taken over this planet? Because they cannot come together in true unity. The sons and daughters of God can do this, and the fallen beings will do anything in their power to prevent this coming together in unity by making you intolerant of each other, based on some outer excuse that they make you believe is so important and is somehow blocking whatever the goal may be.

The key to ending intolerance

Do you not see, my beloved, that there are many groups in America, and elsewhere, who may have a valid vision of what should be manifest? They are led astray into thinking that, in order to manifest a worthy goal, they have to fight against, or at least judge and condemn, a certain other group of people, for they are the ones who are standing between them and the manifestation of their goal. This is, of course, pure illusion, for if you are a co-creator with God, then what you really need in order to manifest your goal is the power of God flowing through you. There is no being on earth, no force on earth, no government on earth, no organization on earth, that can prevent you from going within your heart and developing your heart tie to your I AM Presence. Therefore, you do not need to put down or exterminate any other group of people in order to manifest your co-creative goal and express your abilities. You need to go within.

If you are not willing to go within and take responsibility for going within and looking at your own psychology, then you fall into the trap of the fallen beings of thinking that the problem is out there in these other people. They are the ones who need to be changed so that your goal can be manifest. What nonsense! What utter nonsense! I, Saint Germain, I am here to challenge it. I do challenge it by releasing the violet flame in a greater measure, for truly this violet flame release will make matter sing. When matter sings, that singing, that cosmic hum, expressed even through the atoms and molecules of the matter that makes up the land and the physical bodies of the people, will challenge the mindset of the fallen beings.

When you hear that matter is singing everywhere – and it does not matter whether it is a white, red, black, pink, yellow or a polka-dotted body – they are still singing with the same tune. Therefore, you know that it is the singing that is beyond, which matters and is the foundation of unity. The outer differences simply do not matter. They are not a source of conflict or division because you actually come to the point where you rejoice in each others differences.

The elitist mindset in America

This is what should have happened long ago on this continent. This was my vision when I pulled together those Founding Fathers, but you do understand that even many of the

Founding Fathers had a mindset of elitism. They did not necessarily want to free America from the British out of altruistic motives. They wanted to overthrow the British elite that ruled America so they could form an elite that ruled America.

You see that from the very beginning there was the elitist mindset, and this is indeed not my vision. This is again what I will not tolerate, for I have a Divine intolerance of those who are putting down the sons and daughters of God and the Flame of Freedom and making a mockery of the Flame of Freedom that I used to sponsor this nation. America today is not a bastion of freedom in the world. It is a bastion of tyranny and elitism, and this shall not stand!

I AM Saint Germain, and I AM manifesting my Presence in this land, and I AM making matter sing as you are making matter sing when you make these calls. I say: "Enough is enough!" The power elite of America has had its day on this continent. I will challenge it from this point forward, and when you make the calls and reinforce the challenge, we together will co-create a new future for America.

First, you will see the power elite become exposed is a greater measure than before. You will see the people awaken and accept the existence of the power elite and the need to transcend it. Therefore, we will bring forth a new state of awareness, a new state of freedom.

Surely, this will not happen instantly, you understand, because it is part of the people's learning process that they awaken gradually, that they take command over this nation and that they step up to the plate so that there will not be a vacuum. The power elite cannot be removed if there are not those among the people who are willing to step up and take the positions now held by power elite people. That would not facilitate the learning process where the American people wake up and realize that we, the people, are the government.

A more direct form of democracy

That is why I serve you notice for making your calls and holding your vision that America needs to transcend into a new form of democracy. It is not the highest form of democracy to have what you have now: a representative democracy. This opens you up to a tremendous manipulation by the power elite, for they can manipulate, deceive or even buy or intimidate the representatives that are elected. They can manipulate the entire process of election so that only those representatives who are willing to compromise and go along with the power elite, or who even believe in the agenda of the power elite, can stand for election.

When you look at the candidates that the people can choose from, they have very few, or perhaps even none, who truly represent the people. There is too much room for manipulation. There is too much room for people who have all of their money from corporations or lobbying groups to launch political campaigns where they can basically promise anything they want. Then, once they are elected and in there, they can do whatever the power elite wants and get away with it and even hide it from the people so that they will be re-elected, perhaps several times over.

This is not the form of democracy that I envisioned. It was the only one practical, given the times during the formation of America when communication was so much more primitive than today. Today, you have the Internet. This means that all people of America have the opportunity to educate themselves. People have the opportunity to create websites and put out information that challenges the government's position and the official or mainstream media.

Therefore, I speak into the collective consciousness of America: "Wake up, all Americans, and take upon yourselves the responsibility to educate yourselves about what is truly going on. I also call you to wake up and strive for Christ discernment, for not everything that is out there is true." Not all of the conspiracy theories have validity. In fact, most of them are distorted in some way or another, even though they contain some truth. You, yourselves, who have studied this, know how difficult it is to discern. Therefore, I ask you to make the calls for the increase of discernment of yourselves and the people.

I tell you that there has never been a better opportunity to educate yourselves, and therefore there has never been a better opportunity to take responsibility for the nation. Therefore, I say that there needs to be a more direct form of democracy where you create and use technology so that people can vote over the Internet, can vote directly for issues. There are so many issues in America that should not be decided by a small group of people in Congress, who can all be intimidated, manipulated, bought or persuaded by the power elite. It is not the highest form of democracy. The higher form of democracy is that there are certain big issues that need to be voted on by the people. Then, Congress, the politicians and the government apparatus are simply the servants of executing the details within the framework decided by the people.

Misguided patriotism

This can take different forms, I grant you. There are many technical challenges to overcome. There is a great challenge of overcoming the mindset where people believe that in order to be loyal to the American form of government, in order to be patriots, they need to maintain the status quo. Since when did it ever become loyalty to me to maintain the status quo? I AM the God of Freedom for the earth, and what is freedom?

It is continual, constant self-transcendence. How can you ever claim to be loyal to me or to my cause by seeking to maintain the status quo? It is, as we have said, the fallen beings who want to maintain form over time. I do not. I want to see form continually be transcended into a higher level of expression of the Golden Age, for my vision is so far higher than any human being on earth can currently accept and grasp. Therefore, the only way to manifest my vision is to continually transcend the form that is there now.

This, then, needs to happen. You need to make the calls for this, you need to hold the vision for this, you need to accept this. Now, I know very well that there are those who will say: "Oh, the people are not ready. They are not capable of making the right decisions. They will make terrible decisions. They will make mistakes." Well, my beloved, surely the people will make mistakes, but are you then implying that the current government is not making mistakes? Well then, be willing to let the people make their mistakes and learn from them, for I am willing to let the people make their mistakes and learn from them. I guarantee you that it will be a better government than what you have right now.

A shift in the American mindset

This, of course, requires a mind shift, a shift in your willingness to look at your government a new way. This messenger has, from the moment he came to America many years ago, been struck by the fact that Americans are more suspicious of their own government than many of the people in Europe. He knows well that it is because many of the people in Europe are asleep and are not aware of what is going on, but nevertheless it is true that Americans are more suspicious of their government than most other nations. Why is this so? Look at the birth of America. It started with a suspicion and hostility against the government of the British Empire.

This momentum created the United States, grant you, but this momentum needs to be transcended before the Golden Age can manifest in America. You cannot manifest a Golden Age matrix for America if the people are suspicious or hostile towards their own government, or if they think that their government is hostile towards them. It is a government *of* the people, *by* the people and *for* the people. I am perfectly aware that it is currently a government *of* the elite, *by* the elite and *for* the elite. For the shift to occur, the people must take back their willingness to own the government. You do not do this by projecting that the government is out to get you, or that it is so manipulated that nothing you do would make a difference.

Do you hear me, my beloved? You cannot change things if you will not take responsibility for them, and you cannot take responsibility if you do not accept that change is possible with the power of God, not with the power of men. I AM the power of God, and I am willing to work with those people in America who are willing to transcend the old mindset. Therefore, I say to you: "Wake up and get over this hostility, this suspicion. Accept that this is *your* government—if you take responsibility and claim ownership of it." It is possible, it *is* possible, to shift America almost in the blink of an eye if enough people wake up. I look to you who are the spiritual people, who are willing to listen to me and read my words, to be the first ones to make that shift.

Get out of your focus on conspiracy theories and this hopeless mindset that things are so bad that nothing can be done. Indeed, *something* can be done, for with God, with the God of Freedom, all things are possible. Therefore, I seal you in my flame not only of freedom but of this constant willingness to change, to reach beyond limitations and to manifest the higher matrix that you know is just waiting to be manifest in the three higher realms.

The Golden Age is not far away. It has descended through the identity realm, through the mental realm, almost all the way through the emotional realm, not in its ultimate manifestation but in a high enough manifestation to make an earth-shattering difference in America. There are many people who are beginning to grasp it. I ask you to make the calls and to hold the vision yourselves that a critical mass of people will wake up, grasp this matrix that I am releasing, act upon it and demand and call it into physical manifestation.

Thus, I thank you for your gracious attention, for the use of your chakras and auras, and I seal you in the love of my heart.

27 | INVOKING A MORE DIRECT DEMOCRACY IN AMERICA

In the name of the I AM THAT I AM, Jesus Christ, I use the authority that I have as a being in embodiment on earth to call upon Saint Germain and Portia to reinforce my calls and use my chakras to project the statements in this invocation into the collective consciousness and awaken Americans to the need to go beyond representative democracy. Awaken Americans to the reality that we are spiritual beings and that we can co-create a new future by working with the ascended masters. I especially call for …

[Make your own calls here.]

Part 1

1. America is a process, it is not a result, it is not a static state. It is an ever-self-transcending state, a mindset of wanting to go beyond boundaries, wanting to find greater and greater freedom and manifest a higher level of the Golden Age matrix of Saint Germain.

> O Saint Germain, you do inspire,
> my vision raised forever higher,
> with you I form a figure-eight,
> your Golden Age I co-create.
>
> **O Saint Germain, what love you bring,**
> **it truly makes all matter sing,**
> **your violet flame does all restore,**
> **with you we are becoming more.**

2. I invoke the Presence of Saint Germain in a greater manifestation than before. I invoke a greater intensity of the Freedom Flame than has ever been released on this planet.

> O Saint Germain, what Freedom Flame,
> released when we recite your name,
> acceleration is your gift,
> our planet it will surely lift.
>
> **O Saint Germain, what love you bring,**
> **it truly makes all matter sing,**
> **your violet flame does all restore,**
> **with you we are becoming more.**

3. By the authority of the Christ Flame within me, I draw a line in the sand and say: "Thus far and no farther." The manifestations of intolerance that are dividing Americans are consumed this moment in a greater manifestation than has ever been possible before.

> O Saint Germain, in love we claim,
> our right to bring your violet flame,
> from you Above, to us below,
> it is an all-transforming flow.
>
> **O Saint Germain, what love you bring,**
> **it truly makes all matter sing,**
> **your violet flame does all restore,**
> **with you we are becoming more.**

4. The *United* States of America is meant to be a country united: one nation under God whereby the people of America all see ourselves as the sons and daughters of God.

> O Saint Germain, I love you so,
> my aura filled with violet glow,
> my chakras filled with violet fire,
> I am your cosmic amplifier.
>
> **O Saint Germain, what love you bring,**
> **it truly makes all matter sing,**
> **your violet flame does all restore,**
> **with you we are becoming more.**

5. There cannot be unity, there cannot be one nation under God, when there is such intolerance against those who are

different from ourselves. This mindset of intolerance is directly unamerican and unpatriotic.

> O Saint Germain, I am now free,
> your violet flame is therapy,
> transform all hang-ups in my mind,
> as inner peace I surely find.
>
> **O Saint Germain, what love you bring,**
> **it truly makes all matter sing,**
> **your violet flame does all restore,**
> **with you we are becoming more.**

6. I call forth the judgment of Christ upon those who call themselves patriots but who are more intolerant than almost any other people in America. They do not capture the Freedom Flame of Saint Germain by their hollow rhetoric and their hoarding of guns and ammunition.

> O Saint Germain, my body pure,
> your violet flame for all is cure,
> consume the cause of all disease,
> and therefore I am all at ease.
>
> **O Saint Germain, what love you bring,**
> **it truly makes all matter sing,**
> **your violet flame does all restore,**
> **with you we are becoming more.**

7. This nation may have been built by the use of guns, but it will not enter the Golden Age by the use of guns, bombs or any other kind of force-based device. The Golden Age is not

going to be manifest by force. It is going to be manifest by the power of God that is beyond force.

> O Saint Germain, I'm karma-free,
> the past no longer burdens me,
> a brand new opportunity,
> I am in Christic unity.
>
> **O Saint Germain, what love you bring,**
> **it truly makes all matter sing,**
> **your violet flame does all restore,**
> **with you we are becoming more.**

8. We cannot be free unless we have the power of God flowing through us to consume the forces of anti-love and anti-freedom, which would tie us down in a certain matrix and therefore seek to maintain their illusions over time. They shall not stand!

> O Saint Germain, we are now one,
> I am for you a violet sun,
> as we transform this planet earth,
> your Golden Age is given birth.
>
> **O Saint Germain, what love you bring,**
> **it truly makes all matter sing,**
> **your violet flame does all restore,**
> **with you we are becoming more.**

9. I call forth Saint Germain and a greater release of the violet flame than ever before.

O Saint Germain, the earth is free,
from burden of duality,
in oneness we bring what is best,
your Golden Age is manifest.

**O Saint Germain, what love you bring,
it truly makes all matter sing,
your violet flame does all restore,
with you we are becoming more.**

Part 2

1. I visualize Saint Germain standing on the North Pole and Portia standing on the South Pole. There is a figure-eight flow of violet flame between them, flowing along the four flyways, these four energy currents.

O Portia, in your own retreat,
with Mother's Love you do me greet.
As all my tests I now complete,
old patterns I no more repeat.

**O Portia, opportunity,
I am beyond duality.
I focus now internally,
with you I grow eternally.**

2. I visualize this push-pull, this figure-eight flow of the violet flame. I open my chakras to the release of this into the physical octave on the entire North American continent, the

entire American continent, and flowing around the globe in this release of violet flame that truly brings out joy.

> O Portia, Justice is your name,
> upholding Cosmic Honor Flame,
> No longer will I play the game,
> of seeking to remain the same.

> **O Portia, opportunity,**
> **I am beyond duality.**
> **I focus now internally,**
> **with you I grow eternally.**

3. I visualize that these currents of violet flame consume all energies and records of intolerance in America, all energies dividing the American people and preventing us from being one nation under God.

> O Portia, in the cosmic flow,
> one with you, I ever grow.
> I am the chalice here below,
> of cosmic justice you bestow.

> **O Portia, opportunity,**
> **I am beyond duality.**
> **I focus now internally,**
> **with you I grow eternally.**

4. I call forth the judgment of Christ upon the fallen beings who are intolerant of anyone who has more light than them and who seek to create division and put down certain groups of people in an attempt to stop the lifestreams who have the potential to manifest Christhood.

O Portia, cosmic balance bring,
eternal hope, my heart does sing.
Protected by your Mother's wing,
I feel at one with everything.

**O Portia, opportunity,
I am beyond duality.
I focus now internally,
with you I grow eternally.**

5. Once we allow the mindset of intolerance in a nation, there is no one who is free from being the target of intolerance. When we allow our nation to be taken over by this mindset of intolerance, we all become the targets of it.

O Portia, bring the Mother Light,
to set all free from darkest night.
Your Love Flame shines forever bright,
with Saint Germain now hold me tight.

**O Portia, opportunity,
I am beyond duality.
I focus now internally,
with you I grow eternally.**

6. America was meant to be the gathering place of people from all around the globe, from all kinds of backgrounds, in order to demonstrate that outer differences do not matter, when we have the recognition in our hearts that we are the sons and daughters of God.

O Portia, in your mastery,
I feel transforming chemistry.

In your light of reality,
I find the golden alchemy.

**O Portia, opportunity,
I am beyond duality.
I focus now internally,
with you I grow eternally.**

7. The sons and daughters of God can come together in true unity, and the fallen beings will do anything in their power to prevent this by making us intolerant of each other, based on some outer excuse.

O Portia, in the cosmic stream,
I am awake from human dream.
Removing now the ego's beam,
I earn my place on cosmic team.

**O Portia, opportunity,
I am beyond duality.
I focus now internally,
with you I grow eternally.**

8. Many groups in America have a valid vision of what should be manifest. They are led astray into thinking that, in order to manifest a worthy goal, they have to fight against, or at least judge and condemn, certain other people.

O Portia, you come from afar,
you are a cosmic avatar.
So infinite your repertoire,
you are for earth a guiding star.

> **O Portia, opportunity,**
> **I am beyond duality.**
> **I focus now internally,**
> **with you I grow eternally.**

9. This is an illusion, for if we are co-creators with God, what we really need in order to manifest our goal is the power of God flowing through us.

> O Portia, I am confident,
> I am a cosmic instrument.
> I came to earth from heaven sent,
> to help bring forward her ascent.

> **O Portia, opportunity,**
> **I am beyond duality.**
> **I focus now internally,**
> **with you I grow eternally.**

Part 3

1. There is no being on earth, no force on earth, no government on earth, no organization on earth, that can prevent us from going within our hearts and developing our heart tie to our I AM Presences.

> O Saint Germain, you do inspire,
> my vision raised forever higher,
> with you I form a figure-eight,
> your Golden Age I co-create.

> **O Saint Germain, what love you bring,
> it truly makes all matter sing,
> your violet flame does all restore,
> with you we are becoming more.**

2. We do not need to put down or exterminate any other group of people in order to manifest our co-creative goal and express our abilities. We need to go within.

> O Saint Germain, what Freedom Flame,
> released when we recite your name,
> acceleration is your gift,
> our planet it will surely lift.

> **O Saint Germain, what love you bring,
> it truly makes all matter sing,
> your violet flame does all restore,
> with you we are becoming more.**

3. The trap of the fallen beings is to make people think that the problem is out there in these other people. They are the ones who need to be changed so that our goal can be manifest.

> O Saint Germain, in love we claim,
> our right to bring your violet flame,
> from you Above, to us below,
> it is an all-transforming flow.

> **O Saint Germain, what love you bring,
> it truly makes all matter sing,
> your violet flame does all restore,
> with you we are becoming more.**

4. I call upon Saint Germain to challenge this mindset by releasing the violet flame in a greater measure that will make matter sing. When matter sings, that singing, that cosmic hum, expressed even through the atoms and molecules of the matter that make up the land and the physical bodies of the people, will challenge the mindset of the fallen beings.

> O Saint Germain, I love you so,
> my aura filled with violet glow,
> my chakras filled with violet fire,
> I am your cosmic amplifier.
>
> **O Saint Germain, what love you bring,**
> **it truly makes all matter sing,**
> **your violet flame does all restore,**
> **with you we are becoming more.**

5. When we hear that matter is singing everywhere, we know that it is the singing that matters and is the foundation of unity. The outer differences simply do not matter. They are not a source of conflict or division because we rejoice in each others differences.

> O Saint Germain, I am now free,
> your violet flame is therapy,
> transform all hang-ups in my mind,
> as inner peace I surely find.
>
> **O Saint Germain, what love you bring,**
> **it truly makes all matter sing,**
> **your violet flame does all restore,**
> **with you we are becoming more.**

6. I call upon Saint Germain to challenge the elitist mindset that is against his vision for a united America. I will not tolerate this mindset, for I have a Divine intolerance of those who are putting down the sons and daughters of God and the Flame of Freedom.

> O Saint Germain, my body pure,
> your violet flame for all is cure,
> consume the cause of all disease,
> and therefore I am all at ease.
>
> **O Saint Germain, what love you bring,**
> **it truly makes all matter sing,**
> **your violet flame does all restore,**
> **with you we are becoming more.**

7. I call forth the judgment of Christ upon those who are making a mockery of the Flame of Freedom that Saint Germain used to sponsor this nation. America today is not a bastion of freedom in the world. It is a bastion of tyranny and elitism, and this shall not stand!

> O Saint Germain, I'm karma-free,
> the past no longer burdens me,
> a brand new opportunity,
> I am in Christic unity.
>
> **O Saint Germain, what love you bring,**
> **it truly makes all matter sing,**
> **your violet flame does all restore,**
> **with you we are becoming more.**

8. I call for Saint Germain to manifest his Presence in this land and make matter sing. I say with Saint Germain: "Enough is enough! The power elite of America has had its day on this continent."

> O Saint Germain, we are now one,
> I am for you a violet sun,
> as we transform this planet earth,
> your Golden Age is given birth.
>
> **O Saint Germain, what love you bring,**
> **it truly makes all matter sing,**
> **your violet flame does all restore,**
> **with you we are becoming more.**

9. By the authority of the Christ flame within me, I challenge the power elite and I call for Saint Germain to reinforce the challenge. We together will co-create a new future for America.

> O Saint Germain, the earth is free,
> from burden of duality,
> in oneness we bring what is best,
> your Golden Age is manifest.
>
> **O Saint Germain, what love you bring,**
> **it truly makes all matter sing,**
> **your violet flame does all restore,**
> **with you we are becoming more.**

Part 4

1. By the authority of the Christ flame within me, I call for the power elite to be exposed in a greater measure than before. I call for the people to awaken and recognize the existence of the power elite and the need to transcend it.

> O Portia, in your own retreat,
> with Mother's Love you do me greet.
> As all my tests I now complete,
> old patterns I no more repeat.
>
> **O Portia, opportunity,**
> **I am beyond duality.**
> **I focus now internally,**
> **with you I grow eternally.**

2. I call forth a new state of awareness, a new state of freedom so the people will awaken and take command over this nation. I call for the cutting free of the people who can take the positions now held by power elite people.

> O Portia, Justice is your name,
> upholding Cosmic Honor Flame,
> No longer will I play the game,
> of seeking to remain the same.
>
> **O Portia, opportunity,**
> **I am beyond duality.**
> **I focus now internally,**
> **with you I grow eternally.**

3. I call for Americans to be cut free to see that America needs to transcend into a new form of democracy that is beyond a representative democracy.

> O Portia, in the cosmic flow,
> one with you, I ever grow.
> I am the chalice here below,
> of cosmic justice you bestow.
>
> **O Portia, opportunity,**
> **I am beyond duality.**
> **I focus now internally,**
> **with you I grow eternally.**

4. I call forth the judgment of Christ upon the power elite who are manipulating, deceiving or even buying the representatives that are elected.

> O Portia, cosmic balance bring,
> eternal hope, my heart does sing.
> Protected by your Mother's wing,
> I feel at one with everything.
>
> **O Portia, opportunity,**
> **I am beyond duality.**
> **I focus now internally,**
> **with you I grow eternally.**

5. I call forth the judgment of Christ upon the power elite who are manipulating the entire process of elections so that only those representatives who are willing to compromise and go along with the power elite, or who even believe in the agenda of the power elite, can stand for election.

27 | *Invoking a more direct democracy in America*

> O Portia, bring the Mother Light,
> to set all free from darkest night.
> Your Love Flame shines forever bright,
> with Saint Germain now hold me tight.
>
> **O Portia, opportunity,**
> **I am beyond duality.**
> **I focus now internally,**
> **with you I grow eternally.**

6. I call forth the judgment of Christ upon the candidates who are not truly representing the people because they get all of their money from corporations or lobbying groups to launch political campaigns where they can basically promise anything they want.

> O Portia, in your mastery,
> I feel transforming chemistry.
> In your light of reality,
> I find the golden alchemy.
>
> **O Portia, opportunity,**
> **I am beyond duality.**
> **I focus now internally,**
> **with you I grow eternally.**

7. I call forth the judgment of Christ upon those candidates who, once they are elected, do whatever the power elite wants and get away with it and even hide it from the people so that they will be re-elected.

> O Portia, in the cosmic stream,
> I am awake from human dream.

> Removing now the ego's beam,
> I earn my place on cosmic team.
>
> **O Portia, opportunity,**
> **I am beyond duality.**
> **I focus now internally,**
> **with you I grow eternally.**

8. This is not the form of democracy that Saint Germain envisioned. Today, all people of America have the opportunity to educate themselves. People have the opportunity to create websites and put out information that challenges the government's position and the official or mainstream media.

> O Portia, you come from afar,
> you are a cosmic avatar.
> So infinite your repertoire,
> you are for earth a guiding star.
>
> **O Portia, opportunity,**
> **I am beyond duality.**
> **I focus now internally,**
> **with you I grow eternally.**

9. I speak into the collective consciousness of America: "Wake up, all Americans, and take upon yourselves the responsibility to educate yourselves about what is truly going on. I also call you to wake up and strive for Christ discernment, for not everything that is out there is true."

> O Portia, I am confident,
> I am a cosmic instrument.

I came to earth from heaven sent,
to help bring forward her ascent.

**O Portia, opportunity,
I am beyond duality.
I focus now internally,
with you I grow eternally.**

Part 5

1. There has never been a better opportunity to educate ourselves, and therefore there has never been a better opportunity to take responsibility for our nation.

O Saint Germain, you do inspire,
my vision raised forever higher,
with you I form a figure-eight,
your Golden Age I co-create.

**O Saint Germain, what love you bring,
it truly makes all matter sing,
your violet flame does all restore,
with you we are becoming more.**

2. I call forth a more direct form of democracy where we create and use technology so that people can vote over the Internet, can vote directly about issues.

O Saint Germain, what Freedom Flame,
released when we recite your name,

acceleration is your gift,
our planet it will surely lift.

**O Saint Germain, what love you bring,
it truly makes all matter sing,
your violet flame does all restore,
with you we are becoming more.**

3. There are too many issues in America that should not be decided by a small group of people in Congress, who can all be intimidated, manipulated, bought or persuaded by the power elite.

O Saint Germain, in love we claim,
our right to bring your violet flame,
from you Above, to us below,
it is an all-transforming flow.

**O Saint Germain, what love you bring,
it truly makes all matter sing,
your violet flame does all restore,
with you we are becoming more.**

4. This is not the highest form of democracy. The higher form of democracy is that there are certain big issues that need to be voted on by the people. Then, Congress, the politicians and the government apparatus are simply the servants of executing the details within the framework decided by the people.

O Saint Germain, I love you so,
my aura filled with violet glow,
my chakras filled with violet fire,
I am your cosmic amplifier.

> O Saint Germain, what love you bring,
> it truly makes all matter sing,
> your violet flame does all restore,
> with you we are becoming more.

5. I call for Americans to be cut free from the mindset where people believe that in order to be loyal to the American form of government, in order to be patriots, they need to maintain the status quo.

> O Saint Germain, I am now free,
> your violet flame is therapy,
> transform all hang-ups in my mind,
> as inner peace I surely find.

> O Saint Germain, what love you bring,
> it truly makes all matter sing,
> your violet flame does all restore,
> with you we are becoming more.

6. We are not being loyal to Saint Germain by maintaining the status quo. Saint Germain is the God of Freedom for the earth, and freedom is continual, constant self-transcendence.

> O Saint Germain, my body pure,
> your violet flame for all is cure,
> consume the cause of all disease,
> and therefore I am all at ease.

> O Saint Germain, what love you bring,
> it truly makes all matter sing,
> your violet flame does all restore,
> with you we are becoming more.

7. We are never loyal to Saint Germain and the cause of freedom by seeking to maintain the status quo. It is the fallen beings who want to maintain form over time.

> O Saint Germain, I'm karma-free,
> the past no longer burdens me,
> a brand new opportunity,
> I am in Christic unity.
>
> **O Saint Germain, what love you bring,**
> **it truly makes all matter sing,**
> **your violet flame does all restore,**
> **with you we are becoming more.**

8. Saint Germain wants to see form continually be transcended into a higher level of expression of the Golden Age, for his vision is so far higher than any human being on earth can currently accept and grasp. Therefore, the only way to manifest Saint Germain's vision is to continually transcend the form that is here now.

> O Saint Germain, we are now one,
> I am for you a violet sun,
> as we transform this planet earth,
> your Golden Age is given birth.
>
> **O Saint Germain, what love you bring,**
> **it truly makes all matter sing,**
> **your violet flame does all restore,**
> **with you we are becoming more.**

9. I call forth the judgment of Christ upon the power elite who will say that the people are not ready and will make terrible

27 | Invoking a more direct democracy in America

decisions. I accept that the current government is also making mistakes. I am willing to let the people make their mistakes and learn from them, for this will be a better government than what we have right now.

> O Saint Germain, the earth is free,
> from burden of duality,
> in oneness we bring what is best,
> your Golden Age is manifest.

> **O Saint Germain, what love you bring,**
> **it truly makes all matter sing,**
> **your violet flame does all restore,**
> **with you we are becoming more.**

Part 6

1. I call for Americans to be cut free from the mindset that makes them more suspicious of their own government than many other people.

> O Portia, in your own retreat,
> with Mother's Love you do me greet.
> As all my tests I now complete,
> old patterns I no more repeat.

> **O Portia, opportunity,**
> **I am beyond duality.**
> **I focus now internally,**
> **with you I grow eternally.**

2. This suspicion goes back to the birth of America. It started with a suspicion and hostility against the government of the British Empire. This momentum created the United States, but it needs to be transcended before the Golden Age can manifest in America.

> O Portia, Justice is your name,
> upholding Cosmic Honor Flame,
> No longer will I play the game,
> of seeking to remain the same.
>
> **O Portia, opportunity,**
> **I am beyond duality.**
> **I focus now internally,**
> **with you I grow eternally.**

3. We cannot manifest a Golden Age matrix for America if the people are suspicious or hostile towards their own government, or if they think that their government is hostile towards them.

> O Portia, in the cosmic flow,
> one with you, I ever grow.
> I am the chalice here below,
> of cosmic justice you bestow.
>
> **O Portia, opportunity,**
> **I am beyond duality.**
> **I focus now internally,**
> **with you I grow eternally.**

4. I call for Americans to be cut free to take back our willingness to own the government. We do not do this by projecting

that the government is out to get us, or that it is so manipulated that nothing we do would make a difference.

> O Portia, cosmic balance bring,
> eternal hope, my heart does sing.
> Protected by your Mother's wing,
> I feel at one with everything.

> **O Portia, opportunity,**
> **I am beyond duality.**
> **I focus now internally,**
> **with you I grow eternally.**

5. We cannot change things if we will not take responsibility for them, and we cannot take responsibility if we do not accept that change is possible with the power of God, not with the power of men.

> O Portia, bring the Mother Light,
> to set all free from darkest night.
> Your Love Flame shines forever bright,
> with Saint Germain now hold me tight.

> **O Portia, opportunity,**
> **I am beyond duality.**
> **I focus now internally,**
> **with you I grow eternally.**

6. Saint Germain is the power of God, and he is willing to work with those people in America who are willing to transcend the old mindset.

> O Portia, in your mastery,
> I feel transforming chemistry.
> In your light of reality,
> I find the golden alchemy.
>
> **O Portia, opportunity,**
> **I am beyond duality.**
> **I focus now internally,**
> **with you I grow eternally.**

7. By the authority of the Christ flame within me, I say to all Americans: "Wake up and get over this hostility, this suspicion. Accept that this is *our* government—if we take responsibility and claim ownership of it."

> O Portia, in the cosmic stream,
> I am awake from human dream.
> Removing now the ego's beam,
> I earn my place on cosmic team.
>
> **O Portia, opportunity,**
> **I am beyond duality.**
> **I focus now internally,**
> **with you I grow eternally.**

8. It is possible, it *is* possible, to shift America almost in the blink of an eye if enough people wake up. I call for the spiritual people to be the first ones to make that shift and get out of the focus on conspiracy theories and this hopeless mindset that things are so bad that nothing can be done.

> O Portia, you come from afar,
> you are a cosmic avatar.

So infinite your repertoire,
you are for earth a guiding star.

**O Portia, opportunity,
I am beyond duality.
I focus now internally,
with you I grow eternally.**

9. Indeed, *something* can be done, for with God, with the God of Freedom, all things are possible. By the authority of the Christ flame within me, I call forth the Golden Age matrix of Saint Germain to descend into the physical in a high enough manifestation to make an earth-shattering difference in America. I demand and call this into physical manifestation.

O Portia, I am confident,
I am a cosmic instrument.
I came to earth from heaven sent,
to help bring forward her ascent.

**O Portia, opportunity,
I am beyond duality.
I focus now internally,
with you I grow eternally.**

Sealing

In the name of the I AM THAT I AM, I accept that Archangel Michael, Astrea and Shiva form an impenetrable shield around myself and all constructive people in America, sealing us from all fear-based energies in all four octaves. I accept that the Light

of God is consuming and transforming all fear-based energies that make up the dark forces working against America!

28 | THE JUDGMENT OF CHRIST UPON THE FALSE JESUS

I AM the Ascended Master Jesus Christ. I am the hierarch of the Piscean Age. I am the brother in Spirit of Saint Germain, the hierarch of the Aquarian Age.

How do you think it feels for me to have started the Piscean dispensation on earth – walking in a physical body, taking on everything I took on in order to give that initial impetus for the founding of the Christian movement – and then, here I am today, and there are over a billion people who claim to be my followers, yet so few of them are open to my Living Word, to the living Presence, to the living Spirit that I AM? They worship a dead spirit, a dead idol. They worship a spirit that is not a Spirit of God but a man-made spirit that has been created by the Christian movement, especially since the formation of the Roman Catholic church.

Binding of the false Christ

I have, through this messenger, withdrawn my light from that church. I shall today withdraw my light from all Christian churches in America that are trapped in worshipping the false Jesus that has been created by man. I AM the Living Jesus Christ. I AM the real Jesus. The spirit that has been created by the Christian churches for these many centuries is hereby judged. It is judged by the Living Word and the living Presence of the real Christ, the real Jesus. I therefore, by speaking these words in the physical, command Archangel Michael to send his angels to bind that spirit of the false Jesus. I command you to take it from the earth. I command you to bind and consume all of the demons, all of the fallen beings who have been instrumental in creating, sustaining and reinforcing it. Thus, there is an opportunity for Christianity worldwide and Christianity in America to start on a clean white page.

The creation of false gods

I know well that most Christians are not likely to make use of this opportunity, for they are so attached to this false image of Christ that they will not let go of it, and they will begin to create a new spirit for them to worship. Do you not understand that when it was said to "have no other gods before me," before the one God, it is precisely because people have for a very long time created false gods that they have worshiped before the one formless God? How did it come to be on planet earth that people would create these false gods?

It was introduced here by the fallen beings. They were the ones who wanted to be those false gods, worshiped by as many people as possible. This is not to say that people had not created some gods before, for there is a tendency for people to see divinity in everything, and this tendency can quickly become the worshiping of a particular god, such as a god of nature or certain aspects of nature. This then can cause people to stop worshiping the formless God, to stop always striving to transcend themselves until they touch the hem of the formless God through the Christ consciousness.

False gods can be touched without the Christ consciousness, but the formless God can be touched only through the Christ consciousness. Those who are not willing to transcend themselves, to transcend their egos in order to take on part of the Christ consciousness (to let that living Christ consciousness dwell within them), they will be left to worship these false gods. When enough people have worshiped the false gods for some time, you create a spirit that has enough awareness, consciousness, and momentum that people will feel like they have had a supernatural or even spiritual experience.

America worshiping a false Christ

When you look at America today (and for that matter beyond the borders of America, but I will focus on America for this particular purpose), you see that there are many Christians who go to church, or they do other religious activities, and they feel they have had a genuine spiritual experience of going beyond their normal level of consciousness. There are indeed a few people who have genuine spiritual experiences by going to a Christian church, for they are able to transcend the outer circumstances and reach my heart. I tell you that the vast majority of the people who claim to have such experiences are not having an experience of touching the formless God through the Christ consciousness. They are having the experience of interacting with a man-made god, the false god created by Christianity, or even the false gods, the false spirits, created by specific churches.

This is not who I AM. This is not worshiping me, following me, being loyal to me, acknowledging me. You do not do me any service by indulging in these experiences where you simply go into an ecstatic or trance-like state and your mind can be taken over by lower spirits. This is *not* the Holy Spirit, for *it* is undivided, indivisible, and it always points to the formless God, not a man-made image of God or Christ. What is the difference, you might say? The formless God is beyond any image and so is Christ. This is what people either cannot or will not realize. Why will they not realize this? Because their minds have been trapped by the snares created by the fallen beings. The fallen beings cannot (because they *will* not) experience the formless God or the Christ consciousness. If they could or would experience the Christ consciousness, they would not be fallen beings.

This is, one might say, a black-and-white viewpoint. You understand, or at least I aim to help you understand, that there are certain things on earth that are either/or. Your television is either on or off. It is not in some in-between state. It is either day or night, although there is a brief in-between state. A color is either black or white. It is not black and white at the same time, although it can be a mixture of the two. This is not black-and-white thinking. This is simply distinguishing between various characteristics.

Black-and-white thinking is when you impose a mental image upon reality instead of being willing to experience reality. Black-and-white thinking begins when you create an idol and project that this is God, the only true God, and therefore you refuse to go beyond the idol and experience the formless God. When you experience the formless God or the formlessness of the Christ consciousness, you cannot be in black-and-white thinking. If you are in black-and-white thinking, you cannot experience the formless God.

The scribes and Pharisees in America

What, then, can get you out of black-and-white thinking once you have entered that state of mind? Nothing, nothing from heaven or earth, except your own willingness to question the way you look at life. Surely, you can give people an experience that there is an alternative to black-and-white thinking. This is what I did when I walked the earth in a physical body. This is what many of you can do because you have enough Christ consciousness that you can give people that experience. It still requires the exercise of free will where you are willing to step back, look at your thinking, and say: "Is this all there is to my ability to think? Is this all there is to my mind's ability to grasp reality? Or can I potentially have an experience that is beyond these mental images?"

The scribes and the Pharisees were not willing to question their images, even when I stood before them in the flesh. The leaders of the Jewish religion were not willing to question their images, for they would not let go of the form that they were seeking to maintain over time. Therefore, they would rather kill the Living Christ than change their thinking, transcend their thinking.

The sad fact is that the vast majority of the leaders of Christian churches in America are in exactly the same frame of mind today as the scribes and Pharisees were in when I stood before them in the flesh. Now I again stand, almost in the flesh, and I speak to the mass consciousness of the Christian churches in America. Therefore I say: "Come forth out of the tomb of this false Christianity that worships a man-made spirit that is not the Living Christ!"

The need to make a choice for Christ

Those who are the leaders of these churches will today be confronted with me, with my Spirit at inner levels. My Spirit is able to cover the entire continent and therefore manifest itself to all of the people upon it. I therefore manifest my Spirit at inner levels for all of the leaders of the Christian churches, and I serve them notice:

It is time for you to choose between light and darkness. If you will not choose, then the judgment of Christ will be upon you, and you will be confronted with the full descent of your karma. You may deny karma, you may deny the judgment, you may deny anything you like, but at inner levels you cannot deny that you have been visited by the Living Spirit of Christ.

This is an action that can, and hopefully will, be reinforced by those hearing, reading this dictation, being willing to give the invocation, and therefore calling forth a shift in the Christian churches of America. This does not mean I envision that these churches will begin to accept me as an ascended master or accept this messenger or other teachings. It does mean that the Christian churches in America need to begin to shift out of black-and-white thinking, and they need to do so quickly, or there will be a descent of judgment such as has not been seen before on this continent (or any other, for that matter) since the time of Atlantis. This is beyond playing games.

You have had your day. You have had your day during the Piscean dispensation, to do whatever you wanted with the Christian movement. You, pastors and leaders in America, have had your day since the founding of this nation to play games and think you can define how a Christian church should be.

The abuse of power in Christian churches

Look at the ministers who have abused their power in various ways: money, sex, power, what have you. Look at those who have claimed that certain wars were just wars approved by God or Christ. Look at this circus that has been created by Christian churches in America. Look at the major mega-churches, where people come and are exposed to all kind of pageantry that is nothing but cheap entertainment and has nothing to do with the self-transcendence that is the hallmark of Christ. I for one have had enough of it, and I call upon all those who are the spiritual people, who are open to my Living Word, to decide whether you have had enough of it also. If you have, then make the calls. Use the tools and invocations and make the calls for a shift in the Christian movement in America away from black-and-white thinking.

I tell you that there are many wonderful, loving, kind people in Christian movements. I may sound stern, but I am not unaware of these people. I am not insensitive to their great love for me and for humanity. I am not pushing aside all of the efforts they have made, whether in charity or in other ways. I know I sound uncompromising, and I *am* uncompromising. Despite all of your efforts, you are not fulfilling your highest potential as long as you allow yourself to be trapped in these mockeries of Christian churches, created by those beings that are completely taken over by the consciousness of anti-Christ. Remember what I said to Peter when he told me how my mission should unfold, according to his idolatrous image? I said: "Get thee behind me, Satan!" For Satan is the consciousness that demands that Spirit conforms to its own image or conforms to the current conditions of matter.

This is how matter becomes a self-reinforcing downward spiral: When the people in embodiment begin to allow their Spirits to conform to current conditions and think they cannot be changed. That is why I performed miracles. I wanted to demonstrate that through the Christ consciousness anything on earth can be changed. If you do not accept this, you are caught in the satanic consciousness. Everything is fluid, everything is subject to the power of God, but the power of God can come only through those in embodiment who are willing to exercise their free will and be the open doors for that power.

Satanic forces in Christian churches

This is not a matter of doing good deeds. It is perfectly fine to feed the hungry and clothe the homeless, but unless you are doing it with the Spirit of Christ, you are not fulfilling your highest potential, and therefore it is not the worthy offering. The worthy offering is not measured by a man-made standard of what it means to do good deeds. It is measured by the standard of Christ: your willingness to transcend your consciousness and multiply the talents, instead of burying them in the ground of a man-made idol.

Although I love all people on earth, all those who are doing good deeds, who have pure intentions, I love you with the firmness of a Christic love that will not leave you alone in a lesser state when I know you are capable of manifesting a higher state. Therefore, I am here to shake awake those who are willing to be awakened. There is more to life than what you have been told by these Christian churches. If you could see what is going on behind the visible, physical, conscious level,

28 | *The judgment of Christ upon the false Jesus*

you would instantly remove yourselves from these churches and withdraw your light.

There are forces of darkness, forces of anti-Christ, satanic forces, that are using the Christian churches of America to steal the light of the good and the pure-intentioned people. By going to these churches every Sunday, pouring out your devotion to what you think is me, you are supporting this entire false hierarchy of Christianity that is running most of the Christian churches in America today. This is not working for the cause of Christ, regardless of what you are doing on the outer. I am not saying that all of the beneficial activities need to be stopped. I am saying they need to be transcended so that they can be done from a higher level of Christ consciousness. You need to recognize that the churches and their leaders are taken over by these forces of darkness, and if you will not come up higher, you will continue to give your light to them.

This will mean that you will not be saved after this lifetime, as you believe will be the case. You will be confronted with the absolute reality that you have not qualified to enter heaven, you have not qualified for your ascension, and you will have to come back into embodiment. If you continue to listen to the false preachers who deny reincarnation, it will not change the law of God. No amount of preaching from the pulpit will change the law of God.

There is an absolute reality: You cannot cheat the law of God. The fallen beings would have you believe that there are ways to get around it, ways to force God to accept you into the kingdom of heaven. It is all lies! I have exposed this in enough dictations through this messenger, in books, and on the websites that anyone who is willing can free him- or herself from the illusions promoted by the false pastors of Christianity, the wolves in sheep's clothing, those who may appear beautiful outward but within they are like whitened sepulchers filled with dead men's bones. Stop following them! Awaken and follow me, the Living Christ!

False teachers of the New Age movement

Truly it is time, it is past time, that the spiritual people of America step up. Now I speak not only to those in Christian movements but to those who have rejected Christianity because they saw the falsity of it. It is commendable that you have the discernment to see the falsity of many Christian churches. It is commendable that you have opened your hearts and minds to a teaching that is beyond Christianity and beyond materialism. I tell you: the vast majority of the so-called spiritual, New Age or progressive people in America—instead of following the false idols of Christianity, you are following other false idols. You are following those who are the false teachers of the New Age movement.

I am not saying that all who are in that movement are false teachers, but there are many. Many – too many – people who have the potential to manifest Christhood and qualify for their ascension in this lifetime have tied themselves to these lesser gurus who are not interested in taking you to Christ consciousness. They are interested in having you follow them for whatever reason they have, but it all revolves around taking your light, for they need it. Why? Because they do not have the internal light, for they have not been willing to reach for the Christ consciousness.

They may talk about enlightenment all day and all night, but there is no substitute for the Christ consciousness, even though you may call it other names. The Christ consciousness is self-transcendence. It is being willing to step back and reach for a higher experience, rather than being attached to a mental image and projecting it upon reality. The consciousness of Satan is that of projecting a mental image upon reality and denying or refusing the direct experience of the reality that is beyond images because it is the formless God and the formless Christ.

Enlightenment is an empty concept

Truly, because of Christianity, it is easy to believe that Christ takes on the form promoted by the Christian churches, but it is time for you to know better and realize that Christ is much more. Christ is a universal state of consciousness that can never be trapped in any form or in any name, nor can it be captured by any guru, no matter how outrageous a claim he makes to be enlightened.

Enlightenment is an empty concept. Anyone who claims to be enlightened demonstrates that he or she does not know what enlightenment is. Enlightenment is nothing but a label. For that matter, Christ consciousness is nothing but a label. Any word, any image, that can be grasped by the human mind is nothing but a label. The Christ consciousness – for I have to name it some word that you can grasp and hear – is beyond all words, all images. It is that transcendent experience. You may say: "But is that not enlightenment?" Yes and no, for enlightenment is that which does not and will not conform to any image on earth. You may say: "But can we not then use the word enlightenment as you use the words Christ consciousness?" Sure, you can. Just make sure that, as I know that the Christ consciousness is more than the word, you also know that enlightenment is more than the word and the mental image that certain teachers have built around it. The more you seek to explain it, the more you create an idol that can trap the minds of those who are unaware or unwilling to transcend. There are enough people in the spiritual and New Age movement in America that, if they manifested their Christhood, they could make the decisive difference that many of you dream about making. Because you are running after the false gurus, you are not manifesting your Christ potential, and therefore you cannot make the difference. I have called for 10,000 Christed beings [See the book *The Mystical Teachings of Jesus*] to step forward and consciously accept and manifest their Christhood. That is what it will take to shift the earth to a higher level. Not to the fifth dimension, or any other dimension, or any other fancy label that you run after, thinking: "This is it."

Transcend the false gurus

My beloved, the shift in consciousness is beyond what any guru in the New Age movement has so far been able to envision. It is beyond what we have given in these teachings or any previous ascended master teaching. It is something that is not set in stone. It is something that is co-created as you go along. There is no one in heaven or on earth who can predict exactly how this will be manifest. We who are in the spiritual realm have no need to predict it, for we enjoy seeing it unfold. It cannot unfold as long as those who have the potential to be the forerunners allow themselves to be trapped in these blind alleys, these false images and organizations and movements created specifically to keep you from your Christhood.

Am I saying all movements and all gurus are false? Nay, of course not. I am only calling those who are trapped by false gurus to come out from the tomb and be willing to meet the Living Christ that I AM, rather than the false Christ that you are now following. This is not a matter of following this

28 | The judgment of Christ upon the false Jesus

messenger. It is a matter of following the Living Christ that I AM.

You may say: "We are looking towards the Aquarian Age." Yes, you are, but there is no Aquarian Age on earth without Jesus Christ. I hold the Office of the Hierarch of Pisces, and no one can enter the Aquarian Age or the Aquarian consciousness without going through the office that I hold. It is not in any way associated with Christian churches, but it is a spiritual office, and if you allow the Christian churches and their falsity to cause you to refuse to approach the Living Spirit that I AM, then you cannot enter the Aquarian Age of Saint Germain.

What will you then enter? Only another state of idolatry where you think you are creating the Golden Age, but it is only by degrees different from what has been created by false Christianity over these past centuries. This is not the vision of Saint Germain. Then I, the Living Spirit of Jesus Christ, hereby manifest my Presence in front of all false gurus in America:

It is time for you to make the choice between light and darkness. If you will not, then the judgment of Christ will descend with all of the ramifications this might have. It may not be visible, but it surely will be undeniable.

My beloved, those of you who are here have held a tremendous balance that has allowed me to bring forth this judgment. For that you have my formless gratitude. Although it is formless, it is only formless in a human sense, for it is also timeless. Those who are willing to be part of this movement of manifesting Christhood, those who are willing to use the tools and the invocations to call forth and reinforce the judgment I have pronounced today, I will not forget you. When you most need it, whether it be while you are still in physical embodiment or whether it be after you leave embodiment and need that extra impetus of light to get you to a higher level, you will find that I will be there for you in whatever manifestation you need in order to transcend your current sense of self. As always, you must be willing, but I will be there, for I AM with you always. Truly, my love is the ultimate cure for anti-love.

You may not see this release as loving, but I also have a softer side. If that appeals more to you, then I have given other releases and other tools that will help you tune in to the softness of the Spirit of Jesus Christ. Whatever you need to open your heart to me, you can find it. If you do open your hearts, you will know that I AM with you always.

29 | INVOKING THE JUDGMENT OF CHRIST UPON THE FALSE JESUS

In the name of the I AM THAT I AM, Jesus Christ, I use the authority that I have as a being in embodiment on earth to call upon Jesus to reinforce my calls and use my chakras to project the statements in this invocation into the collective consciousness and awaken Americans to the fact that most Christians are worshiping a false Jesus. Awaken Americans to the reality that we are spiritual beings and that we can co-create a new future by working with the ascended masters. I especially call for …

[Make your own calls here.]

Part 1

1. I call forth the judgment of Christ upon the dead spirit, the dead idol, worshiped by most Christians in America, the spirit that is not a Spirit of God but a man-made spirit that has been created by the Christian movement, especially since the formation of the Roman Catholic church.

> O Jesus, blessed brother mine,
> I walk the path that you outline,
> a great example to us all,
> I follow now your inner call.
>
> **O Jesus, let the Fire of Joy,**
> **consume the devil's subtle ploy,**
> **transfigured is our planet earth,**
> **the golden age is given birth.**

2. Through the Christ flame in my heart, I ratify that Jesus has withdrawn his light from all Christian churches in America that are trapped in worshiping the false Jesus that has been created by man.

> O Jesus, open inner sight,
> the ego wants to prove it's right,
> but this I will no longer do,
> I want to be all one with you.
>
> **O Jesus, let the Fire of Joy,**
> **consume the devil's subtle ploy,**
> **transfigured is our planet earth,**
> **the golden age is given birth.**

3. I ratify that the spirit that has been created by the Christian churches for these many centuries is hereby judged. It is judged by the Living Word and the living Presence of the real Christ, the real Jesus.

> O Jesus, I now clearly see,
> the Key of Knowledge given me,
> my Christ self I hereby embrace,
> as you fill up my inner space.
>
> **O Jesus, let the Fire of Joy,**
> **consume the devil's subtle ploy,**
> **transfigured is our planet earth,**
> **the golden age is given birth.**

4. By the authority of the Christ flame in my heart, I command Archangel Michael to send his angels to bind that spirit of the false Jesus.

> O Jesus, show me serpent's lie,
> expose the beam in my own eye,
> as Christ discernment you me give,
> in oneness I forever live.
>
> **O Jesus, let the Fire of Joy,**
> **consume the devil's subtle ploy,**
> **transfigured is our planet earth,**
> **the golden age is given birth.**

5. By the authority of the Christ flame in my heart, I command Archangel Michael to take it from the earth and to bind and consume all of the demons, all of the fallen beings who have been instrumental in creating, sustaining and reinforcing it.

O Jesus, I am truly meek,
and thus I turn the other cheek,
when the accuser attacks me,
I go within and merge with thee.

**O Jesus, let the Fire of Joy,
consume the devil's subtle ploy,
transfigured is our planet earth,
the golden age is given birth.**

6. I call for Christians in America to be awakened so they can see that they have an opportunity to start on a clean white page.

O Jesus, ego I let die,
surrender ev'ry earthly tie,
the dead can bury what is dead,
I choose to walk with you instead.

**O Jesus, let the Fire of Joy,
consume the devil's subtle ploy,
transfigured is our planet earth,
the golden age is given birth.**

7. I call for Christians in America to be cut free from the false image of Christ so they can see that people have for a very long time created false gods that they have worshiped before the one formless God.

O Jesus, help me rise above,
the devil's test through higher love,
show me separate self unreal,
my formless self you do reveal.

29 | Invoking the judgment of Christ upon the false Jesus

> **O Jesus, let the Fire of Joy,**
> **consume the devil's subtle ploy,**
> **transfigured is our planet earth,**
> **the golden age is given birth.**

8. By the authority of the Christ flame in my heart, I command Archangel Michael to bind the fallen beings who introduced the false gods because they wanted to be those false gods, worshiped by as many people as possible.

> O Jesus, what is that to me,
> I just let go and follow thee,
> with this I do pass ev'ry test,
> to find with you eternal rest.

> **O Jesus, let the Fire of Joy,**
> **consume the devil's subtle ploy,**
> **transfigured is our planet earth,**
> **the golden age is given birth.**

9. I call for Christians in America to be cut free to see that many people who claim to have spiritual experiences are not having an experience of touching the formless God through the Christ consciousness. They are having the experience of interacting with a man-made god, the false god created by Christianity, or even the false gods created by specific churches.

> O Jesus, fiery master mine,
> my heart now melting into thine,
> I love with heart and mind and soul,
> the God who is my highest goal.

> O Jesus, let the Fire of Joy,
> consume the devil's subtle ploy,
> transfigured is our planet earth,
> the golden age is given birth.

Part 2

1. I call for Christians in America to be cut free to see that this is not worshiping Jesus, following Jesus, being loyal to Jesus, acknowledging Jesus.

> O Jesus, blessed brother mine,
> I walk the path that you outline,
> a great example to us all,
> I follow now your inner call.

> O Jesus, let the Fire of Joy,
> consume the devil's subtle ploy,
> transfigured is our planet earth,
> the golden age is given birth.

2. I call for Christians in America to be cut free to see that they do not do Jesus any service by indulging in these experiences where they go into an ecstatic or trance-like state and their minds can be taken over by lower spirits.

> O Jesus, open inner sight,
> the ego wants to prove it's right,
> but this I will no longer do,
> I want to be all one with you.

> **O Jesus, let the Fire of Joy,**
> **consume the devil's subtle ploy,**
> **transfigured is our planet earth,**
> **the golden age is given birth.**

3. I call for Christians in America to be cut free to see that this is *not* the Holy Spirit, for *it* is undivided, indivisible, and it always points to the formless God, not a man-made image of God or Christ.

> O Jesus, I now clearly see,
> the Key of Knowledge given me,
> my Christ self I hereby embrace,
> as you fill up my inner space.

> **O Jesus, let the Fire of Joy,**
> **consume the devil's subtle ploy,**
> **transfigured is our planet earth,**
> **the golden age is given birth.**

4. I call for Christians in America to be cut free to see that the formless God is beyond any image and so is Christ.

> O Jesus, show me serpent's lie,
> expose the beam in my own eye,
> as Christ discernment you me give,
> in oneness I forever live.

> **O Jesus, let the Fire of Joy,**
> **consume the devil's subtle ploy,**
> **transfigured is our planet earth,**
> **the golden age is given birth.**

5. I call for Christians in America to be cut free from the snares created by the fallen beings who cannot and *will* not experience the formless God or the Christ consciousness.

> O Jesus, I am truly meek,
> and thus I turn the other cheek,
> when the accuser attacks me,
> I go within and merge with thee.
>
> **O Jesus, let the Fire of Joy,**
> **consume the devil's subtle ploy,**
> **transfigured is our planet earth,**
> **the golden age is given birth.**

6. I call for Christians in America to be cut free to see that black-and-white thinking is when we impose a mental image upon reality instead of being willing to experience reality. Black-and-white thinking begins when we create an idol and project that this is God, the only true God, and therefore we refuse to go beyond the idol and experience the formless God.

> O Jesus, ego I let die,
> surrender ev'ry earthly tie,
> the dead can bury what is dead,
> I choose to walk with you instead.
>
> **O Jesus, let the Fire of Joy,**
> **consume the devil's subtle ploy,**
> **transfigured is our planet earth,**
> **the golden age is given birth.**

7. I call for Christians in America to be cut free to see that nothing from heaven or earth can get us out of black-and-white

thinking, except our own willingness to question the way we look at life.

> O Jesus, help me rise above,
> the devil's test through higher love,
> show me separate self unreal,
> my formless self you do reveal.

> **O Jesus, let the Fire of Joy,**
> **consume the devil's subtle ploy,**
> **transfigured is our planet earth,**
> **the golden age is given birth.**

8. I call for Christians in America to be cut free to see that the vast majority of the leaders of Christian churches in America are in exactly the same frame of mind today as the scribes and Pharisees were in when Jesus stood before them in the flesh.

> O Jesus, what is that to me,
> I just let go and follow thee,
> with this I do pass ev'ry test,
> to find with you eternal rest.

> **O Jesus, let the Fire of Joy,**
> **consume the devil's subtle ploy,**
> **transfigured is our planet earth,**
> **the golden age is given birth.**

9. In oneness with Jesus, I speak into the mass consciousness of the Christian churches in America: "Come forth out of the tomb of this false Christianity that worships a man-made spirit that is not the Living Christ!"

> O Jesus, fiery master mine,
> my heart now melting into thine,
> I love with heart and mind and soul,
> the God who is my highest goal.
>
> **O Jesus, let the Fire of Joy,**
> **consume the devil's subtle ploy,**
> **transfigured is our planet earth,**
> **the golden age is given birth.**

Part 3

1. I ratify that those who are the leaders of these churches will be confronted with the real Jesus, with his Spirit at inner levels. Jesus is manifesting his Spirit at inner levels for all of the leaders of the Christian churches.

> O Jesus, blessed brother mine,
> I walk the path that you outline,
> a great example to us all,
> I follow now your inner call.
>
> **O Jesus, let the Fire of Joy,**
> **consume the devil's subtle ploy,**
> **transfigured is our planet earth,**
> **the golden age is given birth.**

2. I ratify that Jesus serves the Christian leaders notice: "It is time for you to choose between light and darkness. If you will not choose, then the judgment of Christ will be upon you, and you will be confronted with the full descent of your karma.

You may deny karma, you may deny the judgment, you may deny anything you like, but at inner levels you cannot deny that you have been visited by the Living Spirit of Christ."

> O Jesus, open inner sight,
> the ego wants to prove it's right,
> but this I will no longer do,
> I want to be all one with you.
>
> **O Jesus, let the Fire of Joy,**
> **consume the devil's subtle ploy,**
> **transfigured is our planet earth,**
> **the golden age is given birth.**

3. I ratify and reinforce this action and call forth a shift in the Christian churches of America. I call for the Christian churches in America to begin to shift out of black-and-white thinking, and to do so quickly before there is a descent of judgment such as has not been seen before on this continent.

> O Jesus, I now clearly see,
> the Key of Knowledge given me,
> my Christ self I hereby embrace,
> as you fill up my inner space.
>
> **O Jesus, let the Fire of Joy,**
> **consume the devil's subtle ploy,**
> **transfigured is our planet earth,**
> **the golden age is given birth.**

4. In oneness with Jesus, I say to the Christian leaders who deny the Living Christ: "You have had your day. You have had your day during the Piscean dispensation, to do whatever you

wanted with the Christian movement. You pastors and leaders in America have had your day since the founding of this nation, to play games and think you can define how a Christian church should be."

> O Jesus, show me serpent's lie,
> expose the beam in my own eye,
> as Christ discernment you me give,
> in oneness I forever live.

> **O Jesus, let the Fire of Joy,**
> **consume the devil's subtle ploy,**
> **transfigured is our planet earth,**
> **the golden age is given birth.**

5. I call forth the judgment of Christ upon the ministers who have abused their power through money, sex, power or by claiming that certain wars were just wars approved by God or Christ.

> O Jesus, I am truly meek,
> and thus I turn the other cheek,
> when the accuser attacks me,
> I go within and merge with thee.

> **O Jesus, let the Fire of Joy,**
> **consume the devil's subtle ploy,**
> **transfigured is our planet earth,**
> **the golden age is given birth.**

6. I call forth the judgment of Christ upon the leaders of the mega-churches where people are exposed to all kind of

pageantry that is nothing but cheap entertainment and has nothing to do with the self-transcendence that is the hallmark of Christ.

> O Jesus, ego I let die,
> surrender ev'ry earthly tie,
> the dead can bury what is dead,
> I choose to walk with you instead.

> **O Jesus, let the Fire of Joy,**
> **consume the devil's subtle ploy,**
> **transfigured is our planet earth,**
> **the golden age is given birth.**

7. In oneness with Jesus, I ratify that I have had enough of it, and I call upon all spiritual people to decide whether they have had enough of it also.

> O Jesus, help me rise above,
> the devil's test through higher love,
> show me separate self unreal,
> my formless self you do reveal.

> **O Jesus, let the Fire of Joy,**
> **consume the devil's subtle ploy,**
> **transfigured is our planet earth,**
> **the golden age is given birth.**

8. I call for the cutting free of the many wonderful, loving, kind people in Christian movements, so they can see that they are not fulfilling their highest potential as long as they allow themselves to be trapped in these mockeries of Christian churches,

created by those beings that are completely taken over by the consciousness of anti-Christ.

> O Jesus, what is that to me,
> I just let go and follow thee,
> with this I do pass ev'ry test,
> to find with you eternal rest.

> **O Jesus, let the Fire of Joy,**
> **consume the devil's subtle ploy,**
> **transfigured is our planet earth,**
> **the golden age is given birth.**

9. I call for Christians to be cut free to see what Jesus meant when he said to Peter: "Get thee behind me, Satan!" For Satan is the consciousness that demands that Spirit conforms to its own image or conforms to the current conditions of matter.

> O Jesus, fiery master mine,
> my heart now melting into thine,
> I love with heart and mind and soul,
> the God who is my highest goal.

> **O Jesus, let the Fire of Joy,**
> **consume the devil's subtle ploy,**
> **transfigured is our planet earth,**
> **the golden age is given birth.**

Part 4

1. I call for Christians to be cut free to see that it is fine to feed the hungry and clothe the homeless, but unless we are doing it with the Spirit of Christ, we are not fulfilling our highest potential, and therefore it is not the worthy offering.

> O Jesus, blessed brother mine,
> I walk the path that you outline,
> a great example to us all,
> I follow now your inner call.
>
> **O Jesus, let the Fire of Joy,**
> **consume the devil's subtle ploy,**
> **transfigured is our planet earth,**
> **the golden age is given birth.**

2. I call for Christians to be cut free to see that the worthy offering is not measured by a man-made standard of what it means to do good deeds. It is measured by the standard of Christ: Our willingness to transcend our consciousness and multiply the talents, instead of burying them in the ground of a man-made idol.

> O Jesus, open inner sight,
> the ego wants to prove it's right,
> but this I will no longer do,
> I want to be all one with you.
>
> **O Jesus, let the Fire of Joy,**
> **consume the devil's subtle ploy,**

> transfigured is our planet earth,
> the golden age is given birth.

3. I call for Christians to be cut free to see that Jesus loves us with the firmness of a Christic love that will not leave us alone in a lesser state, when he knows we are capable of manifesting a higher state.

> O Jesus, I now clearly see,
> the Key of Knowledge given me,
> my Christ self I hereby embrace,
> as you fill up my inner space.

> **O Jesus, let the Fire of Joy,**
> **consume the devil's subtle ploy,**
> **transfigured is our planet earth,**
> **the golden age is given birth.**

4. I call for Jesus to shake awake those who are willing to be awakened so they can see there is more to life than what they have been told by these Christian churches. Jesus, cut them free to see what is going on behind the visible, physical, conscious level, so they can remove themselves from these churches and withdraw their light.

> O Jesus, show me serpent's lie,
> expose the beam in my own eye,
> as Christ discernment you me give,
> in oneness I forever live.

> **O Jesus, let the Fire of Joy,**
> **consume the devil's subtle ploy,**

transfigured is our planet earth,
the golden age is given birth.

5. I call forth the judgment of Christ upon the forces of darkness, the forces of anti-Christ, the satanic forces that are using the Christian churches of America to steal the light of the good and the pure-intentioned people.

O Jesus, I am truly meek,
and thus I turn the other cheek,
when the accuser attacks me,
I go within and merge with thee.

**O Jesus, let the Fire of Joy,
consume the devil's subtle ploy,
transfigured is our planet earth,
the golden age is given birth.**

6. I call for Christians to be cut free to see that by going to these churches every Sunday, pouring out their devotion to what they think is Jesus, they are supporting this entire false hierarchy of Christianity that is running most of the Christian churches in America today.

O Jesus, ego I let die,
surrender ev'ry earthly tie,
the dead can bury what is dead,
I choose to walk with you instead.

**O Jesus, let the Fire of Joy,
consume the devil's subtle ploy,
transfigured is our planet earth,
the golden age is given birth.**

7. I call for Christians to be cut free to see that this is not working for the cause of Christ, regardless of what they are doing on the outer. These activities need to be transcended so that they can be done from a higher level of Christ consciousness.

> O Jesus, help me rise above,
> the devil's test through higher love,
> show me separate self unreal,
> my formless self you do reveal.
>
> **O Jesus, let the Fire of Joy,**
> **consume the devil's subtle ploy,**
> **transfigured is our planet earth,**
> **the golden age is given birth.**

8. I call for Christians to be cut free to see that they need to recognize that the churches and their leaders are taken over by these forces of darkness, and if they will not come up higher, they will continue to give their light to them.

> O Jesus, what is that to me,
> I just let go and follow thee,
> with this I do pass ev'ry test,
> to find with you eternal rest.
>
> **O Jesus, let the Fire of Joy,**
> **consume the devil's subtle ploy,**
> **transfigured is our planet earth,**
> **the golden age is given birth.**

9. I call for Christians to be cut free to see that this will mean that they will not be saved after this lifetime, as they believe will be the case. They will be confronted with the absolute

reality that they have not qualified to enter heaven, and they will have to come back into embodiment.

> O Jesus, fiery master mine,
> my heart now melting into thine,
> I love with heart and mind and soul,
> the God who is my highest goal.
>
> **O Jesus, let the Fire of Joy,**
> **consume the devil's subtle ploy,**
> **transfigured is our planet earth,**
> **the golden age is given birth.**

Part 5

1. I call forth the judgment of Christ upon the false preachers who deny reincarnation, thinking their preaching from the pulpit will change the law of God.

> O Jesus, blessed brother mine,
> I walk the path that you outline,
> a great example to us all,
> I follow now your inner call.
>
> **O Jesus, let the Fire of Joy,**
> **consume the devil's subtle ploy,**
> **transfigured is our planet earth,**
> **the golden age is given birth.**

2. I call forth the judgment of Christ upon the fallen beings who want us to believe that there are ways to force God to accept us into the kingdom of heaven.

> O Jesus, open inner sight,
> the ego wants to prove it's right,
> but this I will no longer do,
> I want to be all one with you.
>
> **O Jesus, let the Fire of Joy,**
> **consume the devil's subtle ploy,**
> **transfigured is our planet earth,**
> **the golden age is given birth.**

3. I call forth the judgment of Christ upon the false pastors of Christianity, the wolves in sheep's clothing, those who may appear beautiful outward but within they are like whitened sepulchers filled with dead men's bones.

> O Jesus, I now clearly see,
> the Key of Knowledge given me,
> my Christ self I hereby embrace,
> as you fill up my inner space.
>
> **O Jesus, let the Fire of Joy,**
> **consume the devil's subtle ploy,**
> **transfigured is our planet earth,**
> **the golden age is given birth.**

4. I call for Christians to be cut free to stop following the false pastors and to awaken and follow the Living Christ!

29 | Invoking the judgment of Christ upon the false Jesus

O Jesus, show me serpent's lie,
expose the beam in my own eye,
as Christ discernment you me give,
in oneness I forever live.

O Jesus, let the Fire of Joy,
consume the devil's subtle ploy,
transfigured is our planet earth,
the golden age is given birth.

5. I call for spiritual people to be cut free to see that instead of following the false idols of Christianity, they are following other false idols, they are following those who are the false teachers of the New Age movement.

O Jesus, I am truly meek,
and thus I turn the other cheek,
when the accuser attacks me,
I go within and merge with thee.

O Jesus, let the Fire of Joy,
consume the devil's subtle ploy,
transfigured is our planet earth,
the golden age is given birth.

6. I call for spiritual people to be cut free to see that many people who have the potential to manifest Christhood and qualify for their ascension in this lifetime have tied themselves to these lesser gurus, who are not interested in taking them to Christ consciousness, they are interested in having people follow them.

O Jesus, ego I let die,
surrender ev'ry earthly tie,
the dead can bury what is dead,
I choose to walk with you instead.

**O Jesus, let the Fire of Joy,
consume the devil's subtle ploy,
transfigured is our planet earth,
the golden age is given birth.**

7. I call forth the judgment of Christ upon the false teachers of the New Age movement, those who do not have the internal light, for they have not been willing to reach for the Christ consciousness.

O Jesus, help me rise above,
the devil's test through higher love,
show me separate self unreal,
my formless self you do reveal.

**O Jesus, let the Fire of Joy,
consume the devil's subtle ploy,
transfigured is our planet earth,
the golden age is given birth.**

8. I call for spiritual people to be cut free to see that the Christ consciousness is self-transcendence. The consciousness of Satan is that of projecting a mental image upon reality and denying or refusing the direct experience of the reality that is beyond images because it is the formless God and the formless Christ.

> O Jesus, what is that to me,
> I just let go and follow thee,
> with this I do pass ev'ry test,
> to find with you eternal rest.
>
> **O Jesus, let the Fire of Joy,
> consume the devil's subtle ploy,
> transfigured is our planet earth,
> the golden age is given birth.**

9. I call for spiritual people to be cut free to see that Christ does not take on the form promoted by the Christian churches, for Christ is much more. Christ is a universal state of consciousness that can never be trapped in any form or in any name, nor can it be captured by any guru, no matter how outrageous a claim he makes to be enlightened.

> O Jesus, fiery master mine,
> my heart now melting into thine,
> I love with heart and mind and soul,
> the God who is my highest goal.
>
> **O Jesus, let the Fire of Joy,
> consume the devil's subtle ploy,
> transfigured is our planet earth,
> the golden age is given birth.**

Part 6

1. I call for spiritual people to be cut free to see that there are enough people in the spiritual and New Age movement in

America that, if they manifested their Christhood, they could make the decisive difference that many of them dream about making.

> O Jesus, blessed brother mine,
> I walk the path that you outline,
> a great example to us all,
> I follow now your inner call.
>
> **O Jesus, let the Fire of Joy,**
> **consume the devil's subtle ploy,**
> **transfigured is our planet earth,**
> **the golden age is given birth.**

2. I call for spiritual people to be cut free to see that because people are running after the false gurus, they are not manifesting their Christ potential, and therefore they cannot make the difference. In oneness with Jesus, I call for 10,000 Christed beings to step forward and consciously accept and manifest their Christhood, thereby shifting the earth to a higher level.

> O Jesus, open inner sight,
> the ego wants to prove it's right,
> but this I will no longer do,
> I want to be all one with you.
>
> **O Jesus, let the Fire of Joy,**
> **consume the devil's subtle ploy,**
> **transfigured is our planet earth,**
> **the golden age is given birth.**

3. I call for spiritual people to be cut free to see that this shift cannot unfold as long as those who have the potential to be

the forerunners allow themselves to be trapped in these blind alleys, these false images and organizations and movements created specifically to keep us from our Christhood.

> O Jesus, I now clearly see,
> the Key of Knowledge given me,
> my Christ self I hereby embrace,
> as you fill up my inner space.
>
> **O Jesus, let the Fire of Joy,**
> **consume the devil's subtle ploy,**
> **transfigured is our planet earth,**
> **the golden age is given birth.**

4. In oneness with Jesus, I am calling those who are trapped by false gurus to come out from the tomb and be willing to meet the Living Christ of Jesus, rather than the false Christ that you are now following.

> O Jesus, show me serpent's lie,
> expose the beam in my own eye,
> as Christ discernment you me give,
> in oneness I forever live.
>
> **O Jesus, let the Fire of Joy,**
> **consume the devil's subtle ploy,**
> **transfigured is our planet earth,**
> **the golden age is given birth.**

5. I call for spiritual people to be cut free to see that there is no Aquarian Age on earth without Jesus Christ. Jesus holds the Office of the Hierarch of Pisces, and no one can enter the

Aquarian Age or the Aquarian consciousness without going through the office that Jesus holds.

> O Jesus, I am truly meek,
> and thus I turn the other cheek,
> when the accuser attacks me,
> I go within and merge with thee.
>
> **O Jesus, let the Fire of Joy,**
> **consume the devil's subtle ploy,**
> **transfigured is our planet earth,**
> **the golden age is given birth.**

6. I call for spiritual people to be cut free to see that this office is not associated with Christian churches, but it is a spiritual office. If people allow the Christian churches and their falsity to cause them to refuse to approach the Living Spirit that Jesus is, then they cannot enter the Aquarian Age of Saint Germain.

> O Jesus, ego I let die,
> surrender ev'ry earthly tie,
> the dead can bury what is dead,
> I choose to walk with you instead.
>
> **O Jesus, let the Fire of Joy,**
> **consume the devil's subtle ploy,**
> **transfigured is our planet earth,**
> **the golden age is given birth.**

7. I call for spiritual people to be cut free to see that they will then enter another state of idolatry where they think they are creating the Golden Age, but it is only by degrees different

from what has been created by false Christianity over these past centuries. This is not the vision of Saint Germain.

> O Jesus, help me rise above,
> the devil's test through higher love,
> show me separate self unreal,
> my formless self you do reveal.

> **O Jesus, let the Fire of Joy,**
> **consume the devil's subtle ploy,**
> **transfigured is our planet earth,**
> **the golden age is given birth.**

8. I ratify that the Living Spirit of Jesus Christ is manifesting his Presence in front of all false gurus in America: "It is time for you to make the choice between light and darkness. If you will not, then the judgment of Christ will descend with all of the ramifications this might have. It may not be visible, but it surely will be undeniable.

> O Jesus, what is that to me,
> I just let go and follow thee,
> with this I do pass ev'ry test,
> to find with you eternal rest.

> **O Jesus, let the Fire of Joy,**
> **consume the devil's subtle ploy,**
> **transfigured is our planet earth,**
> **the golden age is given birth.**

9. I call for the cutting free of all those who have it in their Divine plans to be part of this movement of manifesting Christhood, so they will awaken and use the tools and the

invocations to call forth and reinforce the judgment Jesus has pronounced and thereby help shift America into the Golden Age of Saint Germain.

> O Jesus, fiery master mine,
> my heart now melting into thine,
> I love with heart and mind and soul,
> the God who is my highest goal.
>
> **O Jesus, let the Fire of Joy,**
> **consume the devil's subtle ploy,**
> **transfigured is our planet earth,**
> **the golden age is given birth.**

Sealing

In the name of the I AM THAT I AM, I accept that Archangel Michael, Astrea and Shiva form an impenetrable shield around myself and all constructive people in America, sealing us from all fear-based energies in all four octaves. I accept that the Light of God is consuming and transforming all fear-based energies that make up the dark forces working against America!

30 | IS AMERICA A CHRISTIAN OR A BUDDHIST NATION?

I AM the Ascended Master Gautama Buddha, and although you may know me more as the serious Buddha, I come today as the joyful Buddha to share in your joy that you have dared to release.

Truly, it is not only the dictations that are given during a conference, or the invocations or decrees that you give, that release and anchor light. When you freely share of your hearts and your joy-flame, we can use your chakras and auras to release much light and anchor it into the physical octave. Thus, do not fall into the trap of thinking that a free-flowing sharing like you have had, of people talking to each other, is of no value. Do not think that it always has to feel like work in order to have an effect, for truly did not Christ say that unless you become as the little child, you cannot enter the kingdom?

Even the Buddhas are not always serious. We are joyful, maybe not in a way you consider it on earth, but certainly joyful when we observe that those who are the spiritual students can transcend themselves and the seriousness of the world. Do you not realize, my beloved, that in these short days you have been together in this room, you have created a sacred space that is so set apart from the hustle and bustle of the city around you that you are almost not on the same planet. Yet when you walk out that door, you will again be out in the hustle and bustle. You will be in a different space inside, if you will make, not an effort but be aware of the need to maintain it, be aware of the many challenges that come at you from all sides that want to pull you out of your sacred space.

Your inner sanctuary

Truly, we have talked before about your inner sanctuary. In your heart you have what ideally should be a sacred space where no force in this world, no person in this world, no demon, no authority figure, can ever enter. For that matter, no loved one can enter, not even a child, for it is *your* sacred space. What is it that the forces of anti-love seek to do? They seek to invade your sacred space or to pull you out of it so that you are no longer centered, so that you no longer realize you have a sacred space, so that you forget that you are a sacred being.

There are people in America who will say: "What right does the Buddha have to give a dictation on this soil when we are a Christian nation?" What makes you think that the Buddha is not a Christian? What makes you think that Christ did not study and practice Buddhism? The Buddhic consciousness is the Christ consciousness, at a higher level than the Christ consciousness that goes out into the hustle and bustle of the world. It is not higher in the sense of more valuable, but it is a higher level of detachment from the world. The Christ is the one who hears the cries of the world and goes out to minister to the people, giving them whatever they need in order to come up higher. The Buddha stays apart, creates a sacred space, a sanctuary, and therefore lets the people come to him or her. Both are equally needed, both are equally valuable, although certainly many more people in the world need the Christ to minister to them, for they are not yet ready for the Buddha.

Is America a Christian nation?

Certainly, I come to challenge the mindset that America is a Christian nation. As Jesus himself has challenged the false preachers of the Christian churches in America, I come to give my polarity to Jesus' release, not only for the judgment of the false teachers of Christianity but for the judgment of the false teachers of Buddhism that have come to this nation.

The Christ consciousness is a universal state of consciousness, but it is more focused on discerning between light and darkness, reality and unreality. Although the Christ consciousness at the Christic level is not dualistic, it is still focused on the difference between light and darkness, reality and unreality. The Buddhic consciousness has transcended that level and manifested a higher detachment and therefore more of a vision of universality. The Buddhic level of consciousness – the Buddhic level of the Christ consciousness, we might say – is therefore more focused on the universal or formless behind outer forms. The Christ will say: "Get thee behind me, Satan." The Buddha will not say this, for to the Buddha there is no Satan and there is no behind.

When you look at this nation of the United States of America, what do you see? You see that people from all over the world – from all different cultures, races, nationalities, religions, skin colors – have been brought here and put into this "melting pot." There are many tensions between different groups of people in America, not only between blacks and whites but many other groups. This growing tension is a sign that America has not stepped up, that not enough people have stepped up to the Buddhic consciousness. How shall America fulfill its destiny without a critical mass of people holding the spiritual balance by embracing and manifesting the Buddhic consciousness? You see, the Christ consciousness is surely needed in America, but the Christ consciousness is not enough for America to fulfill her destiny.

The Christ consciousness shines a light into the darkness, which reinforces and brings out the contrast. The Buddhic consciousness allows you to see beyond the contrast and see that the contrast is not real for there is a Buddhic essence behind both light and darkness. People cannot overcome their differences through the Christic level of consciousness, but only through the Buddhic level of consciousness. Surely, we do not expect all people in America to attain the Buddhic level of consciousness, for they have barely begun to grasp the Christ consciousness. We do expect a critical mass of people to embrace the Buddhic consciousness and hold the balance for America.

The only way that the cosmic experiment of America can work, the only way that the melting pot can avoid blowing itself up, is that people learn to see beyond the outer differences and embrace the universal aspect within. This is, of course, what the forces of anti-love will do anything in their power to avoid by defining these conflicts and blowing them up out of proportion, stirring up the energies in people's emotional bodies, feeding them illusion after illusion until they are so focused on the outer differences that they have no awareness of the Buddhic nature hiding behind all form.

Problems with Buddhism in America

Who then shall hold this Buddhic balance for America? Certainly, we hope that you who are ascended master students will do so. We also hope that those who have embraced Buddhism in some form in America will be able to do so. Unfortunately, many of them are not manifesting that potential because the Buddhic movements, the Buddhic teachers that have come to America, have been far too focused on the outer form of Buddhism, rather than the universal elements of it.

What sense does it make to build a Buddhist monastery in the mountains of America that looks exactly like a Buddhist monastery in the mountains of India or Tibet? What sense does it make to wear the same robes, to have the same rituals? What sense does it make? What sense does it make for the people in the East to still be, quote-unquote, "worshiping" the Buddha the way they have done for centuries when the modern world has shifted? *That* in itself makes no sense, and it makes even less sense to take that form of Buddhism and try to transplant it to America where the consciousness is so different.

The judgment of Buddhist teachers

Thus, we might say that Jesus' judgment of the false teachers of Christianity was the Omega. I therefore pronounce the Alpha aspect of the judgment of the Buddha upon the false teachers of Buddhism that have come to America and that are working in other Western countries and in the East as well.

You may say: "How can the Buddha, who is non-attached, speak about the judgment?" Non-attachment does not mean that you think everything is equally good or that everything is good. It does not mean that the Buddha does not care, does not discern, does not discriminate, between that which helps people grow and that which stops their growth. Therefore, while the Buddhic judgment is different from the judgment of Christ, it is still valid for the Buddha to say: "Vajra! Vajra! Vajra! Vajra! I claim America for the Spirit of Buddha and not the false spirits created by the false teachers."

I breathe out a cosmic breath to send the energies – to those who can receive them – of an awakening that it is necessary to step up to a higher form of what you might call Buddhism, but which is not Buddhism in a traditional sense. There is a need to recognize that you must embrace the universal aspects of the Buddha's teachings as they were given 2,500 years ago. There is also a need to acknowledge that you must embrace the universal teachings that I, the Buddha, am giving today.

Finding the inner Buddha

Why do we see celebrities running after this or that Buddhic teacher when they have grown up in America, know the American culture and therefore should be willing to embrace the appearance of the Buddha rather than some dead outer ritual? You may think it is great pageantry to take on certain Buddhist customs and rituals, but it is not true Buddhism. You are not worshiping the Buddha by doing so. You are not embracing the Buddha within by being so focused on these completely out-of-place outer rituals, dogmas, doctrines, customs, clothing, building styles, what have you.

Do you think that if the Buddha had manifested in the West, he would have taken on these outer forms? Nay.

Therefore, realize that for the Buddha time is not. I AM manifesting myself in the West for those who are willing to embrace me, but when you are focused on all of these outer forms developed in a different time in a different culture, you are not embracing me. I do not need you to worship me. I need you to embrace me. You need to embrace the living Presence that I AM in order to discover and accept the Buddha nature within yourself.

I, the living Buddha, am not in a golden statue. Nor am I in a mantra in some strange language that you barely understand. Surely, you can use certain mantras, as you did before this dictation, to tune in to my Presence, but be not trapped in thinking that giving the mantra itself is enough for it is not. In order to embrace the Buddha, you need to surrender. Surrender is the only way to overcome an attachment, and it is your attachments to the world that prevent you from embracing the Buddha.

Judging the forces of anti-buddha

I also come to bring forth the judgment of the Buddha upon the many institutions in America that are reinforcing the differences between groups of people, and that are seeking to divide and conquer the people and blow on the fires of conflict between various groups. You have had a very long time to create conflict in this nation. I, Gautama Buddha, will manifest my Presence here so that those who will call for the reinforcement of my Presence and my momentum will contribute to the judgment and the removal of the forces that are distinctly anti-buddha, stirring up conflict based on outer differences. The outer differences do not matter. It is the spirit within. The Christian churches have done this. Businesses have done this.

The government has done this. So many seemingly benign organizations have done the same.

When you start looking with the discernment I am giving you, you will see just how many organizations actually reinforce the sense of separateness between people. Truly, the women's liberation movement claims to have liberated women, but to a large degree it has only cemented the difference, the distinction between men and women. It has done little to overcome the conflict that goes all the way back to what Mother Mary exposed: the deliberate intent to murder the Divine feminine and any representative of the Divine feminine in embodiment, such as you saw during the witch hunts and other events of systematically persecuting or killing women.

You may call for the rights of a certain group of people to be acknowledged, and that may be valid at a certain level, but there comes a point where it is no longer valid for now you are only reinforcing differences. You are locking people into a matrix that creates an inherent conflict between them, and this is not beneficial to the growth of society.

Political duality

It will never be possible to have two political parties that are not locked in a dualistic struggle. They have to set themselves apart from each other, and this almost inevitably leads to them being polarized towards the extremes of any issue. When you then add the black-and-white thinking that is a manifestation of anti-christ, you see that it will always be viewed that, when two viewpoints are in conflict and are opposites, one must be right, the other must be wrong. In the greater vision of the Buddha none of the two are right and none of the two are wrong. They are simply out of touch with reality. They are away from the Middle Way. I hereby call forth the awakening of those who have in their Divine plans the vow to embody in America and discover, walk, and demonstrate the Middle Way, not in a Buddhist context, not by following an Eastern Buddhic religion, but by being the open door for the ideas that are beyond the dualistic extremes.

This is the calling of many people who have embodied in America, not a large number compared to the size of the population, but a sufficient number if they all awaken and embrace what is possible for them. Therefore, I speak into the four levels of matter, and I say: "Wake up! Discover and embrace your dharma. Form the Sangha, and then embrace the Buddha within yourselves and each other."

Do not judge yourselves or each other

My beloved, it is my great joy to seal this conference. You have had such a short time, but you have accomplished so much. Allow yourselves to recognize, without any pride of the ego, that you have accomplished a great work for America. Truly, we rejoice. We rejoice in being with you. We rejoice in observing how you share your presences freely.

Do not fall into the trap of judging each other when one person dares to simply be open and relaxed and express his or her individuality and personality. Observe the messenger who does not judge any of you. Do not judge each other. Truly, the ascended masters are not looking to create a community of mindless minions where everybody is so focused on outer rules that none dare to express individuality.

You have each been given a sacred individuality by your spiritual parents. It is your right to express it. You have developed, during your sojourn on this earth, an outer individuality.

It is also your right to express that individuality in the form it has right now. Surely, you will use our teachings and tools and your own willingness to transcend the outer individuality gradually, but you cannot, my beloved, make maximum progress by falling into the trap of the forces of anti-love, of judging your outer individuality according to some worldly standard.

We of the ascended masters, we see your outer individuality, we see that it is not ultimately real, that it is not something you will keep for the rest of your life or take with you to the ascended state. As long as it does not directly block your growth, we are not concerned about it. Do not fall into the trap seen in so many spiritual communities, even ascended master organizations, where you use the outer teaching to create some kind of standard and then seek to judge yourselves and each other based on that standard. Allow yourselves to be who you are, and instead of being irritated over each other's outer personality, see beyond it and see that it does not matter.

There are some, especially in previous ascended master organizations, who never dared to express their individuality for they were so focused on following the rules. They would sit there quietly, and whenever someone dared to express individuality, they would then judge it. They would put it down, or they would speak about it behind people's backs. Do you not realize that we could judge you? We see how not daring to express anything is not the fastest way to growth, but we do not judge you. We allow you to sit there and judge others, but I will say that judging others can only be done when you judge yourself, and this will hinder your growth.

The control game of judging

Someone expressing their personality, however imperfectly, is still flowing. Expressing your personality, and then perhaps seeing that there could be a higher expression, leads to growth. Not daring to express anything, but instead judging yourself and others, will not lead to growth. Again, I do not judge you. I simply point out to you that this does not help your growth, for it is truly what other masters have talked about: a control game.

What is the essence of a control game? The essence of it is a deficit. You have allowed the fallen beings to put upon you one of the many illusions they have invented. You have allowed yourself to believe that you have a deficit in your being, that you are not worthy, that you are not good enough, that you are not complete, that you do not have what it takes, that you have no right to be here or express yourself. We have, in Holland, talked about the original birth trauma of your light being put down, and this causes you to judge your Divine individuality, anchored in your I AM Presence [See the book: *Healing Your Spiritual Traumas*].

Another way to have a sense of deficit is that you have something in your outer personality that you judge. Perhaps you have been in a negative pattern at some point in your life, and now you believe that, because you have done this thing, you can never be free of it, you can never again be worthy. These are, so to speak, the Alpha and the Omega ways to create the sense of a deficit inside of you.

What the fallen beings have done is create a world where, when you have this sense of deficit, you cannot avoid having it stirred up. There are so many activities that human beings engage in where their inadequacy will be reinforced, even by loved ones in families. This happens all the time. It also happens at the level of society, or even at the level of religion, where the sense that you are a sinner already stirs up this sense of inadequacy.

Well, how can you live with that deficit inside of you? The answer is that you cannot so what must you do? You must find a way to compensate for the deficit, and that is the birth of all control games. They take many different outer forms, but they are all aimed at one thing: compensating for the inner deficit. That is why I say that those of you who are willing to overcome these control games need to look at this sense of inadequacy.

You need to make peace with the fact that you have a Divine individuality. You need to strive to experience your I AM Presence and to embrace that Divine individuality, accepting that you have a right to express it on earth. Before you can really do this, you need to get rid of this sense that your outer personality is inadequate.

I am not – *listen!* – I am not saying that you need to get rid of the outer personality. I am saying you need to get rid of the sense that this outer personality can prevent you from expressing your light because you are somehow not worthy or spiritual enough, according to some worldly standard. If you wait until you are perfect in terms of the outer personality before you dare to express the light of your Presence, then you will never be an open door for the Presence. You will have aspects of the outer personality with you until the moment you ascend. When Christ was hanging up on the cross, he had to give up the last ghost. It is part of what keeps you tied to earth.

Accept yourself as you are right now

Allow yourselves to recognize and accept that, no matter who you are right now, no matter how your personality is right now, you still have a right to be here. You have a right to be a spiritual person. You have a right to express yourself freely and without these encumbrances. Why did Christ say: "Unless you become as a little child?" It is because the child, no matter how imperfect or how distinct its personality might be, is free and unencumbered in expressing it. That is what cannot help but stir the hearts of other people who see that even though the child may be imperfect or have a distinct personality, it is cute, it is loving, it is joyful. Allow yourselves the same freedom. Give that freedom to yourself, and give it to each other.

Truly, my beloved, it is a joy when you overcome this focus on the outer personality, when you are no longer judging yourself and judging others. Be willing to recognize how you have all been brought up to take on this artificial tendency to always evaluate everything you do and everything other people do: Is it good enough? Is it right? Is it acceptable? Is it okay? Why do you evaluate the expressions of other people, seeking to find fault and put them down? It is because you have already evaluated yourself and found fault with yourself. Once you have judged yourself, the only way to get out of this sense of feeling bad about yourself is by making other people as bad or worse. When you have put yourself down to a certain degree, you have to put other people down to a greater degree, and then you somehow feel that there is some kind of balance. If you are not worse than the others, then you are maybe, perhaps somehow okay.

Are you not tired of playing this silly game? Then look at it, use the tools, the teachings, use your ability to tune in to your heart, to your I AM Presence, to your spiritual teachers, and get that perspective on it. See how you are judging yourself, and I promise you that, when you discover this subtle belief of the fallen beings that you have taken on and see the unreality of it, you will feel like the weight of the world has been taken off your shoulders. Literally, the weight of the world's condemnation and judgment *has* been taken off. *Be free!* You will feel so much lighter, so much freer when you stop judging everything and everyone, including yourself.

I would gladly give my all to set one person free from this judgment. Since I own nothing, I have nothing to give. Or perhaps what I have to give is beyond measure and therefore sufficient for each and every one of you, if you will but accept that you are worthy to receive what the Buddha offers you. Will you receive what I offer? [Audience says: "Yes."] Then take the essence, the vibration, of this dictation with you.

If you feel you lose it, then listen to the sound file again and allow yourself to rediscover the sacred space in your hearts where no worldly force can enter. The Buddha is there and has always been there. Whilst the Christ is with you always, I am with you beyond time for to the Buddha time is not. Space is the only reality. Wherever you are in space, there I AM.

I seal you and this conference in the ever-present Presence of the Buddha. I AM Gautama.

31 | INVOKING FREEDOM FROM JUDGMENT

In the name of the I AM THAT I AM, Jesus Christ, I use the authority that I have as a being in embodiment on earth to call upon Gautama Buddha to reinforce my calls and use my chakras to project the statements in this invocation into the collective consciousness and awaken Americans to the need to stop judging ourselves and each other. Awaken Americans to the reality that we are spiritual beings and that we can co-create a new future by working with the ascended masters. I especially call for …

[Make your own calls here.]

Part 1

1. What right does the Buddha have to give a dictation on this soil when America is a Christian nation? What makes you think that the Buddha is not a Christian?

What makes you think that Christ did not study and practice Buddhism?

> Gautama, show my mental state
> that does give rise to love and hate,
> your exposé I do endure,
> so my perception will be pure.

> **Gautama, Flame of Cosmic Peace,**
> **unruly thoughts do hereby cease,**
> **we radiate from you and me**
> **the peace to still Samsara's Sea.**

2. The Buddhic consciousness is the Christ consciousness, at a higher level than the Christ consciousness that goes out into the hustle and bustle of the world. It is not higher in the sense of more valuable, but it is a higher level of detachment from the world.

> Gautama, in your Flame of Peace,
> the struggling self I now release,
> the Buddha Nature I now see,
> it is the core of you and me.

> **Gautama, Flame of Cosmic Peace,**
> **unruly thoughts do hereby cease,**
> **we radiate from you and me**
> **the peace to still Samsara's Sea.**

3. The Christ is the one who hears the cries of the world and goes out to minister to the people, giving them whatever they need in order to come up higher. The Buddha stays apart,

31 | Invoking freedom from judgment

creates a sacred space, a sanctuary, and therefore lets the people come to him or her.

> Gautama, I am one with thee,
> Mara's demons do now flee,
> your Presence like a soothing balm,
> my mind and senses ever calm.

> **Gautama, Flame of Cosmic Peace,**
> **unruly thoughts do hereby cease,**
> **we radiate from you and me**
> **the peace to still Samsara's Sea.**

4. Both are equally needed, both are equally valuable, although certainly many more people in the world need the Christ to minister to them, for they are not yet ready for the Buddha.

> Gautama, I now take the vow,
> to live in the eternal now,
> with you I do transcend all time,
> to live in present so sublime.

> **Gautama, Flame of Cosmic Peace,**
> **unruly thoughts do hereby cease,**
> **we radiate from you and me**
> **the peace to still Samsara's Sea.**

5. In oneness with Gautama, I challenge the mindset that America is a Christian nation. I ratify the judgment of the false teachers of Christianity and of the false teachers of Buddhism that have come to this nation.

Gautama, I have no desire,
to nothing earthly I aspire,
in non-attachment I now rest,
passing Mara's subtle test.

**Gautama, Flame of Cosmic Peace,
unruly thoughts do hereby cease,
we radiate from you and me
the peace to still Samsara's Sea.**

6. The Christ consciousness is a universal state of consciousness, but it is more focused on discerning between light and darkness, reality and unreality. The Christ consciousness is not dualistic, but focused on the difference between light and darkness, reality and unreality.

Gautama, I melt into you,
my mind is one, no longer two,
immersed in your resplendent glow,
Nirvana is all that I know.

**Gautama, Flame of Cosmic Peace,
unruly thoughts do hereby cease,
we radiate from you and me
the peace to still Samsara's Sea.**

7. The Buddhic consciousness has transcended that level and manifested a higher detachment and therefore more of a vision of universality. The Buddhic level of the Christ consciousness is focused on the universal or formless behind outer forms. The Christ will say: "Get thee behind me, Satan." To the Buddha there is no Satan and there is no behind.

Gautama, in your timeless space,
I am immersed in Cosmic Grace,
I know the God beyond all form,
to world I will no more conform.

**Gautama, Flame of Cosmic Peace,
unruly thoughts do hereby cease,
we radiate from you and me
the peace to still Samsara's Sea.**

8. People from all over the world have been brought to America and put into this "melting pot." The growing tension between different groups is a sign that America has not stepped up, that not enough people have stepped up to the Buddhic consciousness.

Gautama, I am now awake,
I clearly see what is at stake,
and thus I claim my sacred right
to be on earth the Buddhic Light.

**Gautama, Flame of Cosmic Peace,
unruly thoughts do hereby cease,
we radiate from you and me
the peace to still Samsara's Sea.**

9. How shall America fulfill its destiny without a critical mass of people holding the spiritual balance by embracing and manifesting the Buddhic consciousness? The Christ consciousness is surely needed in America, but the Christ consciousness is not enough for America to fulfill her destiny.

> Gautama, with your thunderbolt,
> we give the earth a mighty jolt,
> I know that some will understand,
> and join the Buddha's timeless band.
>
> **Gautama, Flame of Cosmic Peace,**
> **unruly thoughts do hereby cease,**
> **we radiate from you and me**
> **the peace to still Samsara's Sea.**

Part 2

1. The Christ consciousness shines a light into the darkness, which reinforces and brings out the contrast. The Buddhic consciousness allows us to see beyond the contrast and see that the contrast is not real for there is a Buddhic essence behind both light and darkness.

> Gautama, show my mental state
> that does give rise to love and hate,
> your exposé I do endure,
> so my perception will be pure.
>
> **Gautama, Flame of Cosmic Peace,**
> **unruly thoughts do hereby cease,**
> **we radiate from you and me**
> **the peace to still Samsara's Sea.**

2. People cannot overcome their differences through the Christic level of consciousness, but only through the Buddhic level

31 | Invoking freedom from judgment

of consciousness. A critical mass of people need to embrace the Buddhic consciousness and hold the balance for America.

> Gautama, in your Flame of Peace,
> the struggling self I now release,
> the Buddha Nature I now see,
> it is the core of you and me.

> **Gautama, Flame of Cosmic Peace,**
> **unruly thoughts do hereby cease,**
> **we radiate from you and me**
> **the peace to still Samsara's Sea.**

3. The only way that the cosmic experiment of America can work, the only way that the melting pot can avoid blowing itself up, is that people learn to see beyond the outer differences and embrace the universal aspect within.

> Gautama, I am one with thee,
> Mara's demons do now flee,
> your Presence like a soothing balm,
> my mind and senses ever calm.

> **Gautama, Flame of Cosmic Peace,**
> **unruly thoughts do hereby cease,**
> **we radiate from you and me**
> **the peace to still Samsara's Sea.**

4. This is what the forces of anti-love will do anything in their power to avoid by defining these conflicts and blowing them out of proportion, stirring up the energies in people's emotional bodies, feeding them illusion after illusion until they are

so focused on the outer differences that they have no awareness of the Buddhic nature hiding behind all form.

> Gautama, I now take the vow,
> to live in the eternal now,
> with you I do transcend all time,
> to live in present so sublime.

> **Gautama, Flame of Cosmic Peace,**
> **unruly thoughts do hereby cease,**
> **we radiate from you and me**
> **the peace to still Samsara's Sea.**

5. Who shall hold this Buddhic balance for America? Those who have embraced Buddhism are not manifesting that potential because the Buddhic movements, the Buddhic teachers that have come to America, have been far too focused on the outer form of Buddhism, rather than the universal elements of it.

> Gautama, I have no desire,
> to nothing earthly I aspire,
> in non-attachment I now rest,
> passing Mara's subtle test.

> **Gautama, Flame of Cosmic Peace,**
> **unruly thoughts do hereby cease,**
> **we radiate from you and me**
> **the peace to still Samsara's Sea.**

6. What sense does it make to build a Buddhist monastery in the mountains of America that looks exactly like a Buddhist

monastery in the mountains of India or Tibet? What sense does it make to wear the same robes, to have the same rituals?

> Gautama, I melt into you,
> my mind is one, no longer two,
> immersed in your resplendent glow,
> Nirvana is all that I know.
>
> **Gautama, Flame of Cosmic Peace,**
> **unruly thoughts do hereby cease,**
> **we radiate from you and me**
> **the peace to still Samsara's Sea.**

7. What sense does it make for the people in the East to still be "worshiping" the Buddha the way they have done for centuries when the modern world has shifted? It makes even less sense to take that form of Buddhism and try to transplant it to America where the consciousness is so different.

> Gautama, in your timeless space,
> I am immersed in Cosmic Grace,
> I know the God beyond all form,
> to world I will no more conform.
>
> **Gautama, Flame of Cosmic Peace,**
> **unruly thoughts do hereby cease,**
> **we radiate from you and me**
> **the peace to still Samsara's Sea.**

8. In oneness with Gautama, I pronounce the Alpha aspect of the judgment of the Buddha upon the false teachers of Buddhism that have come to America and that are working in other Western countries and in the East as well.

Gautama, I am now awake,
I clearly see what is at stake,
and thus I claim my sacred right
to be on earth the Buddhic Light.

**Gautama, Flame of Cosmic Peace,
unruly thoughts do hereby cease,
we radiate from you and me
the peace to still Samsara's Sea.**

9. In oneness with Gautama, I say, "Vajra! Vajra! Vajra! Vajra! I claim America for the Spirit of Buddha and not the false spirits created by the false teachers."

Gautama, with your thunderbolt,
we give the earth a mighty jolt,
I know that some will understand,
and join the Buddha's timeless band.

**Gautama, Flame of Cosmic Peace,
unruly thoughts do hereby cease,
we radiate from you and me
the peace to still Samsara's Sea.**

Part 3

1. In oneness with Gautama, I breathe out a cosmic breath to send the energies of an awakening that it is necessary to step up to a higher form of what we might call Buddhism, but which is not Buddhism in a traditional sense.

> Gautama, show my mental state
> that does give rise to love and hate,
> your exposé I do endure,
> so my perception will be pure.

> **Gautama, Flame of Cosmic Peace,
> unruly thoughts do hereby cease,
> we radiate from you and me
> the peace to still Samsara's Sea.**

2. There is a need to recognize that we must embrace the universal aspects of the Buddha's teachings as they were given 2,500 years ago. There is also a need to acknowledge that we must embrace the universal teachings that the Buddha is giving today.

> Gautama, in your Flame of Peace,
> the struggling self I now release,
> the Buddha Nature I now see,
> it is the core of you and me.

> **Gautama, Flame of Cosmic Peace,
> unruly thoughts do hereby cease,
> we radiate from you and me
> the peace to still Samsara's Sea.**

3. Those of us who have grown up in America and know the American culture must be willing to embrace the appearance of the Buddha rather than some dead outer ritual. We must embrace the Buddha within instead of being so focused on these completely out-of-place outer rituals, dogmas, doctrines, customs, clothing and building styles.

> Gautama, I am one with thee,
> Mara's demons do now flee,
> your Presence like a soothing balm,
> my mind and senses ever calm.
>
> **Gautama, Flame of Cosmic Peace,**
> **unruly thoughts do hereby cease,**
> **we radiate from you and me**
> **the peace to still Samsara's Sea.**

4. If the Buddha had manifested in the West, he would not have taken on these outer forms. For the Buddha, time is not. The Buddha *is* manifesting himself in the West for those who are willing to embrace him, but when we are focused on all of these outer forms developed in a different time in a different culture, we are not embracing him.

> Gautama, I now take the vow,
> to live in the eternal now,
> with you I do transcend all time,
> to live in present so sublime.
>
> **Gautama, Flame of Cosmic Peace,**
> **unruly thoughts do hereby cease,**
> **we radiate from you and me**
> **the peace to still Samsara's Sea.**

5. Gautama does not need us to worship him. He needs us to embrace him. We need to embrace the living Presence that Gautama is in order to discover and accept the Buddha nature within ourselves.

31 | Invoking freedom from judgment

> Gautama, I have no desire,
> to nothing earthly I aspire,
> in non-attachment I now rest,
> passing Mara's subtle test.
>
> **Gautama, Flame of Cosmic Peace,**
> **unruly thoughts do hereby cease,**
> **we radiate from you and me**
> **the peace to still Samsara's Sea.**

6. Gautama is the living Buddha, he is not in a golden statue. Nor is he in a mantra in some strange language that we barely understand. We cannot be trapped in thinking that giving the mantra itself is enough, for it is not.

> Gautama, I melt into you,
> my mind is one, no longer two,
> immersed in your resplendent glow,
> Nirvana is all that I know.
>
> **Gautama, Flame of Cosmic Peace,**
> **unruly thoughts do hereby cease,**
> **we radiate from you and me**
> **the peace to still Samsara's Sea.**

7. In order to embrace the Buddha, we need to surrender. Surrender is the only way to overcome an attachment, and it is our attachments to the world that prevent us from embracing the Buddha.

> Gautama, in your timeless space,
> I am immersed in Cosmic Grace,

> I know the God beyond all form,
> to world I will no more conform.
>
> **Gautama, Flame of Cosmic Peace,**
> **unruly thoughts do hereby cease,**
> **we radiate from you and me**
> **the peace to still Samsara's Sea.**

8. I ratify the judgment of Gautama upon the many institutions in America that are reinforcing the differences between groups of people, and that are seeking to divide and conquer the people and blow on the fires of conflict between various groups.

> Gautama, I am now awake,
> I clearly see what is at stake,
> and thus I claim my sacred right
> to be on earth the Buddhic Light.
>
> **Gautama, Flame of Cosmic Peace,**
> **unruly thoughts do hereby cease,**
> **we radiate from you and me**
> **the peace to still Samsara's Sea.**

9. I call for the reinforcement of the Presence of Gautama and his momentum to bring forth the judgment and the removal of the forces that are distinctly anti-buddha, stirring up conflict based on outer differences. I call forth the judgment of the Christian churches, businesses, the government and any organizations that reinforce the sense of separateness between people.

> Gautama, with your thunderbolt,
> we give the earth a mighty jolt,

31 | Invoking freedom from judgment

I know that some will understand,
and join the Buddha's timeless band.

**Gautama, Flame of Cosmic Peace,
unruly thoughts do hereby cease,
we radiate from you and me
the peace to still Samsara's Sea.**

Part 4

1. I reinforce the judgment of the Buddha upon the women's liberation movement that to a large degree has cemented the difference, the distinction between men and women. It has done little to overcome the conflict that goes all the way back to the deliberate intent to murder the Divine feminine.

Gautama, show my mental state
that does give rise to love and hate,
your exposé I do endure,
so my perception will be pure.

**Gautama, Flame of Cosmic Peace,
unruly thoughts do hereby cease,
we radiate from you and me
the peace to still Samsara's Sea.**

2. It is valid to call for the rights of a certain group of people to be acknowledged at a certain level, but there comes a point where it is no longer valid for now we are only reinforcing differences. We are locking people into a matrix that creates

an inherent conflict between them, and this is not beneficial to the growth of society.

> Gautama, in your Flame of Peace,
> the struggling self I now release,
> the Buddha Nature I now see,
> it is the core of you and me.

> **Gautama, Flame of Cosmic Peace,**
> **unruly thoughts do hereby cease,**
> **we radiate from you and me**
> **the peace to still Samsara's Sea.**

3. It will never be possible to have two political parties that are not locked in a dualistic struggle. They have to set themselves apart from each other, and this almost inevitably leads to them being polarized towards the extremes of any issue.

> Gautama, I am one with thee,
> Mara's demons do now flee,
> your Presence like a soothing balm,
> my mind and senses ever calm.

> **Gautama, Flame of Cosmic Peace,**
> **unruly thoughts do hereby cease,**
> **we radiate from you and me**
> **the peace to still Samsara's Sea.**

4. When we consider the black-and-white thinking that is a manifestation of anti-christ, it will always be viewed that, when two viewpoints are in conflict and are opposites, one must be right, the other must be wrong.

31 | Invoking freedom from judgment

Gautama, I now take the vow,
to live in the eternal now,
with you I do transcend all time,
to live in present so sublime.

**Gautama, Flame of Cosmic Peace,
unruly thoughts do hereby cease,
we radiate from you and me
the peace to still Samsara's Sea.**

5. In the greater vision of the Buddha none of the two are right and none of the two are wrong. They are simply out of touch with reality. They are away from the Middle Way.

Gautama, I have no desire,
to nothing earthly I aspire,
in non-attachment I now rest,
passing Mara's subtle test.

**Gautama, Flame of Cosmic Peace,
unruly thoughts do hereby cease,
we radiate from you and me
the peace to still Samsara's Sea.**

6. In oneness with Gautama, I call forth the awakening of those who have in their Divine plans the vow to embody in America and discover, walk, and demonstrate the Middle Way, not in a Buddhist context, not by following an Eastern Buddhic religion, but by being the open door for the ideas that are beyond the dualistic extremes.

Gautama, I melt into you,
my mind is one, no longer two,

immersed in your resplendent glow,
Nirvana is all that I know.

**Gautama, Flame of Cosmic Peace,
unruly thoughts do hereby cease,
we radiate from you and me
the peace to still Samsara's Sea.**

7. This is the calling of many people who have embodied in America. Therefore, I speak into the four levels of matter, and I say: "Wake up! Discover and embrace your dharma. Form the Sangha, and then embrace the Buddha within yourselves and each other."

Gautama, in your timeless space,
I am immersed in Cosmic Grace,
I know the God beyond all form,
to world I will no more conform.

**Gautama, Flame of Cosmic Peace,
unruly thoughts do hereby cease,
we radiate from you and me
the peace to still Samsara's Sea.**

8. Gautama, help all of these people overcome the control game of judging ourselves and each other, the control game put upon us by the fallen beings. Help us connect to our higher beings and overcome the sense of deficit, the sense of not being good enough according to some standard.

Gautama, I am now awake,
I clearly see what is at stake,

and thus I claim my sacred right
to be on earth the Buddhic Light.

**Gautama, Flame of Cosmic Peace,
unruly thoughts do hereby cease,
we radiate from you and me
the peace to still Samsara's Sea.**

9. Gautama, help all of us become conscious that we are tired of playing this silly game. Help us tune in to our hearts, to our I AM Presences, to our spiritual teachers, and see the subtle beliefs of the fallen beings that we have taken on. Help us experience that the weight of the world's condemnation and judgment has been taken off and that we are so much lighter, so much freer when we stop judging everything and everyone, including ourselves.

Gautama, with your thunderbolt,
we give the earth a mighty jolt,
I know that some will understand,
and join the Buddha's timeless band.

**Gautama, Flame of Cosmic Peace,
unruly thoughts do hereby cease,
we radiate from you and me
the peace to still Samsara's Sea.**

Sealing

In the name of the I AM THAT I AM, I accept that Archangel Michael, Astrea and Shiva form an impenetrable shield around myself and all constructive people in America, sealing us from

all fear-based energies in all four octaves. I accept that the Light of God is consuming and transforming all fear-based energies that make up the dark forces working against America!

32 | CONSUMING THE RECORDS OF WAR IN AMERICA

In the name of the I AM THAT I AM, Jesus Christ, I call upon Saint Germain to send oceans of violet flame to consume all records of war in America, past, present and future. Awaken people to the reality that we are spiritual beings and that we can co-create a peaceful future for America by working with the ascended masters. I especially call for Saint Germain to take command over …

[Make your own calls here.]

Part 1

1. Saint Germain, release oceans of violet flame to consume the cause and the energetic records of all fighting among native Americans before the arrival of Europeans. Heal the souls of all people who are affected by these wars.

O Saint Germain, you do inspire,
my vision raised forever higher,
with you I form a figure-eight,
your Golden Age I co-create.

**O Saint Germain, what love you bring,
it truly makes all matter sing,
your violet flame does all restore,
with you we are becoming more.**

2. Saint Germain, release oceans of violet flame to consume the cause and the energetic records of the American Revolutionary War. Heal the souls of all people who are affected by this war.

O Saint Germain, what Freedom Flame,
released when we recite your name,
acceleration is your gift,
our planet it will surely lift.

**O Saint Germain, what love you bring,
it truly makes all matter sing,
your violet flame does all restore,
with you we are becoming more.**

3. Saint Germain, release oceans of violet flame into the identity body of America to consume the cause and the energetic records of the American Civil War. Heal the souls of all people who are affected by this war.

O Saint Germain, in love we claim,
our right to bring your violet flame,

from you Above, to us below,
it is an all-transforming flow.

**O Saint Germain, what love you bring,
it truly makes all matter sing,
your violet flame does all restore,
with you we are becoming more.**

4. Saint Germain, release oceans of violet flame into the mental body of America to consume the cause and the energetic records of the American Civil War. Heal the souls of all people who are affected by this war.

O Saint Germain, I love you so,
my aura filled with violet glow,
my chakras filled with violet fire,
I am your cosmic amplifier.

**O Saint Germain, what love you bring,
it truly makes all matter sing,
your violet flame does all restore,
with you we are becoming more.**

5. Saint Germain, release oceans of violet flame into the emotional body of America to consume the cause and the energetic records of the American Civil War. Heal the souls of all people who are affected by this war.

O Saint Germain, I am now free,
your violet flame is therapy,
transform all hang-ups in my mind,
as inner peace I surely find.

**O Saint Germain, what love you bring,
it truly makes all matter sing,
your violet flame does all restore,
with you we are becoming more.**

6. Saint Germain, release oceans of violet flame into the physical body of America to consume the cause and the energetic records of the American Civil War. Heal the souls of all people who are affected by this war.

O Saint Germain, my body pure,
your violet flame for all is cure,
consume the cause of all disease,
and therefore I am all at ease.

**O Saint Germain, what love you bring,
it truly makes all matter sing,
your violet flame does all restore,
with you we are becoming more.**

7. Saint Germain, release oceans of violet flame to consume the cause and the energetic records of the Indian Wars. Heal the souls of all people who are affected by these wars.

O Saint Germain, I'm karma-free,
the past no longer burdens me,
a brand new opportunity,
I am in Christic unity.

**O Saint Germain, what love you bring,
it truly makes all matter sing,
your violet flame does all restore,
with you we are becoming more.**

8. Saint Germain, release oceans of violet flame into the identity body of America to consume the cause and the energetic records of World War I. Heal the souls of all people who are affected by this war.

> O Saint Germain, we are now one,
> I am for you a violet sun,
> as we transform this planet earth,
> your Golden Age is given birth.
>
> **O Saint Germain, what love you bring,**
> **it truly makes all matter sing,**
> **your violet flame does all restore,**
> **with you we are becoming more.**

9. Saint Germain, release oceans of violet flame into the mental body of America to consume the cause and the energetic records of World War I. Heal the souls of all people who are affected by this war.

> O Saint Germain, the earth is free,
> from burden of duality,
> in oneness we bring what is best,
> your Golden Age is manifest.
>
> **O Saint Germain, what love you bring,**
> **it truly makes all matter sing,**
> **your violet flame does all restore,**
> **with you we are becoming more.**

Part 2

1. Saint Germain, release oceans of violet flame into the emotional body of America to consume the cause and the energetic records of World War I. Heal the souls of all people who are affected by this war.

> O Saint Germain, you do inspire,
> my vision raised forever higher,
> with you I form a figure-eight,
> your Golden Age I co-create.
>
> **O Saint Germain, what love you bring,**
> **it truly makes all matter sing,**
> **your violet flame does all restore,**
> **with you we are becoming more.**

2. Saint Germain, release oceans of violet flame into the physical body of America to consume the cause and the energetic records of World War I. Heal the souls of all people who are affected by this war.

> O Saint Germain, what Freedom Flame,
> released when we recite your name,
> acceleration is your gift,
> our planet it will surely lift.
>
> **O Saint Germain, what love you bring,**
> **it truly makes all matter sing,**
> **your violet flame does all restore,**
> **with you we are becoming more.**

3. Saint Germain, release oceans of violet flame into the identity body of America to consume the cause and the energetic records of World War II. Heal the souls of all people who are affected by this war.

> O Saint Germain, in love we claim,
> our right to bring your violet flame,
> from you Above, to us below,
> it is an all-transforming flow.
>
> **O Saint Germain, what love you bring,**
> **it truly makes all matter sing,**
> **your violet flame does all restore,**
> **with you we are becoming more.**

4. Saint Germain, release oceans of violet flame into the mental body of America to consume the cause and the energetic records of World War II. Heal the souls of all people who are affected by this war.

> O Saint Germain, I love you so,
> my aura filled with violet glow,
> my chakras filled with violet fire,
> I am your cosmic amplifier.
>
> **O Saint Germain, what love you bring,**
> **it truly makes all matter sing,**
> **your violet flame does all restore,**
> **with you we are becoming more.**

5. Saint Germain, release oceans of violet flame into the emotional body of America to consume the cause and the energetic

records of World War II. Heal the souls of all people who are affected by this war.

> O Saint Germain, I am now free,
> your violet flame is therapy,
> transform all hang-ups in my mind,
> as inner peace I surely find.
>
> **O Saint Germain, what love you bring,**
> **it truly makes all matter sing,**
> **your violet flame does all restore,**
> **with you we are becoming more.**

6. Saint Germain, release oceans of violet flame into the physical body of America to consume the cause and the energetic records of World War II. Heal the souls of all people who are affected by this war.

> O Saint Germain, my body pure,
> your violet flame for all is cure,
> consume the cause of all disease,
> and therefore I am all at ease.
>
> **O Saint Germain, what love you bring,**
> **it truly makes all matter sing,**
> **your violet flame does all restore,**
> **with you we are becoming more.**

7. Saint Germain, release oceans of violet flame into the identity body of America to consume the cause and the energetic records of the Cold War. Heal the souls of all people who are affected by this war.

O Saint Germain, I'm karma-free,
the past no longer burdens me,
a brand new opportunity,
I am in Christic unity.

**O Saint Germain, what love you bring,
it truly makes all matter sing,
your violet flame does all restore,
with you we are becoming more.**

8. Saint Germain, release oceans of violet flame into the mental body of America to consume the cause and the energetic records of the Cold War. Heal the souls of all people who are affected by this war.

O Saint Germain, we are now one,
I am for you a violet sun,
as we transform this planet earth,
your Golden Age is given birth.

**O Saint Germain, what love you bring,
it truly makes all matter sing,
your violet flame does all restore,
with you we are becoming more.**

9. Saint Germain, release oceans of violet flame into the emotional body of America to consume the cause and the energetic records of the Cold War. Heal the souls of all people who are affected by this war.

O Saint Germain, the earth is free,
from burden of duality,

in oneness we bring what is best,
your Golden Age is manifest.

**O Saint Germain, what love you bring,
it truly makes all matter sing,
your violet flame does all restore,
with you we are becoming more.**

Part 3

1. Saint Germain, release oceans of violet flame into the physical body of America to consume the cause and the energetic records of the Cold War. Heal the souls of all people who are affected by this war.

O Saint Germain, you do inspire,
my vision raised forever higher,
with you I form a figure-eight,
your Golden Age I co-create.

**O Saint Germain, what love you bring,
it truly makes all matter sing,
your violet flame does all restore,
with you we are becoming more.**

2. Saint Germain, release oceans of violet flame into the identity body of America to consume the cause and the energetic records of the Korean War. Heal the souls of all people who are affected by this war.

> O Saint Germain, what Freedom Flame,
> released when we recite your name,
> acceleration is your gift,
> our planet it will surely lift.
>
> **O Saint Germain, what love you bring,**
> **it truly makes all matter sing,**
> **your violet flame does all restore,**
> **with you we are becoming more.**

3. Saint Germain, release oceans of violet flame into the mental body of America to consume the cause and the energetic records of the Korean War. Heal the souls of all people who are affected by this war.

> O Saint Germain, in love we claim,
> our right to bring your violet flame,
> from you Above, to us below,
> it is an all-transforming flow.
>
> **O Saint Germain, what love you bring,**
> **it truly makes all matter sing,**
> **your violet flame does all restore,**
> **with you we are becoming more.**

4. Saint Germain, release oceans of violet flame into the emotional body of America to consume the cause and the energetic records of the Korean War. Heal the souls of all people who are affected by this war.

> O Saint Germain, I love you so,
> my aura filled with violet glow,

my chakras filled with violet fire,
I am your cosmic amplifier.

**O Saint Germain, what love you bring,
it truly makes all matter sing,
your violet flame does all restore,
with you we are becoming more.**

5. Saint Germain, release oceans of violet flame into the physical body of America to consume the cause and the energetic records of the Korean War. Heal the souls of all people who are affected by this war.

O Saint Germain, I am now free,
your violet flame is therapy,
transform all hang-ups in my mind,
as inner peace I surely find.

**O Saint Germain, what love you bring,
it truly makes all matter sing,
your violet flame does all restore,
with you we are becoming more.**

6. Saint Germain, release oceans of violet flame into the identity body of America to consume the cause and the energetic records of the Vietnam War. Heal the souls of all people who are affected by this war.

O Saint Germain, my body pure,
your violet flame for all is cure,
consume the cause of all disease,
and therefore I am all at ease.

**O Saint Germain, what love you bring,
it truly makes all matter sing,
your violet flame does all restore,
with you we are becoming more.**

7. Saint Germain, release oceans of violet flame into the mental body of America to consume the cause and the energetic records of the Vietnam War. Heal the souls of all people who are affected by this war.

O Saint Germain, I'm karma-free,
the past no longer burdens me,
a brand new opportunity,
I am in Christic unity.

**O Saint Germain, what love you bring,
it truly makes all matter sing,
your violet flame does all restore,
with you we are becoming more.**

8. Saint Germain, release oceans of violet flame into the emotional body of America to consume the cause and the energetic records of the Vietnam War. Heal the souls of all people who are affected by this war.

O Saint Germain, we are now one,
I am for you a violet sun,
as we transform this planet earth,
your Golden Age is given birth.

**O Saint Germain, what love you bring,
it truly makes all matter sing,**

your violet flame does all restore,
with you we are becoming more.

9. Saint Germain, release oceans of violet flame into the physical body of America to consume the cause and the energetic records of the Vietnam War. Heal the souls of all people who are affected by this war.

> O Saint Germain, the earth is free,
> from burden of duality,
> in oneness we bring what is best,
> your Golden Age is manifest.

> **O Saint Germain, what love you bring,
> it truly makes all matter sing,
> your violet flame does all restore,
> with you we are becoming more.**

Part 4

1. Saint Germain, release oceans of violet flame to consume the cause and the energetic records of the Persian Gulf war. Heal the souls of all people who are affected by this war.

> O Saint Germain, you do inspire,
> my vision raised forever higher,
> with you I form a figure-eight,
> your Golden Age I co-create.

> **O Saint Germain, what love you bring,
> it truly makes all matter sing,**

your violet flame does all restore,
with you we are becoming more.

2. Saint Germain, release oceans of violet flame to consume the cause and the energetic records of the intervention in Yugoslavia. Heal the souls of all people who are affected by this war.

> O Saint Germain, what Freedom Flame,
> released when we recite your name,
> acceleration is your gift,
> our planet it will surely lift.

> **O Saint Germain, what love you bring,**
> **it truly makes all matter sing,**
> **your violet flame does all restore,**
> **with you we are becoming more.**

3. Saint Germain, release oceans of violet flame into the identity body of America to consume the cause and the energetic records of the War on Terrorism. Heal the souls of all people who are affected by this war.

> O Saint Germain, in love we claim,
> our right to bring your violet flame,
> from you Above, to us below,
> it is an all-transforming flow.

> **O Saint Germain, what love you bring,**
> **it truly makes all matter sing,**
> **your violet flame does all restore,**
> **with you we are becoming more.**

4. Saint Germain, release oceans of violet flame into the mental body of America to consume the cause and the energetic records of the War on Terrorism. Heal the souls of all people who are affected by this war.

> O Saint Germain, I love you so,
> my aura filled with violet glow,
> my chakras filled with violet fire,
> I am your cosmic amplifier.

> **O Saint Germain, what love you bring,**
> **it truly makes all matter sing,**
> **your violet flame does all restore,**
> **with you we are becoming more.**

5. Saint Germain, release oceans of violet flame into the emotional body of America to consume the cause and the energetic records of the War on Terrorism. Heal the souls of all people who are affected by this war.

> O Saint Germain, I am now free,
> your violet flame is therapy,
> transform all hang-ups in my mind,
> as inner peace I surely find.

> **O Saint Germain, what love you bring,**
> **it truly makes all matter sing,**
> **your violet flame does all restore,**
> **with you we are becoming more.**

6. Saint Germain, release oceans of violet flame into the physical body of America to consume the cause and the energetic

records of the War on Terrorism. Heal the souls of all people who are affected by this war.

> O Saint Germain, my body pure,
> your violet flame for all is cure,
> consume the cause of all disease,
> and therefore I am all at ease.
>
> **O Saint Germain, what love you bring,**
> **it truly makes all matter sing,**
> **your violet flame does all restore,**
> **with you we are becoming more.**

7. Saint Germain, release oceans of violet flame to consume the cause and the energetic records of the War in Afghanistan. Heal the souls of all people who are affected by this war.

> O Saint Germain, I'm karma-free,
> the past no longer burdens me,
> a brand new opportunity,
> I am in Christic unity.
>
> **O Saint Germain, what love you bring,**
> **it truly makes all matter sing,**
> **your violet flame does all restore,**
> **with you we are becoming more.**

8. Saint Germain, release oceans of violet flame to consume the cause and the energetic records of the War in Iraq. Heal the souls of all people who are affected by this war.

> O Saint Germain, we are now one,
> I am for you a violet sun,

as we transform this planet earth,
your Golden Age is given birth.

**O Saint Germain, what love you bring,
it truly makes all matter sing,
your violet flame does all restore,
with you we are becoming more.**

9. Saint Germain, release oceans of violet flame to consume the cause and the energetic records of all potential for the United States being pulled into future wars, especially in the Middle East, in Africa or a war with Russia.

O Saint Germain, the earth is free,
from burden of duality,
in oneness we bring what is best,
your Golden Age is manifest.

**O Saint Germain, what love you bring,
it truly makes all matter sing,
your violet flame does all restore,
with you we are becoming more.**

Sealing

In the name of the I AM THAT I AM, I accept that Archangel Michael, Astrea and Shiva form an impenetrable shield around myself and all constructive people in America, sealing us from all fear-based energies in all four octaves. I accept that the Light of God is consuming and transforming all fear-based energies in America!

33 | FREEING AMERICA FROM INTOLERANCE

In the name of the I AM THAT I AM, Jesus Christ, I call upon Archangel Michael to cut all people in America free from the intolerance and elitism generated by power elite groups. Awaken people to the reality that we are spiritual beings and that we can co-create a new future for America by working with the ascended masters. I especially call for Archangel Michael to take command over …

[Make your own calls here.]

Part 1

1. Archangel Michael, we call forth the judgment of Christ upon the demons and fallen beings who are using the American government to promote the mindset that women are unfit for positions of leadership. We command you to remove these beings from America.

Archangel Michael, light so blue,
my heart has room for only you.
My mind is one, no longer two,
your love for me is ever true.

**Archangel Michael, you are here,
your light consumes all doubt and fear.
Your Presence is forever near,
you are to me so very dear.**

2. Archangel Michael, we call forth the judgment of Christ upon the demons and fallen beings who are using American churches, especially the Catholic church and fundamentalist churches, to promote the mindset that women are responsible for the fall of man and cannot be trusted. We command you to remove these beings from America.

Archangel Michael, I will be,
all one with your reality.
No fear can hold me as I see,
this world no power has o'er me.

**Archangel Michael, you are here,
your light consumes all doubt and fear.
Your Presence is forever near,
you are to me so very dear.**

3. Archangel Michael, we call forth the judgment of Christ upon the demons and fallen beings who are using the American military to promote the mindset that women are inferior in leadership positions. We command you to remove these beings from America.

> Archangel Michael, hold me tight,
> shatter now the darkest night.
> Clear my chakras with your light,
> restore to me my inner sight.
>
> **Archangel Michael, you are here,**
> **your light consumes all doubt and fear.**
> **Your Presence is forever near,**
> **you are to me so very dear.**

4. Archangel Michael, we call forth the judgment of Christ upon the demons and fallen beings who are using American corporations to promote the mindset that women are not suited for business. We command you to remove these beings from America.

> Archangel Michael, now I stand,
> with you the light I do command.
> My heart I ever will expand,
> till highest truth I understand.
>
> **Archangel Michael, you are here,**
> **your light consumes all doubt and fear.**
> **Your Presence is forever near,**
> **you are to me so very dear.**

5. Archangel Michael, we call forth the judgment of Christ upon the demons and fallen beings who are using the American educational system to promote the mindset that women should fit into a certain role. We command you to remove these beings from America.

> Archangel Michael, in my heart,
> from me you never will depart.
> Of hierarchy I am a part,
> I now accept a fresh new start.

> **Archangel Michael, you are here,**
> **your light consumes all doubt and fear.**
> **Your Presence is forever near,**
> **you are to me so very dear.**

6. Archangel Michael, we call forth the judgment of Christ upon the demons and fallen beings who are using American scientific institutions, especially the National Science Foundation, to promote the mindset that women are less intelligent than men. We command you to remove these beings from America.

> Archangel Michael, sword of blue,
> all darkness you are cutting through.
> My Christhood I do now pursue,
> discernment shows me what is true.

> **Archangel Michael, you are here,**
> **your light consumes all doubt and fear.**
> **Your Presence is forever near,**
> **you are to me so very dear.**

7. Archangel Michael, we call forth the judgment of Christ upon the demons and fallen beings who are using any organization, including Jewish organizations, to promote the mindset that women belong in the home. We command you to remove these beings from America.

Archangel Michael, in your wings,
I now let go of lesser things.
God's homing call in my heart rings,
my heart with yours forever sings.

Archangel Michael, you are here,
your light consumes all doubt and fear.
Your Presence is forever near,
you are to me so very dear.

8. Archangel Michael, we call forth the judgment of Christ upon the demons and fallen beings who are using the American media, including the movie industry, to promote the mindset that women should fill a certain role. We command you to remove these beings from America.

Archangel Michael, take me home,
in higher spheres I want to roam.
I am reborn from cosmic foam,
my life is now a sacred poem.

Archangel Michael, you are here,
your light consumes all doubt and fear.
Your Presence is forever near,
you are to me so very dear.

9. Archangel Michael, we call forth the judgment of Christ upon the demons and fallen beings who are using any individual or organization to promote the mindset that women should tolerate physical and emotional abuse from men. We command you to remove these beings from America.

Archangel Michael, light you are,
shining like the bluest star.
You are a cosmic avatar,
with you I will go very far.

**Archangel Michael, you are here,
your light consumes all doubt and fear.
Your Presence is forever near,
you are to me so very dear.**

Part 2

1. Archangel Michael, we call forth the judgment of Christ upon the demons and fallen beings who are using the governmental apparatus to promote the mindset that African Americans are inferior to White Americans. We command you to remove these beings from America.

Archangel Michael, light so blue,
my heart has room for only you.
My mind is one, no longer two,
your love for me is ever true.

**Archangel Michael, you are here,
your light consumes all doubt and fear.
Your Presence is forever near,
you are to me so very dear.**

2. Archangel Michael, we call forth the judgment of Christ upon the demons and fallen beings who are using the media to promote the mindset that the souls of African Americans are

different from White Americans. We command you to remove these beings from America.

> Archangel Michael, I will be,
> all one with your reality.
> No fear can hold me as I see,
> this world no power has o'er me.

> **Archangel Michael, you are here,**
> **your light consumes all doubt and fear.**
> **Your Presence is forever near,**
> **you are to me so very dear.**

3. Archangel Michael, we call forth the judgment of Christ upon the demons and fallen beings who are using private organizations, including white supremacists, to promote the mindset that African Americans have no right to be in America. We command you to remove these beings from America.

> Archangel Michael, hold me tight,
> shatter now the darkest night.
> Clear my chakras with your light,
> restore to me my inner sight.

> **Archangel Michael, you are here,**
> **your light consumes all doubt and fear.**
> **Your Presence is forever near,**
> **you are to me so very dear.**

4. Archangel Michael, we call forth the judgment of Christ upon the demons and fallen beings who are using religious organizations, including fundamentalist churches, to promote the mindset that the souls of African Americans are created

inferior by God. We command you to remove these beings from America.

> Archangel Michael, now I stand,
> with you the light I do command.
> My heart I ever will expand,
> till highest truth I understand.
>
> **Archangel Michael, you are here,**
> **your light consumes all doubt and fear.**
> **Your Presence is forever near,**
> **you are to me so very dear.**

5. Archangel Michael, we call forth the judgment of Christ upon the demons and fallen beings who are directing a mindset of intolerance and discrimination against Native Americans. We command you to remove these beings from America.

> Archangel Michael, in my heart,
> from me you never will depart.
> Of hierarchy I am a part,
> I now accept a fresh new start.
>
> **Archangel Michael, you are here,**
> **your light consumes all doubt and fear.**
> **Your Presence is forever near,**
> **you are to me so very dear.**

6. Archangel Michael, we call forth the judgment of Christ upon the demons and fallen beings who are directing a mindset of intolerance and discrimination against Hispanics. We command you to remove these beings from America.

33 | Freeing America from intolerance

> Archangel Michael, sword of blue,
> all darkness you are cutting through.
> My Christhood I do now pursue,
> discernment shows me what is true.
>
> **Archangel Michael, you are here,**
> **your light consumes all doubt and fear.**
> **Your Presence is forever near,**
> **you are to me so very dear.**

7. Archangel Michael, we call forth the judgment of Christ upon the demons and fallen beings who are directing a mindset of intolerance and discrimination against people of other nationalities. We command you to remove these beings from America.

> Archangel Michael, in your wings,
> I now let go of lesser things.
> God's homing call in my heart rings,
> my heart with yours forever sings.
>
> **Archangel Michael, you are here,**
> **your light consumes all doubt and fear.**
> **Your Presence is forever near,**
> **you are to me so very dear.**

8. Archangel Michael, we call forth the judgment of Christ upon the demons and fallen beings who are directing a mindset of intolerance and discrimination against people of Asian descent. We command you to remove these beings from America.

> Archangel Michael, take me home,
> in higher spheres I want to roam.
> I am reborn from cosmic foam,
> my life is now a sacred poem.
>
> **Archangel Michael, you are here,**
> **your light consumes all doubt and fear.**
> **Your Presence is forever near,**
> **you are to me so very dear.**

9. Archangel Michael, we call forth the judgment of Christ upon the demons and fallen beings who are directing a mindset of intolerance and discrimination against Muslims or from Muslims towards others. We command you to remove these beings from America.

> Archangel Michael, light you are,
> shining like the bluest star.
> You are a cosmic avatar,
> with you I will go very far.
>
> **Archangel Michael, you are here,**
> **your light consumes all doubt and fear.**
> **Your Presence is forever near,**
> **you are to me so very dear.**

Part 3

1. Archangel Michael, we call forth the judgment of Christ upon the demons and fallen beings who are using the Republican and Democratic parties to direct a mindset of intolerance

towards people with different political beliefs. We command you to remove these beings from America.

> Archangel Michael, light so blue,
> my heart has room for only you.
> My mind is one, no longer two,
> your love for me is ever true.
>
> **Archangel Michael, you are here,**
> **your light consumes all doubt and fear.**
> **Your Presence is forever near,**
> **you are to me so very dear.**

2. Archangel Michael, we call forth the judgment of Christ upon the demons and fallen beings who are using the media to direct a mindset of intolerance towards new political ideas. We command you to remove these beings from America.

> Archangel Michael, I will be,
> all one with your reality.
> No fear can hold me as I see,
> this world no power has o'er me.
>
> **Archangel Michael, you are here,**
> **your light consumes all doubt and fear.**
> **Your Presence is forever near,**
> **you are to me so very dear.**

3. Archangel Michael, we call forth the judgment of Christ upon the demons and fallen beings who are using the educational establishment to direct a mindset of intolerance towards all spiritual ideas. We command you to remove these beings from America.

> Archangel Michael, hold me tight,
> shatter now the darkest night.
> Clear my chakras with your light,
> restore to me my inner sight.
>
> **Archangel Michael, you are here,**
> **your light consumes all doubt and fear.**
> **Your Presence is forever near,**
> **you are to me so very dear.**

4. Archangel Michael, we call forth the judgment of Christ upon the demons and fallen beings who are using religious organizations to direct a mindset of intolerance towards spiritual ideas. We command you to remove these beings from America.

> Archangel Michael, now I stand,
> with you the light I do command.
> My heart I ever will expand,
> till highest truth I understand.
>
> **Archangel Michael, you are here,**
> **your light consumes all doubt and fear.**
> **Your Presence is forever near,**
> **you are to me so very dear.**

5. Archangel Michael, we call forth the judgment of Christ upon the demons and fallen beings who are using the financial elite and the business world to direct a mindset of intolerance towards new economic ideas. We command you to remove these beings from America.

33 | Freeing America from intolerance

> Archangel Michael, in my heart,
> from me you never will depart.
> Of hierarchy I am a part,
> I now accept a fresh new start.
>
> **Archangel Michael, you are here,**
> **your light consumes all doubt and fear.**
> **Your Presence is forever near,**
> **you are to me so very dear.**

6. Archangel Michael, we call forth the judgment of Christ upon the demons and fallen beings who are using the scientific establishment to direct a mindset of intolerance towards ideas that go beyond materialism. We command you to remove these beings from America.

> Archangel Michael, sword of blue,
> all darkness you are cutting through.
> My Christhood I do now pursue,
> discernment shows me what is true.
>
> **Archangel Michael, you are here,**
> **your light consumes all doubt and fear.**
> **Your Presence is forever near,**
> **you are to me so very dear.**

7. Archangel Michael, we call forth the judgment of Christ upon the demons and fallen beings who are using the military to direct a mindset of intolerance towards ideas that are not dualistic. We command you to remove these beings from America.

> Archangel Michael, in your wings,
> I now let go of lesser things.
> God's homing call in my heart rings,
> my heart with yours forever sings.
>
> **Archangel Michael, you are here,**
> **your light consumes all doubt and fear.**
> **Your Presence is forever near,**
> **you are to me so very dear.**

8. Archangel Michael, we call forth the judgment of Christ upon the demons and fallen beings who are using any organization to direct a mindset of intolerance towards a new social awareness, including public health care. We command you to remove these beings from America.

> Archangel Michael, take me home,
> in higher spheres I want to roam.
> I am reborn from cosmic foam,
> my life is now a sacred poem.
>
> **Archangel Michael, you are here,**
> **your light consumes all doubt and fear.**
> **Your Presence is forever near,**
> **you are to me so very dear.**

9. Archangel Michael, we call forth the judgment of Christ upon the demons and fallen beings who are using any organization to direct a mindset of intolerance towards a more direct form of democracy that makes the current political establishment obsolete. We command you to remove these beings from America.

Archangel Michael, light you are,
shining like the bluest star.
You are a cosmic avatar,
with you I will go very far.

**Archangel Michael, you are here,
your light consumes all doubt and fear.
Your Presence is forever near,
you are to me so very dear.**

Part 4

1. Archangel Michael, we call forth the judgment of Christ upon the demons and fallen beings who are promoting the mindset that America is God's chosen nation and has God's support for its wars. We command you to remove these beings from America.

Archangel Michael, light so blue,
my heart has room for only you.
My mind is one, no longer two,
your love for me is ever true.

**Archangel Michael, you are here,
your light consumes all doubt and fear.
Your Presence is forever near,
you are to me so very dear.**

2. Archangel Michael, we call forth the judgment of Christ upon the demons and fallen beings who are promoting the

mindset that America is inferior to Europe and lacks culture. We command you to remove these beings from America.

> Archangel Michael, I will be,
> all one with your reality.
> No fear can hold me as I see,
> this world no power has o'er me.
>
> **Archangel Michael, you are here,**
> **your light consumes all doubt and fear.**
> **Your Presence is forever near,**
> **you are to me so very dear.**

3. Archangel Michael, we call forth the judgment of Christ upon the demons and fallen beings who are promoting the mindset that America is superior to all other nations and has a right to rule the world. We command you to remove these beings from America.

> Archangel Michael, hold me tight,
> shatter now the darkest night.
> Clear my chakras with your light,
> restore to me my inner sight.
>
> **Archangel Michael, you are here,**
> **your light consumes all doubt and fear.**
> **Your Presence is forever near,**
> **you are to me so very dear.**

4. Archangel Michael, we call forth the judgment of Christ upon the demons and fallen beings who are promoting the mindset that America has a responsibility to use its military might to

33 | Freeing America from intolerance

destroy all threats to freedom, democracy and Christianity. We command you to remove these beings from America.

> Archangel Michael, now I stand,
> with you the light I do command.
> My heart I ever will expand,
> till highest truth I understand.
>
> **Archangel Michael, you are here,**
> **your light consumes all doubt and fear.**
> **Your Presence is forever near,**
> **you are to me so very dear.**

5. Archangel Michael, we call forth the judgment of Christ upon the demons and fallen beings who are promoting the mindset that America has a right to dominate the world economy. We command you to remove these beings from America.

> Archangel Michael, in my heart,
> from me you never will depart.
> Of hierarchy I am a part,
> I now accept a fresh new start.
>
> **Archangel Michael, you are here,**
> **your light consumes all doubt and fear.**
> **Your Presence is forever near,**
> **you are to me so very dear.**

6. Archangel Michael, we call forth the judgment of Christ upon the demons and fallen beings who are promoting the mindset that American businesses, even multinational corporations not loyal to America, should receive government support for their

exploitation of other markets. We command you to remove these beings from America.

> Archangel Michael, sword of blue,
> all darkness you are cutting through.
> My Christhood I do now pursue,
> discernment shows me what is true.
>
> **Archangel Michael, you are here,**
> **your light consumes all doubt and fear.**
> **Your Presence is forever near,**
> **you are to me so very dear.**

7. Archangel Michael, we call forth the judgment of Christ upon the demons and fallen beings who are promoting the mindset that America must be first in everything from sports, to the military, to space exploration. We command you to remove these beings from America.

> Archangel Michael, in your wings,
> I now let go of lesser things.
> God's homing call in my heart rings,
> my heart with yours forever sings.
>
> **Archangel Michael, you are here,**
> **your light consumes all doubt and fear.**
> **Your Presence is forever near,**
> **you are to me so very dear.**

8. Archangel Michael, we call forth the judgment of Christ upon the demons and fallen beings who are promoting the mindset that Americans do not need to learn from the mistakes

of older nations. We command you to remove these beings from America.

> Archangel Michael, take me home,
> in higher spheres I want to roam.
> I am reborn from cosmic foam,
> my life is now a sacred poem.

> **Archangel Michael, you are here,**
> **your light consumes all doubt and fear.**
> **Your Presence is forever near,**
> **you are to me so very dear.**

9. Archangel Michael, we call forth the judgment of Christ upon the demons and fallen beings who are promoting the mindset that rejects the teachings of the ascended masters and the Golden Age ideas of Saint Germain. We command you to remove these beings from America.

> Archangel Michael, light you are,
> shining like the bluest star.
> You are a cosmic avatar,
> with you I will go very far.

> **Archangel Michael, you are here,**
> **your light consumes all doubt and fear.**
> **Your Presence is forever near,**
> **you are to me so very dear.**

Sealing

In the name of the I AM THAT I AM, I accept that Archangel Michael, Astrea and Shiva form an impenetrable shield around myself and all constructive people in America, sealing us from all fear-based energies in all four octaves. I accept that the Light of God is consuming and transforming all fear-based energies in America!

34 | FREEING AMERICA FROM BLACK-AND-WHITE THINKING

In the name of the I AM THAT I AM, Jesus Christ, I call upon Archangel Michael to cut all people in America free from the black-and-white thinking generated by demons and fallen beings. Awaken people to the reality that we are spiritual beings and that we can co-create a new future for America by working with the ascended masters. I especially call for Archangel Michael to take command over ...

[Make your own calls here.]

Part 1

1. Archangel Michael, consume the records and bind the demons and fallen beings who spread black-and-white thinking through some Native American tribes.

Archangel Michael, light so blue,
my heart has room for only you.
My mind is one, no longer two,
your love for me is ever true.

**Archangel Michael, you are here,
your light consumes all doubt and fear.
Your Presence is forever near,
you are to me so very dear.**

2. Archangel Michael, consume the records and bind the demons and fallen beings who spread black-and-white thinking through the Revolutionary War.

Archangel Michael, I will be,
all one with your reality.
No fear can hold me as I see,
this world no power has o'er me.

**Archangel Michael, you are here,
your light consumes all doubt and fear.
Your Presence is forever near,
you are to me so very dear.**

3. Archangel Michael, consume the energetic records of the us-versus-them mentality anchored in America through the Civil War and kept alive to this day by certain people.

Archangel Michael, hold me tight,
shatter now the darkest night.
Clear my chakras with your light,
restore to me my inner sight.

> Archangel Michael, you are here,
> your light consumes all doubt and fear.
> Your Presence is forever near,
> you are to me so very dear.

4. Archangel Michael, bind and consume the demons of the us-versus-them mentality produced by the Civil War.

> Archangel Michael, now I stand,
> with you the light I do command.
> My heart I ever will expand,
> till highest truth I understand.

> Archangel Michael, you are here,
> your light consumes all doubt and fear.
> Your Presence is forever near,
> you are to me so very dear.

5. Archangel Michael, I call forth the judgment of Christ upon the fallen beings who spread the us-versus-them mentality through the Civil War and who are still using the conflict between North and South today. I command you to remove these beings from earth.

> Archangel Michael, in my heart,
> from me you never will depart.
> Of hierarchy I am a part,
> I now accept a fresh new start.

> Archangel Michael, you are here,
> your light consumes all doubt and fear.
> Your Presence is forever near,
> you are to me so very dear.

6. Archangel Michael, consume the energetic records of the us-versus-the-people mentality anchored in America through the big industrialists who used all means, including the government, to stop free competition.

> Archangel Michael, sword of blue,
> all darkness you are cutting through.
> My Christhood I do now pursue,
> discernment shows me what is true.
>
> **Archangel Michael, you are here,**
> **your light consumes all doubt and fear.**
> **Your Presence is forever near,**
> **you are to me so very dear.**

7. Archangel Michael, bind and consume the demons of the us-versus-the-people mentality produced by the big industrialists.

> Archangel Michael, in your wings,
> I now let go of lesser things.
> God's homing call in my heart rings,
> my heart with yours forever sings.
>
> **Archangel Michael, you are here,**
> **your light consumes all doubt and fear.**
> **Your Presence is forever near,**
> **you are to me so very dear.**

8. Archangel Michael, I call forth the judgment of Christ upon the fallen beings who spread the us-versus-the-people mentality through the big industrialists and who are still using American

business and multinational corporations. I command you to remove these beings from earth.

> Archangel Michael, take me home,
> in higher spheres I want to roam.
> I am reborn from cosmic foam,
> my life is now a sacred poem.
>
> **Archangel Michael, you are here,**
> **your light consumes all doubt and fear.**
> **Your Presence is forever near,**
> **you are to me so very dear.**

9. Archangel Michael, consume the energetic records of the us-versus-the-people mentality anchored in America through the big bankers and financiers, especially the banks who make up the Federal Reserve.

> Archangel Michael, light you are,
> shining like the bluest star.
> You are a cosmic avatar,
> with you I will go very far.
>
> **Archangel Michael, you are here,**
> **your light consumes all doubt and fear.**
> **Your Presence is forever near,**
> **you are to me so very dear.**

Part 2

1. Archangel Michael, bind and consume the demons of the us-versus-the-people mentality produced by the big bankers and financiers.

> Archangel Michael, light so blue,
> my heart has room for only you.
> My mind is one, no longer two,
> your love for me is ever true.
>
> **Archangel Michael, you are here,**
> **your light consumes all doubt and fear.**
> **Your Presence is forever near,**
> **you are to me so very dear.**

2. Archangel Michael, I call forth the judgment of Christ upon the fallen beings who spread the us-versus-the-people mentality through the big bankers and financiers who are still manipulating the economy. I command you to remove these beings from earth.

> Archangel Michael, I will be,
> all one with your reality.
> No fear can hold me as I see,
> this world no power has o'er me.
>
> **Archangel Michael, you are here,**
> **your light consumes all doubt and fear.**
> **Your Presence is forever near,**
> **you are to me so very dear.**

3. Archangel Michael, consume the energetic records of the us-versus-the-people mentality anchored in America through the government, especially Congress, the Senate, the Supreme Court and the people around the president.

> Archangel Michael, hold me tight,
> shatter now the darkest night.
> Clear my chakras with your light,
> restore to me my inner sight.
>
> **Archangel Michael, you are here,**
> **your light consumes all doubt and fear.**
> **Your Presence is forever near,**
> **you are to me so very dear.**

4. Archangel Michael, bind and consume the demons of the us-versus-the-people mentality produced by the government.

> Archangel Michael, now I stand,
> with you the light I do command.
> My heart I ever will expand,
> till highest truth I understand.
>
> **Archangel Michael, you are here,**
> **your light consumes all doubt and fear.**
> **Your Presence is forever near,**
> **you are to me so very dear.**

5. Archangel Michael, I call forth the judgment of Christ upon the fallen beings who spread the us-versus-the-people mentality through the government. I command you to remove these beings from earth.

Archangel Michael, in my heart,
from me you never will depart.
Of hierarchy I am a part,
I now accept a fresh new start.

Archangel Michael, you are here,
your light consumes all doubt and fear.
Your Presence is forever near,
you are to me so very dear.

6. Archangel Michael, consume the energetic records of the us-versus-the-people mentality anchored in America through all power elite groups, especially multinational corporations.

Archangel Michael, sword of blue,
all darkness you are cutting through.
My Christhood I do now pursue,
discernment shows me what is true.

Archangel Michael, you are here,
your light consumes all doubt and fear.
Your Presence is forever near,
you are to me so very dear.

7. Archangel Michael, bind and consume the demons of the us-versus-the-people mentality produced by all power elite groups.

Archangel Michael, in your wings,
I now let go of lesser things.
God's homing call in my heart rings,
my heart with yours forever sings.

> Archangel Michael, you are here,
> your light consumes all doubt and fear.
> Your Presence is forever near,
> you are to me so very dear.

8. Archangel Michael, I call forth the judgment of Christ upon the fallen beings who spread the us-versus-the-people mentality through all people and groups who feel they are superior to others. I command you to remove these beings from earth.

> Archangel Michael, take me home,
> in higher spheres I want to roam.
> I am reborn from cosmic foam,
> my life is now a sacred poem.

> Archangel Michael, you are here,
> your light consumes all doubt and fear.
> Your Presence is forever near,
> you are to me so very dear.

9. Archangel Michael, consume the energetic records of the us-versus-the-people mentality anchored in America through the educational system, especially the Ivy League colleges.

> Archangel Michael, light you are,
> shining like the bluest star.
> You are a cosmic avatar,
> with you I will go very far.

> Archangel Michael, you are here,
> your light consumes all doubt and fear.
> Your Presence is forever near,
> you are to me so very dear.

Part 3

1. Archangel Michael, bind and consume the demons of the us-versus-the-people mentality produced by the educational system.

> Archangel Michael, light so blue,
> my heart has room for only you.
> My mind is one, no longer two,
> your love for me is ever true.
>
> **Archangel Michael, you are here,**
> **your light consumes all doubt and fear.**
> **Your Presence is forever near,**
> **you are to me so very dear.**

2. Archangel Michael, I call forth the judgment of Christ upon the fallen beings who spread the us-versus-the-people mentality through the educators who feel they know better than anyone. I command you to remove these beings from earth.

> Archangel Michael, I will be,
> all one with your reality.
> No fear can hold me as I see,
> this world no power has o'er me.
>
> **Archangel Michael, you are here,**
> **your light consumes all doubt and fear.**
> **Your Presence is forever near,**
> **you are to me so very dear.**

3. Archangel Michael, consume the energetic records of the us-versus-the-people mentality anchored in America through the media and those who own the media.

> Archangel Michael, hold me tight,
> shatter now the darkest night.
> Clear my chakras with your light,
> restore to me my inner sight.

> **Archangel Michael, you are here,**
> **your light consumes all doubt and fear.**
> **Your Presence is forever near,**
> **you are to me so very dear.**

4. Archangel Michael, bind and consume the demons of the us-versus-the-people mentality produced by the media.

> Archangel Michael, now I stand,
> with you the light I do command.
> My heart I ever will expand,
> till highest truth I understand.

> **Archangel Michael, you are here,**
> **your light consumes all doubt and fear.**
> **Your Presence is forever near,**
> **you are to me so very dear.**

5. Archangel Michael, I call forth the judgment of Christ upon the fallen beings who spread the us-versus-the-people mentality through those media people who feel they have a right to manipulate public opinion. I command you to remove these beings from earth.

Archangel Michael, in my heart,
from me you never will depart.
Of hierarchy I am a part,
I now accept a fresh new start.

**Archangel Michael, you are here,
your light consumes all doubt and fear.
Your Presence is forever near,
you are to me so very dear.**

6. Archangel Michael, consume the energetic records of black-and-white thinking anchored in America by many religious groups, especially the Catholic church and Christian fundamentalist churches.

Archangel Michael, sword of blue,
all darkness you are cutting through.
My Christhood I do now pursue,
discernment shows me what is true.

**Archangel Michael, you are here,
your light consumes all doubt and fear.
Your Presence is forever near,
you are to me so very dear.**

7. Archangel Michael, bind and consume the demons of black-and-white thinking produced by religious groups.

Archangel Michael, in your wings,
I now let go of lesser things.
God's homing call in my heart rings,
my heart with yours forever sings.

**Archangel Michael, you are here,
your light consumes all doubt and fear.
Your Presence is forever near,
you are to me so very dear.**

8. Archangel Michael, I call forth the judgment of Christ upon the fallen beings spreading black-and-white thinking through religious groups. I command you to remove these beings from earth.

Archangel Michael, take me home,
in higher spheres I want to roam.
I am reborn from cosmic foam,
my life is now a sacred poem.

**Archangel Michael, you are here,
your light consumes all doubt and fear.
Your Presence is forever near,
you are to me so very dear.**

9. Archangel Michael, consume the energetic records of the us-versus-them mentality anchored in America through the military and the military-industrial complex.

Archangel Michael, light you are,
shining like the bluest star.
You are a cosmic avatar,
with you I will go very far.

**Archangel Michael, you are here,
your light consumes all doubt and fear.
Your Presence is forever near,
you are to me so very dear.**

Part 4

1. Archangel Michael, bind and consume the demons of the us-versus-them mentality produced by the military.

> Archangel Michael, light so blue,
> my heart has room for only you.
> My mind is one, no longer two,
> your love for me is ever true.
>
> **Archangel Michael, you are here,**
> **your light consumes all doubt and fear.**
> **Your Presence is forever near,**
> **you are to me so very dear.**

2. Archangel Michael, I call forth the judgment of Christ upon the fallen beings who spread the us-versus-them mentality through the military that seeks to produce conflict. I command you to remove these beings from earth.

> Archangel Michael, I will be,
> all one with your reality.
> No fear can hold me as I see,
> this world no power has o'er me.
>
> **Archangel Michael, you are here,**
> **your light consumes all doubt and fear.**
> **Your Presence is forever near,**
> **you are to me so very dear.**

3. Archangel Michael, consume the records and bind the demons and fallen beings who spread black-and-white

thinking through the Republican party and some conservative organizations.

> Archangel Michael, hold me tight,
> shatter now the darkest night.
> Clear my chakras with your light,
> restore to me my inner sight.

> **Archangel Michael, you are here,**
> **your light consumes all doubt and fear.**
> **Your Presence is forever near,**
> **you are to me so very dear.**

4. Archangel Michael, consume the records and bind the demons and fallen beings who spread gray thinking through the Democratic party and some liberal organizations.

> Archangel Michael, now I stand,
> with you the light I do command.
> My heart I ever will expand,
> till highest truth I understand.

> **Archangel Michael, you are here,**
> **your light consumes all doubt and fear.**
> **Your Presence is forever near,**
> **you are to me so very dear.**

5. Archangel Michael, consume the records and bind the demons and fallen beings who spread black-and-white thinking through white supremacist groups and other anti-black groups, especially the Ku Klux Klan.

> Archangel Michael, in my heart,
> from me you never will depart.
> Of hierarchy I am a part,
> I now accept a fresh new start.
>
> **Archangel Michael, you are here,**
> **your light consumes all doubt and fear.**
> **Your Presence is forever near,**
> **you are to me so very dear.**

6. Archangel Michael, consume the records and bind the demons and fallen beings who spread black-and-white thinking through survivalist groups and the gun lobby.

> Archangel Michael, sword of blue,
> all darkness you are cutting through.
> My Christhood I do now pursue,
> discernment shows me what is true.
>
> **Archangel Michael, you are here,**
> **your light consumes all doubt and fear.**
> **Your Presence is forever near,**
> **you are to me so very dear.**

7. Archangel Michael, consume the records and bind the demons and fallen beings who spread black-and-white thinking through science and all organizations who promote a materialist view on life.

> Archangel Michael, in your wings,
> I now let go of lesser things.
> God's homing call in my heart rings,
> my heart with yours forever sings.

> Archangel Michael, you are here,
> your light consumes all doubt and fear.
> Your Presence is forever near,
> you are to me so very dear.

8. Archangel Michael, consume the records and bind the demons and fallen beings who spread black-and-white thinking through some environmentalist organizations.

> Archangel Michael, take me home,
> in higher spheres I want to roam.
> I am reborn from cosmic foam,
> my life is now a sacred poem.

> Archangel Michael, you are here,
> your light consumes all doubt and fear.
> Your Presence is forever near,
> you are to me so very dear.

9. Archangel Michael, consume the records and bind the demons and fallen beings who spread black-and-white thinking through Muslim organizations or terror groups and anti-muslim organizations.

> Archangel Michael, light you are,
> shining like the bluest star.
> You are a cosmic avatar,
> with you I will go very far.

> Archangel Michael, you are here,
> your light consumes all doubt and fear.
> Your Presence is forever near,
> you are to me so very dear.

Sealing

In the name of the I AM THAT I AM, I accept that Archangel Michael, Astrea and Shiva form an impenetrable shield around myself and all constructive people in America, sealing us from all fear-based energies in all four octaves. I accept that the Light of God is consuming and transforming all fear-based energies in America!

35 | FREEING AMERICA FROM ELITISM

In the name of the I AM THAT I AM, Jesus Christ, I call upon Archangel Michael to cut all people in America free from the elitism generated by demons and fallen beings through power elite groups. Awaken people to the reality that we are spiritual beings and that we can co-create a new future for America by working with the ascended masters. I especially call for Archangel Michael to take command over …

[Make your own calls here.]

Part 1

1. Archangel Michael, we call forth the judgment of Christ upon the elitist mindset that causes some people to feel they belong to an elite and that they know better than the people, even better than God, and can therefore define how the world should work.

Archangel Michael, light so blue,
my heart has room for only you.
My mind is one, no longer two,
your love for me is ever true.

Archangel Michael, you are here,
your light consumes all doubt and fear.
Your Presence is forever near,
you are to me so very dear.

2. Archangel Michael, we call forth the judgment of Christ upon the demons and fallen beings who are spreading the elitist mindset through the Founding Fathers and those who promote patriotism today. We command you to remove these beings from America.

Archangel Michael, I will be,
all one with your reality.
No fear can hold me as I see,
this world no power has o'er me.

Archangel Michael, you are here,
your light consumes all doubt and fear.
Your Presence is forever near,
you are to me so very dear.

3. Archangel Michael, we call forth the judgment of Christ upon the demons and fallen beings who are spreading the elitist mindset through Freemasonry. We command you to remove these beings from America.

Archangel Michael, hold me tight,
shatter now the darkest night.

Clear my chakras with your light,
restore to me my inner sight.

**Archangel Michael, you are here,
your light consumes all doubt and fear.
Your Presence is forever near,
you are to me so very dear.**

4. Archangel Michael, we call forth the judgment of Christ upon the demons and fallen beings who are spreading the elitist mindset through the early American industrialists. We command you to remove these beings from America.

Archangel Michael, now I stand,
with you the light I do command.
My heart I ever will expand,
till highest truth I understand.

**Archangel Michael, you are here,
your light consumes all doubt and fear.
Your Presence is forever near,
you are to me so very dear.**

5. Archangel Michael, we call forth the judgment of Christ upon the demons and fallen beings who are spreading the elitist mindset through the Rockefeller dynasty. We command you to remove these beings from America.

Archangel Michael, in my heart,
from me you never will depart.
Of hierarchy I am a part,
I now accept a fresh new start.

> **Archangel Michael, you are here,**
> **your light consumes all doubt and fear.**
> **Your Presence is forever near,**
> **you are to me so very dear.**

6. Archangel Michael, we call forth the judgment of Christ upon the demons and fallen beings who are spreading the elitist mindset through the Morgan dynasty. We command you to remove these beings from America.

> Archangel Michael, sword of blue,
> all darkness you are cutting through.
> My Christhood I do now pursue,
> discernment shows me what is true.

> **Archangel Michael, you are here,**
> **your light consumes all doubt and fear.**
> **Your Presence is forever near,**
> **you are to me so very dear.**

7. Archangel Michael, we call forth the judgment of Christ upon the demons and fallen beings who are spreading the elitist mindset through the Kennedy dynasty. We command you to remove these beings from America.

> Archangel Michael, in your wings,
> I now let go of lesser things.
> God's homing call in my heart rings,
> my heart with yours forever sings.

> **Archangel Michael, you are here,**
> **your light consumes all doubt and fear.**

> Your Presence is forever near,
> you are to me so very dear.

8. Archangel Michael, we call forth the judgment of Christ upon the demons and fallen beings who are spreading the elitist mindset through the Bush dynasty. We command you to remove these beings from America.

> Archangel Michael, take me home,
> in higher spheres I want to roam.
> I am reborn from cosmic foam,
> my life is now a sacred poem.

> **Archangel Michael, you are here,**
> **your light consumes all doubt and fear.**
> **Your Presence is forever near,**
> **you are to me so very dear.**

9. Archangel Michael, we call forth the judgment of Christ upon the demons and fallen beings who are spreading the elitist mindset through all families who consider themselves part of the elite and superior to the people. We command you to remove these beings from America.

> Archangel Michael, light you are,
> shining like the bluest star.
> You are a cosmic avatar,
> with you I will go very far.

> **Archangel Michael, you are here,**
> **your light consumes all doubt and fear.**
> **Your Presence is forever near,**
> **you are to me so very dear.**

Part 2

1. Archangel Michael, we call forth the judgment of Christ upon the demons and fallen beings who are spreading the elitist mindset through the Rothschild dynasty in and out of America. We command you to remove these beings from America.

> Archangel Michael, light so blue,
> my heart has room for only you.
> My mind is one, no longer two,
> your love for me is ever true.
>
> **Archangel Michael, you are here,**
> **your light consumes all doubt and fear.**
> **Your Presence is forever near,**
> **you are to me so very dear.**

2. Archangel Michael, we call forth the judgment of Christ upon the demons and fallen beings who are spreading the elitist mindset through the financial elite, especially on Wall Street, who think they can define how the economy should work. We command you to remove these beings from America.

> Archangel Michael, I will be,
> all one with your reality.
> No fear can hold me as I see,
> this world no power has o'er me.
>
> **Archangel Michael, you are here,**
> **your light consumes all doubt and fear.**
> **Your Presence is forever near,**
> **you are to me so very dear.**

3. Archangel Michael, we call forth the judgment of Christ upon the demons and fallen beings who are spreading the elitist mindset through large corporations, especially multinational corporations. We command you to remove these beings from America.

> Archangel Michael, hold me tight,
> shatter now the darkest night.
> Clear my chakras with your light,
> restore to me my inner sight.
>
> **Archangel Michael, you are here,**
> **your light consumes all doubt and fear.**
> **Your Presence is forever near,**
> **you are to me so very dear.**

4. Archangel Michael, we call forth the judgment of Christ upon the demons and fallen beings who are spreading the elitist mindset through the banking system, especially the private banks who make up the Federal Reserve system. We command you to remove these beings from America.

> Archangel Michael, now I stand,
> with you the light I do command.
> My heart I ever will expand,
> till highest truth I understand.
>
> **Archangel Michael, you are here,**
> **your light consumes all doubt and fear.**
> **Your Presence is forever near,**
> **you are to me so very dear.**

5. Archangel Michael, we call forth the judgment of Christ upon the demons and fallen beings who are spreading the elitist mindset through all international financial organizations seeking to control the American economy. We command you to remove these beings from America.

> Archangel Michael, in my heart,
> from me you never will depart.
> Of hierarchy I am a part,
> I now accept a fresh new start.
>
> **Archangel Michael, you are here,**
> **your light consumes all doubt and fear.**
> **Your Presence is forever near,**
> **you are to me so very dear.**

6. Archangel Michael, we call forth the judgment of Christ upon the demons and fallen beings who are spreading the elitist mindset through the presidency and people around the president. We command you to remove these beings from America.

> Archangel Michael, sword of blue,
> all darkness you are cutting through.
> My Christhood I do now pursue,
> discernment shows me what is true.
>
> **Archangel Michael, you are here,**
> **your light consumes all doubt and fear.**
> **Your Presence is forever near,**
> **you are to me so very dear.**

7. Archangel Michael, we call forth the judgment of Christ upon the demons and fallen beings who are spreading the

elitist mindset through the Supreme Court. We command you to remove these beings from America.

> Archangel Michael, in your wings,
> I now let go of lesser things.
> God's homing call in my heart rings,
> my heart with yours forever sings.

> **Archangel Michael, you are here,**
> **your light consumes all doubt and fear.**
> **Your Presence is forever near,**
> **you are to me so very dear.**

8. Archangel Michael, we call forth the judgment of Christ upon the demons and fallen beings who are spreading the elitist mindset through Congress. We command you to remove these beings from America.

> Archangel Michael, take me home,
> in higher spheres I want to roam.
> I am reborn from cosmic foam,
> my life is now a sacred poem.

> **Archangel Michael, you are here,**
> **your light consumes all doubt and fear.**
> **Your Presence is forever near,**
> **you are to me so very dear.**

9. Archangel Michael, we call forth the judgment of Christ upon the demons and fallen beings who are spreading the elitist mindset through the Council on Foreign Relations and the Trilateral Commission. We command you to remove these beings from America.

> Archangel Michael, light you are,
> shining like the bluest star.
> You are a cosmic avatar,
> with you I will go very far.
>
> **Archangel Michael, you are here,**
> **your light consumes all doubt and fear.**
> **Your Presence is forever near,**
> **you are to me so very dear.**

Part 3

1. Archangel Michael, we call forth the judgment of Christ upon the demons and fallen beings who are spreading the elitist mindset through all government or private think tanks or secret societies. We command you to remove these beings from America.

> Archangel Michael, light so blue,
> my heart has room for only you.
> My mind is one, no longer two,
> your love for me is ever true.
>
> **Archangel Michael, you are here,**
> **your light consumes all doubt and fear.**
> **Your Presence is forever near,**
> **you are to me so very dear.**

2. Archangel Michael, we call forth the judgment of Christ upon the demons and fallen beings who are spreading the

elitist mindset through all lobbying groups. We command you to remove these beings from America.

> Archangel Michael, I will be,
> all one with your reality.
> No fear can hold me as I see,
> this world no power has o'er me.

> **Archangel Michael, you are here,**
> **your light consumes all doubt and fear.**
> **Your Presence is forever near,**
> **you are to me so very dear.**

3. Archangel Michael, we call forth the judgment of Christ upon the demons and fallen beings who are spreading the elitist mindset through corruption or the "old boys network." We command you to remove these beings from America.

> Archangel Michael, hold me tight,
> shatter now the darkest night.
> Clear my chakras with your light,
> restore to me my inner sight.

> **Archangel Michael, you are here,**
> **your light consumes all doubt and fear.**
> **Your Presence is forever near,**
> **you are to me so very dear.**

4. Archangel Michael, we call forth the judgment of Christ upon the demons and fallen beings who are spreading the elitist mindset through conservative organizations. We command you to remove these beings from America.

Archangel Michael, now I stand,
with you the light I do command.
My heart I ever will expand,
till highest truth I understand.

**Archangel Michael, you are here,
your light consumes all doubt and fear.
Your Presence is forever near,
you are to me so very dear.**

5. Archangel Michael, we call forth the judgment of Christ upon the demons and fallen beings who are spreading the elitist mindset through all liberal organizations. We command you to remove these beings from America.

Archangel Michael, in my heart,
from me you never will depart.
Of hierarchy I am a part,
I now accept a fresh new start.

**Archangel Michael, you are here,
your light consumes all doubt and fear.
Your Presence is forever near,
you are to me so very dear.**

6. Archangel Michael, we call forth the judgment of Christ upon the demons and fallen beings who are spreading the elitist mindset through all humanists and their organizations. We command you to remove these beings from America.

Archangel Michael, sword of blue,
all darkness you are cutting through.

My Christhood I do now pursue,
discernment shows me what is true.

**Archangel Michael, you are here,
your light consumes all doubt and fear.
Your Presence is forever near,
you are to me so very dear.**

7. Archangel Michael, we call forth the judgment of Christ upon the demons and fallen beings who are spreading the elitist mindset through Jewish organizations. We command you to remove these beings from America.

Archangel Michael, in your wings,
I now let go of lesser things.
God's homing call in my heart rings,
my heart with yours forever sings.

**Archangel Michael, you are here,
your light consumes all doubt and fear.
Your Presence is forever near,
you are to me so very dear.**

8. Archangel Michael, we call forth the judgment of Christ upon the demons and fallen beings who are spreading the elitist mindset through the Catholic church. We command you to remove these beings from America.

Archangel Michael, take me home,
in higher spheres I want to roam.
I am reborn from cosmic foam,
my life is now a sacred poem.

**Archangel Michael, you are here,
your light consumes all doubt and fear.
Your Presence is forever near,
you are to me so very dear.**

9. Archangel Michael, we call forth the judgment of Christ upon the demons and fallen beings who are spreading the elitist mindset through the Anglican church. We command you to remove these beings from America.

Archangel Michael, light you are,
shining like the bluest star.
You are a cosmic avatar,
with you I will go very far.

**Archangel Michael, you are here,
your light consumes all doubt and fear.
Your Presence is forever near,
you are to me so very dear.**

Part 4

1. Archangel Michael, we call forth the judgment of Christ upon the demons and fallen beings who are spreading the elitist mindset through all Christian fundamentalist churches. We command you to remove these beings from America.

Archangel Michael, light so blue,
my heart has room for only you.
My mind is one, no longer two,
your love for me is ever true.

35 | Freeing America from elitism

**Archangel Michael, you are here,
your light consumes all doubt and fear.
Your Presence is forever near,
you are to me so very dear.**

2. Archangel Michael, we call forth the judgment of Christ upon the demons and fallen beings who are spreading the elitist mindset through the Mormon church. We command you to remove these beings from America.

Archangel Michael, I will be,
all one with your reality.
No fear can hold me as I see,
this world no power has o'er me.

**Archangel Michael, you are here,
your light consumes all doubt and fear.
Your Presence is forever near,
you are to me so very dear.**

3. Archangel Michael, we call forth the judgment of Christ upon the demons and fallen beings who are spreading the elitist mindset through Muslim organizations or jihadist groups. We command you to remove these beings from America.

Archangel Michael, hold me tight,
shatter now the darkest night.
Clear my chakras with your light,
restore to me my inner sight.

**Archangel Michael, you are here,
your light consumes all doubt and fear.**

> Your Presence is forever near,
> you are to me so very dear.

4. Archangel Michael, we call forth the judgment of Christ upon the demons and fallen beings who are spreading the elitist mindset through white supremacist, survivalists or Neo-Nazi organizations. We command you to remove these beings from America.

> Archangel Michael, now I stand,
> with you the light I do command.
> My heart I ever will expand,
> till highest truth I understand.
>
> **Archangel Michael, you are here,
> your light consumes all doubt and fear.
> Your Presence is forever near,
> you are to me so very dear.**

5. Archangel Michael, we call forth the judgment of Christ upon the demons and fallen beings who are spreading the elitist mindset through all New Age organizations, including ascended master organizations. We command you to remove these beings from America.

> Archangel Michael, in my heart,
> from me you never will depart.
> Of hierarchy I am a part,
> I now accept a fresh new start.
>
> **Archangel Michael, you are here,
> your light consumes all doubt and fear.**

**Your Presence is forever near,
you are to me so very dear.**

6. Archangel Michael, we call forth the judgment of Christ upon the demons and fallen beings who are spreading the elitist mindset through the American educational system. We command you to remove these beings from America.

Archangel Michael, sword of blue,
all darkness you are cutting through.
My Christhood I do now pursue,
discernment shows me what is true.

**Archangel Michael, you are here,
your light consumes all doubt and fear.
Your Presence is forever near,
you are to me so very dear.**

7. Archangel Michael, we call forth the judgment of Christ upon the demons and fallen beings who are spreading the elitist mindset through Ivy League colleges, especially Yale and Harvard. We command you to remove these beings from America.

Archangel Michael, in your wings,
I now let go of lesser things.
God's homing call in my heart rings,
my heart with yours forever sings.

**Archangel Michael, you are here,
your light consumes all doubt and fear.
Your Presence is forever near,
you are to me so very dear.**

8. Archangel Michael, we call forth the judgment of Christ upon the demons and fallen beings who are spreading the elitist mindset through the scientific establishment, including the National Science Foundation. We command you to remove these beings from America.

> Archangel Michael, take me home,
> in higher spheres I want to roam.
> I am reborn from cosmic foam,
> my life is now a sacred poem.
>
> **Archangel Michael, you are here,**
> **your light consumes all doubt and fear.**
> **Your Presence is forever near,**
> **you are to me so very dear.**

9. Archangel Michael, we call forth the judgment of Christ upon the demons and fallen beings who are spreading the elitist mindset through the media and those who own and control the media. We command you to remove these beings from America.

> Archangel Michael, light you are,
> shining like the bluest star.
> You are a cosmic avatar,
> with you I will go very far.
>
> **Archangel Michael, you are here,**
> **your light consumes all doubt and fear.**
> **Your Presence is forever near,**
> **you are to me so very dear.**

35 | Freeing America from elitism

Sealing

In the name of the I AM THAT I AM, I accept that Archangel Michael, Astrea and Shiva form an impenetrable shield around myself and all constructive people in America, sealing us from all fear-based energies in all four octaves. I accept that the Light of God is consuming and transforming all fear-based energies in America!

www.ingramcontent.com/pod-product-compliance
Lightning Source LLC
Chambersburg PA
CBHW021412300426
44114CB00010B/463